ART YOUNG
HIS LIFE AND TIMES

ART YOUNG   *Harry Godfrey*

ART YOUNG

HIS LIFE AND TIMES

by

ART YOUNG

Edited by

JOHN NICHOLAS BEFFEL

NEW YORK

SHERIDAN HOUSE

1939

COPYRIGHT 1939 BY ART YOUNG

PRINTED IN THE UNITED STATES OF AMERICA
BY J. J. LITTLE AND IVES COMPANY, NEW YORK

ACKNOWLEDGEMENT

Without the assistance of John Nicholas Beffel the writing of this book might possibly have been finished sometime around 1950.

Although it was earnestly undertaken I found myself involved in debates with my own ego to such an extent I had to have the first dead-line moved ahead one year, then another year, and no doubt would have continued indefinitely asking for extensions of time. Then, too, I had periods of indifference as to whether it was worth doing at all. But Beffel was a stimulating adviser and an agreeable companion in helping me retrace my steps to look at it all again. Indeed it was he in the first place who proposed the book. Beffel kept me interested, took notes of my memory talks, assembled my long-hand pages in proper sequence, and conferred with me on many occasions to discuss contents and weigh values. I found it best to let him have his own way when I couldn't see the best way myself to present some of the phases of a long life overcrowded with memories.

If there is any show of vainglory in the book, I'll blame it on Beffel. The modesty, if any, is mine.

And if there are any mistakes as to names or dates, they, too, are mine, for Beffel will find the right date or the correct spelling of a name if they can be found in any place on earth. He will not rest until a statement of fact is authenticated by checking up with other chroniclers of the same period of American history.

In writing personal names of the old home town, however, it was often a hit-or-miss recollection and not always strict identity that resulted.

Special thanks are due also to Ruth Collat for her thoughtful reading of the proofs of this narrative; to Charles

ACKNOWLEDGEMENT

Scribner's Sons and Harper & Brothers for permission to quote respectively from *Mr. Dooley Says* and *Mr. Dooley's Philosophy;* and to the publishers of the *Encyclopedia Britannica* for leave to use some paragraphs from the author's article therein on the theory and technique of the cartoon.

A.Y.

Chestnut Ridge Road,
Bethel, Connecticut,
October, 1939.

CONTENTS

CHAPTER	PAGE
1. Sunlight and Shadow in Paris	3
2. A Chinese Army Gets in My Way	17
3. Back to the Old Home Town	27
4. Any Boy Could Become President Then	35
5. A Small-Town Lad Chooses a Career	49
6. I Capture the Nimble Nickel	62
7. The Stage is Set for a Supreme Tragedy	74
8. I See Chicago Justice at Close Range	82
9. Melville E. Stone Sends for Me	88
10. Four Dissenters Silenced by the Rope	101
11. Patterson of the Tribune Fires Me	109
12. I Go to New York with High Hopes	115
13. We Learn About the English and Welsh	126
14. On the Stage; Pictures Set to Music	136
15. Return to Health and Chicago	144
16. I Work With Thomas Nast	155
17. Altgeld Pardons the Anarchists	165
18. Mayor Harrison is Shot Down	169
19. I Marry Elizabeth North	175
20. Helping the Yellow Press Start a War	188
21. Matrimony Hits a Reef	200
22. I Become Aware of the Class Struggle	213
23. Another Child and New Worries	225
24. But the Back-to-Nature Experiment Fails	243
25. All Too Slowly I See the Light	254
26. At Last I Know Where I'm Going	269
27. In Washington for the Metropolitan	282
28. The A. P. Robes Itself in White	295
29. War-Makers Beat Their Drums	302
30. The Censorship Picks on the Masses	318
31. We Go to Trial in Tense Days	328

CONTENTS

CHAPTER	PAGE
32. Stifling the Voices Against War	340
33. Some Optimists Launch Another Magazine	352
34. Successful Publishing Requires Hardness	364
35. My Younger Son Picks a College	378
36. Battles on the Liberator Board	386
37. An Art Gallery and Two Books	395
38. I Move Along a Shadowy Road	408
39. Among the Silk Hats at Brisbane's Funeral	424
40. Overflow Meeting of Memories	433
Epilogue: Watching the Old Order Crack	450
Index	461

ILLUSTRATIONS

Art Young . . . . *Frontispiece*	
	PAGE
Buffalo Bill in Paris, 1889	7
Bougeaureau	9
End of the Paris Exposition, 1889	13
My Day Nurse	19
My Boyhood Home	28
Remembrance of My Father and Mother . . .	32
Scene in Father's Store Around 1886	39
Old Fashioned Grandpa	44
Youthful Entry in a Prize Contest	55
Early Art School Drawings, Chicago, 1884 . . .	63
My First Published Cartoon	64
William Frederick Poole	71
Judge Joseph E. Gary	84
Fashion in 1886	90
Booth and Barrett	91
Finley Peter Dunne	96
Before the Bicycle	97
The Chatsworth Train Wreck	99
The Haymarket Prisoners in Jail	103
When I Was Misled	107
Eugene Field's Letter	114
Arrival in New York, 1888	117
Joseph Keppler, Sr.	122
Bernard Gillam	122
Clarence Webster and His Kodak	132
When I Was on the Stage	141
Preview of World's Columbian Exposition . . .	157
Elizabeth North	176
Vanguard of Coxey's Army	182
Keir Hardie	185

ix

ILLUSTRATIONS

	PAGE
A Comic Suggested by My Wife	189
From an Early Art Young Book	194
The Terrible Teddy	197
Artists and Editors:	
Frederic Remington, Arthur Brisbane, Thomas Nast and Bob Davis	203
Frederick B. Opper	204
When 'Hiram Pennick' Was Merely Comic	211
Just Alike	226
Connecticut Crime Against Art	234
Mark Twain	241
A Success	246
Shots at Truth	248
All Is Vanity	250
Graduation Night at Cooper Union, 1906	254
Ella Reeve Bloor	257
Alexander Irvine	258
American Mothers	259
The In and Out of Our Penal System	261
Charles Edward Russell	263
Some Day. A prophetic cartoon	265
Piet Vlag	270
Just People	273
Time to Butcher	278
Holy Trinity	280
The Lawrence Way	282
Taft: "Eyes Front!"	284
At the 1912 Socialist Convention	286
Oscar Ameringer	287
When the Village Rich Man Dies	290
Susan B. Anthony	292
"He Stirreth Up the People"	294
When I Was Under a Cloud	300
Mother Jones	303
Not Harmonious	304
Where Will It Strike?	306
Charles A. Lindbergh	309

ILLUSTRATIONS

	PAGE
The White Man's Burden	312
Terence V. Powderly	316
Having Their Fling	325
The Boss	326
A Case of Heresy	329
Morris Hillquit	333
Bill Haywood	344
The Sower	348
Charles W. Ervin	353
A Good Morning Poster	358
Small Favors Thankfully Received	361
James Eads How	365
Fixing Up the World War Soldiers	367
The Poor Fish	370
The Harding Inaugural Parade	373
A Private View for the Best People	376
Bonus or No Bonus	377
Looking On	379
Convention Notes	380
Fight La Follette	381
Editor of the County Gazette	382
Hope Springs Eternal	384
Steffens Reports On His Visit to Russia	393
My Art Gallery	401
Mary Heaton Vorse	403
Defeat	404
Sketching Devils	417
Ghosts	419
One Bystander to Another	420
Heywood Broun	422
A Greek Fable Up to Date	426
My Slouch Hat	427
Remember Whence You Came	430
For Adoption	431
Rounding Up the Unbridled Past	433
The Joke Is On You, Baby	435
O. Henry	436

	PAGE
Robert G. Ingersoll	436
Carlo Tresca	438
Sacco and Vanzetti	439
Alexander Woollcott	441
For an Upton Sinclair Book	443
Elizabeth Gurley Flynn	445
Clarence Darrow	446
Self-Portrait of Thomas Nast	448
Over They Go	454

ART YOUNG
HIS LIFE AND TIMES

Chapter 1

SUNLIGHT AND SHADOW IN PARIS

PARIS was like some lovely young hostess with arms outstretched that September afternoon as Clarence Webster and I strolled along the boulevards, crossed the bridges over the Seine with its gay Exposition-bound boats, and revelled in the sound of the animate voices all around us, the musical cries, the bright faces, and the cracking of cabmen's whips—a continual cracking above all other sounds. For months I had been hungering for all this, but my visions had never come near the reality.

Clear skies and a fresh breeze, and Chicago and New York far behind. Exquisite women passed in magnificent carriages, and on the wide walks were men of leisure topped by silk hats; trim nursemaids with their convoys of children; artists and their girls, known as *grisettes,* whom my dictionary describes as having "lively and free manners but not necessarily of immoral character." Spreading green trees, statues of historic figures at every turn, fountains pouring forth sun-drenched water. And in the distance, dominating the whole scene, the black outline of the Eiffel Tower. The year was 1889, and I was twenty-three.

As a small boy at home in Monroe, Wisconsin, I had seen only one person who had been to Paris. This was Mrs. Cook, an old lady who occasionally called at our house. She had traveled widely in European countries, an unusual thing for an American sixty years ago, before the day of popular cruises. Mother told me that Mrs. Cook had spent many months in Paris, and had played cards with Victor Hugo. I didn't know who Victor Hugo was, but he sounded important, and Mrs. Cook seemed to me a remarkable woman just to look at because she had traveled and met famous people. Afterward, when I attended art schools in Chicago and New York, the talk was often about Paris—the shining goal of those students who wanted to finish off their education. My instructors in Chicago and New York—J. H. Vanderpoel, Kenyon Cox, Carroll Beckwith, and others—had studied abroad. Both Paris and Munich in their time were close rivals for aspiring artists.

"We won't think about work for a week," Webster insisted. "We're going to examine this widely advertised town and see if it lives up to all we've heard about it."

I was not so sure about spending more time in loafing; for I was eager to enroll in the *Académie Julien*, where I would study drawing and painting and continue my art training generally. But all things considered I decided it best to be an idle wanderer for a while longer, and get oriented. We had already been to the picturesque town of Chester in England on the day after landing in Liverpool, and had gone over into Wales to do some sketching and because Web was keen to learn if Welshmen really could pronounce the names of their towns. Then we explored London, particularly some of the places made familiar in Dickens's writings, for Web was an ardent Dickens fan. And overnight the boat had brought us from Dover to Calais, with me curled up on a big coil of rope on deck, sicker than any dog; after which we had proceeded on a wheezing and halting train to the French capital.

Everywhere we went Web jotted down his impressions and observations in a notebook. For he was doing a series of travel articles for the *Chicago Sunday Inter-Ocean* under the *nom de plume* of Conflagration Jones, and I was illustrating them with pen and ink drawings. Pale faced, and with a dark vandyke beard, Webster had been mistaken in Hyde Park for John Burns, leader of the London dockworkers' strike. Carrying a camera under his arm, as Burns had carried a portfolio, he was followed for blocks by an admiring group of workers until he finally discovered why they were doing it, and explained—with some difficulty—that he was not John Burns. Webster's camera was the novelty of that season—a kodak.

My own appearance in Paris that first day is a strange memory picture to look back upon. I wore a flat-top black derby hat, cutaway coat with tails, trousers which flared around the feet in the current fashion, a cream-colored Windsor tie, and a winged collar, and I carried a cane, swinging it in the manner of one who thought he had the world by the tail. The flat-top hat—I think it was called a "shell derby"—was in the prevailing mode, but the other items of attire I had adopted in New York because I didn't want to look like other young men, which was, I suspect, an act of protest against the herd instinct. But to my discomfiture in Paris I saw so many men queerly dressed that my own garb attracted no special attention; no one turned to look after me, saying: "I wonder who that is." Nobody cared how you dressed. I was introduced to an artist who wore a plug hat, a short velvet coat, and wooden shoes, and who passed anywhere without comment.

A dyspeptic who at home was regarded by many acquaintances as a grouch, Webster had excellent qualities, and his surface cheerfulness on our travels was doubtless often a screen for internal misery. Certainly much of the cooking we encountered in England must have depressed him. He liked tarts and pies—especially the British pork pie—and suffered in consequence, then resorted to taking Carter's Little Liver Pills, which he always carried.

He had been my best friend in Chicago during the four years that I worked as cartoonist and news sketch artist on the dailies there. After I went to New York to study, I kept in close touch with him by letter, and he knew that I was restless. When he arranged the joint assignment I approved of the plan instantly. Web was a versatile individual—journalist, art critic, humorous writer, lecturer. From the beginning of this European trip we both made sketches, and I attempted some painting with a water color outfit which my companion carried. We had sailed from New York on the maiden voyage of the Cunard liner *Teutonic*. I had funds enough to carry me along for several months in France—and I felt that it would be simple to earn more when needed, remembering that I had made money easily in Chicago; earned more at eighteen than I had supposed came to men twice that age.

While Web commented jocularly on people and incidents that afternoon, I was lost in daydreaming. This was life, and life was good. Here was the Queen City of the world, with lovely parks and boulevards, glorious women, and all about one the marks of a culture centuries old. And what traditions lingered! Here Doré, Daumier, Steinlen, and Millet had worked, here one could see the drawings of the masters of the Renaissance, here Napoleon had shaken the foundations of the world's empires. (Later I was to discover that Paris also had slums, but we didn't see these on that day.) . . . Breathing in that romantic air, I was whispering to myself a vow: "I'm going to be recognized as an artist—and nothing can stop me." Hovering in my mind, though not definitely a part of the vow, was a thought of rich rewards to come; in that hour everything, for me, was wreathed in dazzling golden light.

I wanted to go at once to the Louvre, and Web assented. "We'll ask the first *gendarme* we see." Having the greater initiative, he voiced the questions, and got profuse answers, with elaborate gestures. The answers were not clear to me, but they appeared adequate for my companion who had given much time to a French dictionary on the ship, though his pronunciation didn't sound at all like that of a native. Seizing me by the arm, he guided me triumphantly in the direction indicated, only to learn from an Englishman an hour later that the famous museum was in another part of the city—in fact, not far from our hotel—and by the time we arrived at its doors it was closed.

Web amused himself by asking many *gendarmes*: "Where is *la Tour Eiffel?*" This always brought a look of quizzical amazement to the face of the one addressed, since the tallest man-made structure then in the world, 984 feet high, towered above everything else, and was visible all over Paris. But we kept straight faces and Web would say *"Oui! Oui!"* when the guardian of law and order pointed impressively to that giant steel spire.

Earlier that summer Bill Nye, who had come to Paris to do some articles for the *New York World*, had been taken into custody for some inadvertent infraction of the law, and wrote that he "would willingly go a hundred miles to be arrested by a John Darm—they are so courteous."

"How about going to the Exposition this morning?" Web inquired on our second day in France.

"Let's just walk around the streets," I urged. "The Exposition will keep until tomorrow." Next day it was postponed again, there being so many other things to see, and we kept postponing it. I had read so much about it, and had looked at many illustrations of that spectacle, in *Harper's Weekly* and other periodicals, that my thought had been that I would rush to the Exposition grounds as soon as I reached Paris. But now there seemed no special reason to hurry.

We had taken rooms in the Hotel de Nice, a small quiet establishment in the Rue des Beaux Arts, a short street in the Latin Quarter, traversed at one end by the Rue Bonaparte

BUFFALO BILL IN PARIS. 1889.

and the other by the Rue de Seine. In that street also there had lived Prosper Merimee, author of the *Carmen* libretto; Corot; and Fantin La Tour, who had painted flowers and done masterful lithographs of scenes from the operas of Wagner.

Web learned that Oscar Wilde was staying in the Hotel Alsace, almost opposite our quarters. He essayed to interview Wilde, and presented his card to the *concierge*, who told him that the playwright was too ill to see anyone. This was five years before Wilde's trial and disgrace, but he was well known as a public figure, who during his lecture tour in the United States in 1882 had reaped perhaps the largest array of unfavorable press comment, ridicule, derision, and cat-calling of any foreign-born individual who had ever visited this country. Web's day was spoiled for him by that disappointment, as another day had been clouded in London when he tried to get an audience with James McNeill Whistler, and found him "busy with a sitting."

Buffalo Bill's Wild West show was holding forth in a tent in an open field near the Exposition, and we were taken to see it by Theodore Stanton, Paris correspondent for the *Inter-Ocean*, son of Elizabeth Cady Stanton, the pioneer suffragist, and brother of Harriot Stanton Blatch. Colonel Cody was then in his prime, a dashing and dramatic figure. The Parisians called him *Guillaume Boofalo,* cheering him madly as he shot glass balls in air from a galloping steed. We were thrilled, and thought it a great show. Cody introduced American popcorn balls to the French, who didn't take to them. It was amusing to see the people outside the tent hesitatingly buy the pink and white balls and nibble on them.

Day after day Web and I moved about the streets, having fun. We were looking chiefly for the comic aspects of life for the *Inter-Ocean* series, for it was the comic that was wanted back in Chicago. With that attitude, I realize now that we saw only surfaces. If there was a social problem anywhere in Paris then, if people on mean streets were hungry, we never knew it. Even in the Whitechapel district of London, where we saw hordes of ragged and lean people, they had no social meaning for me. It was poverty, but what could be done about it? My eyes had not then been opened to the realities of the human struggle.

We sampled some of the night life of Paris, and once we went to a theatre which had a reputation for being risqué, but found nothing that was any bolder than the offerings of Chicago burlesque houses. True, we were importuned by guides with mysterious eye-winks to go with them to see things behind locked doors in out-of-the-way corners, but we were wary, suspecting they might be runners for robbers' dens.

After the week of loafing I signed up at both the *Académie Julian,* where I studied by day, drawing chiefly from the nude, and at the Colarossi School, which I attended in the evenings, sketching models in costume. At the *Julian* I studied under Bougeaureau and Tony Robert Fleury. Bougeaureau was then the high priest of French painters. I liked his work, for its thoroughness of draftsmanship and his ability to impose beauty over realism, though his art was being assailed as sentimental "candy-box stuff" by both realists and impressionists.

Though I lived in the Latin Quarter on friendly terms with the other students, I did not enter Parisian life with the Bohemian abandonment you read about in novels of the

BOUGEAUREAU. From a pencil sketch made when I was studying in the *Académie Julian*.

Quarter. I was in deadly earnest about developing my talent, and carousing had no lure for me.

I applied myself assiduously to the work in hand, and as I proceeded I became more and more convinced that graphic art was my road to recognition. Painting interested me no less, but I thought of it as having no influence. If one painted a portrait, or a landscape, or whatever, for a rich man to own in his private gallery, what was the use? On the other hand, a cartoon could be reproduced by simple mechanical processes and easily made accessible to hundreds of thousands. I wanted a large audience. . . . The prevailing art of that period embraced a thorough, almost photographic, lens-like observance of detail. Gerome, Messonier, Cabanel,

Vibert, and Bougeaureau were in the forefront of the art-world then, because they were good composers and accurate, precise draftsmen. In a sense they were the forerunners of colored photography, though of course their work was superior to the candid camera as imaginative-selection always is when an individuality, not a machine, reveals a scene.

I enjoyed working in the schools, but the days were not all pleasant. I was angrily resentful when a poor girl, anxious to qualify as a model for a week of posing, would be hooted as she disrobed for approval on Monday morning before a class of more than a hundred young men. Many times I saw some sad, inexperienced girl jeered down because her hips were too large or too small, according to majority opinion. I had heard much about French courtesy, but in the Julian classroom it was often found wanting, when cries of *"La Bas!"* and worse were hurled at the innocent who hoped that her figure was good enough to earn the paltry sums paid for this tedious labor of posing.

One day I had sketched a big-muscled male, and Bougeaureau came around inspecting our work. When he saw my drawing, he commented, with vigorous shoulder-shrugging. I didn't understand French, and it was my custom to ask a fellow-student named Robert Henri what the instructor had said. "He says your drawing is too brutal. The model looks brutal enough without making him more so."

But I knew that Hogarth, Daumier, and Doré also had been brutal in portraying brutality, and that caricature meant the ability to exaggerate. Indeed, that all good art had this quality in some degree.

Web's wife was soon to have a child and one day, after receiving a letter, he left for home with a wave of the hand, and when he was gone I felt rather lost. I had depended upon him in my daily life much more than I had realized. I now found myself overwhelmed by Paris. The few words of French I had learned failed me at every turn, and north always proved to be south, except when the sun was setting beyond the Eiffel Tower—one direction I had learned was west. Looking back I can see how ill-prepared I was for the Gay City, and how much more I might have got out of it had I obtained a proper background of understanding by intensive reading. I had read some of Hugo's and Balzac's works, and a few other books by artists who had lived in France, but of the things of deeper significance in the past of that nation I knew little. I had never heard of Francois Villon then, nor did I know that Dante had once been a student at the University of Paris.

In those first days of being alone I dared not venture far from the bronze statue of Voltaire, in front of the Institute of France, which was around the corner from my hotel. There he sat on his pedestal and smiled across the blue-black Seine. Often I gazed up at that strong lean face, and pondered the wisdom and courage reflected there, recalling a line from Hugo: "Jesus wept, but Voltaire smiled."

But as the days rolled by I shed some of my timidity and made excursions farther from my base. Just to look at all those ancient surroundings enchanted me—the crooked and winding streets of the Quarter, through which the wind howled on stormy nights; the more ponderous statues, many bearing names I did not know; the Punch and Judy shows in the Champs Elysees; the book-stalls flanking the Seine; the tall, narrow dwellings centuries old. Down some of those little streets clear rivulets ran all the time, so clean that women washed clothes in the gutters; I never learned where all that water came from.

And of course the art galleries. On Saturdays and Sundays I would haunt the Louvre, which was just across the Seine from the hotel. There I would contemplate the paintings and drawing of Raphael, Millet, Delacroix, Gericault, and others—weighing with what I hoped was an intelligent eye the good and bad features in each.

One day I paid the long delayed visit to the Exposition. It was big, but I was less thrilled than I had hoped to be. The decorative scheme was rococo and too much jeweled like a gaudy wedding cake. I hunted out the United States exhibit, and there met with disappointment; it was too small to do justice to our country, I thought, and not at all up to the showing made by England and Germany. The most important exhibit there, to my mind, was the Edison phonograph, to which several persons could listen at once through ear-tubes. It was uncanny, to hear the human voice coming out of a machine, both in song and speech, and band music.

This machine used the cylindrical record which preceded the later disk form.

Naturally I was interested in watching the crowds, and especially in hearing the comments made by American visitors. And as I moved about I found a good many things that were worth stopping to look at—outlandish weapons, queer foodstuffs, exotic color schemes in the buildings and booths occupied by the darker peoples.

Several times that day I paused at the foot of the Eiffel Tower, gazing up at its incredible height. But I did not enter for a ride in its elevator. I knew that many of the famous artists of France had protested against its erection, on the ground that it would violate the canons of art. Bougeaureau, Dumas, Sardou, de Maupassant, Gounod, and other well known men had spoken out in an open letter "in the name of our national good taste, against such an erection in the very heart of our city, as the monstrous and useless Eiffel Tower." Yet everywhere in Paris one met with reproductions of the tower in every conceivable material—chocolate, celluloid, pewter, wood, pasteboard, *papier mache*, glass, china, even in gold. The commercially minded section of the French people had overlooked no chance to cash in on the Eiffel idea.

My hotel was notable for good food, bad coffee, and a motley assortment of guests. Like many Paris hotels then it had what Webster disparagingly called "he-chambermaids" —men who made the beds and polished the floors with brushes attached to their shoes. Two women conducted the establishment—Madame Medard and Madame Franklin, the first a handsome Frenchwoman and the second an Englishwoman, heavy and business-like but kindly disposed, especially toward art students.

Thomas Corner of Baltimore, a Quaker boy who later became well known as a portrait painter, was a fellow-boarder. He and I had a good deal in common. One person whom I sketched often was a woman of grand manner from New York whose daughter was studying art and who liked to tell everybody about it. She sat opposite me at the dinner table, and never gave the good looking blonde daughter a chance to talk, but insisted on regaling us with reminiscences

THE LAST OF THE PARIS EXHIBITION

Pall Mall Budget

END OF THE PARIS EXPOSITION, 1889. I was the last spectator to leave.

of her travels. At the dinner table she would always assure us that "cheese digests everything but itself."

In the several weeks since Webster left, I had made no drawings for publication, feeling that it was well to concentrate on study. But now I had a bright idea: I would attend the Exposition on the closing night, and be the last person shooed off the grounds. I did that, and it was a curious experience, watching the spirit of antic play shown by visitors from many lands. There was something both joyous and sad about that farewell to a world event. I looked back into the grounds as two *gendarmes* politely but firmly closed the main gates—the walks were cluttered with newspapers, candy boxes, and other litter. Ahead of me were students, arms over shoulders, dancing in single file across the nearest bridge over the Seine. Behind them some peasants singing. And an old gentleman in high hat and shawl, moving along with spry step.

I had made numerous pencil sketches during the evening, and next day I re-drew them in ink, grouped them on a large sheet of paper, and sent them post haste to the *Pall Mall Budget* in London, which was edited by W. T. Stead. To my surprise that publication devoted a full page to a reproduction of my pictures, and sent a prompt check.

That called for a celebration. I took Corner to dinner on a Saturday evening in a cafe where there was good wine. Talking across the table, I dwelt upon things I was going to do—romantic and bizarre features for the papers in London, Chicago, and New York. The market was waiting; all I had to do was turn out the stuff.

Next day I was up early, whistling merrily, and after breakfast hastened forth to walk along the *Quai* in the sunshine and gaze over the stone parapet at the busy boating on the Seine. My emotions were riding high; I needed room for my wings. Ahead of me through the years lay glamorous adventure. I would study diligently as long as need be, but presently I would begin going to other places over weekends and holidays and sketching my observations for publication, doing enough writing to counterbalance the pictures in print. Perhaps I would take trips to Brussels, Vienna, the seacoast, and maybe Florence. Already my name meant something to Chicago editors—and now here was London showing receptivity. I could have everything I wanted in life. . . . I wrote to my mother and father in Wisconsin, sending them a marked copy of the *Budget,* and telling of my plans.

For weeks I worked with great enthusiasm. Christmas approached, and I sent home souvenirs of Paris, and wrote Mother telling of the festive observance of the holidays there. At Madame Medard's suggestion I attended Christmas morning mass in the Cathedral of Notre Dame, and was stirred by the music. January and February passed, with my thoughts of future success still soaring. I was living in a dream-world.

Never had I felt more fit, physically and mentally, than I did as I came downstairs one morning in March. My descent was a dance. For I had awakened with a brilliant visualization of certain pictures that I knew I could do—a series of pen-and-ink drawings which would express the spirit of Paris from the viewpoint of a dozen different types of humans of whom I had made note in the streets. I had lain in bed for a few minutes, clear-eyed and vibrant with the joy of prospective creation.

But at breakfast the talk of the others was anything but cheerful. There was a new outbreak of *la grippe,* a virulent form of influenza. Some of my fellow-lodgers were down with it, and I remembered that several students both at the *Julien* and at Colarossi's had been absent on that account. In the previous year there had been an epidemic of *la grippe* in Paris, and I heard that certain scientists had seen in it a counterpart of a plague lately raging in China, though health officials denied this. Directors of the Exposition had indignantly repudiated the theory that Asiatic visitors to the Fair had brought the germ of the disease into France.

Talk of sickness always annoyed me; I had never been ill. I was in fine trim, weighing around 140, with no excess fat then, and with muscles in good condition. I would be immune to *la grippe,* partly because I wasn't afraid of it. Days passed, with more and more students falling ill, and I remained untouched.

One afternoon at school, however, I became aware of a crowded feeling in my chest, then pain, which steadily grew worse. I kept on working for an hour, until the suffering became so intense that I asked to be excused. Madame Franklin's face paled as I staggered into the hotel. "You are ill!"

she cried. "You should be in bed . . . Jean, go at once and call young Dr. Delbet." The Delbets, father and son, lived near by.

Madame Franklin and the servants helped me upstairs to my third floor room. Woozily I managed to undress and get into bed. When the doctor came he examined me and looked grave. "Did you strain yourself, by lifting or falling?" No, I had not. I could not recall any strain. . . . "Pleurisy," the doctor said, and so badly was the pleural cavity swollen that my heart was beating on the right side. Young Dr. Delbet tried to reduce the inflammation with plasters. No use! But I got through till next morning. Then Delbet called in his father, a noted physician of that time, and also Dr. Peters of *Hôpitál de la Charité*. More tests, head-shakings, consultation outside my room. Then the elder Dr. Delbet came in alone. My condition was "serious", he explained. Did I have any relatives in Paris? No? Too bad. An immediate operation was imperative. He and the others would "do everything possible" for me. He tried to be casual about it, but his efforts could not hide the gravity of my condition. I could read it in all of the faces around me. I felt like one doomed to the scaffold.

Nurses came. Madame Franklin tried to cheer me as preparations for the operation were made. Thomas Corner had cabled my father. Madame Medard assured me she would pray to the Blessed Virgin for my recovery. Corner said: "Don't worry, Art, you'll get through all right."

I was not so sure. I thought I ought to send some kind of a message to the folks at home, but I didn't know what to say. I dared not tell them what was in my mind. I was on fire with the fever, but my legs were like ice. All the golden dreams of the future had faded; no dazzling light before my closed eyes—only blackness. I tried to lift my arms to reach out and grasp something tangible. But I was powerless. . . . Outside somewhere a bell was tolling. I could hear my own footsteps, going to somebody's funeral—maybe my own.

Chapter 2

A CHINESE ARMY GETS IN MY WAY

THEY moved me on a stretcher into a large front room. I could hear Madame Medard praying in the hall. Such a shuffling and concern—over an art student from the prairies of Wisconsin—it was comical. But I knew I was terribly ill. Low but insistent voices kept calling out: *"Attendez! Attendez!"* . . . The pain lessened, then came again in repeated stabs. Tom Corner was bending over me, and I was trying to tell him what to write to my folks. But I gave it up. "Never mind . . ." It would take more than two weeks for a letter to reach home. The Quaker artist's face was hazy to my eyes. . . . I heard him say: "Your father is coming." He would be too late, I was sure.

Then the three doctors came in, and a nurse. All of them advanced toward my bed; I felt them closing in on me. I tried to cry out, but no words would come from my throat. Now some one was holding a sponge close to my nostrils. Chloroform, sickishly sweet. My body became light; I was floating in air, high above the roof-tops and the church-spires. I heard a crash like thunder, and I sank into darkness, down, down, down.

Long afterward I was fighting my way upward through the blackness, choking until I found light once more. But instantly the light blinded me. I could hear voices, all jumbled. They were talking about me, I was certain, but I could make out nothing that they said. . . . After a long time Dr. Peters's voice grew distinct. "How do you feel, young man?" I struggled to answer, uttering something I've forgotten—probably: "Awful."

There was a new pain in my body, a roving pain. Each time I wondered about it, the pain leaped to another region. Ice packs on my head. Nausea.

Somebody at some time explained to me that there were three rubber tubes in my side, instead of the usual single tube for draining the pleural cavity, and that I must be careful not to turn my body and not dislodge them. So I had to lie for hours in unchanging position, until I would plead for relief, and the nurses would shift me.

Time passed leadenly, in my conscious periods. Then the fever would rise again, and days and nights would chase each other, like silhouetted figures on a shadow-lantern. All the persons who entered the room, if I could see them at all, were like shadows. All food tasted alike. Damp cold was coming in from outside, and the skies were gray. The room was heated by a charcoal grate, which gave uneven results, and required much tending. I learned one French phrase from the doctor, *"Fermer la porte, s'il vous plaît."*

My hearing became supersensitive, whispers on the far side of the room being audible to me. Sounds outside came in from great distances—bells, whistles of boats on the Seine. In the street below a goat-milk peddler, cab drivers incessantly cracking their whips, a hand-organ grinder playing doleful tunes from grand operas, and, this being a time of a governmental crisis—with a dictatorship headed by General Boulanger threatened hourly—cavalry troops clattering by.

Often thirst was upon me, my throat always parched. Thoughts carried me back to the cool clear water in a trough on my Uncle Aly's farm, where the horses drank. I thought, too, of my mother, father, and sister, and the pony of my boyhood. I wondered dimly about God, if there was one, as I heard Madame Medard pray; I didn't mind her doing that, because she meant it kindly, but I had no inclination to pray myself, although I remembered Hugo's phrase, something like this: "There are times when the soul prays though the body does not kneel."

I had two nurses, both English. The one who served by day, whose name escapes me, was a large woman curiously resembling Mrs. Sairey Gamp in *Martin Chuzzlewit*. She was a devout Catholic, and one day I saw her jabbing holes with a hat-pin through a newspaper picture of Martin Luther. But she was conscientious in carrying out the doctors' orders, sometimes a bit too conscientious, I thought. Talkative when I was able to listen, she told of seeing Victor Hugo lying in state during the great public funeral ceremonies in 1885. She hadn't a good word to say of him—

lying dead, she declared, "looked like a mean old bear." Her pet hatred, however, was Gambetta, the liberal Premier, who was accidentally shot and killed in 1882; she was glad of that. Naturally I didn't form any special liking for my day nurse; she was mostly venom.

MY DAY NURSE. From a pencil sketch made in bed. She jabbed a picture of Martin Luther with a hatpin.

But Mrs. Stone, who watched over me at night, was a joy serene. She was kind, and lovely for a sick artist just to look at. She had an industrious husband, whose photograph she showed me proudly, and six small children. One line I remember from her quiet talk was: "You ought to see me 'usband and the rest of us a-walking out of a Sunday."

Days of rain and fog came, and gloom pressed into the room. The elder Dr. Delbet appeared daily, gave me hypodermic injections, and conversed in anxious whispers with the nurse and Madame Franklin. I was only half-conscious, and presently was clutching at dark shapes in ugly dreams. Some time later Madame Franklin was at my bedside saying, "Your father is half way across the ocean."

That night I grew worse. Could I last till my father arrived? If I should have a relapse I was sure I would not live; I had not enough strength left. It was hard to hold on to reality. The room seemed too warm and I needed oxygen. I tried to breathe deeply, but found that it brought pain to the lung area, and seemed likely to disturb the tubes. So I breathed with exceeding care, taking in all the air I could without doing damage inside. That was something to think about, something constructive; oxygen was life-giving; the more I got of it the better. I wanted a window open. Mrs. Stone demurred at that; but after an argument she opened one window a little and I felt better.

Corner came in whenever permitted, trying to interest me with reminders that Father was steadily coming nearer. "I'll go to the *Gare du Nord* and meet him. What kind of a looking man is he?" I was able to answer that question, in a half-lucid interval. "He resembles General Grant and wears a blue broadcloth suit." After that a long blank.

When my father arrived, I recognized him, although I was in a mental haze and my talk was incoherent. I felt no surprise at his being there; I had a notion that he had been close by all the time, and it seemed as if he had just dropped in from around the corner instead of crossing the Atlantic. But there was a vague comfort in knowing that he was near. He would come and go, sitting by my bed for hours, sometimes far into the night. He would bring in fruit, which I could not then eat freely, but it was cheerful to see it, and Sairey Gamp was fond of fruit.

There was trouble with the drainage from my wound, the fever mounted again, and my mind rambled. Late one night, after Father had gone to sleep in his room down the hall, I reached the high point of delirium.

For hours, it seemed, I had been conscious of marching steps, and the shadows of passing people. I heard voices in a strange tongue, commands, the clash of cymbals, and the clatter of horses' hoofs. I asked the nurse what the excitement was all about. She said it was nothing. Then, far off, I could hear drums, coming closer and closer. More commands, below my window.

Suddenly I knew what all these maneuvers meant: There was going to be a war—a Chinese army, led by a giant general on a white horse, was coming across the Seine, around the Institute of France, and past our hotel. The general wore a huge and fierce looking mustache, and held a ponderous broad sword across his loins. Sweeping all obstacles aside, he and his soldiers were pushing on to seize the Eiffel Tower and set up a new empire with Li Hung Chang at its head.

Where were all the French patriots who should be here dying for France? Why hadn't the bridge over the Seine been guarded? Why hadn't the garrisons on the frontier kept back these barbarian hordes? Somebody must do something about this. By God, I would do it myself. I would go out there on the window balcony and stop these Chinese soldiers from advancing another foot. . . . I tried to jump out of bed and hurry to the window. Mrs. Stone sought to stop me, and her face seemed to change. Ah! I saw her now as a Chinese spy.

I struck at her, and struggled with her, determined to get out on the balcony and stop the invasion. But the nurse had strong arms, and managed to get me back to bed, and after a while quieted me. In the morning I was clearer-headed. The elder Dr. Delbet was there again, very solemn, as he talked with Father and Mrs. Stone.

After this delirium I began to show marked improvement. My mind cleared and I was able to carry on intelligent conversations.

"How is Mother?" was my first question.

"She's well, and anxious for you to come home."

I had inquiries to make about my sister Nettie, my brothers Charles and Will, and other people and institutions in our town. And as I sat propped up against pillows and ate milk toast—the first food that tasted right—Father began remembering things that had been happening at home since I visited there the previous summer.

"Charlie recited some poetry at the fire department's entertainment," he said. . . . "We went to see Uncle Dave the Sunday before I left. He's had his whiskers cut short, and you wouldn't know him. . . . Old Man Meyers confided to me lately that he's on the point of discovering perpetual motion."

All this talk of home lifted my spirits. My eyes must have lighted up, for Father was encouraged to go on, with a chuckle now and then.

"There's a new iron gate at the poorhouse. . . . Ab Keeler says he's going to sign the pledge next time a temperance lecturer comes to town. . . . Hank Hussig found an

Indian hatchet with a head ten inches long in his cornfield. . . . The county officials are going after the fast drivers. Judge Dobell fined two men from Clarno five dollars each for driving faster than a walk across the Pecontonica River bridge."

More news of similar kind came as the days went by, in letters from my mother and sister. And they sent copies of the *Weekly Sentinel*. Father now read from it such items as these:

"Carl Marty of New Glarus sent a carload of cheese to Milwaukee. . . . The young folks report Julia Moore's party a success. . . . Monroe Band concert at Turner Hall next Thursday night. Hear Strawn Shrake play 'The Palms.' . . . Fred Geiger was a pleasant caller Tuesday from Blanchardville. . . . Henry Puffer is on the sick list. . . . George Wagner of Orangeville and Billy Blunt, our popular townsmen, are going to start a gents' furnishing store on the south side of the Square. Good luck, George and Bill. Don't forget to advertise in the *Sentinel*. We need some haberdashing. . . . Mr. and Mrs. Bat Niles of Spring Grove are the proud parents of a son, born last Friday. . . . Steve Klassy drove up to New Glarus Tuesday to look at a cow."

Thus the history of Monroe and the surrounding countryside, important to those named and important then to me as I took hold of life again.

During the long slow weeks of convalescence I saw my father in a new light, developing an appreciation for his capacities which I had never had before. Here was Dan Young, a small-town general storekeeper, who knew little of the world, suddenly uprooted by a crisis, and sent hurtling across 4,000 miles of land and water to a country where the language and customs were alien to him—yet doing everything that needed to be done, quietly, effectively. In those first days when I was babbling in delirium he scarcely left my side, even though there was always a nurse on duty. And when my senses were restored he was constantly thoughtful.

Presently it occurred to me that he must be tired staying indoors so much, and I persuaded him to go out exploring on his own. Having a natural instinct for direction, he walked a lot and saw numerous landmarks that I had never got around to see—including the Tomb of Napoleon. His French was as bad as mine, though he too had been trying to fathom a co-language dictionary. Going to a barber-shop, he asked for a haircut in carefully rehearsed syllables, but was not understood. So he had to fall back upon the sign language, imitating scissor-blades with two fingers, gesturing with them around his head.

I never asked him how much my operation cost; I hadn't the courage.* And there were the nurses' services, and the hotel expense. My morale was in no condition then to concern myself with financial problems. Father had assumed all the responsibility, and I let things take their course. Each day he wrote my mother and sister. It was understood without discussion that I was to go home as soon as I was able to travel. I offered no objections to this; it was easier to let some one else make all my decisions.

Toward the end of April, I was definitely on the upgrade, and it was possible to dismiss both nurses. The tubes had been removed, and the wound was healing. Madame Medard and Madame Franklin looked in occasionally to talk with Father, and Corner came in each evening. But I was alone a good deal of the time, and I welcomed that. I wanted to think, to re-plan my shattered future. My ego had been dealt a devastating blow. *Ego* was not a layman's word in that day; we called it self-esteem. I remembered a sermon I had once heard in the Presbyterian church at home, about the deadly sin of pride. And I had been the cock of the walk in Chicago—and now had been laid low.

Lying there weighing all that had happened to me, I knew that it was too early for any planning. I was not even sure that I would be able to do any drawing when I got back on my feet. I searched my brain for ideas for pictures, but none would come. Hitherto ideas had flowed easily.

So I began making mental journeys back to the scenes of childhood. What a marvelous instrument the brain, when it performs normally—a magic carpet, annihilating time and space. . . . Gazing across the distance at my self of earlier

---

* As these pages were written, a letter from my sister gave me the answer to that question, almost fifty years after the fact. She wrote: "The doctors would not operate on you until Father had cabled $700."

years, I thought that if I could live life over again I would do it better, would be more considerate of my parents, more helpful in the store and on the farm.

"Why do the French say *'Oui! Oui!'* when just one *'Oui!'* would do?" Father wanted to know.

"That is one of the mysteries of this strange land," I told him. "Clarence Webster devoted a great deal of time and energy trying to learn the answer to that question, and he was never able to get any light on it. He has a theory that the old rhyme about one of the ten little pigs saying 'wee, wee, all the way home' was written by a Frenchman."

Father displayed more humor in Paris than I had ever suspected him of having. In my boyhood he had usually appeared rather glum, while the rest of us laughed a good deal. I couldn't understand that. Yet perhaps, I reflected, as I stared at the ceiling of my room, raising a family of four children was a pretty serious business. . . . He had a free and easy way now, as of one on a holiday, which amused me—especially when he would say to the elder Dr. Delbet (dignified member of the Legion of Honor): "Well, Doc, how do you think the boy is today?"

Late April brought warmer weather and sunshine again, and my strength increased. Soon I was able to get out of bed, sitting up for fifteen minutes one day, and next day trying my legs in the hall. A week later I was permitted to go out of doors; and leaning on Father's arm, I moved slowly and carefully around the corner of the Institute to the Voltaire statue. After lying in bed so long, I felt as if I were on stilts ten feet tall, and in danger of falling at every step. We stood for a little while and looked over the parapet into the Seine with its brisk traffic; then sat on a bench and watched some children at play.

When I felt equal to a longer walk, we visited the Louvre together, and Father seemed a bit abashed when we came to a room full of paintings of nudes, mostly of beautiful women. Yet I noticed he wasn't in any hurry to get away.

"I suppose it's all right," he said, as we finally left, "to have pictures like that in a big city, but if they were exhibited in Monroe it would be kind of embarrassing if the minister and his wife happened to come in while a fellow was looking at them."

On a fine day in May we boarded a boat and went up the river to the Exposition grounds. When Father wanted to go up in the Eiffel Tower, I said nothing about my previous indifference to it. By this time I felt that perhaps a duty was involved. When I got back home it might be hard to explain why I hadn't gone up when every other visitor to Paris presumably had.

It cost five francs to make the ascent. The elevators accommodated fifty passengers at a time, and were so solidly constructed that there was a fine sense of security as one was propelled upward. The day being clear, France was spread out below us like a relief map. Lecturers on the lofty observatory floor, 750 feet above ground, pointed out towns, rivers, battlefields, and other landmarks as we gazed through fieldglasses. I had to admit to myself that Alexandre Gustave Eiffel had great engineering skill; and better than skill—imagination.

I was still shaky as the ship bore us homeward, although the sea air helped. And I was humbled. There was still much doubt in my mind about the future. It would depend on how far I succeeded in building back to normal strength. I had no immediate wish to do any drawing. Yet I had no thought of any other career. I was gripped by the same inertia which had held me during those last weeks in Paris. Nothing seemed worth doing which required any effort.

But my father's spirits were high. He was taking me home upright and not horizontally, and I was going back to fresh country air and sunshine and good food. That anxious journey to France and the return with his son alive was of course the high point in Father's life. He had never before been away from his Wisconsin home farther than Iowa. . . . And now he was enjoying himself. He was interested in everything on the ship—the machinery, the pilot house, the changing of watches by the seamen, the crisp commands, the clock-work routine, and the luxurious meals. We did a turn around the deck morning and afternoon, and it was exhilarating for him to feel the surge of the seas when the bow of the liner climbed a wave as we rounded the forecabin. I tried to pretend that I felt exhilaration too, but my pretense had a poor foundation.

Much of the time I sat in a deck chair and had little to say, even when Father was close by. I was still trying to recover my old whistling confidence.

Chapter 3

BACK TO THE OLD HOME TOWN

I FELT a good deal stronger when we landed in New York, but I was miserably sunburned. We put up at the Murray Hill Hotel, and I took Father to see the outside of the Art Students' League building, where I had studied, viewing it from across the street; it was then at Twenty-third and Lexington avenue. I had no wish to meet anyone I knew, because I didn't want to do any explaining about Paris. That was mostly a nightmare to be forgotten—the wreck of a golden dream.

We walked over to Madison Square, where I grew wobbly again, and we sat for awhile on a bench. Though he did not say it in words, Father was plainly concerned about those spells of weakness which kept recurring, and he was not so much interested in seeing New York as in getting on to Wisconsin. I felt the same way.

There was something friendly about the front of the Grand Central station next morning. We of course referred to it as "the depot", as railroad stations were called fifty years ago. Father stocked up with fruit. I went to bed early in the Pullman berth that evening, and succeeded in sleeping a good deal. The elder Dr. Delbet had said: "Rest as much as you can."

Clarence Webster was waiting for us when we pulled into Chicago, and took us to lunch at the Grand Pacific Hotel. Web had much to tell about the boys I had worked with, and plied me with questions about Paris. "You're looking great, Art, for an alleged invalid," he said heartily. "You'll soon be back at the drawing board."

I must have smiled wanly, for I wasn't so sure. I had not touched a pen since my last day at the *Julian*. My hands were clumsy. And I was still many pounds underweight, although my hair, which had been largely burned out by the fever, had grown in again and was curling naturally. Sometimes in the nights on the ship there had been a dull, pressing pain beneath the four-inch scar where the incision had been made in my left side. Often I said to myself: "Oh, Gosh, suppose I had to go through all that again!"

We were met at the train in Monroe by the rest of our family and a little group of friends. What I recall particularly is that I gave way to tears when I caught sight of my mother. Weeping is frowned upon among males generally, but I seem to be about fifty-two per cent weepy. Mother held me close, with no words. My sister and the boys did the talking. "Hello, Art, glad them foreign doctors didn't kill

MY BOYHOOD HOME.

ye," the village hackman remarked. And Frank Chenoweth, volunteer booking agent for the town's brass band, explained that "We were going to have the band boys here, but Scott Darling is out of town." Scott was the pride of Monroe as a drummer. He could rat-tat-tat the snare-drum like nobody else I ever heard, and the band was no good without him.

In the family carriage we drove to our home, known as the Evergreen Fruit Farm. Carrie, our Scandinavian hired girl, had supper all ready for us. But first I had to see Nig, the pony which Father had bought for me when I was around 10 or 11; he was still frisky and recognized me with delight when I patted his head.

Supper was a gay affair, with much talk. Elizabeth North, my favorite Monroe girl, was there, sitting next to me. Father, and not I, answered most of the questions. He told them how kind Mrs. Stone, the night nurse, had been, and he took out of his pocket a thermometer which he had brought away from my sick-room as a souvenir, because there was a story attached to it. When he found that the room was ten degrees cooler than he thought it ought to be, he arranged with the *concierge* to have more heat, then cooled the thermometer in a glass of water just before Dr. Delbet's arrival, to make it register the lower temperature the latter had ordered. When the doctor came, he said: "It's too warm here," but on looking at the thermometer he said: "No, it's correct. It must be I."

He recalled incidents of the sea voyages. When he was leaving the boat at Havre, a sailor pointed to his collar as if something were wrong—and Father suspected that the young man was alarmed at thinking that he had forgotten to put on his necktie, an article of apparel he had never worn in all his life. He was past fifty before he would consent to put on a tie, and I never saw him wear any kind of clothes except dark blue broadcloth.

I had a good chance to observe him from my sick-bed and on the boat and now back home. A ruddy, handsome face, with a close-cropped beard. His crudities often amused me, but I wondered then and later why it had not been Father's fate to be a celebrity. To my mind he was a great man. And sometimes I think that just character, regardless of ambition to achieve, ought to be the principal test of fame.

My father had no worldly ambition. I couldn't understand why one of his popularity among the townspeople and farmers did not want to get into political office where he could exercise an influence for good in the community. Everybody knew Dan Young, knew him to be a man who had his own ideas of what was right and friendly to all—but for political distinction of any kind, he had no yearning. As a youngster of ambition I thought that just to be a good man, a forthright citizen, was not enough—why was he not mayor, as the local managers of political affairs wanted him to be, at least in one campaign when he was a favorite with the Republican leaders? Now I know that to be honored as this or that in the *Who's Who* of political affairs is not always the way of a wise man. It may take as much courage not to be "distinguished" as to become so—it depends on one's own idea of integrity and usefulness.

Next day I went into town with my younger brother Will, visited Father's store, noting improvements there; and looked in at the court house and other establishments where old acquaintances held forth. Charlie Booth, editor of the *Weekly Sentinel,* interrupted a printing job to welcome me; a genial man, he appeared glad always to have his work interrupted, so he would have an excuse for conversation. There was the usual group discussing politics around the courthouse, in various dialects. Fred Lund, the Populist, was detailing the wrongs suffered by the farmers under the Harrison administration.

On the west side of the Square I met up with the Methodist preacher, who inquired sedately after my welfare. Bill Hoesly, the postmaster, wanted to know when I'd have another exhibition of pictures to hang in the post office. I said I appreciated the invitation, but that I lacked inspiration and didn't know when I'd get at my drawing again. Elmer Peasley told me he had intended to go to Paris when he was twenty, but changed his mind after being seasick while crossing Lake Michigan.

Talking with a lot of the old-timers and listening with a fresh ear to their voices, I realized clearly for the first time what a racial conglomerate was this town in which I had grown up. In having this mixture of people from many lands, it was of course akin to countless other towns that had been formed in pioneer days in Wisconsin, Illinois, Minnesota, and Iowa. Here were New Englanders who had left the East for good and found southern Wisconsin about right; Germans from a fatherland where war had been flaring up, and who liked the idea of peace and democracy; Swiss, who came to this region of hills and lakes, seeing it as dairy country resembling their own; Norwegians, Swedes, and Danes, who stopped here instead of continuing their migration toward the upper Mississippi in Minnesota; and a goodly proportion of Irish, Scotch, English, and Welsh.

Having made the rounds of familiar spots in Monroe, I was inclined to spend most of my time on the farm in the days that followed. It was good to wander in the fields and see green things sprouting. I drank in the clean air as if it were wine.

June and fine weather, and arrangements were being made for a lawn party at our place, in honor of my return from Paris. My sister Nettie, who for five years had been Mrs. Clyde Copeland, was the moving spirit behind this celebration. The idea pleased me, and gave me an incentive to draw some pen-and-ink pictures to herald the event, the first I had attempted to draw since my illness. My pen-hand worked well, and that was good for my morale. These pictures were sent to Chicago by Charlie Booth to be engraved, and were reproduced in the *Sentinel* with an announcement of plans for the party. One of the drawings depicted certain leading citizens of Monroe coming to the big event. These citizens I had often made sketches of before I left home. Some of them I now pictured walking on our telephone wire, with balancing poles in their hands, to get to this brilliant social affair.

Horse-drawn buses brought the guests to the farm. Loads of them came—the young folks and some of the older ones. The party was a distinct success, as those things go—the grand picnic event of that summer in Monroe. I had never realized before how many good-looking girls there were in our town, and for once I was the center of attraction. Everybody present seemed carefree, and I was congratulated over and over again upon having come safely through a critical illness—and was asked a hundred times if it didn't feel good to be home again. And of course the boys and girls wanted to hear all about Paris and the Exposition and the Eiffel Tower—and was the Latin Quarter as naughty as reports would lead you to believe?

Nettie was at her best that day, and Mother was bright-eyed and youthful looking as she moved from one group to another, to make sure that everyone had enough ham sandwiches, coffee, lemonade, strawberries fresh from our field, ice-cream, and cake. Father shared the honors, having left the store in charge of the clerks.

Sundays were pleasant days. Father would be at home and would trim his beard in the morning with ceremonious regularity, while Mother would busy herself with preparations for dinner. Hammock, chairs, and a buffalo robe would be out on the lawn. Charles and Will and I would read the *Chicago Sunday Inter-Ocean* and George W. Peck's *Milwaukee Sun,* in which the "Peck's Bad Boy" stories were running, and then perhaps try our hand at croquet. After

REMEMBRANCE OF MY FATHER AND MOTHER.

dinner Mother would join us on the lawn, and in due time somebody would make a pail of lemonade. Often Nettie and her husband would join us.

Sometimes we would get Father and Mother talking about pioneer days, and there was rich drama in their memories. Father was born in 1838, only six years after the Black Hawk War, on a farm near Orangeville in Oneco township, Stephenson County, Illinois, a few miles south of the Wisconsin line and only ten miles from Monroe. This, too, was the spot where I came into the world. As a boy Father had plowed with oxen, when the settlers thereabouts were still fearful of possible Indian raids, despite government guarantees that there would be no more. Father was the son of Stephen and Louisa Miner Young, and Stephen had come overland from somewhere in northern New York. Family legend says that both the Youngs and the Miners originally hailed from rural England.

My mother's people were Pennsylvania Dutch, which means German; her great grandparents had hailed from the Palatinate. Her father was Jacob Wagner, her name being Amanda. When she was five, her parents and her several brothers and sisters traveled by prairie schooner to northern Illinois, where they took up a homestead in Stephenson county in the same township where my father's people lived.

When Mother was a young girl on a farm, she and her three sisters would go barefooted to the pasture to milk the cows. On frosty autumn mornings, once the cows were made to stand up, the girls would plant their feet on the ground that had been warmed all night by bovine heat. Young people went to church, carrying their shoes to save sole-leather and putting them on at the church door. Traveling cobblers in those days repaired and sold shoes of their own make.

Father served as a mounted usher at the second of the Lincoln-Douglas debates in 1858; this in Freeport, the seat of Stephenson county. Some 15,000 people attended, coming from as far away as Chicago. The railroads gave excursion rates, and the crowds came on special trains, as well as in wagons, on horseback, and on foot.

Stephenson county had been divided on the slavery question, and thus there were big demonstrations for both these notable candidates for the United States Senate. Stephen A. Douglas had been a member of that body for eleven years, and was seeking re-election. On the previous evening the Democrats welcomed his arrival from Galena with a long torchlight procession. But there was a greater throng on hand when a train from Dixon brought Lincoln, the Republican nominee, in the morning.

Lincoln was much the better humored of the two debaters that day, my father remembered. He towered almost two feet above his rival. Despite the apparent enthusiasm for Douglas shown by the parade, jeers met some of the Senator's assertions. When he complained that the interrupters were lacking in respect, Lincoln retorted that Mr. Douglas would be given respect if *he* were careful to be respectful to his audience.

Some man in the overflow crowd back of the speakers' platform called out while Abe was voicing an argument, asking him to turn around oftener so those in the rear could hear him.

"I'd like to talk to you folks behind me," Lincoln answered, "but I think I'd better talk to the majority."

Father was always receptive to mechanical progress. Ours was the first telephone in Monroe. It connected the store and the farm, being powered by storage batteries. Mother didn't like it, and said she wouldn't talk into the thing. It got out of order easily, but we could sometimes hear simple statements like: "Can't get home for supper"— the words vague and accompanied by such electric sputterings as to cast much doubt on the early Bell phones ever being practical. Years before that innovation a wire had been strung from store to farm over which we sent dots-and-dashes messages by hammering with a potato masher, or an implement that looked like one, on metallic diaphragms encased in walnut boxes.

To keep up to date, Father never neglected to renew his subscription to the *Scientific American*. He was inventively inclined, and got one of the earliest patents on an automatic gate-swinger, designed to save farmers the trouble of getting out of a buggy or wagon every time they wanted to enter or leave their enclosed acres. It didn't work very well, however, and I remember how patiently and hopefully I tried to manipulate the leverage, hoping that in time Father would perfect the device and make money out of it. But after repeated trials I found that it was simpler to get out of the wagon or dismount from my pony when I wanted to open the gate. Yet I still think the underlying theory of that invention was all right, and simply needed further experiment to have made it practicable.

The leading farm periodicals also came to us regularly, and Father was always among the first in that vicinity to cultivate any new variety of strawberry, raspberry, potato, or other vegetable or fruit.

Chapter 4

ANY BOY COULD BECOME PRESIDENT THEN

I HAVE no recollection of my birthplace, but once when I was a young man, on a visit home from Chicago in the Eighties, I drove out there with Father. The house was gone, its site being marked by a depression which showed the outlines of the foundation. Father traced the boundaries of the farm for me; pointed out the East Forty, and the cow pasture. We found the old well, now almost filled in; and only a single tumbledown shed remained of the outbuildings. A wagon wheel was sunk into the grass. And down by the creek, still gurgling on its way, we stood where the springhouse had been. That was the prototype of the ice-box and frigidaire. A simple stone house built around a cold bubbling spring, in which to keep eggs, milk, and butter cool through the summer heat.

I was raised on a bottle—as they used to put it—when a mother's breasts went dry. And I can remember playing with the artificial breasts that women wore in those days to build up a thin bosom. These were heavy round pads with white linen covers, filled with sawdust, and were meant only for wear on the street or at social functions. But we children, getting into everything, bandied them about the house. My recollections of the colored fashion plates in *Godey's Lady's Book* seem to go back to the age of three. That publication was a regular visitor in our house, for my mother, like most pioneer women, was taking notice of correct appearances. Reveling in "the pretty pictures," I turned the pages again and again. My favorite toys were not soldiers, but Noah's Ark and the animals that went in two by two.

Mother attended the Lutheran church when we lived in Illinois. After we moved to Monroe, however, when I was a year old in 1867, she went to the Methodist church, which was across the way from our house, and she took me along for Sunday school. All I remember about this religious experience is that one Sunday we each were given a colored card with tinseled angels on it.

My father was not a churchgoer in those days, and when I became older I learned that he was an agnostic. But he contributed to the local churches regardless of creed, and he liked to discuss religion with the local ministers when they came into our store. He was well versed in the arguments of Robert G. Ingersoll, whose books he had read. In his old age he got into the habit of going with Mother to the Universalist church every Sunday.

I must have been about five when there occurred the first manifestation of sex that I can recall in my life. Mother took me to the home of one of her friends, beyond the railroad tracks south of town. It was fairyland to me as we moved along a garden walk, amid blue and pink flowers.

A girl of my own age was there, and we romped together while the two women gossiped. I felt like some playful animal, chasing this girl around and into secret places, especially under a bed. Why couldn't I go on chasing her until something happened? There were a couple of similar experiences with the same girl when I was eight or nine. Female-like—or shall I say cat-like—she was still on the defensive and unyielding. She was on my mind for a long time as a citadel to be taken. When I saw the citadel many years later, I didn't think it worth taking. But she was the essence of all that was beautiful in the world and comes back in my dreams even now. If this interests the Freudians, let them make what they can of it.

Mother doted on my blond curls, and made me wear them much longer than I wanted to, as she did my kilts. I must have been five and a half before I got rid of both—and she was tearful, of course, when the curls were sheared off. She had them saved and kept them for years. Now that my hair was cut I made definite declarations of my masculinity.

After I grew up my mother would recall the time she started to put a kind of Red Riding Hood cape on me. She was wrapping it over my shoulders as she had done before on rainy days. I protested, saying, "I won't wear it 'cause I wore that when I was a girl."

Sometimes Pa would let me ride with him to the store,

where he would give me candy, or an orange. The store looked out upon the Square, in the center of which was the courthouse. Public celebrations and mass-meetings were held there, and parades on Fourth of July and Decoration Day always moved through the Square. There, too, the fire department held exhibition drills, including speedy ladder scaling. A lofty flagpole rose near a bandstand.

Traveling men, pausing in the act of selling a bill of merchandise, would make much of me. They were impressed by the pictures I was constantly drawing. In the store many objects attracted my eyes, especially the picture labels on packages and the advertising placards. And I enjoyed looking at the Chinese posters which were enclosed in chests of tea.

From infancy I had been fascinated by books, magazines, and newspapers with pictures in them. Long before I was able to write I had begun to copy those pictures with a pencil on any scraps of paper I could find. There was a picture advertisement of a livery stable in the *Sentinel*. That seemed to me more interesting and amusing than anything else in its columns. It was nothing but a wood-cut of a horse and buggy, but the horse was going. Because of continued printing of that cut for years the whip sticking up from the dashboard had thickened until it looked like a heavy club.

We had fine times—we kids. There were four of us. When I was five, Charles was eight, Nettie seven, and Will three. Charles kept us laughing with tales of fun at school, and repeated the "pieces" he spoke on Friday afternoons or the last day of a term. We had an Estey organ, which Nettie learned to play by note at an early age.

Fred Darling, the boy next door, knew a lot of valuable things. He was eight or nine when I was five, could pick up snakes by the tail without fear, and had stories to tell as good as many of those in the books that Charles read to me. One day Fred had gone with his father out to Big Prairie, beyond the poorhouse, to fish for suckers and bullheads in the creek. Coming back, he told me he had seen a camp of Indians, and he imitated one of their dances and their war whoops: "*Yea yu! yea yu!*" Another time he said he saw an Indian in the Square shoot pennies from between the fingers of his small son. I asked Father to take me to see the Indians when they came to town again. He agreed to, but the redskins did not reappear, and I never managed to see them emulate William Tell. No doubt they had learned at last that they hadn't really belonged in southern Wisconsin after the Black Hawk War, and were on their way farther west.

At intervals Mother would feel a need to get away from home and would hitch up and drive to Orangeville, to see her sisters, taking along one of us children—choosing the one who had been "the best this week." Those trips were joyful, when I was the lucky one, for Aunt Mary would welcome us with cookies and jam and maybe salt-rising bread. In after years James Whitcomb Riley's "Out to Old Aunt Mary's" seemed to me to have been written about my own lovable relative.

The first book I ever owned was *The Three Bears*, with colored illustrations. Other books which were mine in childhood, and which contained pictures, were *Robinson Crusoe*, *Aladdin and the Magic Lamp*, and *Aesop's Fables*.

My father had a considerable library, or what was called a library in those days. That is, he had a collection of books which he kept in a locked case called "the secretary," with an overflow of several volumes resting on a table in the sitting room. I remember especially *The Gilded Age*, by Mark Twain and Charles Dudley Warner; *Struggles and Triumphs, or Forty Years' Recollections*, by P. T. Barnum; *Sunshine and Shadow in New York*; *Barriers Burned Away* by E. P. Roe; *Robert G. Ingersoll's Lectures*; *The Farmer's Almanac*; *The Lady of the Lake*, by Sir Walter Scott; and Will Carleton's *Farm Ballads*—most of them illustrated with wood-cuts.

In school my studies were often interrupted by ideas for pictures, and I would lose myself in drawing. Geography and history interested me more than other school books, because the text was relieved by engravings on wood blocks. Even at an early age I delighted in the wood-cut. It had direct strength and simplicity. I liked a firm line—no hesitancy. Technical-teasing or whispering in art has never appealed to me. Whatever the artist has to say he ought to say out loud.

I had no thought of taking drawing lessons; the pictorial urge had come naturally. Often I copied pictures out of magazines or books, to see if I could improve upon them or vary their features. But when I was twelve or so I gave up copying, and made it a point to do original work, either from observation of people or things or from imagination. My schoolmates watched over my shoulders while I drew behind the screen of a geography. I was just being polite to my teachers when I used such a screen, for none of them appeared to mind if drawing encroached upon the studies I was supposed to be pursuing. One day I drew a comic picture on the long white hair-ribbon of Alice Treat, who sat in front of me. I thought she would be annoyed, but she was complimented, and I heard that she hung the ribbon over the mantel-piece at home.

To the people of Monroe the long two-story establishment on the north side of the Square was Dan Young's store, but at home we always spoke of it as "our store." It was a gathering place for politicians and other leading citizens, and for farmers who came in from the country for miles around. Here they swapped horses, told off-color stories, discussed the Civil War and the hard times which followed, and talked about crops. Their tales were apt to become tall when boys were listening, and often I had reason to be skeptical of the war reminiscences of some of the veterans.

SCENE IN FATHER'S STORE AROUND 1886.
The cronies hear the funny cracks.

All these debaters were rugged individualists, who believed there was equal opportunity in the world for everybody who was willing to work hard and keep an eye open for the main chance. And indeed there was some truth in the will-to-power theory in the Eighties. Garfield, widely emblazoned as an ex-canal-boat boy, got into the White House, and the Monroe Hot Stove Club echoed the stump-speakers and editors who held that "any boy born in the United States" might become President. I was frequently reminded that a farm boy who looked much like my father also had attained to the nation's highest office. . . . The exponents of persevering industry and unwavering ambition of course never mentioned opportunities for women. Their place was still in the home, and the few who stepped out of it for public careers met with raised eyebrows if not bitter hostility.

While the veterans vocalized the part they had played in freeing the slaves, and the other talkers figured out what was wrong with the country, I stood behind a nearby showcase and put their portraits on paper, with contours usually exaggerated. The subjects of such caricature were apt to be startled by my emphasis on whatever was personal, but usually they were flattered by the attention given them by the town's only artist. And I was never too busy with customers to draw a picture of any one. I was quite willing to postpone delivering groceries, or sweeping out the store, or cleaning the lamp chimneys. This was at times exasperating to my father, but it hastened my artistic education.

New chances for adventure loomed when Father bought the farm a mile north of town. This was about the time when I was finishing first grade in school. Father figured that he could raise fruit and vegetables in quantity and sell them in the store, besides having plenty for ourselves. The farm comprised only 20 acres, but it seemed boundless, especially when I grew old enough to attempt plowing and was assigned to pick potato-bugs off the vines.

Our house was white, with green blinds, and part of it was two-storied. There was an attic with a window where on rainy days I would explore amid a hodge-podge of old furniture for cast-away clocks and forgotten toys. Out in front was a broad, clean lawn on which one could roll a long way. A line of evergreen shrubs along the roadside added a note of decorative charm.

In the barn we soon had a cow in addition to our horse; later chickens, ducks, and turkeys were added. We raised a good deal of sweet corn, which was sliced from the cob by knives and then dehydrated (though that word was not used then) in a drying house heated by a furnace. Father had invented this process, and the dried corn, which would of course keep indefinitely, was sold in the store.

Wagons loaded with grain and produce moved past; creaking wheels indicated when a farmer was too poor to buy axle-grease or was negligent. "Bummers" in faded army uniforms would stop in to ask for a drink at our well, and maybe get a meal also. The hired girl was likely to be impatient, classing them when they were out of earshot as "lazy good-for-nothings," but my mother was sympathetic and kind to these uninvited visitors. Once one of them mapped the Wilderness battlefield for me, with a stick on the ground, and explained the general strategy of Grant's and Lee's forces. He was wounded and left for dead on the field, he said—and after he got out of the hospital he never could find his regiment again.

I was industrious then, and tried to help the hired girl with churning—but I wasn't fast enough to suit her. She said I was "as slow as molasses in January." This term to describe slowness was a mid-western idiom—and another to describe speed was doing a task "in two jerks of a lamb's tail."

My mother got the notion when I was about 10 that I ought to take piano lessons. She talked with Carrie Bloom, the town's leading pianist, who consented to see what she could do with me. She taught me to play two short exercises, but somehow I couldn't play and look at notes at the same time. The notes were in the way. Subsequently Mother thought I'd better try again, this time with an out-of-town teacher, Clara Porter from Janesville.

By dutiful application I improved considerably, and in due time was billed with Miss Porter's other pupils for a public concert. In a crowded hall before the elite of Janesville, I walked to the piano, sat down, and began to play *The Maiden's Prayer* with an affected boldness. Before me was the music, and my teacher stood alongside ready to turn the leaves. The first few notes went over with a resounding confidence. Then suddenly a tremulous stage fright seized me. I could go no further. I left the stage—a failure—and Miss Porter's reputation for bringing out the musical talent of fond mothers' boys and girls got a setback that night. I never recovered from this defeat. I couldn't talk about it for years.

My recitations and impersonations were better than my piano-playing, and various townspeople who heard them said I ought to study for the stage. But the actor of the family was my brother Charles. I had a deep admiration for him when he acted in school plays and other local-talent productions. I thought he was of star caliber, and still think so. His voice had a noble resonance when he declaimed Mark Antony's oration over the body of Caesar: "Look you here . . . This was the most unkindest cut of all . . . Put a tongue in every wound of Caesar, that should move the stones of Rome to rise and mutiny." I hear again the rhythmic echo of his tones in lines like "Men shut their doors against a setting sun" and when he cried: "Art thou that Thracian robber?"

Looking at him on or off the stage, I felt that if Booth or Barrett only knew him they would say: "Charles Young has no equal on the American stage." He never got any further, however, than Turner Hall in Monroe and a few theatres in nearby towns. Perhaps he didn't take his own histrionic talent seriously enough. But I shall always think of my brother Charles as a potential interpreter of drama who should have become widely known. To the mute inglorious Miltons, one can add the inglorious Booths and Macreadys and the unsung of all the arts.

One of the great days of my boyhood was that on which my father presented me with an Indian pony called Nig. Father paid $25 for him. Such ponies were brought to our part of the country in droves. Nig was coal-black. Two or three times a week I rode him, sometimes far into the country, and would mount him at a moment's notice, to go on some hurried errand—provided only that I was not busy drawing.

I can remember how resentful and stubborn I was at times when Mother would ask me to go to town for a beefsteak—if I was absorbed in a picture. I thought she should know that my artistic development was more important than a steak. She would use diplomacy then, perhaps reminding me that Nig looked lonesome and needed exercise. That was her best appeal.

My passion for riding Nig had become theatrical. No doubt about it, I was an exhibitionist. Whether anybody saw me or not as I rode, I was "the man on horseback" of the future. Especially on Sundays, on long stretches of level road, I would let Nig out, and he would run a close race with the liveliest wind. I liked to feel his prancing under me, see the proud curve of his neck, and hear his fretful hoofbeats when he was all lathered up and apparently enjoying it as much as I. No one ever saw us in the Square except when my mount was dancing.

Once he threw me—I had become too dictatorial and he resented it. I was sprawled upon the ground a half mile from town on a back street, and Nig ran wildly through the Square. People knew from this that something had happened to Dan Young's boy—and doubtless felt that it served him right for getting his pony all het up.

Father scolded me for letting myself get thrown. "The idea! Can't you hang onto a horse? You ought to be ashamed."

I was humiliated and was never thrown again. Nig had taught me a lesson. I never gave him cause to repeat his anger, for it had suddenly dawned upon me that he had rights which deserved respect. And after he had cooled down that day, Nig was my friend always. I curried him daily and fed him his oats for several years. I missed him when I went away. In my letters from Chicago and New York I wanted to know: "How's Nig?" He lived to be twenty-six years old. We owned him more than twenty-three years.

Another companion of mine then was a coach dog named Van, a black-and-white polka-dot Dalmatian who was too good for his own good. When I think of the way I batted Van around—pulling his ears; using him for a pillow when I was inclined to rest, especially on winter nights behind the stove; making him jump high for food; fooling him in numberless ways, I marvel that he never turned on me in mad revolt.

I tried to interpret what he would say if he could talk. He had a wise look when in repose, as if thinking things over. And with what patience he followed under the wheels of the family buggy, close to Nig's heels. No matter how far we drove, how hot the day, nor how much dust he breathed in, he would keep on to the end of the journey.

Although we had cats, cows, pigs, chickens, geese, ducks, etcetera, they were not enough to satisfy Will and myself, so we caught woodchucks, owls, and gophers, keeping them for a few days to study their habits, and then turning them loose again. I was good at mimicking animal voices, and one day I was trying to outdo a rooster that was crowing. My mother saw me in the act and said to Nancy Grant, our washerwoman, "Hear the rooster, Nancy?" and Nancy answered, "Yes, a two-legged rooster."

Often I wonder if being raised in daily contact with animals is not vitally important in the development of a child—whatever his future calling may be. One curse of city upbringing, I would say, is not to know the constant kinship of soil, vegetation, birds, and the so-called dumb creatures.

Monroe had its share of eccentric characters, mention of whom would invariably bring a smile to the faces of their townsmen.

Bob Crow was one of these. We boys would cross his farm when we went to Banty's Mill to swim in the pond there, which had been created by damning up a creek. He always contended that a man was not dressed up unless he wore a silk hat. And whenever he came to town he was adorned with a stove-pipe head-piece such as Abe Lincoln used to wear.

Casper Disch lived out at the poor farm. He had a sunny nature, laughing a great deal.

"Let's see you stand on your ear, Casper," we would say when we met him as we cut across the poorhouse grounds to gather walnuts or hunt for birds' eggs.

And he would immediately oblige. That is, he would try energetically to stand on his ear, though he never quite succeeded. He seemed to think we were complimenting him by making the request. We would say, "All you need is a little more practice, Casper," and he would believe us.

Billy Rean, the village grouch, was an early subject of my caricaturing. He could just sit silently in the Square and exude grouchiness like a drum-stove throwing off heat.

OLD-FASHIONED GRANDPA

In boyhood I cherished a fond ambition to attain the majestic dignity of George Banks, the druggist, who had a "bay window" in front and who walked down Main Street with his shoulders far back and with the air of a man who owned the whole town. Often I would walk behind him and imitate his manner, to the great amusement of my mother and of others who happened to see my performance.

Father wanted at least one of us three boys to grow up and look after the farm. But none of us leaned toward tilling the soil. I tried being an agriculturist, but it soon palled upon me. The days were too long and the tasks endless—currying and harnessing the horses; watering, feeding, and milking the cows; feeding hogs; weeding potatoes; making boxes to be filled by the hundred berry pickers we employed in season; plowing; husking corn, cutting wood; picking potato-bugs from the vines and burning them in kerosene.

There was no money to be made by a farmer's son in farm-work. Father had no thought of offering me any incentive; he would pay our hired man, but he regarded it as a son's duty to help his parents all he could without wages. Of course I got my board, lodging, clothes, but I was interested also in having some money to spend. I never could keep my mind on the job before me. When I went plowing I would put a copy of *Puck* in one pocket and *Harper's Weekly* in another, and would sit down at the far end of the furrows and enjoy myself.

Charles, my eldest brother, was ambitious to be a soldier. He also was fond of reciting poetry. When the Spanish-American War broke out he was in the state militia, and was quickly promoted to Lieutenant-Colonel. He never caught up with the war, but like William Jennings Bryan he got sidetracked in Jacksonville, Florida, where he enlivened informal camp gatherings with dramatic recitations. Returning home, he resumed his partnership with Father in the store and continued it until after 1918.

Will, who was three years younger than I, wanted to go to college, and got his wish. He attended the University of Wisconsin, was co-founder of the *Daily Cardinal* there, and subsequently was a special feature writer on the *New York World,* managing editor of *Hampton's Magazine,* author of a history of the cigarette, editor of the British government's official war films, and producing director of the first "Alice in Wonderland" film and of "The Mystery of Life," a sound movie dealing with evolution, in which Clarence Darrow was narrator.

Circuses made every boy's heart beat faster, and perhaps they had the same effect on the girls, though I never thought to inquire about that. Every boy who was footloose was up at the Fair Grounds watching the canvas-hands put up the "big top" and unload the animal wagons, but few girls had the temerity to hang around; if they did they'd be called tomboys. Forepaugh's circus had its winter quarters in Janesville, 35 miles east. Heralded by flamboyant posters, it came to Monroe when I was ten or eleven. The town's whole population was standing on the sidewalks around the Square when the parade came down the hill. Farmers held tightly to their horses lest they bolt and run away when the smell of the camels and elephants reached them. A man with a silk hat in a carriage made a speech repeatedly inviting everybody to a free show at the Fair Grounds, to be given by "the Tightrope King."

Generally I got money from Father and went with my tall chum, Harry Everett. School had been let out for the afternoon. I liked the waxworks in the sideshow, and the animals, and fell in love with the winsome girl who danced on the cushioned back of a galloping white horse. Harry went into the circus in the midst of a half dozen other boys, bending his knees so he could get in for a quarter. If he had stood straight up they would have charged him full admission price.

Next day I did an artistic production at school which was a nine days' sensation. All along the blackboards in my room I drew a circus parade with chalk—band-wagon, elephants, camels, horses, wild animals in cages, clowns, calliope, and the rest. Emma Van Wagenen, my teacher, brought in Mr. Donaldson, the principal, to see this pageant, and numerous boys and girls brought their parents to marvel at it. Miss Van Wagenen was apologetic when it finally became necessary to have the parade erased, and in fact it was removed only one section at a time. But I didn't mind seeing those chalk pictures destroyed. I could draw others just as good any time. My ego was flowering.

And in another school vacation I did better than that, with my brother Will's energetic aid. With several other boys we were putting on a show at the home of Eddie Mack. Having constructed a tent out of old carpets and other stray pieces of cloth, Eddie's father allowed us to pitch it on the spacious Mack lawn.

This was to be no ordinary kid-show, but one on a grand scale, like Barnum's. So we must have a street parade. Will borrowed all the available boys' wagons and topped them with cages made of wooden grocery boxes. In these we put various animals and birds that we had caught—woodchucks, rabbits, hawks, gophers, and snakes.

I decorated the cages with tropical scenes—one being a tiger hunt—with bright red, green, purple, and yellow predominating. This presentation was designed to impress the beholder with the idea that our menagerie was the most wonderful collection of wild beasts in captivity.

My masterpiece of our glittering enterprise was the cage containing a water-snake, which I adorned with a depiction of an Indian shooting a boa-constrictor with bow and arrow. To the wagon which bore that exhibit we hitched Fred Schuler's dog.

With an improvised brass band, drum major, clowns, and my pony Nig, we paraded through the principal streets and around the Square, amid the plaudits of Monroe's business men, who remembered that they were once boys themselves.

At the show grounds we took in about 50 cents, the admission price being one cent. It was a great day.

This experience might well stand as an epitome of many an artist's life—fun in the doing of his job but with small returns on the investment of talent, time, and energy.

One summer the Wisconsin countryside was swept by a revival of religion. Widely advertised evangelists held forth at meetings in a tented grove outside the town. Here they would exhort their congregations day and night, making scarlet sinners "white as snow." Scores of people I knew, including two of my cousins, "got the power." These cousins seemed so happy that I went with them to the camp meeting, and tried to get it. But in spite of the hard work of the eloquent soul-saver on the platform, the "power" evidently was not for me.

The best part of the revivals, I thought, was the songs, such as *Bringing in the Sheaves* and *Shall We Gather at the River?* and the sad, sweet longing for some place to go to that sounded better than Monroe, in that rousing old hymn, *Sweet Beulah Land*. It was easy for me to play those tunes on our family organ, by ear.

In Turner Hall we saw *Uncle Tom's Cabin*, *East Lynne*, Hy Henry's Minstrels, *Diabolo the Fire Demon*—and once we had Janauscheck, a noted Polish actress. Topping all these, to my mind, was a comedian named Jake Simons, whom I picked for success but who never arrived. The charm of his funniness lay in its simplicity. He could make his audience laugh by just standing still and saying nothing, doing nothing except letting his feelings play across his face as he listened to the talk of other performers on the stage. He knew the value of slow motion.

What an enviable life actors and actresses led, traveling all over the country, seeing the sights, meeting important people, having their names on show-bills, and being applauded nightly! I had grown restless early in my teens, and the theatrical companies which came to town fed my urge to get away to the bigger world outside.

Chapter 5

A SMALL-TOWN LAD CHOOSES A CAREER

ONE of my sorrows in adolescent days was a nose with the habits of a chameleon.* If I had been born with a club-foot or a stammering tongue it could not have caused me more worry than that unruly beak. From childhood it would take on the color of blue, pink, plain red, or carnation, depending upon sluggish circulation or the weather, or both. Too much sun or too much cold would make it conspicuous over my other features.

A spanked and cry-baby complexion was my booby-gift from the gods, while all other Youngs near or distantly related were endowed with normal coloring and were pleasing to look at under all adversities of digestion, liver complaint, or extremes of climate. My cheeks were often pink and my mouth usually a juicy red, but the flush of full rosy dawn seemed to prefer hitting me right on the snoot.

Yet despite that nose I was always popular, especially with the girls. They still tell in Monroe how this odd boy was the cause of a battle royal between two of the village belles, Lena Myers and Nettie Booth. On the south side of the Square, with people looking on and enjoying the show, they fought and scratched and tore each other's clothes, all for the honor of being the sweetheart of yours truly.

This affair was the talk of the town. All other honors I have received since pale into insignificance beside it. I cannot remember now which girl was considered victorious, and perhaps the outcome was not clear. Enough for me to know that I was the cause of such a sensation, a gossip subject for weeks. Doubtless it was my ability to draw pictures which

---

* After reaching the age of 60 I began to be described by various metropolitan writers as one who "looks like an angel much the worse for wear and tear", as "a Santa Claus without whiskers", and again as "one who might pass for the kind of capitalist he likes to ridicule." Peggy Bacon states in her book, *Off With Their Heads*, that I have "a light comedy nose." But to have that invaluable part of my anatomy dismissed with such a casual observation by that merciless analyst of looks, was not Peggy at her best.

led them to forget my comic nose and to contend for my favor. Is it because women are themselves creative (or better say procreative) that they are inclined to admire those who can create in the arts? I think there is something to that.

After I got out in the world, so conscious did I become of the blushing shine of my nose on occasions, that I took to carrying in my vest-pocket a piece of chamois laden with talcum powder. With this I would surreptitiously tone down the offending organ if I had to attend a public affair. Close friends told me that I exaggerated the importance of personal appearance, and harbored unduly high ideals of physical perfection. And perhaps I was inclined to look too closely for my own defects and eccentricities as I looked for them in others as a caricaturist.

Disgust with my facial map was lessened somewhat, however, when I began to read history and learned about the bodily shortcomings of the great—that Lincoln's ears were abnormally large, that Alexander Pope was a hunchback, Sir Walter Scott had a lame leg, Michelangelo a broken nose, and so on. And talking with people, I could see that often those really worth while were excessively freckled, had too much mouth, or were lacking in some other way.

With all my self-consciousness about looks (and it may be a feminine streak that is said to be in every artist), I have long had a dislike for individuals who judge others by surface aspects, whether it be a matter of clothes regarded as incorrect for the occasion, a spot on a shirt-front, or need of a shave. Keeping up appearances all too often is the concern of persons who have nothing else worth keeping up.

My contacts with girls when I was a growing boy were of course necessarily superficial. However much I felt the need of some sex association, I was hemmed in on all sides by the religious, puritanical taboo that young people must not mate in advance of marriage. That taboo was always sounding, like a bell-buoy in the seas, always warning me lugubriously against the traditional "evil." It kept me living in a world of self-deceptive morality. On every hand I was told of the evil of sex indulgence, and "lost manhood" advertisements by quack doctors helped build up fear within me of sexual diseases.

When I was about fourteen I heard a sermon by the Rev.

Mr. Bushnell in the Methodist Church on "Carnal Sin." Carnal was a new word to me, but there was no mistaking what he meant. He condemned the sexual act without qualification. Quoting the Bible, he skipped the pages where the tribes of Israel seemed to do nothing but "begat" day and night. All this I read in later years. My youthful mind began struggling with the problem of how Mr. Bushnell could be the father of seven children without having gravely sinned. Why didn't he say that over-indulgence in sex or excess gratification of any physical or emotional appetite was evil? But no; it was wrong any way you looked at it. And his sermon had the effect of making me think of him ever afterward as a pulpit-pounding fraud, full of sin himself but demanding that others remain pure.

Despite all the apparent hypocrisy of certain leaders of moral conduct in our town, I was infected during those formative years with the thought that sexual union was really a sin. The grown folks said so—so it must be so. And this dictatorship of bourgeois morality in the life of a small community made of one young man something of an ascetic —who loved vicariously all the girls he looked at and who looked at him, that being as far as he dared go.

I hark back to my first feeling for poetry. In a schoolbook was a line: "The wind came howling over the mountain." What the story was I don't recall. Lines in another book which conjured up a poetic sense within me were:

> Over the river they beckon to me—
>   Loved ones who've crossed to the farther side;
> The gleam of their snowy robes I see,
>   But their voices are drowned in the rushing tide.

That was a long poem, and sad, but it sounded pretty good to my crude young mind.

Then I got hold of a volume of Longfellow. "The Bridge at Midnight" and "The Old Clock on the Stairs" were quite up to my country-boy standard of real poetry. But I never read novels nor serial stories. I saw my brother Will reading *Golden Days* and the *Youth's Companion,* and I felt that my lack of interest in them marked me as mentally deficient. Novel reading called for wading through too much type. I had no patience for that. The very word "fiction" I abhorred. I wanted truth. Short stories, poems, paragraphs, brief essays, picture books—anything boiled down was more to my liking.

Dante's *Inferno* was the first book to give me a real thrill. I thought Doré's drawings in it remarkable, and I became exceedingly curious about his work. No one in town owned a Doré Bible, the highest priced table book of the period, but I soon began to see Doré's pictures in magazines. Who was he? Then a man came to town opportunely and lectured about Doré in Wells's Opera House. Admission 15 cents. It seems strange that the visiting lecturer on that subject could have hoped to draw much of an audience in a town of 2,000 in 1881. But there was a goodly turnout—and I suppose the explanation is that anyone coming to a town of that size to lecture about anything was an event.

That was a great night for me. I was the town's fifteen-year-old prodigy in art, and I remember the people turning to look in my direction as the speaker proceeded. Edith Eaton leaned over and said: "This ought to interest you, Artie." I sat there fascinated, especially by the lantern slides of the imaginative Doré's paintings and illustrations. Fires of ambition flamed within me. I must escape from the humdrum life of Monroe, and get away to Chicago. There, I felt, lay my big chance. Chicago newspapers were just beginning to use pen drawings. If I could only get to the Windy City and show samples of my work to an editor, I was sure I could get a job. I thought of mailing some specimens, but reconsidered. The proper way, I decided, was to go forth with a flower in my buttonhole, a portfolio of pictures under my arm, and compete on the ground.

I didn't graduate. Professor Twining, the high school principal, who was my last teacher, apparently wasn't concerned about that. He knew that I spent most of my time drawing, and was tolerant when I flunked in my classes. Evidently he deemed it more important for me to follow my artistic bent than to gain marks in the cut-and-dried curriculum of those days. Spelling was the one study at which I was good. I had another year to go when I quit school—

but I felt that I was getting dumber and dumber each term, and that it would be a waste of time to continue.

No matter what other possible careers I contemplated in day-dreams, I always came back to making pictures. I practiced on all the town's personalities which were in any way distinctive or eccentric, caricaturing every one of consequence around the Square. My subjects included Strawn Shrake, leader of the Monroe brass band; John Bolender, grocer and mayor; Arabut Ludlow and Joe Treat, bankers; Dr. Hall and Dr. Loofborough; Charles Booth, editor of the *Weekly Sentinel;* A. C. Dodge, Pete Wells, and Bill Rean, local business men; fat Louis Schutze, proprietor of the Green County House, and Alderman Fred Wettengel. Most of them took it in good part, no matter how loosely I played with their features.

But my *chef d'œuvre* of that time was a pen sketch in color, portraying our leading lawyers—Colin Wright, A. S. Douglas, H. J. Dunwiddie, and P. J. Clawson—in characteristic attitudes before the Green county bar. This was exhibited in the window of Father's store, where for weeks it constantly drew onlookers.

I had been doing a lot of such pictures at home, showing them to a few people, and then putting them aside. I was drawing more and more, day and night—especially night, by the light of a kerosene lamp. One day, however, I handed Bill Hoesly, our postmaster, a sketch of himself, in no sense complimentary. But Bill said:

"I don't think I'm that good lookin', Art. But I hear you got quite a gallery of pictures of better lookin' fellers than me at home. How about letting the public see them? There's a nice blank wall goin' to waste. I guess Uncle Sam wouldn't object if you tacked up some of your masterpieces."

That was real encouragement. I hurried home and was back in an hour with several drawings that I felt proud of. The only one I can remember now was that of a sergeant drilling a squad of soldiers, and each soldier a comic of some young man I knew about town. Bill helped me tack them up, chuckling. Everybody in town saw those pictures, and everybody I met commented on them. I enjoyed that taste of recognition.

An offer of a substantial cash prize by the Waterbury

Watch Company to amateur artists for the best pen-and-ink illustrated advertisement of its popular dollar watch caused me to get busy. Painstakingly, and with considerable imagination for a boy of fourteen, I worked out a somewhat elaborate but symmetrical and rather impressive sketch designed to occupy a full page of some current magazine. I got no prize for this effort, but received a letter commending my picture. I still feel that mine was as good as the prizewinner. Artists will notice in this drawing the influence of the Thomas Nast cross-hatch technique.

I got into a jam over one picture I made when I was sixteen. P. J. Clawson, then district attorney, was running for re-election. His opponents prevailed upon me to draw a cartoon showing P. J. before and after election. In the first scene he was shaking hands with his constituents and beaming upon them. In the second he was walking along as if he were the only person on earth. That was not a diplomatic move on my part—for I was enamored of the district attorney's daughter Sophia, and had been spending some of my evenings at their home.

My lampoon was exhibited in an upright showcase in Father's store, and P. J. almost burst with indignation when he heard about it. He forbade his daughter ever to see me again, and walked into the store brandishing his cane, demanding to know where I was. Hearing that he was gunning for me, I stayed at home for a few days, working industriously on the farm.

Despite the manifest truth in my cartoon, P. J. was elected again—and having emerged from the campaign "triumphant over traducers," as he said in a victory speech, he soon cooled down. Presently I was going around with Sophia once more, but whenever P. J. saw me, for a long while after that, he always scowled and looked as if he still owed me a beating.

Not long after this I made a sketch, the effects of which taught me that propaganda may sometimes stir people into action, but produce an undesirable result. I drew in water colors a likeness of myself addressing a classic figure of a woman emblematic of public opinion, while members of the Green County bar were grouped around her. Beneath were the words: "Here you have lawyers to be proud of. Why

YOUTHFUL ENTRY IN A PRIZE CONTEST. Modestly I signed my name backward.

don't you wake up and build a courthouse you also can feel proud of?" . . . Eventually the citizens did bestir themselves (or rather the politicians and contractors did), tore down the old courthouse, and built a new one; and my cartoon which set them thinking hung for many years in the office of the county clerk, Frank Corson, who had always been an admirer of my work. But the new courthouse, while much larger and more adequate to the needs of the growing town, never looked so picturesque as the old one. That edifice had simple lines and the mellowness of a weather-beaten landmark. I wish I had let it alone.

Clerking in Father's store began to pall upon me. I knew I was not a good clerk, and so did everybody else. For a time I thought it might be sensible to apply for a job in one of Monroe's three carriage shops. It would be easy to make stripes and rococo flourishes on carriages and wagons. And if I could just be around where others were using brushes and paint, I could develop in my own way and perhaps make a little money.

A handsome old gentleman named Austin, an Englishman, was an expert carriage painter in one of those shops. He had a private studio on a side street, where he made enlarged copies from chromo reproductions of popular paintings. Knowing that he was rather gruff and taciturn, I watched him from outside of his front window, but never ventured inside. Often I stood fascinated, while he slowly brushed on his oil colors as he copied Landseer's famous "Monarch of the Glen," or "The Stag at Bay," which were his specialties. Some of these faithful copies he sold in town —others, I imagine, he gave away. At a party one evening in the home of the well-to-do McCrackens I saw Austin's duplicate of the "Monarch of the Glen" hanging above their new piano.

I wondered then if I couldn't open a studio and make a living. Mr. Austin had, and managed to support a family. I must become master of my own fate—no more clerking in a store.

While I pondered this desire, Clyde Copeland, the town's leading photographer, suddenly discovered that he could make a place for me in his establishment. Clyde was an alert, genial fellow, who had been keeping company with my sister Nettie. He couldn't pay much, he explained—maybe $3 a week—but I would have a chance to learn the photograph business. Though I was secretly doubtful whether I would care to devote my life to photography, I accepted the job readily.

One inducement to make the Copeland studio my headquarters was the fact that Elizabeth North was employed there as reception girl. She was the daughter of F. B. North, who owned a livery stable near the American House. Fred North was a favorite of mine, not only because he had a rugged face I liked to draw, but because he knew so much about horses and had raised them on a farm of his own. I had known Elizabeth casually in school. Now I learned that she had certain cultural leanings. She read good books, and showed keen interest in my work. I liked to make pencil drawings of her head with its wavy, dark brown hair and large, well-lashed eyes.

Clyde patiently explained to me the whole technique of his profession. I listened attentively, but the process seemed intricate and formidable. I don't know how much Clyde really expected me to learn about photography—but if he expected much, I must have disappointed him.

This experience among photographs impelled me to do a lot of thinking about the value of the creative draftsman. Of what use was my talent? What could I do that a photographer could not? I was drawing "by hand," painstakingly, while here was a machine that merely winked its eye and there was a picture. Where was this invention leading? I was not much interested in the technical side of photography. About all I became proficient at in the Copeland gallery was taking tintypes. Occasionally I would do retouching and watch photographic prints in the process of developing and fixing.

Joshua Sweifel, a Swiss boy with a marked dialect, did most of the work requiring skill. He spent a good deal of time in the dark room "devil-upping," as he called it, while I puttered around with odd jobs, "devil-upping" in my own way, and wondering if my hand-drawn pictures would ever find a place in the world.

Clyde knew, of course, that my strongest interest lay in

drawing, and with his co-operation I had a booth (which I called a "studio") built for myself. Little larger than a modern telephone booth, it was covered with canvas and was on wheels, so that it could easily be moved about. Sitting in this cubicle, I could close myself in and make cartoons in complete seclusion.

The more I thought about photography, the more I was troubled by it. Was it the open sesame to visual truth? I was skeptical, and yet I was being lured into a false regard for the product of this machine, as something to emulate. Often I would think: "If I can't draw as realistically, and catch light and shade accurately enough so that my pictures will beat a camera, then I'd better give up." Wasn't my eye as sharp and sensitive as a lens?

Above all things I knew I wanted the truth, and it appeared, except for color, right here in a photograph. It fooled me, and I tried to make pictures with the detail-quality of photographs. I even tried pasting facial photographs of village acquaintances on my drawing paper and doing their bodies and surroundings in free-hand draftsmanship. But I didn't like the result. The photograph spoiled the whole picture.

My fear of the camera as a competitor was relieved, however, by humorous incidents in the gallery, especially the posing of people to whom it was a new experience. There were many pictures of couples just married—the barbered groom sitting and the bride standing just so, with a hand modestly gripping her husband's shoulder but nevertheless conveying the idea that she had finally caught him. No bride and groom could be posed in any other way. That was the law of the new photographic art.

Sometimes a wife and her daughters would bring the head of the household to be photographed, and he would register deep pain in the process. As a rule the early settler didn't want to be bothered having his picture taken, but the others would insist upon it as a social duty. They would comb the chaff out of Pa's hair and whiskers in a dressing-room and lead him to the slaughter, watching him closely as he posed in the clamp of a head-rack for his family's sake.

If photography has become an "art," what kind is it? Let me inject here my mature conclusions for what they may be worth, on this phenomenon—the candid camera which has almost overwhelmed the graphic arts.

A photograph is the surface of something. Of course an artist is concerned with surface appearances, but only as a means of penetrating to the spirit of the thing. Through his own temperament he reveals the way he is impressed as a beholder of the scene. The artist's emotional reactions to the subject before him, and his obligation to stress its essentials, are the main factors in a work of art. Sensitive to every element in nature, the draftsman finds his hardest task in sacrificing the extraneous detail of his subject, and he is forced to perform many difficult operations, while holding fast to that which is good for his purpose.

Real art transcends the personal and the particular. The photographer cannot make a portrait nor anything else that is not a documentary picture of a particular thing, however skilful he may be in the professional tricks of subduing and heightening the effects of light and shade. He cannot make a picture that is not specific—and therefore lacks universality. Art must transcend positive truth to reveal it.

A photograph of your grandfather or mine may show a noble head and features of unusual character, but it does not belong in the realm of great art, because it is only *one* grandfather, documented and exact. Even a silhouette of a person in the foreground of a photograph, though the detail is lost in the darkness and therefore something is left to the imagination, also looks too much like a certain person. A good illustrator may draw from models but knows how to forget them.

A painter knows how to draw human beings, but he uses them not so much to identify individuals as to represent the kind of human beings they are. The best portraiture is not the accurate measurements up and down and across the face, but the sensation created in the artist's mind from watching the subject, and his ability to capture whatever is characteristic. A photograph does not stimulate the imaginative mood as good music, poetry, or painting does. In short, photography is too literal. And yet I would call it one of the greatest inventions of the nineteenth century—because of its usefulness to science and its documentary utility in all the arts. As a pictorial feature of magazines it has been vastly overdone and is tiresome.

I grew steadily more confident in those early days of photography that it would never successfully compete with the art of the cartoon, and that there would be no invasion by the camera of that field of art where ideas, imagination, fancy, and symbolism are factors of supreme importance. There the hand-drawn pictures would always find an appreciative public.

In the decade following the Civil War the American people lauded Thomas Nast's cartoons of Boss Tweed, and the story goes that Tweed, fleeing from the law, was captured in a Spanish port because he was identified through Nast's well-known caricatures. For the police records, no doubt, photographs would have been better. Nast's cartoons did not look so much like Tweed if you compared them with photographs; they were more than mere realism. The person of Tweed was recreated and emphasized by Nast, who knew the powerful truth of figurative expression. He found that he could exaggerate Tweed's jowls and general facial construction in a way to suggest a money-bag and still further convey the idea with a belly-front that resembled another big bag of cash. And he showed the boss of New York City in arrogant postures defiantly saying: "What are you going to do about it?"

To add to the marvelous realism of the camera in my boyhood there was the stereoscope, to be found on the parlor table in nearly every home. Everybody enjoyed looking through this device, which made photographs three-dimensional. One had the feeling that the camera had pictured the very atmosphere. I would peer through the lenses of our stereoscope spellbound at a man standing on the bank of a tree-girt lake—it was so true to life—the last word in pictorial representation, except for motion and color. And now in this epoch, color, three dimensions, and sound are becoming the common additions to photographic actuality.

Clyde Copeland never complained that he didn't get the worth of his money while I "worked" in his gallery, so perhaps I earned what I got. Or maybe he felt that he was helping a deserving youth toward an art career.

Will Monroe, a school-chum of my brother Charles, was studying to be a doctor at Bellevue Hospital in New York. Will had always been interested in my pictures. He wrote to Charles, saying that if I would send him some drawings he would take them around to the magazines. He was sure they were marketable.

Judge liked a picture I had made of a boy dragging a dog by the neck while a meddlesome old pedant protested: "Why, this is an ignominy." To which the boy answered: "Naw, 'tain't neither, it's nothin' but a common pup." Not a very good joke, but it should be remembered that at that time the comic papers were fond of jests that ridiculed literary Bostonese. *Judge* sent me a check for seven dollars, and I was prancing along the road to fame and fortune.

Monroe could not hold me long after that. I was convinced that Opportunity was knocking insistently at my door. A few weeks passed, punctuated by debates with my parents on the relative chances of an artist in a big city and in a town of 2,250 population. Then I packed a valise, wrapped up the best of my drawings, and bought a ticket for Chicago. I was then seventeen.

My mother was tearfully concerned lest some dark evil befall me in the city. The old story: "breaking home ties." I had said goodbye to Elizabeth the night before. Father came over to the train with me. "You'll get along," he said. Mr. Puffer, the cheerful station agent, yelled: "Don't buy any gold bricks, Art," and old Joe Gleissner, who drove the bus to and from the depot, and who always got the well-known maxims twisted, said: "Vell, Artie, a rolling stone gathers some moss—yah!" My brother Charles rode down to Chicago with me to see that I was comfortably located. The sky was bright as the train sped across the miles toward the promised land.

Chapter 6

I CAPTURE THE 'NIMBLE NICKEL'

MY first residence in Chicago was a dump of a boarding house on Wabash Avenue near 15th Street. The place had been recommended by Mel Morse, railroad baggageman in Monroe, who happened to know the landlady. From my window, which faced the West, I could see slums and low life, and also the constant movement of the masts and riggings of boats in the Chicago River nearby. At this window I began my professional career as a cartoonist, with an improvised easel and the handicap of having no heat in winter. Whatever the hardships, I was determined to get ahead and to make my way without asking for money from home.

In the next room was an old fellow from Texas who thought he knew politics and considered himself an unrecognized statesman. Immediately he set out to enlist my talent on an idea he had for a cartoon. He was sure that *Harper's Weekly* would jump at the chance to publish it. I drew the picture, mailed it to *Harper's*, and it came back in a few weeks with regrets from the editor. I have that cartoon yet, and looking at it now I can see that there was a good deal of merit in the old Texan's idea.

Immediately I signed up at the Academy of Design, which was later merged with the present Art Institute. Here I began to learn the fundamentals of anatomy under John H. Vanderpoel. Short and deformed, and voicing tart humor, this instructor was crisp and direct in his criticism. When a student's drawing was bad, he would go over it with a firm black line and point out the mistakes. He gave each of us individual attention.

Soon after entering the Academy, I went forth with a portfolio of drawings and called on the W. M. Hoyt Company, a wholesale grocery house which published a trade paper called the *Nimble Nickel*. I had seen this periodical in

Diana Robing *Venus Victrix.*

EARLY ART SCHOOL DRAWINGS. CHICAGO, 1884.

my father's store and had sent some sketches to the editor, receiving in return a friendly letter indicating the possibility of my drawing regularly for him. His name was Eugene J. Hall. His handshake was hearty, and after we had talked a few minutes about the aims of the Hoyt house-organ and the power of attraction which lay in illustrations, he took me in to meet A. C. Buttolph, the business manager, who looked over my samples and saw humor in several of my Monroe caricatures.

It was readily agreed that comics were needed to liven up the *Nimble Nickel,* and I was told to go ahead and submit whatever I thought would fit into its editorial scheme. The

Nimble Nickel

MY FIRST PUBLISHED CARTOON, bought by a Chicago wholesale grocery company's publication. 1884.

pay would be according to the firm's idea of value in each instance. In three days I was back with some drawings, including one of a man wearing a plug hat and brandishing a big cleaver, labeled "Great Slaughter of Prices." These offerings were immediately accepted, and I wrote home jubilantly. The next Monday morning a check for $5 came. Week after week I submitted other pictures to Mr. Hall, with slogans or text designed to pull business from retail grocers, and nearly all were taken. Sometimes I was paid $7, and occasionally $10, and this regular income covered the cost of two terms in the Academy.

To the stand-up collar which I had adopted before leaving home, I had added to my wardrobe an artist's flowing black bow tie, and began buying clothes a bit different from the conventional style. I made friends easily, probably because I was interested in everybody and everything, and I imagined people saying behind my back: "Rather queer, but he means well." Anyhow, I hoped they were saying something like that.

Chicago was fascinating, the crowds downtown amazing. The corners at State and Madison streets were crowded with people at all hours, like nothing, I thought, except the business section of Monroe on circus day. I wandered around in the evenings seeing the sights—the Clark Street Dime Museum; the old Exposition Building on Michigan Avenue, when something was going on there; McVicker's Theatre, where drama and melodrama were played; and occasionally, Sam T. Jack's burlesque house, that being a time when big-hipped women were the rage among male connoisseurs.

Then there was the Battle of Gettysburg cyclorama, in a round brick building, on Wabash Avenue. I passed it daily on my way to the Academy, and after a couple of weeks could no longer resist the temptation to go inside. It was a circular mural showing the various phases of that decisive battle, a curious mixture of romanticism and realism, painted by the French artist Henri Philippoteaux. A lecturer recounted the movements of the armies on the field. Glory of war was portrayed here, but the bloodiness of the scene should have been sufficient antidote to cure any onlooking youth of a wish for a military career. Cavalry dashed across the broken terrain, men and horses fell dying, billows of cannon-smoke rolled across the field, infantry pressed on to bayonet charges in the enemy's trenches, a flag had fallen and was being picked up again. That cyclorama stayed a long time, and was well patronized by visitors from the country.

On Sundays I would find new streets to explore, or would take a cable car to one of the parks. When walking I was always on the lookout for displays of pictures in art store windows, confident that some day mine also would be shown thus. And constantly I was sketching scenes along the way. Foreign faces and the picturesque garb of aliens were much in evidence in Chicago then, for great numbers of immigrants were arriving every year—Germans and Irish mainly, also Jews, Italians, and Poles.

During my first year in Chicago, it seemed to be my fate that no matter where I moved I would find myself living in a bawdy house. After a few months in the place on lower Wabash Avenue, I moved two blocks north, where there was a row of houses with dignified doorways, stone steps, and front yards with trees and iron fences. In one of these houses I took a room. Compared with my first quarters, this was like dwelling in a palace.

The landlady who rented me the room had moist eyes and painted cheeks, and lots of rings on her fingers. I hadn't seen women dressed like this in Monroe, but I was prepared to encounter odd customs in the city, and thought nothing of her appearance except to admire her for putting on an abundance of jewelry, lace, and paint, if such was her taste. For she was pleasant-voiced and cordial.

I hadn't been at my new address more than a few weeks when I observed that a well-dressed man who looked and acted like one who was *incognito* appeared there each Saturday and slept late on Sunday. Two or three times I saw him in the landlady's room when the door happened to be ajar.

"Aha!" said this Wisconsin youth to himself. "It doesn't look respectable around here." I felt a bit self-conscious, and pondered what my parents would say if they knew where I was living.

There was a cab out in front a few days later, and an attractive blonde girl alighted and tripped up our steps, carrying a satchel. I was just coming downstairs. The landlady beamed on me and introduced her younger sister, who had come to visit her from St. Joseph, Michigan.

"Mr. Young is the artist I told you about in my last letter."

"Oh!" the blonde exclaimed sweetly. "I want so much to see your pictures. May I?"

I was a little embarrassed by her curiosity, but I managed to say: "It will be a pleasure."

Next day there was a knock at my door while I was drawing. She had come to pay a call, in a gay pink frock.

"Helloo!" she said. "Am I interrupting your work? Or may I come in?"

Again I was embarrassed, for I wasn't used to entertaining young women. But her self-assurance was refreshing, and I asked her to sit down. We immediately found a good deal to talk about—what she had seen and liked or disliked in Chicago (she had been over on State Street shopping with her sister), the fun she had had coming across Lake Michigan on the boat, and what life was like in St. Joe. Then she reminded me of the pictures, and I brought forth many sketches that I had stored up, copies of the *Nimble Nickel* containing my stuff, and the exhibit which I always put foremost—the copy of *Judge* in which the dog joke had been published.

Her name was Clara and she did not gush over my work, but displayed just the right amount of enthusiasm over the drawings that she particularly liked. Sometimes our hands accidentally touched and she didn't seem to mind. Her fingers were slim and tapering and well cared for.

Then we talked some more, and I asked questions about her. She was about my age, and since she left high school she had been keeping house for her parents. She didn't know yet what she wanted to do, whether to take a business course and become a stenographer, or go into training as a hospital nurse.

Watching Clara's face from many angles, I had been struck by the beauty of her profile, and told her so. She blushed, but readily agreed to come back next day to let me do a sketch of her.

Posing her for the sketch, in the right light and at the proper angle, gave me an excuse to touch her arms and her shoulders. Then I said: "Now forget that I am here."

"But I can't," she insisted.

Before I was through I did two sketches of her, so that we each could have one. Afterward she was standing near the door, thanking me and saying she must go, but lingering. When she had said that three times, we both laughed, and suddenly I found her in my arms. Then that cursed demon of inhibition began to ring its warning bell, and I let her go, and was soon back at my work.

Now I wondered: was she in love with me? Did she intend to marry some day? Probably, for most girls had that on their minds. Above all, I knew that I must not get too deeply involved with her. A few days later I met her in the hall and was relieved when she told me she was going back to St. Joe.

"I would like to cross the lake and visit you," I said. I half meant that at the moment, but I never made the trip, and never saw her again.

After a few months, Clay Bennett, a boyhood chum, came from Monroe to study dentistry, and we decided to look for a rooming house where we could live together for the sake of economy. We found one on Clark Street, opposite Kohl and Middleton's Dime Museum. It was called a hotel.

We hadn't been there long before I began to suspect that it was another one of those places. Soon I had ample evidence to prove it. Again I began to think of myself as a lost soul if my environment should get the best of me. Noises in the next room persisted—sounds of hilarity, varied by quarreling. One forenoon I was impelled to peer through a crack in the thin board walls. In that other room I got a good view of a lovely looking girl in the near nude.

An artist has one great advantage over others—he can always justify his inquisitiveness, and his curiosity about all the quirks and perversities of human nature because it's the *summum bonum* of his profession to see life. Without a keen curiosity no one can be an artist. And seeing what is unposed and unconscious in the actions of individuals or groups affords more inspiration than any formal posing or conscious parade.

Now I set out to show my work to editors of various publications, and found a market for drawings with the *American Field,* a sportsman's magazine—chiefly comics relating to hunting or fishing, but occasionally illustrations for a story. Then somebody started a Sons of Veterans periodical, which bought joke drawings from me at $5 each.

Having made good on the *Nimble Nickel* and the *American Field,* I began looking around for other worlds to conquer. I had waited nearly a year before visiting any of the newspaper offices, for I wanted to be sure of my technical facility and of being able to face editors and listen to their critical judgement. When I left Monroe, excited over the sale to the popular *Judge,* it seemed it would be easy for me to walk right in to the office of the editor of any daily and convince him that he needed my services. But my confidence had been sadly deflated by the time I stood in front of a newspaper building. It took me a long time to screw up courage enough to enter. Then the editor would ask me: "How much experience have you had?" and I would show him the *Judge* drawing, and some of my pictures in the *Nimble Nickel* and the *American Field*—hoping these would impress him. I no longer felt like "the wonder" that folks thought I was back home. Thus had my ego been flattened out by the weight of the city's vast impersonality.

All that of course was mental. I had to become a fullfledged Chicagoan before I could generate the requisite bravado to beard those giants of the sanctums.

But the thing seemed easier as my free-lance sales continued. Having studied the contents of the various dailies carefully for months, I picked the *Evening Mail* as the one most likely to be receptive. Bundling up my best pictures, I called on Clinton Snowden, editor of that paper. It was published by Frank Hatton, who had been First Assistant Postmaster General under President Arthur. Midafternoon, with the *Mail* news-room quieting down after the day's rush. My knees were shaky, but I made a show of boldness. Snowden was cordial, looked at my work, told me it had "promising qualities."

"We may be able to use some of your stuff," he said. "But we have no engraving plant. You'd have to draw on chalk plates. Do you know how to handle them?"

I had a general idea, having heard them discussed by a newspaper artist who was a classroom visitor at the Academy.

Snowden took me into a back room. Here flat steel plates were covered with a layer of hard chalk on which you traced your drawing and then plowed your way through the design with a sharp steel pencil—after which molten lead was poured over the plate. When it cooled you had a cut ready to print. As you plowed you had to blow the chalk dust away—and some artists contended it was dangerous to the lungs to breathe in that dust. I didn't like this roundabout way of making a picture ready for printing, but nevertheless I couldn't pass up the chance when Snowden offered to try me out.

I had brought in some sketches of street scenes, with action in them, and these I now transferred to chalk. The result was better than I had expected from this experiment with a medium new to me, and Snowden liked the pictures; published them all during the next week, and gave me an order on the cashier for $12. I made more chalk sketches, which he took, and presently he began giving me an occasional assignment, sometimes to illustrate a story about a news event or to sketch some celebrity who was being interviewed. The pay varied, but some weeks it was pretty good, and I felt that I had practically a staff job, while still being free to do odds and ends for magazines and trade papers.

On one of the *Mail* assignments, I fell in with a cheerful person named Eugene Wood, who had been a country boy in Ohio, but who had by this time made a reputation as a reporter on the Snowden paper. After a month's acquaintance Wood irreverently addressed me as Nosey, referring to my beak, when it was brilliant from too much sun. His ambition was to be a magazine writer. In later years we met often in New York, and became close friends.

Having finished the dentistry course in record time, Clay Bennett returned to Monroe to set up an office, and my next move was back to Wabash Avenue and the familiar sound of the cable cars—the purring of the cable underground and the imperious clanging of the gripman's bell as he tried to push his way through clogged wagon traffic. The cable cars were like short railroad trains—first an open grip car, on which the seats faced in four directions on front, back and sides; and then one or usually two closed trailer cars. In the grip car the driver stood in all weathers with no protection against the icy winds of winter, and operated long heavy upright levers, one of which clutched the moving cable beneath, the other controlling the brakes. Only in warm weather did the gripmen appear to find life agreeable; in winter they were grim looking, red-faced, wind-whipped.

Safety campaigns hadn't been thought of in those days,

and the ways of crowds were free and easy. When there was some great gathering in good weather, with not enough street cars available to accommodate the homeward bound throng afterward, men and boys would climb to the roofs of the cars and ride there. Seldom did the police interfere, and the conductors wouldn't trouble too much to collect fares. They would collect all within reach, and forget the rest.

WILLIAM FREDERICK POOLE, head of Chicago Public Library. 1885.

On the east side of Wabash Avenue, near Van Buren Street, I found a small second-floor room just large enough for a bed, bureau, and chair, and by acrobatic twisting of my body managed to work on a drawing board leaned against the window ledge. (I must remind the reader that I haven't always been fat.) Here I worked hard, turning out a good many pictures beside the sketches for the *Evening Mail*.

Sometimes in the evenings I went to the public library, then near the City Hall. On my first visit there I found an engaging subject for a sketch—William Frederick Poole, the librarian, a distinguished looking personage, who wore long

Dundrearian whiskers and peered over his nose-glasses. I could easily draw him from memory now, fifty-three years afterward. It was he who established that invaluable reference work, *Poole's Index of Periodicals,* forerunner of the present-day *Readers' Guide.* Mr. Poole was always obliging, always ready to give all the time needed to help an inquirer find an elusive book or magazine.

I delved into every available picture book, especially those containing drawings by Doré, whose fame had become world-wide. I also liked to look at the annual illustrated catalogue of the Paris Salon, and both current issues and bound volumes of the *London Graphic, Harper's Weekly,* the *Illustrated News* of London, and *Punch.* I admired the powerful drawings of R. Caton Woodville; the character sketches of F. Barnard, especially his illustrations for the household edition of Dickens; the cartoons of John Leech, Sir John Tenniel, George Cruikshank, and Harry Furniss. People speak of my woodcut style, and doubtless this early absorption in the work of the graphic artists of the middle nineteenth century had its effect upon my technique.

Many of the best artists of that period in Chicago made their living by painting scenery for the theatre. There was Walter Burridge, whose canvases were usually hung on the line at the Academy of Design annual shows, but whose principal activity was producing background curtains for the shows at McVicker's, and for the Dave Henderson productions in the Grand Opera House when Eddie Foy was the big laugh. One Sunday we went sketching together in the country out beyond LaGrange, and Burridge said: "The way to see a landscape is to bend down frontward, and look at the scene between your legs." I tried it, and certainly found that one's legs helped to frame the view, but there was danger of having a rush of art to the head.

Then there was Jules Guerin, also doing stage scenery, whose work became notable in art circles after his Chicago days. He was slim and nimble, an accomplished artist in profanity as well as in paint, and later developed that remarkable talent for seeing and co-ordinating large spaces of flat color, as opposed to the fretful brush-tapping school of the impressionists. He painted the interior of the Pennsylvania station in New York City.

I exhibited a few times at the Academy of Design annual shows, but to this day have never had much enthusiasm for exhibitions. To go to the trouble of having your picture framed, carted, and then if accepted—to be just one among hundreds, no matter how much your work is acclaimed, with always the doubtful chance of a sale—is an unsatisfactory way of becoming a recognized artist. A solo exhibition is more sensible, but that, too, has its penalties. The art agents have their own peculiar methods of promoting artists, and all things considered, I have thought it best to exhibit my work in periodicals and books.

Chapter 7

THE STAGE IS SET FOR A SUPREME TRAGEDY

SNOWDEN'S occasional assignments to me were varied, though for the most part I was allowed to suggest the pictures I wanted to draw. Moving about the city pretty much at will, I knew that labor was stirring, was beginning to raise its voice. Sometimes I attended a mass meeting on the lake front at the foot of Adams Street, and heard some impassioned speaker denounce the capitalists and the daily press, accusing the newspapers generally of systematically misrepresenting the facts about the conditions under which the working masses toiled and lived. I was not convinced by these fiery charges. Certainly, I felt, the *Evening Mail* could not be as black as it was painted; Snowden struck me as an honest fellow, who in conversations had expressed considerable sympathy for the underdog; and the *Mail* now and then published editorials voicing such sympathy.

A rugged Swede who had come from Seattle a few years before, Snowden was understood to have worked with his hands in his youth. He was tireless as director of the news staff, which was small, but which gave everything it had to help this appreciative chief build up the paper. Once in particular Snowden showed a crusading spirit for the benefit of the common people akin to that shining exemplar of enterprising journalism, Joseph Pulitzer. For many months the *Mail* fought for a three-cent fare on street cars. I remember that a date was set for the people to refuse to ride at the five-cent rate. The boycott, as I recall it, was to begin in a specified area. Snowden and others in our office had it all figured out that this action would bring the company to terms once it saw an indignant populace walk out in protest. But the crusade failed. Only a few persons refused to use the street cars, while the many rode and paid five cents as usual. When the disappointing reports came in, there was gloom in the office of the *Evening Mail*.

Early in 1885 three of Jay Gould's railroads, including the Wabash, had given notice of a 10 per cent cut in shopmen's wages. These workers were organized in the Knights of Labor, which was headed by Terence V. Powderly. In a few days some 4,800 shopmen quit their jobs, and the trainmen on all three lines backed this action with a threat of a sympathy strike. Gould gave in; there was no wage cut: and the managements agreed that there would be no discrimination against any of the strikers. Within six months that agreement was repudiated, and many of the shopmen were fired by the Wabash.

Immediately the Knights of Labor announced a boycott against that road, all men on other lines being ordered to move no Wabash freight cars, while union loaders and teamsters throughout the country were ordered to co-operate. Gould knew that the Knights were strong enough to enforce that boycott, and that it would play havoc with the Wabash line's operations; so he promptly capitulated. The discharged men were reinstated, and the K. of L. ban was called off.

This victory gave a strong impetus to labor organization in all the nation's industrial centers. In those times of bitter negotiations, Jay Gould was often quoted as having said: "I could hire half of the working class to kill the other half." And William H. Vanderbilt, another rail king, had attained dark fame by his retort to a *Chicago Daily News* reporter who tried to interview him in his private car: "The public be damned!"

For more than a year there had been "hard times." Strikes followed wage cuts, employers retaliated with lockouts, and great numbers of men were out of work. Many of them took to the roads as tramps (the term *hobo* was not yet in use), begging their way from town to town. The newspapers spoke editorially of "the tramp menace." Speakers in the outdoor meetings and in labor union halls advocated the eight-hour day as a cure for the growing unemployment. Eight Hour Leagues were springing up in various parts of the country, and Chicago, as the nation's chief industrial city, became the center of this movement. The soap-box speakers told of "starvation wages," long hours of toil, and of working conditions "worse than slavery."

That summer a strike of street-car men was broken by

police clubs; the police heads declared that "we will continue to put down disorder wherever it shows itself." Workers' meetings were often broken up by the forces of "law and order."

"Unprincipled foreigners" and "Anarchists" were blamed by the daily press for the eight-hour-day demand. The editors saw "dirty aliens undermining American institutions." Readers began to hear of the "Black International," as the papers called the International Working People's Association, which had been organized in London several years before, and which was now active in New York, with Johann Most as its leader. Bloody revolution was near at hand, unless something was done to stop it, according to the ominous editorials in the dailies.

Now and then, when I had turned in a layout of pictures to Snowden, I would sit down in a corner of the *Evening Mail* local room to talk with the reporters. Usually the conversation was frivolous, but sometimes it took on a serious cast. Louis Seibold was then a star boy reporter on our paper. An Irishman, one of the older men, whose name I've forgotten, but who read a good deal, occasionally made comment which gave me something to think about.

"There's a limit to how far the police can go in the name of law and order," he said once. "They'll go too far with the clubbing one of these days, and the workers will strike back. Even a worm will turn. Captain Schaack has a lot of gall to talk about 'trouble-makers.' You can bet your life if there was no trouble Schaack would make some. He's a glory hunter and a bastard of the first order!"

Albert Parsons had become well known in the city newspaper offices as the editor of the weekly *Alarm*, organ of the International Working People's Association, and as a militant speaker at mass meetings. A good-looking man with dark hair smoothed back tight on his forehead, a dark moustache, earnest and passionate in his attacks upon the "exploiters of labor," there was no mistaking his sincerity. Even Ed Monahan, cynical young reporter who scoffed at all reformers and agitators, conceded that.

What I knew then about the working masses and their problems, at the age of twenty, was fragmentary, gleaned from hearing occasional speeches and from desultory reading.

No clear realization of what labor was up against had yet sunk into my consciousness, nor did it for many years afterward. I lacked a foundation for such understanding; nothing I had learned in school gave me anything on which to build. In a vague way I sensed that the social system was not perfect, but all that seemed remote from my life. The questions raised by the soap-boxers were disturbing at the moment, but there was little I could do, so far as I could see, to better the situation. I would give a hungry man on the street the price of a meal and a bed, but that would help him only for the time being. And if I drew pictures of hungry people, as such, the *Evening Mail* certainly wouldn't publish them. It might use a news report of some man dying in the street from starvation, but it wouldn't go out of its way to air the causes which led to deaths of that kind. Such happenings were depressing to think about, anyhow. Instinct led me to hope that the Knights of Labor would win the fight for the eight-hour day; that would put many jobless men back to work.

My thoughts turned to more pleasant things as spring came in 1886, and I sketched people at their ease on Sunday in the parks, pioneer residents of Chicago, quaint street scenes, important guests in the larger hotels, sandlot baseball games, and other innocuous if colorful phases of the city's life.

And I had been home in March for my sister's marriage to Clyde Copeland, "by Elder Daniel R. Howe of the Christian Church, at the residence of the bride's parents." My wedding gift was a water color drawing of the bride and groom, surrounded by ornate decorations, with cupids rampant over the heads of wedding guests, and myself in the foreground, dismissing the affair with a wave of the hand and saying: "No wedding bells for me."

Lingering in Monroe for a few days, I enjoyed myself. My friend the postmaster was displaying clippings of some of my recent pictures from the *Mail* on the government's wall, and so everybody in town was kept posted about my productions. But old Bill Sutherland, retired plasterer, was surprised to hear that I'd been away. "I don't get downtown much nowadays, on account of my sciaticy." Then he told me "I've tried Swift's Specific, St. Jacob's Oil, Packard's Pain

Killer, and Peruna, but it still ketches me right here," gesturing around to his back.

From my store of collected material I have come across a yellowed copy of the Monroe *Sentinel* which reported my sister's wedding. Scores of compact paragraphs of news of the outside world were in that issue of Charlie Booth's weekly:

"Again is the assertion made in New York dispatches that ex-President Arthur is in very bad health, and not likely to recover. . . . A strike of street-car employees is in progress at Columbus, Ohio, and plans for a revolt at Pittsburgh have been made. . . . Duke Calabeitti, who was exiled from Italy for fighting with Garibaldi, died Wednesday in Hoboken, N. J., where he was a hotel manager. . . . The eight-hour ordinance passed by the Milwaukee common council, affecting all persons paid by the day, has been signed by Mayor Wallber. . . . An affliction resembling epizoot is so prevalent at Canton, Ohio, as to confine 1,000 school children to their beds or homes.

"Distress prevailing among the unemployed of Great Britain is not deemed by Mr. Gladstone a sufficient reason for asking the Queen to appoint a day for national humiliation and prayer. . . . A dispatch from Scituate, Mass. reports the death of Miss Abigail Bates, one of two heroines who in the war of 1812 drove away the British by playing a fife and drum in the bushes. . . . H. M. Hoxie, vice-president of the Missouri Pacific, in a letter to T. V. Powderly, declined to hold a conference with the Knights of Labor, and argues that the strike is devoid of a redressable grievance. . . . Both houses of Congress have passed the pension bill which increases the pensions of soldiers' widows and dependent relatives from $8 to $12 per month. It will require about seven million dollars to meet the provisions of the bill."

Back in Chicago after that vacation, I stuck close to the drawing board. I was doing pretty well on the *Mail,* but I wanted to do better, to put money in the bank and have a substantial cash reserve. Many of the newspaper men I knew spent their spare time in gambling and drinking. I was not inclined in that direction. This was not at all a moral attitude. I simply found no fun in it. I saved my money by holding to the small room on Wabash Avenue, for which I paid $3 a week. Few friends came there, and I had no wish to have large and impressive quarters as an accompaniment to success.

Easter came on April 25, and I watched the parade that morning in the vicinity of one of the South Side churches where the wealthy attended. All was right with the world, if one could judge from the beaming faces of the well-dressed churchgoers as they moved along the walks homeward or got into their carriages. Swelling organ music poured through the open church doors as the congregation made its exit, and a sleek clergyman shook hands with many of his flock, uttering polite, stereotyped phrases.

But in the downtown section some 3,500 workers, bearing flags and union banners, and headed by a band, marched through the streets to the lake front, to join in a demonstration in behalf of the eight-hour work day, in which 20,000 persons or more took part. Speeches were made by various leaders of the movement, including four whose names were soon to become symbols in a mighty social conflict—Parsons, Schwab, Spies, and Fielden.

The speakers dwelt at length upon the wrongs that labor had suffered at the hands of the railroads, manufacturers, and other employers; they told how animosities had been fostered by agents of the bosses between one nationality and another, such as the Germans and the Irish, to keep them from organizing; they excoriated the police for brutal attacks upon the toilers who produced the wealth for capitalists to enjoy.

All this reminded the newspapers and the police heads acutely that May 1 was near, and that organized labor had planned strikes in major industries on that day, to enforce its demand for the eight-hour day. Chicago employers urged Mayor Carter H. Harrison to have state troops in readiness, and he said no, as he had in the past. The police were competent to meet any emergency, he averred. Elected largely by the workers, Harrison was in his fourth term, and he had kept his head, despite all the alarmist talk by merchants and financiers that revolution was at the city's gates.

So bitter and far-reaching had been the attack upon the eight-hour-day movement that the local executive board of the Knights of Labor, that week, rescinded its approval of the plan for the May Day strikes. For this the board was assailed as cowardly by many rank-and-file members. The *Alarm* and another militant labor paper, *Die Arbeiter Zeitung,* called on the workers to defend themselves—with force if need be—against the assaults of the police and the Pinkertons who served the capitalists.

Word was given out at police headquarters on Friday night, April 30, that the whole force would be on reserve all next day, and that arrangements had been made to muster hundreds of special policemen "in the event of any serious outbreak."

"Captain Schaack will be sadly disappointed," said my Irish co-worker on May Day morning, "if his men can't find an excuse to smash a lot of skulls today."

But there was no outbreak, no disorder of any kind. More than 60,000 workers paraded or took part in gatherings that day, and no occasion arose for arrests. The "celebration" of that May Day, however, lacked any aspect of joyousness. Defiance was its keynote, the paraders and the police eyeing each other with sullenness.

Whatever reassurance there was for the general public in Saturday's peacefulness, new trouble blazed forth on Monday at the McCormick harvester works out on Blue Island Avenue, known to old-timers as the Black Road. For many weeks this had been a sore spot for the workers. Fourteen hundred striking employees there had been locked out in February, the company bringing in scabs and 300 Pinkerton thugs to guard them. Cyrus H. McCormick told the press that "the right to hire any man, white or black, union or nonunion, Protestant or Catholic, is something I will not surrender."

Protest meetings arranged by Albert Parsons and his associates near the gates of the McCormick works had repeatedly been broken up by the police with clubs. On that Monday, May 3, August Spies, editor of the *Arbeiter-Zeitung,* was one of those who addressed such a meeting. He called upon the strikers to stand solidly together. Soon afterward there was a clash between the locked-out men and a group of scabs. Police to the number of 150 came, fired into the throng, killing one striker and wounding at least five others.

Spies went back to the *Arbeiter-Zeitung* office, and wrote an account of all this for his paper. He had seen the strikers fall before the police bullets, and that afternoon he read in the *Daily News* that six men had been killed in that attack. This report was not accurate, but Spies had ample reason to believe that it was. Finishing his news story, he talked with others about the situation, and then wrote copy for a leaflet announcing a mass meeting of protest to be held in Haymarket Square on the West Side the next night. This was headed: "Workingmen! To Arms!" Without consulting Spies, the compositor who set the type inserted ahead of that slogan and as a part of it the word "Revenge!" Thousands of copies of this leaflet were distributed overnight wherever workers gathered.

I was reading about the industrial turmoil, or hearing about it from members of the *Mail* staff, but I was not getting assignments to illustrate any news stories dealing with it. My social awareness remained undeveloped. I had no perspective on the human conflict, and had not found out how to connect up an effect with its underlying causes.

When I came from the country I had a strong belief that the newspapers of the big cities were oracles, beacon lights. I still clung to that belief, though a bit shakily. Of course I knew their policies were inconsistent, but perhaps that couldn't be helped—it was best not to expect it. In one election a Chicago daily would thunderingly assail some candidate, and a year later would be lauding him, with no explanation of its reversal. And the same newspaper would attack the railroads for victimizing both their employees and patrons, but would assail the eight-hour day movement and organized labor's program. The press blew hot and cold at will. I was often bewildered by that.

Chapter 8

I SEE CHICAGO JUSTICE AT CLOSE RANGE

I NEED not dwell at length upon what happened in Haymarket Square on the night of May 4, 1886. The story has been told many times—the mass-meeting of some 1,500 persons in protest against the wanton shooting of workers by the police; Mayor Carter H. Harrison in attendance; Albert Parsons speaking, then leaving with his wife for a beer garden two blocks away; Samuel Fielden mounting the wagon used as a rostrum: rain beginning to fall, and the crowd dwindling; the Mayor departing, and visiting the nearby Desplaines Street police station to report to Captain John Bonfield that there had been no disorder at the meeting; Bonfield disregarding the Mayor's words, and in a few minutes leading 125 reserve policemen to the scene, and ordering the remaining audience of some 200 persons to disperse; then from above or behind the wagon a whizzing spark; a tremendous explosion; many policemen falling; their comrades firing into the panic-stricken crowd, killing and wounding. Seven of the police died; how many civilians were killed by police bullets that night was never definitely known, and nothing was ever done about it.

Then a hue and cry—widespread police raids; arrests of hundreds of men and women known as or suspected to be Anarchists, Socialists, or Communists; announcements of the discovery of various dynamite "plots" and of the finding of bombs and infernal machines; indictment of Albert Parsons and others as conspirators responsible for the Haymarket explosion and deaths.

Newspaper editors and public men generally cried for a quick trial of the defendants, with speedy executions to follow, and there was every reason to believe from the published reports that the accused were guilty. Public opinion was formed almost solely by the daily press, and in its columns "evidence" was steadily piled up against these labor agitators. Parsons had disappeared on the night of the bombing—police all over the country were watching for him; was not his flight confession of guilt? Rudolph Schnaubelt also was gone; he had been arrested twice and questioned briefly, but had been released—and Police Captain Schaack was incensed at the "stupidity" of the detectives who had let him go; Schnaubelt specifically was suspected of the actual bomb-throwing. And the daily newspapers reproduced a leaflet announcing the Haymarket meeting, which bore a black-faced line urging workers to come armed.

Like the great mass of Chicagoans, I was swayed by these detailed reports of the black-heartedness of the defendants. Outstanding business and professional men, and prominent members of the clergy, denounced the accused, who were now all lumped together as "Anarchists," and condemned the killing of the seven policemen as being "the most wanton outrage in American history." In the bloody and gruesome descriptions of the tragedy of May 4, the city's people forgot the needless killing and wounding of workers by the police on May 3. I, too, saw "evidence" against Parsons in his running away. He had spoken at the mass-meeting, and the explosion had come only a few minutes after he left—and then he had vanished. Innocent men do not run away when a crime has been committed (so my youthful mind reasoned then); they stay and face the music.

But when on the opening day of the trial, June 21, Albert Parsons walked into court and declared that he wanted to be tried with his comrades, my sympathies began to lean in the other direction. He had been in seclusion in Waukesha, Wisconsin, working as a carpenter and living in the home of Daniel Hoan, father of the present Mayor of Milwaukee. If Parsons were guilty, I reasoned now, he would not have come back; he needn't have come; the police had been unable to find any trace of him.

Shortly after the jury had been selected, Clinton Snowden assigned me to make some pictures of scenes in the courtroom for the *Evening Mail*. The place was crowded, but I managed to get a seat with the reporters at a table near the defense attorneys. The prosecution was putting in its case, and there were continual objections by the defense to the line of questioning by Julius S. Grinnell, the State's Attorney.

Usually these objections were overruled, in a rasping voice, by Judge Joseph E. Gary. When Grinnell uttered some opinion which the defense considered prejudicial, Gary would say: "The jury will disregard the State's Attorney's remark" —but Grinnell kept on with bold assurance that he was master of the situation.

Many well-dressed men and women, obviously from the city's better families, were spectators, craning their necks to

JUDGE JOSEPH E. GARY, who presided at the trial of the Haymarket case defendants.

get a view of the eight defendants. But I was interested quite as much in the lawyers battling on both sides of the case. It was common knowledge that it had been difficult to find reputable and competent attorneys in Chicago willing to defend the accused; their cause was too unpopular; notice had been plainly served that only a pariah and an enemy of society would try to save those men from the gallows. In the face of this warning, three courageous members of the bar, who hitherto had handled only civil cases, had agreed to undertake the Anarchists' defense. William P. Black was chief of these; a captain in the Union Army during the Civil War, he was known as a fighter; tall, dark, and handsome, with a pronounced jaw that shook a short beard, he was often the center of all eyes in court. Assisting Black were William A. Foster, said to be capable as a finder of evidence, and Sigismund Zeisler, an earnest and studious young man with a blond vandyke beard, red lips, and wavy hair.

On the other side of this desperate contest was Grinnell, the State's Attorney, who was understood to aspire to the Governor's chair; and several assistants, whose names got into print much less often than Grinnell's. He had a fresh, healthy face and a big well-curled moustache.

At that stage of the fight the *Evening Mail* was particularly interested in the make-up of the jury, for it had been selected only after the examination of almost a thousand talesmen, during a period of four weeks. That jury was representative of the middle class.

Frank S. Osborne, the jury foreman, was a salesman for Marshall Field and Company; and the other eleven "good men and true" answered to these descriptions: former railroad construction contractor, clothing salesman, ex-broker from Boston, school principal, shipping clerk, traveling paint salesman, book-keeper, stenographer for the Chicago and Northwestern Railway, voucher clerk for the same railroad, hardware merchant, seed salesman.

Watching the accused men in court, I wondered whether it was indeed possible that any of them had anything to do with the throwing of that bomb, which wounded countless working people as well as killing the seven policemen. There were reports, repeatedly published, that members of the Anarchist group were mortally injured on the night of May 4, but that they were "spirited away" by friends.

The defendants were neatly dressed, each with a flower in his buttonhole. They sat in their chairs with dignity, and with the apparent self-confidence of men who expected to be exonerated.

There was a breathless tension to the court proceedings, the air electric. Grinnell talked much about "protecting society and government against enemies bent on their destruction." Captain Black was on his feet often with objections.

Back at the *Evening Mail* office, I re-drew my sketches

on chalk plates. By this time I had acquired a ready hand for working with this process, though I never liked it. These pictures of the trial attracted considerable attention, both among the *Mail* staff and outside. Word came to me a little later that Melville E. Stone, editor of the *Daily News,* had commented favorably upon that day's work of mine. And Snowden praised my courtroom pictures.

Having attended a few sessions of the trial, and in a sense having been for several days a part of that dramatic spectacle, I followed the newspaper reports of the case with deep interest. "Evidence" steadily mounted against them. Of the real quality of that "evidence" I knew nothing then.

After the prosecution had rested its case, the defense attorneys moved that the jury be instructed to return a verdict of not guilty for Neebe, on the ground that the State had failed to connect him in any way with either the bomb-throwing or the alleged conspiracy. But Judge Gary overruled the motion.

When the defense was putting in its evidence, I was in court again, and now the accused men were having their inning. The structure which the State had built up seemed to be breaking down. I took note of Parsons's wife in the audience, with her striking Indian-hued face; of Nina Van Zandt, sweetheart of Spies; and of the relatives of other defendants. They all seemed buoyed up by new hope.

Reading in next morning's papers about the sessions I had attended, however, the case appeared in a much different light than it had in the courtroom. Did the reporters have sharper ears and keener eyes than I? Perhaps so; they were trained in this kind of work while I was new at it. Yet why was one side of the case over-emphasized, and the other subordinated? I know now, but I didn't know then.

And a few days later, the State had the last word blasting the defendants in its closing arguments, repairing any damage the defense had done to the prosecution's case. Grinnell spoke all one day and part of the next. Out over night, the jury brought in a verdict finding all the defendants guilty of murder "as charged in the indictment." That verdict specified a penalty of death for Spies, Schwab, Fielden, Parsons, Fischer, Engel, and Lingg; and fifteen years' imprisonment for Neebe.

I listened to the opinion among the men on the *Mail* staff as to the guilt or innocence of the Anarchists. Argument over that question went on heatedly for days in the news room. The champions of the defendants, who were in the minority, cited various alleged flaws in the State's case. I remember there was a good deal of skepticism over the testimony of a *Tribune* reporter, a prosecution witness, who told what was said by speakers at the Haymarket meeting, and swore that he took notes with a pencil down inside of his overcoat pocket! But even if the prosecution was weak on that point, the conservatives declared, there was plenty of other evidence of guilt—and they cited it, point by point. "I'll trust that jury," Fred Martin insisted. "All of them are guilty as hell."

Newspaper editorials and prominent citizens in interviews lauded the jury for "intelligent service to the State" and the *Tribune* printed a letter from an ardent reader urging the raising of a $100,000 fund to be presented to the jurors as a fitting reward for their fearless integrity, etcetra.

Immediately after the verdict the defense gave notice that it would appeal to the higher courts, and with the convicted men locked in their cells in the county jail, the press began devoting its front pages to other affairs.

I was to see more of the class struggle in the near future without knowing what it meant. Indeed, at that time, when I was 20 years old, I knew hardly anything except that I had a knack for drawing pictures and was pretty good at reciting selections from books of poetry.

Chapter 9

MELVILLE E. STONE SENDS FOR ME

NOW I got word that Melville E. Stone wanted to see me. Waiting a few days so as not to seem too anxious, I went over to the *Daily News* office, taking along samples of the best of my drawings. Stone looked them over with a critical eye.

"I've been watching your work," he said, "and I was impressed particularly by your sketches of the Anarchists' trial. I think we could make a place for you here. The *Daily News* is expanding, and we need pictures—good pictures. We've just put in a zinc etching plant, and we've stopped using chalk plates. . . . How would you like to come and work for us in the art department?"

I favored the idea.

"How much money do you want?"

That was a trying moment. I was still afraid of editors, and for many years thereafter my heart sank whenever I approached any of them. I had read a book, *Getting on in the World,* by William Mathews. Whether it fortified me at this juncture, I don't know, but I kept saying to myself: "Look your listener right in the eye and don't sell your talent too cheap." Stone's question was a tactical error. I had been getting only about $12 a week from the *Evening Mail* for my free-lance contributions; and if he had offered me $15 or $20 a week I would have accepted without haggling, for the chance to work on such an enterprising paper as the *Daily News*.

But boldly I said: "I think I am worth $35—a week."

"Well, you *are* worth that if you can do the work," Stone answered.

Instantly I thought: "My God, what have I done? I've got to make good."

So I was given a key to the art department and a salary that was large for a country boy, in those days before artists and pictures were thought to be much of an asset to newspapers. J. C. Selanders had been doing most of the work in that department, but he was soon to leave for a tour of Europe.

Stone was editor and part owner of the *News,* with Victor F. Lawson as partner. Tall and slim, and son of a small-town clergyman, Stone was an energetic and ambitious person, obviously proud of the contacts with notables that he made through his position.

Most of my assignments came from Charles H. Dennis, the managing editor, and from Butch White, city editor; but occasionally they were given directly by Stone, in his nasal voice. Once I said to him, after proposing a certain kind of picture: "I think the public likes such pictures." "Never mind what the public likes," Stone answered. "I'll take care of that."

Like the *Evening Mail,* the *Daily News* was in an old dingy building. In fact all the Chicago papers were then in such rookeries. My working environment was raw, but it didn't matter. The adventure of being in a bustling metropolis constantly took on new color. The city was smoky and blatant, sprawled out and smelly—with odors both savory and repellent: blindfold, I could have told with a high percentage of accuracy what part of town I was in. There were the spice mills and coffee roasting plants around the Hoyt company's quarters near the Rush Street bridge; the fish, poultry, fruit, and vegetable markets along South Water Street; the poisonous river, which with its two branches divided the city into three segments; and more potent than all else, when the wind was from the Southwest, the unmistakable breath of the stockyards. Another odor which, however, might be found anywhere in Chicago was sewer gas.

Newspaper standards in that time were low, though I didn't know it, having no yardstick for comparison. The dailies were emotional in their news columns as well as in editorials, profuse with derogatory epithets even on the front pages in political campaigns. They fawned upon visiting celebrities, often grew maudlin in eulogies of them. Some of the papers systematically stole telegraph news from the others; one way of achieving such theft was the bribery of a telegraph operator in one office to provide an unofficial client with carbon copies of all material coming over the wires. A good many outlandish fake news stories found their way into print, and were all too often believed by a gullible public. Many reporters were careless with their use of facts. The less prosperous dailies, weak in their supply of telegraphic intelligence and with small local staffs, brought invention into play; anything to keep up with, or beat, their rivals.

FASHION IN 1886, from one of my sketch-books.

It was good sport to sit around with the reporters after hours, in the local room or over in police headquarters, and hear the news-hounds boast about their achievements—how one landed a big story by hiding under a sofa in an alderman's office; how another impersonated a federal officer and thus got an interview with a fugitive not yet caught by the authorities; how a third crouched in water in a rainbarrel while he eavesdropped on a well-known couple who a little later were airing dirty linen in the divorce court. There were gory tales, too, of suspects in crime cases being beaten almost to death in the police stations to force them to talk; these were horrifying.

Assignments on the *Daily News* gave me entree everywhere that I wanted to go, and my life moved along smoothly. From men and women whose names were known internationally for their achievements, I learned much. True,

Chicago Daily News

BOOTH AND BARRETT. Two great actors view the Lincoln statue by St. Gaudens.

the information I was picking up was in unrelated pieces; and I had to become much older before I could put these jigsaw pieces together and make a clear composite of them.

Frances Willard, long president of the Woman's Christian Temperance Union, made a deep impression on me when I sketched her. She was the first woman publicist of any consequence that I ever saw. It was a rare thing in those days for a woman to do battle on social questions in the public arena. Except for those who braved ostracism by going on the stage, most of the gentler sex either remained in the home, concerned themselves with non-controversial activities like music, became missionaries or collected money for the heathen, taught school, or went into nunneries. Miss Willard, a finely moulded individual, was a torch of eloquence.

I listened spellbound as she addressed a convention of several thousand people in the old Exposition building. She was attacking the exploitation of the masses by the rich, and her statements seemed unanswerable. Some years later I got hold of a pamphlet in which she advocated such radical steps as nationalization of transportation and communication; public ownership of newspapers, with every editorial bearing the signature of its author; compulsory arbitration in industrial disputes; and minimum wages for workers. This was one of the first Socialistic appeals that I ever read, although I am sure there was no mention of Socialism in Miss Willard's utterances. I could see nothing fanatical about this magnetic woman or her ideas. But she was expected to stick to the subject of temperance and let economics alone.

President Grover Cleveland and his wife came to town, and I made sketches of them, as they were driven along Michigan Avenue in a four-horse carriage. Cleveland was so bulky that he looked slightly comic, especially because of his habit of wearing his silk hat tilted a bit forward.

One day in Lincoln Park, by sheer chance, I came upon Edwin Booth and Lawrence Barrett, his fellow actor, seated in a carriage viewing the St. Gaudens statue of Abraham Lincoln, which was being made ready for dedication. I sketched that scene and it was reproduced in the *Daily News*. Booth had often been hooted when he appeared on the stage after his brother Wilkes had killed Lincoln, but he nevertheless had continued his career, and finally regained public esteem.

One rarely hears of Eugene Field nowadays, save when some old-timer harks back in reminiscence to him and his work. But in the Eighties he was an institution in Chicago; and like all who are in the limelight he had detractors as well as panegyrists. Day after day the local scene was enlivened by his column in the *Daily News*, which bore the title, "Sharps and Flats."

His writings therein, like those in most columns of the kind in newspapers, were words traced in sand, forgotten soon afterward. Most of his poems have faded out, except "Winken, Blynken, and Nod," "Little Boy Blue" and "Seeing Things at Night." Another favorite with me was "That Was Long Ago," in which a father relates youthful memories to his child. He could recite his own poems better than any of the professional elocutionists. I knew many of them by heart.

"I don't write poetry," he said to me. "Call it just verse." Yet some of it *was* poetry, with depth of feeling and a lilt of beauty that compels remembrance.

I can look back fifty years and see him clearly in his cubby-hole, exchanging quips with a side-whiskered crony— Dr. Frank Reilly of the editorial staff, later Chicago's health commissioner. Field has an architect's drawing board on his knees. That is the desk on which he does his writing; and his penmanship is as clear and fine as copper-plate print. The walls are plastered with newspaper clippings, most of them about himself and his friends. He was sixteen years older than I, but having youngsters like myself around seemed to be his idea of right living.

Field had inherited $8,000 from his father at the age of twenty-one, and set out immediately to see how fast he could get rid of it. With a brother of the girl he was to marry, he went abroad, "spending six months and my patrimony" in France, Italy, Ireland, and England.

"I just threw the money around," he said, in recalling that splurge. "I paid it out for experience—and experience was lying around loose everywhere I traveled. When I got back life was a good deal simpler than when I thought myself rich. Practically broke, I went into newspaper work in St. Louis."

After I had come to know him he made a second visit to England, and declared on his return that he didn't care much for the English. Yet he had brought home a lot of souvenir photographs of British men of letters whom he liked— among them Andrew Lang—and an axe presented to him by Prime Minister Gladstone, who had chopped down numberless trees with it for exercise.

Field asked Lang to translate a Latin epigram which had

accompanied the axe, and Lang promptly obliged with the translation, adding: "If your countrymen admire Mr. Gladstone, I wish they had owned him; but the just anger of God sent him to punish our imperial hypocrisy and humbug. Every nation has the Gladstone it deserves."

I spent many pleasant hours with Field at his home in suburban Buena Park. Here, in a spacious "den," he did a great deal of his work, flanked by books and piles of newspapers, and surrounded by thousands of curios, beautiful or grotesque, which revealed a collector's passion. Especially was he fond of canes from all countries. He sat in an arm-chair which had belonged to Jefferson Davis, and on his table was an inkstand that Napoleon had used and scissors formerly Charles A. Dana's. And on shelves and in glass-fronted cabinets were hundreds of dolls, old china, odd-shaped bottles, mechanical toys, small images, and strange pewter dishes.

"Some of the best of these things I got for nothing," he explained. "When a fellow becomes known as a collector, and can show just the right shade of enthusiasm for some object that another person has, he finds that a lot of people are glad to contribute to his collection."

When Field knew you well enough he would show you his most unusual treasure—an album of pornographic pictures, curious examples of erotica from many lands, in which both men and women and dumb animals were portrayed in amorous ecstasies. I am sure that Anthony Comstock would have burned with envy had he known of that garner of forbidden photographs in Buena Park.

Field had canaries in his den, but their cage-doors were left open. They flew about the room, alighting on his shoulders or anywhere they pleased, while he wrote or read.

He thought of himself as a hard man to get along with, and once told me of a dream he had had the night before. "I was in Heaven, walking along the golden streets," he said, "and somebody introduced me to an old codger he called Job. 'What,' said I, 'are you the man who had so much trouble, as told in the Bible?' . . . 'I'm the man,' said Job. . . . 'Well, Job,' I said, 'you don't know what trouble is. Wait until you meet the woman who had to live with me—Mrs. Eugene Field.'"

Field was an inveterate practical joker, and no one in

the *Daily News* office was immune from his humorous frame-ups. He perpetrated some jokes on the editor which delighted the staff. Once when he felt the need of a salary increase, he rounded up several ragged children from the back streets, gave dimes to them, cautioned them not to talk, and marched them up the stairs and into Stone's presence.

"Is it right," he demanded, "that my children go ragged in the streets because the *Daily News* won't pay me a decent wage?"

Stone pretended to weep over the columnist's sad plight, and instructed the cashier to step up his pay envelope.

Field would cheerfully invite any uninitiated caller to sit in a chair with a camouflage cushion of a few newspapers. It originally had had a cane seat, but this had long since worn out, and the caller's stern would sink into the aperture along with his dignity. Eugene always apologized profusely for not having had the chair fixed, while the victim struggled to extricate himself.

A man of reading and discernment, Field was at the same time Wild-Western and raw, an odd combination. He chewed tobacco with avidity and swore convincingly, often inventing unique profane phrases which aroused admiration among his less imaginative co-workers.

Like Mark Twain, Field was an ardent dissenter against the prevailing social order in private conversation, although not much of that dissent was found in his writings—nor in Twain's. Both of those men were born too soon, or perhaps were just naturally cautious of being combative in public. They were cast by Fate into a period which we know today as the era of rugged individualism—a nation marching behind a banner bearing the legend: "Self conquers all!" Meaning, of course, that it's up to you alone—a doctrine which practically everybody across the land took for granted, and one which hangs on in spite of its falsity.

Yet Field and Twain occasionally exhibited signs of doubt and wrote satirical comment on American life. Field poked fun at the shallow culture of the Chicago pork packers, and Mark Twain indulged in brief outbursts of anarchistic protest. None of their onsets, however, was incisive enough to make the big financiers question their loyalty to the existing economic and social system.

Finley Peter Dunne was on the *Daily News* staff then, writing editorials and paragraphs about current affairs. He had not yet conceived the Mr. Dooley series, those pithy comments on the uneven course of the human race still being ten years in the future. Dunne's small office was on the second floor, one of several formed by eight-foot partitions. I remember dropping in one day to show him a picture I had just finished. He laid down a book he had been reading—the story of a trip up the Hudson and to New York summer resorts, by Charles Dudley Warner. Looking at me through

FINLEY PETER DUNNE, before the Dooley articles brought him fame.

spectacles set against a bulbous nose, Dunne said: "I've been wasting my time reading this. Some critics say Warner is a genius. Genius hell!"

Irish wit often cropped out in his daily talk even then, and so the Dooley philosophy had a familiar ring when it was being featured afterward when Dunne was on the *Evening Journal*. I followed the observations of "the sage of Archey Road" with delight, and Mr. Dooley frequently scored a bull's eye with his verbal shafts. He managed to get in a lot of side-swipes at the financiers, the politicians, the war-makers, and other evil figures and institutions in American life, in the guise of humor. In his Dooley articles he called attention to stupidity on our side of the fence in the conduct of the Spanish-American War; he voiced skepticism that the Standard Oil Company would ever have to pay the famous $29,000,000 fine, and it never did; and he dealt with the national tendency to begin crusades against social wrongs and never finish them. He knew the value of ridicule as a weapon.

Some of the sayings of Mr. Dooley deserve recalling now:

"High finance ain't burglary, an' it ain't obtaining money be false pretinses, an' it ain't manslaughter. It's what ye might call a judicious seliction fr'm th' best features iv thim ar-rts."

WOMEN ON THE TRICYCLE.

Chicago Daily News

BEFORE THE BICYCLE. Young women sped along on tricycles in 1887.

"I'll niver go down again to see sojers off to th' war. But ye'll see me at the depot with a brass band whin th' men that causes wars starts f'r th' scene iv carnage."

"Don't ask f'r rights. Take thim. An' don't let anny wan give thim to ye. A right that is handed to ye f'r nothin' has somethin' the matter with it. It's more than likely it's only a wrong turned inside out."

And when his friend Hennessey asked: "What's all this that's in the papers about the open shop?" Mr. Dooley answered:

". . . Really, I'm surprised at yer ignorance, Hinnissey. What is th' open shop? Sure, 'tis where they kape the doors open to accommodate th' constant stream av min comin' in t' take jobs cheaper than th' min that has th' jobs. . . ."

"But," said Hennessy, "these open-shop min ye minshun say they are fur the unions if properly conducted."

"Sure," said Mr. Dooley, "if properly conducted. An' there we are. An' how would they have thim conducted? No strikes, no rules, no conthracts, no scales, hardly any wages, and damn few members."

Robert B. Peattie and his wife Elia also were energetic members of the *News* staff in my time. With his white face and nose glasses, Peattie moved about the office like an absorbed professor. Elia had school-girl cheeks. In summer she edited the news of the Wisconsin resorts. Whenever she entered the art department all four artists (the staff was growing) stopped their work to gaze upon a woman as pretty as a rose fresh from outdoors. I had heard of the literary evenings in their home, and was invited to one of them, but gave an excuse to stay away. I felt I was still a bit too crude to mingle with the elect.

My most important assignment on the *Daily News*, up to that time, came on August 11, 1887, when I was sent down to Chatsworth, Illinois, some ninety miles, to cover the aftermath of an appalling disaster there. On the previous night an excursion train on Jay Gould's bankrupt railroad, the Toledo, Peoria & Western, had piled up in a corn-field when a burning wooden trestle gave way.

First reports stated that more than 100 persons had been killed, and 400 injured. The actual number of dead was eighty.

I went first to the wreck scene, three miles east of the town. One sleeping car had somehow remained right side up, and was still largely intact. But the others were mostly smashed or burned. Amid the corn rows were a lot of car-seats, on which the injured had been laid until they could be taken to Chatsworth. Many men and boys and a few women moved about amid the debris, some of them picking up bits of charred wood or scraps of twisted metal as souvenirs.

THE WRECK AFTER RECOVERING THE BODIES.

SCENES ON THE LOWER FLOOR OF THE TOWN HALL AT CHATSWORTH.

FREIGHT-ROOM IN THE DEPOT AT CHATSWORTH.

Chicago Daily News

THE CHATSWORTH TRAIN WRECK. Aftermath of an 1887 Illinois disaster in which 80 persons were killed.

That train had left Peoria at 8 p.m. on the 10th, loaded to the limit with 960 passengers, all bound for Niagara Falls on a $7.50 round-trip excursion. Six sleepers, six day coaches and chair-cars, three baggage-cars—all of wood, of course, then—and two locomotives. Being an hour and a half behind time, the train was running nearly a mile a minute when it passed Chatsworth.

The wooden trestle was only 15 feet wide, bridging a dry creek-bed 10 feet below. Sparks from some other train supposedly had set it afire. The engineer on the first locomotive saw the flames too late. The first locomotive got across; the trestle crumpled under the weight of the second, and the cars piled up behind it, quickly taking fire.

Many of the injured were women and children. Among those unhurt were only about fifty able-bodied men. They did all that they humanly could to rescue people trapped in the burning cars, and for some four hours they fought the flames with earth carried in their bare hands. Not a drop of water was available, and the dying suffered from thirst.

Arriving in Chatsworth after dark, I had already steeled my emotions against the sights which met my eyes. Newspaper men take on fortitude in the presence of catastrophes as do doctors and nurses. The city hall, depot, and another building had been turned into hospitals, serving also as morgues, with the dead lying on the floor covered with sheets or other pieces of cloth. Homes of the townsmen had been opened to survivors of the wreck who had to remain there with injured members of their families. I made sketches in the light of flickering lanterns and oil lamps. I can remember the sobbing of women and the groaning of the sufferers on the cots.

Men who stood around waiting to learn whether some loved one would live discussed the cause of the crash. Some of them were outspoken in blaming Jay Gould, notorious for exploiting railroads and the railroad-using public. He had let the T. P. & W. run down, one man said, until anybody who rode on it was in danger of being killed.

My drawings were used in the *Daily News* next day. Done under difficult conditions, I can see now that they were crude. But they evidently were all right for that day, and they satisfied the editors. Stone complimented me, saying I had done a good job.

Chapter 10

FOUR DISSENTERS SILENCED BY THE ROPE

MEANWHILE the attorneys for the convicted Anarchists had carried their case to the State Supreme Court.
The city had cooled down; one no longer heard of plots to blow up police stations, nor of plans for revolution. A defense committee had collected money to cover the expense of the appeal; in the *Daily News* office we understood that it was having tough going; most people in Chicago accepted the jury's verdict as just, and thought the convicted men ought to be hanged: only a few intrepid souls argued otherwise.

In the local room, occasionally during lulls in the pressure of work, controversy over the kind of evidence presented would flare up again. Bits of the speeches made by the defendants in court would be quoted. Doubt would be cast upon some of the "plots" uncovered by Captain Schaack. But the defenders of "law and order" among the reporters would cite an array of evidence developed by the prosecution, to show that "the jury did right."

When in November, 1886, the high Illinois tribunal granted a stay of execution of the sentence, bets at considerable odds were offered by knowing newspapermen that the courts would affirm the verdict. I recall no takers. But when the appeal was filed and arguments were heard in Springfield the following March, the prisoners and their counsel were hopeful of winning a new trial. The lawyers had cited numerous alleged errors in Judge Gary's procedure, and offered affidavits to prove that the jury had been "packed."

Six months passed before the court handed down its decision. It unanimously upheld the judgement. Discussing the case at great length, it gave many technical reasons for approving the jury's findings. This decision was of course featured in the Chicago dailies.

But the defense would not yet admit defeat. Preparations

were immediately begun to carry the fight to the United States Supreme Court, on constitutional grounds. General Benjamin F. Butler was one of the attorneys who presented the argument in Washington late in October, 1887. After five days' consideration by the full bench, Chief Justice Waite read its decision. No cause for reversal, it said.

Earlier Judge Gary had sentenced the seven men in the county jail to die by hanging there on November 11. This left them only nine days to live. Counsel and members of the defense committee began circulating petitions addressed to Gov. Richard Oglesby urging commutation to life terms in prison. Many prominent individuals wrote the state chief executive to that end, and various delegations visited him in behalf of the doomed men.

It was apparent now that sentiment concerning the Anarchists had changed a good deal. Appeals in their behalf were signed by notables including Lyman J. Gage, later Secretary of the Treasury; William Dean Howells, Robert G. Ingersoll, Henry Demarest Lloyd, General Roger A. Pryor, and George Francis Train. From England protests against the impending execution were cabled by William Morris, Walter Crane, Annie Besant, Sir Walter Besant, and Oscar Wilde. And 16,000 members of working-class organizations in London, on a single day, signed a plea to Oglesby to save the doomed men. George Bernard Shaw was one of those who circulated that petition.

While all this desperate activity was being generated by the defense, various well-known Chicago citizens were saying publicly that "the killing of the Haymarket martyrs must be atoned"; that "the safety of our whole community demands that these executions proceed"; that "those who defend anarchy by speaking in behalf of these red-handed murderers ought to be run out of the country."

On Wednesday, November 9, two days before the scheduled hanging, Butch White, city editor of the *News*, assigned me to go to the county jail and do pictures of the "Anarchists." The jail was adjacent to the criminal court building in which the trial had been held. After my credentials had established my identity at the entrance, I climbed the stairs to the tier where the seven were confined, and was allowed to roam freely there while I drew my sketches. Other visitors also were present (presumably friends of officials), and they gazed into the cells of the doomed labor leaders curiously, as if at animals in a zoo.

Albert Parsons sat writing at a table piled with books and papers. He reminded me of a country editor—and, in

Chicago Daily News

THE HAYMARKET PRISONERS IN JAIL. I sketched them there shortly before the date set for the executions, and these drawings were published on that day.

fact, he *had* edited a weekly in Waco, Texas, before coming to Chicago. . . . Adolph Fischer, who had been a printer, looked like an eagle—peering up through the bars of his cell, still hopeful. . . . George Engel, also a printer, had less the appearance of an intellectual than the others. His eyes seemed dull, as if all feeling had gone from him. . . . August Spies, editor of the *Arbeiter Zeitung,* was strikingly good looking and straightforward in his talk. . . . Michael Schwab, spectacled editorial writer, had a solemn, sad face. . . . Samuel Fielden, a bearded ex-Methodist preacher from a country town in England, was a familiar speaker in halls and working-class street meetings, with the voice and intensity of a born orator. . . .

But it is Louis Lingg that I remember best. Perhaps my memory of him is clearest because a ray of sunlight, coming through a little high window, was shining in his cell as I sketched him. Only twenty-two, a pale blond, he had a look of disdain for all. He sat proudly in his chair, facing me with unblinking eyes, and silent. Had he opened his lips, I thought, he probably would have said: "Go ahead, you reporters, do what your masters want you to do. As for me, nothing matters now."

Engel was fifty-one, Fielden forty. The others were in the thirties or twenties. Schwab's beard and Lingg's moustache could not disguise their youthfulness.

Thursday brought word of an explosion in the jail—it was reported that Lingg had put a bomb into his mouth and lighted the fuse, and was dying. Considering all the precautions taken by the authorities, the searching of visitors, and the frequent searching of the Haymarket defendants' cells, no one has ever satisfactorily explained how that bomb got past the guards. I was chilled with the horror of the story as details kept coming in. Suffering untold agony with his face terribly mutilated, Lingg remained conscious while three physicians worked over him, and lived six hours.

Melville Stone was in the local room a great deal that day, directing arrangements for covering the execution. Friends of the prisoners, some of them prominent and influential in civic affairs, were in Springfield, trying to get the Governor to intervene, but our correspondent wired that Oglesby could find no reason for such action. Late in the afternoon, however, the Governor issued a formal statement, commuting the sentences of Fielden and Schwab to life imprisonment, but refusing to interfere with the sentences against the other four. (Oscar Neebe, the eighth defendant, was already serving a 15-year term.)

Wild rumors were in circulation, which the newspapers

made the most of, increasing the fears of the populace. Police Captain Schaack had announced the discovery of a plot to rescue the prisoners. Detective Herman Schuettler was supposed to have heard, through a peep-hole cut in a wall of a North Side rooming house, the discussion of a plan to blow up the jail. The force on guard there was doubled, and Schaack's men searched under the sidewalk for mines. Destruction of the city waterworks, a few blocks away, was asserted to be a part of the alleged conspiracy, and it was carefully protected.

Many wealthy citizens had left town, for the rumors had it that if the four prisoners were hanged vengeance would be taken against the rich. Anarchists from other cities were declared to be streaming toward Chicago to join in the rescue attempt.

I was much relieved when I learned that another artist, and not I, had been assigned to witness the execution and sketch the scene. I would have gone, of course, had I been ordered to, however gruelling the task. But Butch White gave the assignment to William Schmedtgen, an older man, who had joined the staff after me. I never knew why he was chosen, but figured that White thought I was too young.

Next morning I saw Schmedtgen put a revolver in his hip pocket and noticed that he was pale and trembling. Outside in the streets an ominous quiet prevailed. Business seemed to have come to a halt. Pedestrians were comparatively few, and every face was tense. We who stayed in the office didn't talk much, and when we spoke our voices were subdued. It was like sitting near the bedside of some one who is dying. When a copy-boy was heard yelling to another boy out in the corridor, one of the staff hurried out to shut him up.

Reporters worked in relays covering the news in the vicinity of the jail. One by one they came into the office and wrote their individual angles of the story for the early editions, then returned to the scene of action. Thus we got frequent bulletins on what was happening there.

Three hundred policemen had formed a cordon around the jail, a block away from it on all sides, keeping the curious crowds back of a line of heavy rope. Only those persons who could satisfy the cops that they had *bona fide* passports could get through. Once a newspaperman got into the jail, the police would not let him out.

There was no attempt at rescue. The hanging proceeded efficiently, from the viewpoint of officialdom. When the four men had dropped from the scaffold and the doctors had pronounced them dead, the tension of months suddenly was gone. All over town that afternoon there were drunken policemen, in and out of the saloons. Their honor as defenders of law and order had been vindicated.

My pictures of the executed men and their fellow-defendants were used in the *Daily News* that day. Schmedtgen's sketch of the hanging also was rushed into print. I saw him early that afternoon. He was white and silent. We were good friends for years afterward, but I never heard him speak of what was done in the jail-yard.

Long detailed accounts of the hangings were published in the dailies, with the last words of the four Anarchists. . . . The general tenor of those accounts was that their final speeches were stage effects, that they were posing as martyrs.

When another night had passed and no reprisals had been attempted, the mass fear of the populace lifted, the skies were clear again, and people returned to their normal ways of life. Now the whole episode seemed like some weird dream.

Stone congratulated the staff on its "excellent work" in covering the Haymarket case. "It was a good job well ended," he said.

Our circulation had been steadily climbing in recent months.

I didn't know until long afterward about the part that Melville Stone had played in the prosecution of the accused men. Not until 1921, when his autobiography was published, did I know that he wrote the verdict of the coroner's jury, although he was not a member of it.

Called in for advice by the prosecutor, the city attorney, and the coroner, Stone took the position that it did not matter who threw the bomb, but that inasmuch as Spies, Parsons, and Fielden had advocated the use of violence against the police, "their culpability was clear." Then he wrote the verdict for the coroner's jury, which formed the basis for the

Anarchists and Bomb Throwers

ONE HUNDRED AND TWENTY-EIGHT PAGES.

SIXTEEN PAGES ILLUSTRATIONS.

The Greatest Murder Trial on Record, with Speeches in Full of the Attorneys for the Prosecution and Defense. Profusely Illustrated.
Price 25 Cents. Agents Wanted.

G. S. BALDWIN, PUBLISHER, 199 CLARK STREET, CHICAGO.

WHEN I WAS MISLED. Carried away by propaganda against the Haymarket case defendants, I drew this illustration for the cover of a book upholding their conviction. I regret that now.

theory of "constructive conspiracy," on which the prosecution's case was based. It held that Mathias Degan (one of the seven policemen killed in the Haymarket Square explosion), had come to his death from a bomb thrown by a person or persons acting in conspiracy with Spies, Parsons, Fielden, and others unknown.

Everything I read about the Chicago Anarchists in 1886 and 1887 and nearly everything I heard about them indicated that the accused men were guilty. The news reports of the case in the dailies were quite as biased against the defendants as were the editorials. Few who read the charges that some of them had advocated violence against the police realized that they were driven to that extreme by the wanton clubbing, shooting, and killing of workers by the police in the fight of the big industries against the eight-hour day movement.

Not until several years later did I discover that there was another side to the story. So when asked by a publisher to draw a cover for a paper-bound anti-Anarchist book I readily assented. *Anarchists and Bomb-Throwers* was the title of this volume, and it upheld the convictions. My picture showed Law and Order, personified as an Amazonian woman, throttling a bunch of dangerous-looking men.

If the dead can hear, I ask forgiveness now for that act. I was young and I had been misled by the clamor of many voices raised to justify a dark and shameful deed.

Chapter 11

PATTERSON OF THE TRIBUNE FIRES ME

STEADILY the *Daily News* was forging ahead. Its circulation was far in the lead among Chicago's eight English dailies, and it took delight in flaunting its figures. In 1885 its daily average sale had been 131,992 copies, as attested to the American Newspaper Directory; the *Tribune, Times,* and *Herald* each claimed "more than 25,000"; the *Mail* and *Inter-Ocean* had "more than 22,500." In 1886 the *News* average had increased to 152,851, while the *Tribune* had climbed above 37,500. The *Times* and *Inter-Ocean* had stood still, the *Herald* was down to 22,500, and the *Mail* had dropped to 20,000.

The *Tribune* was a sixteen-page morning paper, with the 24-page Sunday edition; the *News* had only eight pages, appearing both morning and evening six days a week; the *Mail* had only four pages.

Much older than the *Daily News,* the *Tribune* (owned by Joseph Medill) obviously was envious of the strides made by the Stone-Lawson paper since its establishment in 1876. One story told with glee by men on the *News* had to do with a trap engineered by that paper to catch the *Tribune* in a theft of exclusive news. Repeatedly the Medill sheet had helped itself to good foreign dispatches originated by the *News;* also its New York correspondent found the press there a ready source of intelligence from all over the United States and from other countries as well.

Matthew Arnold had lately completed a lecture tour in this country, with Chicago as one stop on his itinerary, and remembering his tendency to caustic criticism, the *Daily News* executives saw in him an ideal peg on which to hang a story which would tempt the pirates over on Dearborn Street. Under Melville Stone's instructions a supposed cable dispatch from London was written, quoting from an article concerning the English poet's impressions of Chicago, declared to have just been published in the *Pall Mall Journal*. In that "article" Arnold was represented as assailing various prominent Chicagoans for boorishness and thickheadedness.

Stone sent the purported dispatch to the editor of the *New York Tribune* with a confidential letter of explanation, and soon the alleged criticism of Windy City notables was printed in a single copy of Whitelaw Reid's paper. That copy quickly reached the desk of the *Chicago Tribune's* correspondent, who put the story on the wire. The *Daily News* solemnly sent reporters to interview the citizens whose toes had been stepped on, and all of them were indignant. Meanwhile Stone cabled to Matthew Arnold explaining the hoax, and he answered saying he had not written any such article. Then the *News* let the public in on the secret, pointing out that the *Pall Mall Journal* was non-existent.

But three years had passed since that incident, and the *Tribune* was showing new verve. It had spruced up the entrance to the building it occupied at Madison and Dearborn Streets, and had put in an elevator, the *Daily News* not having yet installed one. And that winter the *Tribune* revealed that it had taken notice of me.

Robert Patterson was running the *Tribune*. He was a son-in-law of Joseph Medill. Patterson sent for me, indicated special interest in my pictures, and offered me a job. I had no trouble in getting $50 a week. Giving Stone notice, I explained that I felt this was an opportunity that I couldn't pass by. He said he was sorry I was leaving, and added: "If at any time you get tired of the *Tribune* there will be a place open for you on the *Daily News*."

Assignments on the *Tribune* were often vague; the editors seemed to have trouble in deciding what they wanted. But one order that challenged my imagination was for sketches of the great blizzard in New York City in March, 1888. "See if you can make a few pictures of that storm," was Patterson's request. Of course I had seen various woodcut illustrations of New York streets and some photographs, but now I had before me not a shred of graphic material—for in that day the *Tribune* had not developed a reference library. With nothing to go on except the telegraphic reports, I drew from word descriptions several pen-and-ink sketches which at least caught the spirit of the mighty snowdrifts in the

East and gave the *Tribune* an aspect of worthy enterprise.

With money from my increased salary piling up in a savings bank, I had a fine sense of well-being. I went to Monroe for a weekend, and basked in the warmth of admiring glances. But I knew that this admiration was not caused so much by my drawings that my fellow Monroeites had been seeing in the Chicago papers as by the fact that Dan Young's boy was making $50 a week. My imagination was soaring on the new job, and I think that the quality of my work decidedly improved.

Shortly after this, however, Robert Patterson informed me that "circumstances have compelled us to make some readjustments in the staff," and that it was necessary to dispense with my services. "Illustrations in newspapers are just a passing vogue," he said. "People will get tired of them." I was stunned, of course, but I asked no questions, did not inquire what was the real reason for my being discharged. I have never asked an editor why he didn't want my work; it would have been too much like asking a woman why she didn't love me. I had a suspicion that the *Tribune* had hired me away from the *Daily News* simply to weaken the staff of the latter.

Stone's offer to make a place for me at any time had sounded pleasant when he uttered it. Yet now I had no thought of going back to the *News*. Having ample money in reserve, I was inclined to relax and free-lance for a while.

My living quarters were still in the little room on Wabash Avenue. But though my own room was cramped, I found ease and comfort in leisure hours in visiting upstairs with a fine looking blonde of about thirty. She managed a department in one of the big State Street stores, but never talked shop. Her two rooms were above mine. Edith knew about me, from our landlady, and had seen my drawings in the newspapers.

When her evenings were lonely, she would signal to me by tapping on the floor. On my first visit she had thoughtfully turned the lights low when they appeared to annoy my eyes, and soon, without quite knowing how it happened, I found her in my arms. She had a healthy outlook, and laughter in her soul. Presently I (or perhaps it was she) had broken down all the barriers of convention that keep a man and woman apart. For me it was akin to standing on a precipice and suddenly gathering courage for a dive into strange waters below.

Knowing much more of life than I, Edith was unafraid, and her ecstasy was like wine to my senses. Here was romantic adventure about which I had wondered and for which I had often longed. But quickly afterward, there was a letdown. As I lay alone in my own room later that night, I was shaken. Had I been wise? Echoes of the Rev. Mr. Bushnell's voice, thundering against the iniquity of carnal sin, swept in to haunt me. Next morning uncertainty lingered. Yet when on another of Edith's lonely evenings she again tapped the signal, I could not say no. Once more the tingling caresses of a free soul lifted me to mountain-tops.

But the reaction followed as before, taking my mind off my work. I saw that, for all of Edith's charm and the joy of being with her, I was steadily being drawn into an impossible situation. Walking down Michigan Avenue in the fresh air to think things out, I determined not to become involved in any other passion but the creating of pictures. All else must be subordinated to that. It was not economic fear which deterred me then; not until later in life did I collide with the frightening financial consequences of love. At that time I simply did not want to assume any emotional responsibilities other than that of pursuing my own artistic development; my career must not become sidetracked by a sentimental attachment.

Overnight I decided that it was time for me to pack up and go to New York. I would study in the art schools there. Newspaper work now seemed commonplace; I wanted to go far beyond it—paint, experiment with color, deal with subtleties, weave into my pictures the undertones and overtones of life.

New York City had something, I was sure, that one with artistic leanings could never find in Chicago. Suddenly that city had grown crude in my eyes. My work was not appreciated, and I was out of a job. Now what? All the world's great lived in or visited New York at some time or other; not nearly so many reached Chicago.

I could see myself growing vastly in creative stature in the atmosphere of the metropolis. There was nothing to hold me back. I had saved enough money to carry me along for many months, while I was working out plans for the future. Eugene Field gave me a letter to Col. John A. Cockerill, who had attained renown as the "fighting editor" of the *Cincinnati Enquirer* and the *Washington Post,* and who at that time was managing editor of the *New York World* under Joseph Pulitzer. Gene laid it on thick. He wrote:

Dear Colonel Cockerill:
This will introduce Mr. A. H. Young, by all odds the brightest and best caricaturist and artist we have had here in Chicago. Inasmuch as he intends to make his home in New York, you will do the smart thing if you get a first mortgage on him. God bless you.
Eugene Field

Also I had an invitation from the art editor of the *New York Graphic* to join his staff. This was the first daily newspaper anywhere to emphasize the importance of pictures with text reduced to a minimum. The *Graphic* staff included such able cartoonists and humorous illustrators as Kemble, Cusachs, Frost, and the inimitable Hopkins ("Hop"), who after the fall of the *Graphic* went to Australia and was that country's leading cartoonist for many years.

Before making the 900-mile jump to the East, I went home to Monroe to say goodbye to the folks, and to lounge around town for a couple of days and tell various friends and acquaintances about my intentions. My father's eyes lighted up as he told customers that his son had not only been working for Chicago newspapers, but that I had saved enough cash to carry me for a year or more through art school in New York. My mother voiced anxiety about my going so far away from home, but I could see that she too was quietly proud of my progress. I spent the evenings with Elizabeth North, agreeably. "I always knew you'd be a success," she said.

The town seemed smaller now than before. And there had been changes—some of the old characters that had frequented our store had died. Bill Blunt had been appointed town constable, a big cherry tree in Frank Shindler's yard had been cut down after being struck by lightning, and the Milwaukee & St. Paul depot had a fresh coat of paint.

Charlie Booth, editor of the *Sentinel,* as usual, knocked off work for a half hour to talk with me. He'd always had ambitions to go to New York himself, he said, but had been too busy to get around to it. Jim Fitzgibbons, poolroom proprietor, asked me to keep an eye open for a cousin of his who at last accounts was driving a street car somewhere in New York City.

Back in Chicago, to cut my moorings, I had another long evening with Edith, and was relieved when she raised no tearful fuss about my going away. But my laughter wasn't real when she said gayly: "I may send you a nice little boy some day. How would you like that?" It was as if I were fleeing from the devil when I boarded a Michigan Central train. Yet as the clicking wheels bore me Eastward, I was warmed anew by the thought of her laughter and her supreme self-assurance. I knew she was no more of a sinner than I— and that has been my attitude toward intimate relations between the sexes ever since.

I wish I could brag about my prowess in the matter of sex in those growing years. I wish I had had more experience in amorous affairs, not so much as my friend Frank Harris claimed to have had, but anyhow bolder and with less regard for the consequences. The Puritan bourgeois ideas of a country town pressed heavily upon me, and affected my approach to life. Gloomy admonitions were my heritage: *Thou shalt not!* and *Beware of disease!*

Having such a background of morality and fear, it was fortunate that I also had a talent to look after, which helped me to forget the flesh. But I saw many girls whom I wanted to love. Vicariously I have loved and still love thousands of them. Through most of my years sex in my life has been repressed. Whether I am the better or worse for it is just idle speculation now. . . . Often I am skeptical when I hear of the vaunted reputations of certain authors and artists as *conquistadores* among women. I doubt their emotional capacity to keep up the pace of which they boast.

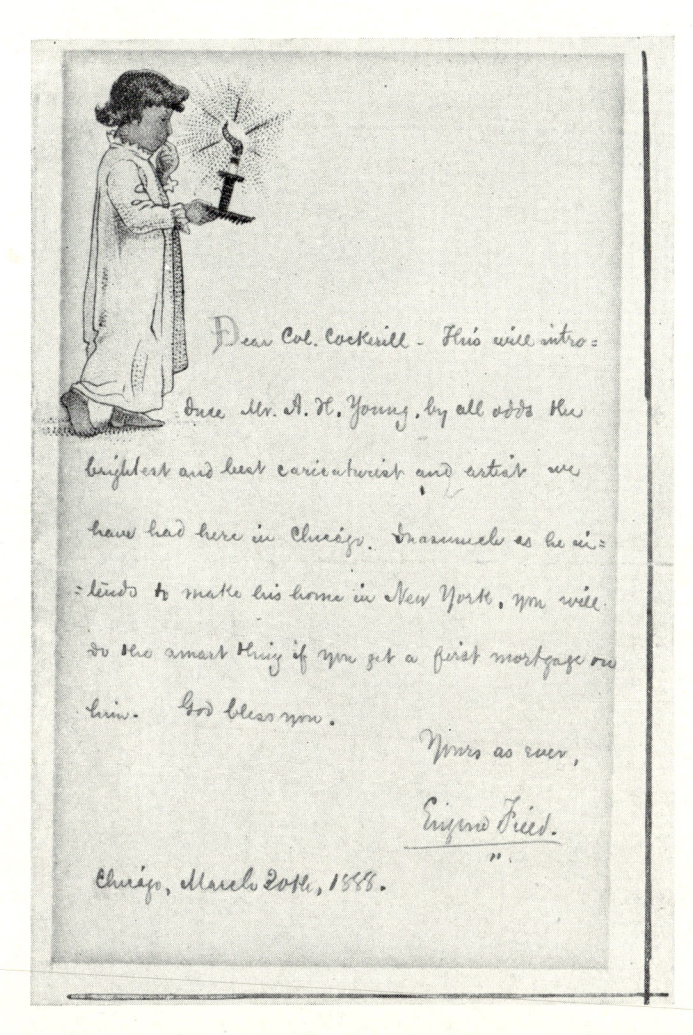

EUGENE FIELD'S LETTER
recommending me to the editor of the *New York World*.

Chapter 12

I GO TO NEW YORK WITH HIGH HOPES

AS the train sped eastward I sat in the luxurious diner and reveled in the scene, as the green-and-brown panorama of the fields flitted past. I liked to see farmers wave their straw hats, and horses out to pasture kick up their heels and run as the train sped by, as if they were showing off and saying: "Think you're going fast? Look at us!" As we went a bit slower through small villages I liked to see the girls and boys at stations and cross-roads, gazing at this express train bound for New York. I suspected they were envious of us lucky passengers, and were hoping that some day they, too, would be riding on a fast train to a fast city.

I read again the letter from Eugene Field to Colonel Cockerill, and the invitation from the *Illustrated Daily Graphic* editor to work for him. There was satisfaction in knowing that I had such letters to fall back upon if needed. But there was no hurry about my getting a job. I wanted to study for a while.

My emotions flared high. I whistled a tune in rhythm with the rumble and click of the wheels. At ease in the Pullman, the first I had ever ridden in, I felt that boyhood dreams were coming true. Towns and cities were momentary incidents along the way. We left Indiana behind and were in Michigan. One knew that only because the time-table said so; the character of the country remained unchanged. A humorous conception of my childhood came back—the thought that each state was of a different color, as in maps, and that between them was a clearly marked boundary.

I had brought along some reading matter—*Harper's Weekly*, the *Daily Graphic*, *Judge*, *Puck*, and *Scribner's*. As usual I went through their pages more than once—scanning the pictures first, then the text and the advertisements. The quality of the illustrations varied considerably, and they seemed much below the standard of the European draftsmen of the graphic arts—in social satire, political cartoons, and comics.

Advertisements of that time included names of firms and products which are still familiar—Pear's Soap; Pond's Extract; Spencerian Pens; Ayer's Cherry Pectoral; Baker's Breakfast Cocoa; Columbia Bicycles; Mellin's Food; Cuticura Soap; Royal Baking Powder, and Castoria: "Children Cry For It." After I had studied the illustrations in the magazines, and read the short pieces of text, I got out my sketchbook and began drawing the faces of my fellow-passengers, and setting down memoranda for jokes about travel. Then, and for many years, I made about ten drawings with a joke comment or dialogue for every one that I finished and sold. Thus I kept exercising my hand and eye.

We reached Detroit after dark, and here the train was broken up into sections, run onto a huge flatboat, and ferried across the river to Windsor. The Canadian shore seemed far away, the Detroit harbor limitless. There was a stiff wind blowing, and there was a sense of pushing into an unknown sea. I wondered what all the fuss was about, as we were towed across to the rail-dock on the other side.

On Clarence Webster's advice I had taken a lower berth, and was glad of this when I saw that the uppers had no windows. Marveling, I watched the porter transform the double seat into a sleeping section . . . In the washroom several traveling men were smoking and indulging in small talk about business, politics, and the state of the crops, and uttering commonplaces of banter.

My berth was comfortable, but it was not easy to go to sleep. After I put out the light I lay awake for hours, it seemed, looking out the window at the countryside, mysterious under the stars. I had hoped to see Niagara Falls, but was on the wrong side of the car, and anyhow I was sound asleep when we passed that famed wonder, before dawn. . . . There was a thrill in seeing the Erie canal, about which I had read a good deal. The railroad was a stiff competitor, but there were still numerous barges moving both east and west in "Clinton's ditch."

When we turned southward at Albany, my heart pounded faster. Here was the historic Hudson, which grew lovelier as we hurried on into the Highlands. I thought of the legends of Rip Van Winkle and the gnomes with whom he played at tenpins, and other tales that Washington Irving told of this majestic valley. But the long run into the city after we passed the outskirts made me conscious of an approach to something ominous—maybe the end instead of the beginning.

Outside Grand Central Station were a flock of men with badges on their hats, all offering to take me to a choice hotel.

ARRIVAL IN NEW YORK, 1888.
I whistled a great deal in those days.

But I knew where I was going. Some one had recommended the Morton House in Union Square as home-like and cheap. So I hunted around till I found a policeman, learned how to get there, and then took a hansom cab.

After I got settled in the hotel, I went out and looked around a little. That afternoon and evening I walked miles. New York was full of wonders, different from Chicago, brighter, cleaner. The clear sunlight was a startling contrast to the smoky atmosphere of the crude city I had left, which

Mayor Carter Harrison excused for being so dirty by saying: "Chicago is like a growing boy who doesn't like to bother keeping himself clean."

Although I went to particular places, I found almost any place interesting during those first days in the metropolis. Just looking on, wherever I happen to be, even to this day, is sure to reveal something that holds me with some dramatic import. From the Morton House I would go over to Brentano's on the west side of Union Square, to scan the latest magazines. Then there was Tiffany's on the southwest corner of Fifteenth Street, where the Amalgamated Bank is now. Here coaches would drive up, letting out women shoppers dressed in style, meaning that they wore bustles. The flaring hoop-skirt had had its day, but complete coverage was still the fashion, woman's form being left to one's imagination.

I walked up to Nineteenth Street on Broadway, and gazed into the windows of Lord and Taylor, about which I had heard so much. They reminded me of a poem about Broadway that I had read in school about "silks and satins that shimmer and shine" and opals that gleam "like sullen fires through a pallid mist."

In a few days I took a room in a boarding house on Sixteenth Street, west of Fifth Avenue. W. J. Arkell, publisher of *Judge,* had just put up his new building at the northwest corner of that intersection. I clipped one of Thomas Nast's cartoons from a copy of the *Daily Graphic* and tacked it on my wall, and one day in conversation with the servant girl who made up my room, I found that she had worked in the Nast household in Morristown, N. J. She told me stories about the Nast family. Surely now I was near the heart of things.

New York agreed with me. I liked the sea-air. I was having fun. For two weeks I just loafed and wandered about town. I wasn't ready to begin systematic study yet, nor to attempt selling pictures, though of course I made sketches everywhere of people and scenes.

I explored Chinatown, and went down to see the site of P. T. Barnum's museum at Broadway and Ann streets. And one day I walked across Brooklyn Bridge, and was stirred by the sight of those tremendous arches and the monumental grace of the whole structure. I was curiously interested, too, in the Richard K. Fox building, in which the *Police Gazette* was published near the bridge on the Manhattan side.

Another time I loafed along the water's edge in Battery Park, and was impressed by Castle Garden, then a landing station for immigrants, and now the Aquarium. Boats were plying to the Statue of Liberty, unveiled only three years before. But I was satisfied to view that at a distance, even though an old Irishman standing on the wharf informed me that Bedloe's Island, on which the statue stands, had "a great history." His father, he said, was one of thousands in excursion boats who saw Hicks, the last pirate in those waters, hanged there.

As in Chicago, everywhere in New York's principal business streets then there were networks of overhead wires strung on poles. These were chiefly for telegraphic purposes, although some of them carried telephone conversations. Newspaper editors frequently urged the city council to compel the owning companies to put those wires underground, since they were a grave handicap in fighting fires. Horse-cars moved along Broadway from the Battery to some point far north. Steve Brodie had lately jumped from Brooklyn Bridge into the East River—or had not, depending on which party to that controversy one belonged to. And now he was reported to be preparing to go over Niagara Falls in a barrel.

Remembering that to my regret I had never got around to visiting the Chamber of Horrors in Chicago, I made it a point to go to the Eden Musee on Twenty-third Street, a similar institution. Here were figures of famous and notorious individuals, amazingly modeled in wax—Queen Victoria, Jesse James, Oscar Wilde, Brigham Young, Horace Greeley, the Prince of Wales, Jay Gould, Boss Tweed, Garibaldi, John Brown, U. S. Grant, Abraham Lincoln, John Wilkes Booth, Robert G. Ingersoll, Jenny Lind, Guiteau, who murdered President Garfield, and a host of others.

But the exhibit which intrigued me most was the glass enclosed Dying Gypsy Maiden. Just why she was dying was not stated, but the expiring heave of her bare bosom was so realistically achieved by hidden mechanism that I felt almost tearful.

Everybody from out of town was drawn to this wonder

palace. It was the high spot of interest in New York. If a farmer was seen standing on a street corner apparently lost, it was taken as a matter of course that he wanted to be directed to the Eden Musee. Once I saw an old fellow standing near the site of the present Flatiron Building, stroking his whiskers and looking first one way and then another. I walked over to him and said: "The Eden Musee is right down there—on the uptown side of the street." He thanked me.

Soon, however, I had my fill of loafing and decided that for my own good I must get down to work again. So I signed up at the Art Students' League, and began studying there industriously, to develop thoroughness, for I knew that my flip sketches needed a basic understanding, especially of anatomy. Teaching-routine at the League was much the same as at the Academy of Design in Chicago, but I found no one among the instructors who would give the same individual attention to the groping student as Vanderpoel had.

Here, too, we had to draw from casts, which always bored me. I did this solemn drafting conscientiously, none the less, though I considered it a waste of time, and found compensation for such tedious labor by sketching comic pictures around the margin of the paper on which the serious effort awaited criticism. After a few weeks I decided to graduate myself to the life classes of Kenyon Cox and Carroll Beckwith on the floor above, and strangely enough, no one objected; I just walked in as if I belonged.

Inspiration from my youthful partial knowledge of Doré's work had carried me a long way. But now I was becoming acquainted with the political and social satires of other leading graphic artists in England and France—Hogarth, Rowlandson, John Leech, George Cruikshank, John Tenniel, Daumier, and Steinlen, and all of these held important and increasing values for me.

Feeling financially secure and being engrossed in study, I neglected to present Eugene Field's letter to Colonel Cockerill of the *World,* and had no inclination to submit my work to the magazines. But I kept close watch on all periodicals as well as the newspapers, for the trend in cartoons and illustrations. *Puck, Judge,* and *Life* were at their best. *Harper's*

Weekly was beginning to slip, and that year the *Illustrated Daily Graphic* folded up.

Journalism today is for the most part gentlemanly and decorous, in so far as the relations among newspapers in the big cities are concerned. But in that day the New York dailies openly assailed one another's actions and motives with all the contempt that lily-white citizens might express toward horse-thieves and road agents. Dana of the *Sun* and Pulitzer of the *World* fought a long feud, widely talked about, and the *World* and *Herald* frequently snarled at each other.

I knew, of course, that it was the *World* that had collected $300,000 to provide a base for the Statue of Liberty after the city, state, and federal governments had all failed to make it possible for the French people's gift to be set up on this side of the Atlantic. The *World* was fighting Tammany. Frequently it assailed the municipal administration for mismanagement, pointing to the failure to clean the back streets, the fire-trap tenements, sweat-shops, and the conditions which bred tuberculosis.

Now and then I meandered into the heart of the East Side. Here was stark poverty, even worse than I had seen in the slums of Chicago. Great numbers of children played amid filth and debris in the narrow streets. Old people sat on doorsteps or moved listlessly along the walks. They seemed to have lost hope. Gangs of toughs congregated on corners.

But looking at all this squalor I felt instinctively that most human beings did not prefer dirt to cleanliness, and they did not like stealing better than earning, nor a bad name better than a good one. I made sketches here and there, but did not remain long in one spot. There was a sense of escape in getting back to my room. The *World's* editorials had not exaggerated. Yet what could one do about it? Nothing, it seemed to me, except through reforms: cleaning streets, paying good wages, providing for cheap carfare, etcetera. I could come no nearer to an answer than that.

I continued to read *Harper's Weekly*, following the work of W. A. Rogers therein (Nast had severed his connection with that periodical a couple of years earlier); and watched *Life, Judge,* and *Puck*. The latter contained topical cartoons, and editorial comment with many pages of drawings to illustrate what are known today as gags. The cartoons by Joseph Keppler, Bernard Gillam, Frederick Opper, and Zim were leading features. *Puck*, too, was agitating for civic virtue, and for the sending of bribe-taking aldermen to Sing Sing. But it viewed the Single Tax movement as akin to anarchy; had fought Henry George and his coworker, the heroic Catholic, Father Edward McGlynn, when the former ran for mayor; and attacked Greenbackism as spelling national ruin. Frequently it ridiculed the United States Senate as a servant of the moneyed interests. It was

JOSEPH KEPPLER, SENIOR, founder of *Puck*.

BERNARD GILLAM, an outstanding illustrator in the Eighties.

strong for civil service reform and a low tariff, and intentionally "mugwump", as liberal Republicans were then called.

Whatever the mixed social ideas I was thus absorbing, the lessons I gained from studying Keppler's drawings were valuable. He was less cumbersome than Nast, having that swing of line reminiscent of the early nineteenth century German draftsmen. Today, as one turns back to the pages of *Puck* in the years from 1870 to 1890, it will be seen that, though dated in subject, Keppler's pictures have an arresting quality of color and a spontaneity agreeable alike to student and layman. But for individuality, and for ability to "make fun of something", Nast was pre-eminent. It was said in those days that his cartoons of Horace Greeley during the Greeley-Grant campaign for the Presidency were a large factor in causing the death of that brilliant but eccentric editor within a month after his defeat in 1872. I didn't believe this, but I knew that his darts of satire were sharp.

P. T. Barnum was then living in New York, in his old age. One bright Sunday I saw him attending services in Robert Collyer's Unitarian church at Park Avenue and 34th Street. I sketched him as he bowed his head in prayer, and as he talked with friends afterward in the sun outside. He was round-shouldered, and had a curly fringe of gray hair left under the rim of his silk hat. Doubtless he would have been pleased if he had known that I was making pictures of him. In these days the venerable showman often stopped people on the streets and engaged them in conversation. At the end he would say: "Do you know who you've been talking to? . . . You've been talking to P. T. Barnum." . . . I had no idea then that years later I would own a home in Bethel, Connecticut, the town in which Barnum was born.

As the months went on I thought a great deal about the possibility of going to Paris, for I had been hearing of the art schools there ever since I signed up with the League. It seemed to be the ambition of most of my fellow-students to study in the French capital, though others dreamed of Munich. They talked much, also, of the unrestricted life in the Latin Quarter, as something else to look forward to.

Clarence Webster knew from my letters that I had considerable yearning to continue my art education abroad. Although I knew that art schools could not make artists, I enjoyed the environment and the thought that I had an aim in life. And one day in the early summer of 1889, Web wrote me saying: "I am planning to go to Europe for a couple of months. England, Wales, and France. The *Inter-Ocean* is willing to let me do a series of travel articles, which will cover my living expense over there. How would you like to go along and illustrate my writings? I am sure that I could arrange with the office to get steamship passage for both of us through the advertising department."

I answered that I would think about it. And the more I pondered the idea, the more it appealed to me. I began to see myself as an art student in Paris for at least a year. So in a few days I packed up and took a train for Chicago. There Web and I conferred with one of the *Inter-Ocean* editors, and we agreed that I would go home to Wisconsin for a short visit before we started East.

In Monroe I spent a few days with the folks, and had some evenings with Elizabeth North, who looked more attractive than ever. Now that I had become a New Yorker, my parents had taken to reading every bit of New York news, and *Harper's Weekly* continued to be a regular visitor at home. Father was interested in having me compare the Art Students' League with the Chicago Academy of Design—which had benefited me the most?

Monroe appeared still smaller. But the cheese business was growing in Green County, with the steady increase in the number of Swiss immigrants. Old George Banks, the druggist, whose walk I used to imitate to the great amusement of my mother—he walked like a king on parade—had grown fatter, but dignity triumphed with his every step. Everybody in Monroe was talking about the Johnstown flood in Pennsylvania which had drowned nearly 2,300 persons a few weeks before.

My sister Nettie and Clyde Copeland had set up a comfortable home over on the north side of town, and my "No wedding bells for me" picture was in plain sight in the parlor when I was there for supper; I never knew whether Nettie displayed it only when I was around, but I grant that she would have been justified in hiding it at other times. Mother seemed less anxious when I left this time, even though I was soon to cross the ocean, than she had when I was going only to Chicago the first time. Perhaps she felt that I was able to take care of myself.

We had railroad passes also, and on the Baltimore & Ohio train, Web posted me on recent happenings in Chicago. . . . Melville Stone was traveling in Europe, spending some of the money he got from Victor Lawson for his interest in the *Daily News*. . . . The jury was being picked for the trial of the alleged *Clan-na-Gael* conspirators for the murder of Dr. Cronin. He had been lured from his home at night by a purported call to attend a sick person, and his body had been found in a catch-basin on the outskirts of the city. The doctor had been a member of the Clan, and was supposed to have been killed because he had betrayed some of its secrets and charged Alexander Sullivan, a lawyer, and others with misappropriating the Clan's funds. . . . There was new talk of building a broad ship canal from Lake Michigan to the Mississippi. . . . Temperance advocates were trying to get an ordinance passed to abolish free lunch in the saloons, with widespread opposition. . . . The police were investigating a report that Rudolph Schnaubelt, who was supposed to have thrown the Haymarket bomb, had been seen in South America. . . . A man named Garfinkle was trying to finance a balloon trip to the North Pole. . . . And Web told me the gossip in art circles, and around the Chicago Press Club, where I first met Opie Read, Stanley Waterloo, and Ben King. It was Ben who wrote that classic parody of the popular poem: "If I Should Die Tonight."

Arriving in New York, I was feeling hot, sooty, sticky, and sick, and I said to Web, "If a B. & O. train can make me miserable, what will an ocean liner do to me?"

Chapter 13

WE LEARN ABOUT THE ENGLISH AND WELSH

LIVERPOOL was our destination, on the Cunard Line's *Teutonic,* newest and finest ocean liner afloat. With the gentlemanly Bruce Ismay, president of the line, modestly receiving congratulations on board, we sailed on August 21 from a pier in the Hudson River. Our tickets were second class, but we had an outside cabin with permission (a courtesy to the press) to roam anywhere on the ship.

Web sauntered about the decks locating notables and interviewing them, everything and everybody being grist to the mill of the *Inter-Ocean's* humorous correspondent with the pen-name "Conflagration Jones." But we spent some of our time sketching, especially down in the steerage. I did not care to meet many people, for I soon verified my fears that I was not a good sailor. There were days and nights when the steamer rared up and pranced, and it was no fun to be rolled around in a ship's cabin like a marble in a pigs-in-clover puzzle. . . . On calm days, however, I managed well with the drawings, and the voyage netted me numerous pictures of those about us. Among the dignitaries riding first class I sketched the railroad magnate, Collis P. Huntington, and his wife. I talked with a woman devoted to a small daughter who would recite on the slightest provocation, "Curfew Shall Not Ring Tonight"; and an evangelist who annoyed people by asking them: "Have you found Christ?" When he asked me, I thought of the Swede in the old story who was asked the same question and answered that he "didn't know he was lost."

I had several chats with a ruddy Englishman who had been traveling in the States and had not been favorably impressed. His main objection was: "Your bloomin' country is all full of 'ills and 'oles." Then there was the man who was always keeping tabs on the ship's course, which was no concern of mine.

We landed in Liverpool a week later. Walking around the streets, my legs still felt as if swayed by the steamer's roll. I made sketches of boys selling matches, and turned to gaze at tall, stately girls with rose-petal complexions who passed. To Web I said: "DuMaurier is right. He knows how to draw the English girls, and Burne-Jones knows how to paint them." We went to the Walker art gallery, where I saw a Doré oil painting of an English flower girl—and it stimulated my desire to see the Doré gallery in London. I had not known that he had mastered painting as well as illustration.

But before going on to London, Web had a notion that we ought to take a look at the old town of Chester, and then visit Wales. At the railway station a hand-swung school-bell was rung by the conductor when it was time for our train to start. The ride to Chester took only an hour. And here I was looking at rural England of which I had seen so many woodcuts and steel engravings. The fences were mostly hedges, though I saw a few of barbed wire, and wrote home that they looked as uncomfortable to sit on as the American brand. Trees in this section were mostly gnarled and twisted oaks, and the old broken-down stiles, with their frames of overgrown hedges, were just as the English artists had time and again pictured them.

We walked up the narrow main street of ancient Chester, wending our way through the slow traffic, where people were all jumbled together with donkey-carts, horses, wagons, and market-baskets. Our eyes were kept peeled looking for a place to stop, as Webster said, "off the trail of the deadly tourists." I remember passing Blossom's Hotel. I wonder if it is still there. A sturdy, weathered looking establishment. But we didn't stop. It seemed a likely place to run into tourists.

The buildings in that picturesque city may have been erected in the time of King Arthur, for all I know—their upper stories jutting out over the sidewalks, propped up, but sagged into complacency as if ready for another century. The general effect of this street upon my eye was like seeing a stage-set for a play of the time of Cromwell—in the days of old "when knights were bold and robbers held their sway."

After going some distance from the main thoroughfare

we discovered a hotel called the Red Lion. Here we stayed four days. Both of us began to realize that we were a long way from home. No letters from loved ones. Of course it was too soon to expect any, but "nobody loves us," we thought, and we could have eaten worms or paid any penance then for the rash conduct of quitting our native soil.

Proceeding to the historic Chester Cathedral, we found the portal open wide, so we walked in and sat down. There we slumped, shafts of sunshine slanting through the stained glass windows, but not for us. I knew I wasn't getting religion, but I was sad with homesickness.

After our morning in the cathedral we began to get hold of ourselves. We found a boat and took a row on the River Dee. That night I started a letter to the *Monroe Sentinel*—which wasn't finished until we reached Paris—and it told a good deal about our adventures that day. In my early childhood I heard a poem recited (or maybe it was a song sung) the refrain of which was: "Mary, call your cattle home across the sands o' Dee." In my letter I reported that "it would take a good deal of loud calling, even by a husky English girl, to get a drove of tired cows across the sands of Dee. The sand of this country is what we call plain mud at home."

We passed at least a dozen boatloads of boys and girls in a half mile, dressed in proper boating clothes, the girls rowing as efficiently as the boys. I wrote that "the American contingent cut quite a figure on the River Dee that beautiful morning. Mr. Webster, with a big sombrero on his head and a section of an American flag around his neck, did the rowing, while I sat at the helm and did all the steering and grumbling."

Chester was surrounded by a high stone wall supposed to have been originally built by the Romans. I remember standing on the very stone of the wall where Charles I stood watching while his army was being defeated by Cromwell's troops on the moor below. That of course is the Baedeker thing to do and a guide who caught me at it charged me three pence.

Taking a cab on another day, we rode through the Duke of Westminster's estate, my companion remarking as we passed deer, grouse, and other wild game, "all for his Royal

Nibs to shoot." We walked around outside the ancient wall, and I made a pencil drawing of the cathedral by moonlight. We had planned to go out to Gladstone's summer home, Hawarden Castle, six miles from Chester, but the fourth day we concluded we'd better see something of Wales.

Back at the hotel, however, we learned that Wambold's circus, then swinging through the provinces, had come to town, and we decided to stay another day. Web had a sudden notion that it would be worth our while to travel with Wambold's aggregation. His idea was that maybe they would take on two live Americans. He would lecture on the American Indian, while I would draw easel pictures to illustrate the lecture as he talked. We went in the evening, and found the performance much like that of the small wagon shows at home. We were interested particularly in the animal tent— and saw a caged stork resent being pointed at and catch a man's forefinger in the grip of its vise-like bill.

But what I most enjoyed here was catching fragments of conversation—just as I did at the hotel—and as I do today wherever I go. Around the bar of the Red Lion, old-timers talked much about the Isle of Man, which was only sixteen miles off shore. "I 'ear 'Awkins went to the h-island today." Hall Caine had not then written his play, *The Manxman*, for Wilson Barrett to produce and play the leading role. Some years later I saw the play and met Hall Caine in New York; the play made me cry—but just what it was about I don't remember.

Next day we journeyed by train down into Wales. Our first stop was Llangollen. Arriving after dark we registered at the hotel and went early to bed, not knowing what the town was like. No scene actual or painted ever looked more beautiful to me than the morning view from that hotel window. A sun-tinged river winding and laughing its rocky course through the town, while a street musician playing a pipe in the foreground gave just the right touch to this decorative bit of Wales.

We conversed with some of the natives, and found that none of them could or would explain why a word spelled Llowainwlmjdfsllwgd was pronounced Gwillid, as we had been informed by non-Welshmen. Walking along a canal, we met up with two ragged boys who said their father worked in the slate mines. They asked if we would like to hear them sing. Of course we said yes, so they sang a folk song, not knowing that I was also putting them down in my sketch book. For singing and posing I hope that we paid them generously. Hardly knowing one English coin from another, I wasn't sure. But they went on their way happy with arms around each other, and it was pleasant to see. I do not think they expected a fee—but like most Welsh children for centuries past, they enjoyed singing.

Then we went to Conway Castle and to Holywell, where we saw the "miraculous well," and the church nearby where hundreds of crutches of the cured had been left as proof. This part of Wales abounded in ancient abbeys and ruined castles. Webster said: "The trouble with our country is that we're shy on ruins. We ought to blow up a lot of old breweries, let the ivy and owls have their way, and call them something historic."

Three days in Wales were all too short for this charming country, but Web's time was limited and the next stop on our schedule was London. When we arrived there we found lodgings in Bloomsbury Square, in a rooming house near the British Museum. Being a Dickens enthusiast, Web was interested in searching out landmarks and streets mentioned in that author's novels. I was more immediately interested in visiting an exhibition of a hundred years of English caricature lately opened in the Royal Arcade Gallery. Dickens could wait. We compromised by going to the caricature exhibition first.

It was inspiring, for it comprised many originals by all the outstanding English draftsmen from before the time of Hogarth. Thus I was able to study at first-hand the work of Rowlandson, the most prolific and versatile of British caricaturists; Gillray, Isaac and George Cruikshank, Leech, Barnard, Howitt, Thackeray, DuMaurier, Keene, Phiz (Hablot K. Browne), and various others. It was Phiz who illustrated most of the Dickens narrative when they first appeared. Of all the drawings on the walls, I was impressed most by those of Hogarth, Rowlandson, Gillray, George Cruikshank, and Frederic Barnard, who illustrated *The Pilgrim's Progress* long after Bunyan's day, and who did pictures for some of the Dickens novels.

I thought Barnard the greatest character artist of all. And to think that I was face to face with Hogarth's originals, and his own engravings—the picture propagandist for good conduct and morals, a preacher with paint. Rowlandson's themes were much more varied. He depicted the lighter side of London life, the gambling parlors and the cockpits, and was less inclined to moralize, but not without taking notice of the misery all about him. Both he and Gillray were well represented by a series of lampoons on Napoleon Bonaparte, which helped to deflate the little emperor's ego and pull down his star. George Cruikshank's works which we saw that day covered a wide range of subjects, done with an etching needle tipped with fanciful satire. I felt that this exhibition alone was worth the trip across the Atlantic, for all those sad "Oh, why did I leave home?" days of both sea- and homesickness.

And now we were looking around at the more romantic parts of Old London. I took a good look at the sacred Bank of England. Moving about wherever our noses led us, we saw Whitehall Palace, where Charles I was tried and in front of which he was beheaded; Westminster Abbey, where I was glad to see a bust of my fellow countryman, Henry Wadsworth Longfellow, amid the tombs of ancient kings, St. Paul's Cathedral, the Royal Academy, Buckingham Palace, and the Houses of Parliament; Petticoat Lane, that famous pushcart market, where bargain-sellers of many nationalities gathered to take the public's money; the Tower of London; Trafalgar Square; the Thames embankment; and Westminster Bridge.

Having steeped himself in Dickens lore, Clarence Webster was able to rattle off a great deal of remembered detail which lighted up London history for me in rich colors. *Barnaby Rudge* of course occupied a much larger stage than any other of the Dickens novels, for it dealt with the Gordon Riots in the time of George III. Its central character was a member of Lord George Gordon's "No Popery" mob of 60,000 persons who gathered in the open fields east of the city where Gordon harangued them, then marched them in divisions across Westminster Bridge, London Bridge, and Blackfriars Bridge. For six days and nights the mob held all London at its mercy, besieged Parliament, emptied the prisons, pillaged the homes of well-to-do Catholics, raided the distilleries and set them on fire. Benjamin Franklin was then in France as a U. S. emissary, and wrote home about the vast destruction.

Most of the buildings in Whitechapel were old and doubtless had been there in the days when Dickens wrote of Bill Sikes murdering Nancy. Men and women in those mean

CLARENCE WEBSTER AND HIS KODAK. New picture-making device creates a sensation in London's Whitechapel district.

streets also seemed of an era far in the past; from their looks they might have been the very people who moved through the pages of *Oliver Twist* or followed Lord George Gordon.

When the natives heard that Web was carrying a picture-taking machine, they surrounded us in droves. A large, slatternly woman, with her abdomen thrown out proudly, cried: "Tike me, Mister!"

Many places we came to in London were instantly connected up with Dickens's writings by Web's extensive memory, and some of them were known to me also—not so much from my reading, for I cared little for novels, but from the hundreds of illustrations over which I had often pored. The whole scene was rich in picture stuff, a constantly changing panorama, as we pushed along. I remember the Tower, Billingsgate Fish Market, St. Paul's Cathedral, the Marble Arch, Regent's Park, Cheapside, and various inns—the Cheshire Cheese, the Blue Bull, the Maypole, the Rainbow Tavern, the Old Ship, the Red Lion, and Jenny's Whim. One fog-enveloped night Webster was sure we had found the Seven Dials, and I made a sketch of two outcasts, an old man and an old woman talking it over in the blear gas light of a foggy night. I showed it to Webster and he said: "Here's Dickens and Doré, all in one picture."

It may have been because I was fed on the latter's drawings in my adolescence, that I admired his work with a kind of awe. And one day, when we again visited the Doré gallery on Bond Street, it was with difficulty that Web finally got me to leave it for other London sights. I thought then and still think that if ever there was a born artist it was the Alsatian Gustav Doré. He was an engine of energy; handsome; with an Oedipus complex, but having futile love affairs with Adelina Patti and Sarah Bernhardt; the talk of Paris at twenty for his Dante, Rabelais, and Balzac illustrations, his paintings and comic drawings. At forty he had outdistanced all other artists, not only illustrating but enhancing the text of his favorites in classic literature. But long before his fiftieth year he was a miserable melancholic, mainly, it is said, because the critics would not recognize him as a great painter.

Doré had at least one admirer who accepted all that he did—painting, cartoons, statuary, and illustrations—as beyond criticism. A young man from Wisconsin who thought he understood him and counted him the greatest artist of his time. I estimated the gift of imagination in all of the arts as supreme. And Doré had it. Rowlandson, George Cruikshank, the elder Peter Breughel, Gillray, Callot, Durer, and Oberlander also had it in the graphic arts, as did most of the Renaissance painters. But Doré's torrential ambition and his over-production not only killed him at fifty-one—it deadened a decent appraisal of his work. He was a sensation, and it may have been only "for the day thereof." Time will tell whether much of his work will survive.

Thomas Nast was a great admirer of Doré. Once, so Nast told me, they almost met. He was going into the Bond Street Gallery and Doré was coming out. "He looked at me," Nast said, "as if he ought to know me, and I looked at him as if I ought to know him—and we let it go at that." I am quoting this from a conversation I had with him when I visited Nast at his home in Morristown, New Jersey, in 1897. Nast had many Doré drawings on his walls there. He told me that the editors of *Harper's Weekly* had accused him of plagiarizing Doré's mannerisms. Anyone who looks through that magazine in the years from 1862 to 1870 will see early Nast drawings which certainly have the powerful dramatic effects of light and shade associated with the work of Doré. But Nast had an original style that no plagiaristic admiration could conceal.

Being older than I, and supposedly better versed in the ways of the world, Web usually took the initiative in arranging our travels. But I found it necessary to prod him to make sure that we didn't miss trains and got to places on schedule; for he had a faulty sense of time. One day, however, he had a laugh on me when I essayed to bargain with the driver of a cab who had deposited us at our house in Bloomsbury Square after an hour of sight-seeing. He demanded half a crown for the ride. That sounded like a lot of money, although I was muddled about money matters, rate of exchange, and all that.

I objected that it was too much, and offered the man four shillings. He looked at me strangely, but said: "Orl right, Guv'ner, 'av it yer own wye."

"I'm not going to let any of these grasping Britishers overcharge us," I said with a glow of victory when the cab had gone.

"How much do you think half a crown is, in American money?" Web inquired.

"I—I don't know."

"Just 61 cents. You've paid him 36 cents more than his price."

After that I let Web handle the finances.

Though our lodgings were near the British Museum, I never managed to visit that institution. It was on my list, but somehow I never found time to go there, and was sorry afterward.

We had set a limit of three weeks for our stay in London. When I realized that we were going next into a foreign-language country, and knowing no word of French except *Oui*, I was a bit timid. Not to know the value of a country's money is bad enough, but not to know its language is to be helpless, I thought—and I said to Web, "Maybe I'd better stay right here."

But in this mood I was forgetting my objective, which was to study at the *Académie Julien*. In a few days we were off for Paris by way of Dover and that churning ride across the English Channel.

Chapter 14

ON THE STAGE; PICTURES SET TO MUSIC

AFTER my illness in Paris, the journey home to Wisconsin, and the strawberry festival which celebrated my return, I found myself with time on my hands and the problem of how best to occupy it. First of course I knew I must look out for my health. I liked the walk to town (about a mile), not on the main road but cross-cutting through Ludlow's farm—stopping perhaps to lie on the bank of the creek—and sometimes sketching cows. I don't know of any animal more difficult to draw than a cow lying down.

Arriving at the Square, I would go to our store, hang around for an hour and look at catalogs and other advertising matter that had come in the mail, help myself to candy or fruit, and then perhaps go upstairs to the *Sentinel* office, and chin with the editor, Charlie Booth. My itinerary also included the Court House and the stand in the post office where Chicago newspapers were sold.

At home I did chores around the farm, whereas in younger days I had usually dodged them, especially when I was engrossed in making pictures. The whole family now cautioned me not to overdo, but I knew that I needed physical activity. I was still much underweight, and naturally my mother undertook to cure that with tasty home-cooked food.

Croquet was *the* outdoor sport in that day, and I thought it fun, playing with my brother Bill. Then I found a pair of Indian clubs in the attic, a reminder of an earlier passion of Bill's, and I began exercising with these, doing fancy gyrations in the front yard. This was a decided mistake. Farmers going by in their wagons disapproved of it. Sometimes I could hear their acid comment; or it was relayed to me promptly by others. "If he was my boy," said one of these critics, "he'd exercise out in the fields with a hoe." I didn't want people to think I was a playboy and a loafer. I had been a great expense to my family; I knew that, and the townspeople knew it. And I *did* try hoeing, dutifully; but a couple of hours of it daily was enough to wear me out.

So I took things more easily for a while. And as the weeks went by, I had to learn that lesson more than once. There were stretches of good weather when I would move along in fine fettle; then I would have days with a pain in my side, and a feeling of dread. Father had Dr. Loofborough, our family physician, come in to see me. He was cheerful and reassuring. "Nothing wrong with you, Art. Just a matter of time and patience—and you'll be all right again. Get plenty of rest—not necessarily at night, but whenever you feel tired—and keep your mind occupied. And if what you're doing seems a task, switch to something else. Don't feel that you have to do today anything that you can put off until tomorrow."

My chief diversion, as always, was drawing pictures, and in running through any illustrated books or magazines that I could get hold of. *Harper's Weekly* came to us regularly, and I was first to look it over. At intervals all too long a show would come to Turner Hall, and usually I would go to renew my childhood; for I had been through enough trouble to make me feel like one who was getting along in years.

Letters from Clarence Webster kept me informed about what the fellows I knew in the Chicago newspaper offices were doing, and made me lonely for the color and movement of the city. Yet when I thought of the possibility of going back, I knew I wasn't equal to it yet. The fine self-confidence that I had had for a few years while things were going well, was lacking now. But I was keenly interested in what Web wrote about preparations for a World's Fair to celebrate the discovery of America by one Christopher Columbus—the question of his right to the title of "discoverer" not having been raised in that era. The Fair would mean a great boom, my friend and advisor said, with the newspapers riding on the crest of the tide. . . .

And now I began toying with an idea that had long been in the back of my mind—the writing and illustrating of a book dealing with intimate affairs in the Hell of my own time, as Dante (with the subsequent pictorial aid of Doré) had done. I figured that Hades must have changed a good deal through the centuries, in view of outside influences, just as the upper world had changed for better or for worse. Looking through the Dante-Doré volume that rested on the parlor table, I was sure that many of the local institutions shown therein would now be obsolete.

I gave attention with my drawing pen to various arrivals in Hell since the Florentine poet's day. New subjects of Satan took form on the paper before me—small-town gossips, cornet-fiends, farmers who failed to blanket their horses in winter, chronic kickers, botch tailors, hypocritical church pillars, bunco-steerers, and kindred souls eligible for membership in the society of the nether regions.

Fitting punishments were set forth in other pictures—quack doctors gulping down their own poison; boodle aldermen, each in a superheated oven; confidence-men on a sandpaper slide; the chronic kickers being kicked by machinery; the monopolists and snobbish rich sitting in frying pans over fires.

Many of those drawings I would now reject as inferior to my present standard. Yet some of them I like much, and would not change. One which I prize (if one may unblushingly admire a self-created work) is my portrait, drawn of course from imagination, of the inventor of the barbed-wire fence, naked except for a high silk hat and a walrus moustache sitting through eternity on his bare behind on one of the fences he devised. As a boy in farm country I used to see cattle and horses gashed and bleeding from encounters with those cruel steel points.*

There was tonic for me in all this. But when I had completed several dozen new views of Gehenna, I made no move to place the material with a publisher. That seemed a formidable task—and remembering the doctor's advice, I set the whole thing aside to be taken up again when I happened to

---

* Until this was written I had no idea who invented barbed-wire. Then word came that his name was Jacob Haish, and that he died in 1926 in DeKalb, Illinois, only sixty miles from where I was born. He was 99 years old, and had made millions from his invention, the idea for which came to him around 1851, as he wound pasture fences with osage, which had stiff thorns. When he died the Illinois Historical Society described him as a "man of peace", who had lived to see the farmer's fence turned into a "tangle of horror and death that ran like a rusty snake through northern France."

be in the proper mood. Yet I mentioned it in a letter to Eugene Field, and I asked him how he would like to write some reading matter to go with the pictures. "Don't be so modest," he replied. "Write it yourself. You know a lot more about Hell than I do. Anybody who went through an illness like yours in Paris ought to have no hesitation in describing the tortures of Hades."

Webster and I had a friend in Chicago who bore the curious name of Wyllys S. Abbot, and who was interested in the stage as well as in journalism. At this point Abbot had what he considered a scintillating idea, about which he first wrote, then came up to see me. He proposed to organize a traveling company, of which I would be the headliner, to edify the people of various cities and towns with a combination of art, song, and music. He dwelt strongly upon my having "a talent which ought to be capitalized." My part would be to draw quick sketches of well-known persons and familiar scenes in time and keeping with music. Webster knew of this stunt of mine and had told him about it.

I was hesitant about carrying out the scheme, but Abbot painted its advantages in such glowing colors that I agreed—and then we went around and enlisted Grant Weber as one of the company. Grant, who had been studying music in Germany, was the boy who had remembered his notes on the day I got stage fright and forgot mine at the Janesville concert when I was ten.

Abbot promptly lined up other performers in Chicago and arranged for a tryout at the Press Club there. Admission was by invitation only, and the membership turned out in force. Suzanne Ella Wood, soprano, described as "a popular young society woman on the South Side," sang well. Grant Weber played creditably; he had developed a fine technique, with both power and delicacy.

We should have had an orchestra accompanying my act to make it effective, but I managed to get along with the solo support of one Signor Tomaso, a find of Abbot's, who used a mandolin. While he rendered appropriate selections, I drew quick charcoal sketches on large sheets of white paper of Napoleon Bonaparte, General William T. Sherman, Richard Wagner, General Boulanger, and Bob Ingersoll, with a pitchfork tossing him into flames. I also made "evolution sketches" —with a few swift strokes of my crayon. I rhythmically changed a watermelon into the face of a grinning darkey while the long-haired Signor obliged with the tune "Dancing in the Barn."

The press did well by us, so that we were able to quote favorable comment from the *Daily News, Tribune, Inter-Ocean,* and *Herald* in a leaflet—"novel exhibition . . . pleasant entertainment . . . clever . . . artistic . . . rare finish and brilliancy . . . refreshing."

Abbot got us a booking at Plymouth Church, and here we added a chorus of young women. This brought us more publicity, and soon we were billed to appear at the Grand Opera House in Bloomington, Illinois. Then Abbot spread himself on a poster, topped by the bold-lettered words: *"Good Morning, have you seen Art Young?"* Below was some bragging about my facility, which, however, I was sure I could live up to. Abbot said: "We've got to do it that way, Art. Everybody does it. You're not heralding your own virtues. I'm doing that, as your manager."

His ballyhoo knew no limit: "Art Young's political satires have widened and strengthened the influence of many journals, among them the *Tribune, Daily News,* and *Inter-Ocean* of Chicago, *Texas Siftings* and *The Judge* (sic) of New York, and the *Pall Mall Budget* of London. His artistic pencil has accompanied Lieutenant Swatka in Alaska, Rider Haggard in Africa, and 'Conflagration Jones' abroad, but—

"His greatest triumph is the presentation of the most unique entertainment ever presented to American audiences in which, keeping time and tune with his crayon, he presents to the eye an artistically beautiful or laughable sketch . . . suggested by the melodious strains. . . .

"The performance is wonderful—the effect is magical. Among his spectators cheers, laughter, and tears seem at his bidding. Once seen, his marvelous talent is never forgotten. *No man has ever before displayed it."*

We appeared in Bloomington on May 22, 1891. The posters had said: "While the band plays he draws a picture of a song." But this must have been press agents' license, for no band or orchestra is mentioned on the program. Instead a Signor Carolla is down for a violin solo, and I seem to remember that he supplied the accompaniment for me. I drew pictures illustrative of the *Marseillaise, Boulanger's March, Marching Through Georgia, In the Sweet Bye and Bye, Lohengrin's Wedding March, McGinty, Annie Rooney, We Won't Go Home Until Morning, Hail Columbia, Tenting Tonight, Nearer My God to Thee,* and others. I am amused now at the memory of having done a portrait of Napoleon to illustrate the *Marseillaise,* but it got across with that audience.

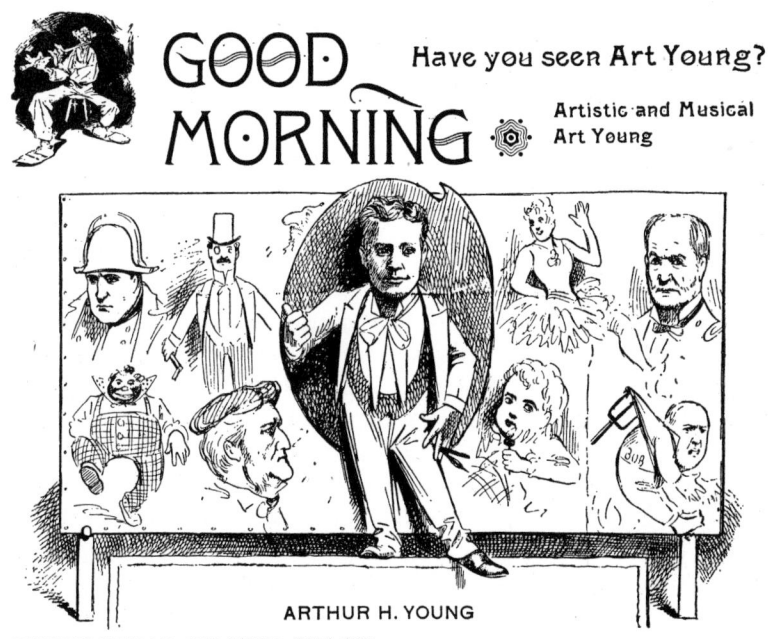

WHEN I WAS ON THE STAGE.

The *Bloomington Daily Leader* said that "the critical audience applauded long and loud," and the local correspondent of the *Chicago Inter-Ocean* reported the concert as "an event of much social importance" and said the audience was "not only large but containing the very elite of the city." Some now forgotten co-worker whom I had known on the *Daily News* in Chicago, had hooked up with the *Kansas City Star,* and he wrote a story for that paper, dwelling upon my method of drawing a picture of Mr. McGinty in rhythm with "the orchestra" as it played the tune lamenting that unfortunate worthy's descent to the bottom of the sea.

With all this favorable comment, Abbot contended that it was time for us to move on my home town. I was reluctant to appear in Monroe, especially in view of my manager's proposal that we stage our performance as a benefit to a home-town boy who had come through a desperate illness. Finally Abbot agreed to omit any mention of a benefit from the advertisements, and I consented to let him go ahead with arrangements.

So he got out a large four-page leaflet, with pen-sketches of the principals, and with five bold cuts of myself, all alike, spread across one page. "Admission 35 and 50 cents. Tickets for sale at the Post Office and at D. S. Young & Co.'s."

June 11 was the date, and Turner Hall was packed. We gave the audience a long program for its money, and those present demanded more from every performer. But I was not happy that night. I felt that even though the ads had not called the show a benefit, it was generally understood that it was intended to be that—and that perhaps all the generous applause was not based strictly on the merits of our offerings.

Clarence Webster was on hand, billed as " 'Conflagration Jones,' the famous humorist of the *Chicago Inter-Ocean*," and gave, in his best style, a recitation entitled "Pizen Jim," with encores. Suzanne Wood, Grant Weber, and others also were on the program. I appeared on the stage with two sets of sketches, repeating what I had done in Bloomington.

Many friends told me that the performance was a great success, but to me that evening was one of the worst ordeals I ever went through. As I stood before the people of Monroe, I felt that everyone there was a super-critic. I wondered whether my clothes were all buttoned properly, and if my necktie was still straight. But the music helped a lot, and I went through all the motions of the routine that I had rehearsed so many times.

On the leaflets heralding our Monroe concert was an announcement of a forthcoming Chicago magazine, the *Ahkoond of Swat*, projected by Abbot, with Webster and myself as associate editors. This was planned as a monthly, the title being borrowed from George Thomas Lanigan's poem. In 1878, when he was on the night news desk of the

New York World, the cable brought the bare announcement of the demise of a king in a small country in India. Unable to find data in any reference books upon which to base an obituary, Lanigan was impelled to write that now famous threnody. The first stanza read:

> What, what, what
> What's the news from Swat?
>   Sad news,
>   Bad news,
> Comes by the cable led
> Through the Indian Ocean's bed,
> Through the Persian Gulf, the Red
>   Sea and the Med-
>   Iterranean—he's dead:
> The Ahkoond of Swat is dead!"

The *Ahkoond of Swat* started bravely, and flamboyantly, as such publications do. It was largely humorous, but also contained editorials dealing with political and other affairs. The first issue contained two of my Hell pictures, each occupying half a page. Abbot predicted a great future for this periodical, but found it difficult to get advertising for it. There were only three issues. So far as I know I have the only copy of the *Ahkoond* that has survived.

About the same time an Englishman we knew in Chicago launched a magazine called *Push*, and Web and I were in on the ground floor there also. But it didn't have enough push to pay its way, and soon gave up the ghost.

There had been talk of our concert company going to Janesville and other Wisconsin cities, but after the Monroe appearance we all felt we had enough of it, and the plan was scrapped.

I went back to work on the Hell book, and resumed the physical exercises. Sometimes the old weakness recurred, but the intervals of well-being were much longer. My share of the proceeds of the concerts was enough to justify my loafing at home for a while longer.

Chapter 15

RETURN TO HEALTH AND CHICAGO

IT seems strange now that I lingered in Monroe convalescing for a year and a half—but it took that long before I was my normal self again. Around Christmas in 1891 I realized that I had been on the sidelines long enough; I must get out into the world once more. A national campaign was coming on; and there was likely to be a hot fight, particularly over the tariff. I didn't know much about the tariff question, but I wanted to be where there was action.

New York seemed my best bet. I still had that letter of introduction from Eugene Field to Colonel Cockerill of the *World,* and there was *Puck,* in which a good many pictures dealt with politics and topical affairs. There ought to be a place for me somewhere in the metropolis. I had been waiting for something to happen which would give me a legitimate excuse to write to eastern editors and ask if there was an opening. But I figured now that my chances would be better if I pulled up stakes and saw the editors in person. My strength had returned and I was a new man, ready for anything.

So I said goodbye again and started east, stopping in Chicago, of course, to look up my friends. I told Field some new anecdote at which he laughed, and he said: "Write it." I did, and also made an illustration for it, and both were published next day in his column, "Sharps and Flats."

Dropping in at the *Inter-Ocean* office to see Web, I was hailed in friendly fashion by William Penn Nixon, the editor and part-owner whom I had met before. He inquired solicitously about my health and plans. Then he asked how I would like to do political cartoons for the *Inter-Ocean,* which at that time was as influential as the *Tribune.* It was, in fact, known as "the farmers' Bible", so completely did the people in the rural districts read and believe in it.

Evidently Nixon had heard about my being let out by

the *Tribune.* He knew my work on the *Daily News,* and also that his managing editor, Mr. Busbey, and Webster wanted me on the staff. He offered me $50 a week, to start at once if I was ready, and it took me no more than a couple of minutes to say yes. This was a definite job, offered without being asked for, and I liked the idea of being so close to home. Elizabeth North was now living in Milwaukee with an uncle, which fact also had had something to do with my acceptance.

Webster took me out to dinner to celebrate, and then we went to look at the two great new skyscrapers that had sprung up in my absence—the Masonic Temple, twenty-one stories high, the tallest building in the land, and the Auditorium, in which were combined a magnificent opera house, hotel, and office floors. And with the stupendous World's Fair coming on in the fall, this surely was the place for me. I had no regret about not going on to New York. Web and his wife had a house out in LaGrange and next day he invited me to share it with them. This arrangement was agreeable and advantageous to me.

Nixon wanted me to do a cartoon every day. This was new to the Mid-West, although Walt McDougall, whom I was soon to meet, had been drawing one a day for the *New York World* as early as 1884. Most of the cartoons which I drew for the *Inter-Ocean* were my own ideas, but occasionally Mr. Busbey would suggest a subject, and I would devise a way to present it. Usually politics was my theme, varied now and then, on an off day, by some travesty on prevailing fads.

The *Inter-Ocean* was Republican, and of course for tariff-protected industry. I had some knowledge of its past, for I had seen that past dug up by enemy papers. They could not forget that in 1880 the *I-O* had supported the Greenback party, an act classified by the righteous as involving gross moral turpitude, and as treason to society, business security, and prosperity—but the farmers liked it. By 1892 the *Inter-Ocean,* like the *Tribune* (which once had published militant editorials by Henry Demarest Lloyd, Socialist), had pulled in its horns, and was now generally regarded by the business interests as respectable and level-headed on most issues.

I had found no reason in that day to regard money-reform as anything but nonsense and it was necessary for me to become much older to get straightened out on that. And I must add that in 1933, fifty-three years after the sweeping defeat of this movement which had reaped so much editorial and oratorical abuse, its supposed evil nature had been forgotten, and Congress voted for the payment of government bonds in currency, one of the demands of the Greenback convention in 1880. And in the intervening years other planks in the Greenback platform had been embodied in government policies or had been generally approved in principle.

H. H. Kohlsaat, proprietor of a chain of busy lunchrooms in the downtown district, was then principal owner of the *Inter-Ocean*. Active in Republican politics, it was well known that he had an ardent dislike for President Benjamin Harrison, who hoped to be nominated to succeed himself.

The Republican convention was scheduled to be held in Minneapolis in the second week of June, 1892, and Kohlsaat, who had taken full charge of the newspaper, assigned me to cover the pictorial side. He was to be a delegate. Shortly before his departure for Minneapolis, he reached his office one morning to discover a large number of Negro men and women waiting to see him. All of them had seen a notice in Eugene Field's column in the *Daily News* which stated that Kohlsaat was going to Minneapolis to urge the nomination of a colored man as Vice-President, and that he was ready to pay the expense of any Negro who would go to the convention to help achieve that end. Kohlsaat had long shown a philanthropic interest toward the black race. He had to explain that this announcement was a joke by a writer with an odd sense of humor—and it was difficult for the hoaxed Negroes to understand that joke. Many southern editors quoted and no doubt believed the story invented by Field.

I remember no hotter place in my life than the vast temporary wooden building in which the Minneapolis conclave was held. Rosin dripped from the new lumber of which it was made, and perspiration dripped from the 15,000 or more persons in attendance. William McKinley of Ohio was chairman. He tried to cool himself frequently with a palm-leaf fan, as did everybody else. It was a fan-fluttering convention. The thousands of fans in evidence had been presented by the enterprising Kohlsaat, who had had them stamped with an advertisement: "Keep cool and read the *Inter-Ocean.*" I was amazed at the emotional heights to which the delegates worked up in that atmosphere.

The fight for the nomination was a three-cornered one, the main contestants beside Harrison being McKinley and James G. Blaine, the "Plumed Knight" of Maine. Thomas B. Reed, also of Maine, and Robert T. Lincoln of Illinois, son of Abraham, were lesser favorites in the balloting. A great experience for me, watching that first of many national conventions which I was to attend during the following forty years. It was spectacular drama. Blaine had been ambitious for years to attain the Presidency, and the disappointment of his followers as they saw him losing another contest was intense.

I sat at the press table with Walt McDougall of the *New York World* and other cartoonists of the dailies. And what was most important, I met Thomas Nast, who was doing some special pictures for the *Inter-Ocean* for his friend Kohlsaat. Nast was then fifty-two. I introduced myself to him, and we talked at length. He stayed only a day.

Listening to speeches, watching the thunderous demonstrations staged by the delegates, and playing a silent part while the correspondents and artists around me speculated on what was happening behind the scenes, I accumulated a large stock of material for use in the campaign. Here were the leaders and the statesmen (not always synonymous) of the Republican party—the best minds, in action at close range.

Chauncey M. Depew made a clear and forceful speech, proving that he was a good speaker on serious subjects as well as a humorist. At the end he placed Harrison in nomination, and then the band played lustily. Several men hurried down the center aisle with a big portrait of the President, adorned with the national colors, and fastened it to a standard on the platform. . . . In one of the demonstrations for Blaine, the cheering was led by the portly Thomas B. Reed, who for many years had been Blaine's implacable enemy; he had succumbed to the pressure of what is known as political expediency. . . . A slim girl in light gray aided the Harrison cause with an oft-repeated Indian war-whoop, recalling the President's grandfather "Old Tippecanoe."

On the fourth day the nomination went to Harrison on the first ballot. He got 535 1-6 votes, while McKinley received 182 1-6; Blaine, 182; Reed, 4; and Lincoln 1. The Vice-Presidential choice was Whitelaw Reid, editor of the *New York Tribune,* who was chosen by acclamation.

Two weeks later I attended the Democratic national convention at the Exposition building on the lake front in Chicago, at which Grover Cleveland was picked to head the ticket, with Adlai E. Stevenson as his running mate. . . . A clergyman with a weak voice delivered the invocation, amid cries of "Louder!" Before the prayer was ended the Horace Boies Club, which had been vociferously championing Iowa's favorite son and Governor, started to march down the aisle to the platform. The club was halted and quieted by the police. . . . One ludicrous incident stands out in memory—a *faux pas* of a German bandmaster. He was a capable musician, but evidently had come to this country some time after the Civil War, and his education in American history was incomplete. For just as the Georgia delegation was entering the hall, his band started to play *Marching Through Georgia.* Immediately there was a riotous demonstration of protest among the mint-julep fanciers in Section K and only the fact that the band playing the hated reminder of General Sherman's march was in the gallery saved the leader and his men from physical violence.

Tammany's representatives were drenched by a downpour of rain through a hole in the roof. Richard Croker and Charles F. Murphy were among those who got their clothes wet. The Tammany crowd was backing former Governor David B. Hill of New York, and fighting with every possible weapon to defeat Cleveland. . . . The band got a big hand when it played *Dixie* and *Ta-ra-ra boom de-ay.*

Representative William L. Wilson of West Virginia was the chairman, and made the keynote speech, saying: "Whoever may be chosen leader by our party in this campaign, no telegram will flash across the sea from the castle of absentee tariff lords to congratulate him. But from the home of labor, from the fireside of the toiler, from the hearts of all who love justice and do equity, who wish and intend that our matchless heritage of freedom shall be the common wealth of all our people and the common opportunity of all our youth, will come up prayers for his success and recruits for the great Democratic host that must strike down the beast of sectionalism and the moloch of monopoly before we can ever again have a people's government run by a people's faithful representatives."

That sounded reasonable to me, but I was a Republican employed by a Republican paper for $50 a week and not to be influenced by the siren song of our opponents. Nevertheless I have always been sensitive to competent oratory, and from that year to the present time have heard all kinds—most of it I would say, as one of Plutarch's noble Grecians or Romans put it, "tall and lofty like a cypress tree, but bearing no fruit."

My work at the office was a consistent day-after-day show-up of the iniquities of the Democrats. On all sides the campaign was bitter, and grew more and more vituperative as the months went on.

My scrap-book for that year contains all of my cartoon attacks on Grover Cleveland and the Democratic party. On one of these the caption reads: "The political Darius Green and his flying machine: The greatest invention under the sun. 'And now,' says Darius, 'hooray for some fun.'" Cleveland, with makeshift wings attached to his shoulders, labeled: "My letter of acceptance" . . . "Meaningless platitudes." . . . "Speeches with no sense." Grover stands on the Democratic platform, labeled: "Free trade . . . No pensions . . . Wildcat currency . . . Fraudulent elections." He is about to try a flight to the White House in the distance.

Remembering that Tammany Hall fought tooth-and-nail to keep Cleveland from being nominated in Chicago, there is a queer ring now to another of my *Inter-Ocean* cartoons entitled *The Beggars*. This depicts Joseph Pulitzer, with accented nose, playing a hand-organ labeled "New York World" and leading the Tammany tiger, which carries a plate in its mouth. The tiger holds in a claw a paper bearing the words: "We must buy votes for Cleveland and free trade", while Pulitzer flaunts a banner reading: "Please give a helping hand to the democracy of the Northwest; it is all going to smash."

Another picture was headed *The Latest from the South*, with an underline: "Adlai Stevenson is still grinding out his one speech to large and enthusiastic audiences." The candidate, adorned with a silk hat, stands on a tree stump grinding a hand-organ. Attached to his coat are ribbons labeled "Knight of the Golden Circle" (the Knights were a secret society of Democrats opposed to the Civil War) and "Greenback record." His sole listener is a Negro seated on a rail fence eating watermelon.

In July the story of the battle between Pinkerton thugs and locked-out Carnegie Steel Company workers in Homestead, Pennsylvania, screamed from the front pages. When men who had struck against a wage-cut gathered to prevent 300 Pinkerton men on barges from landing at the plant, the leader of the thugs gave an order to fire and ten workers fell, two being instantly killed. That was the beginning of an all-day fight, in which the aroused steel workers met repeated attempts of the Pinkertons to land with rocks, bullets, dynamite, and burning oil cast adrift on the waters of the Monongahela River. Other men died that day on both sides of the battle, ten in all, with many wounded.

Around three o'clock the Pinkertons ran up a white flag. It was shot full of holes by the enraged strikers. A second white flag met the same fate. But when a third one was run up cooler heads among the strikers agreed to a truce. With women and children jeering at them, the captured thugs marched with their hands in air several blocks to an old skating rink, where they were held "prisoners of war" for twenty-four hours. Then they were taken to the edge of town and told to "hit the road." Overnight the strikers had burned the Pinkerton barges. Henry C. Frick, manager for Andrew Carnegie, demanded that Governor Pattison of Pennsylvania send in troops. But Pattison was slow to act.

Of course the press dispatches were not so explicit as the summary of the battle that I have given here. The facts of the situation were slow in coming through, as they usually are in such situations, and the emphasis of the telegraphic reports was on "labor rioting."

Editorially the daily newspapers displayed two distinct

attitudes toward that episode, depending on whether they were Republican-tariff-protection or Democratic-free trade organs. We of the *Inter-Ocean* made the most of the battle and its aftermath. From the dispatches I drew a front page cartoon-spread of the tragedy, and underneath it the editor put this caption: "Who's to blame?"

I note three cartoons that I drew in the next few days. One has this underline: "What a regiment—if all the men who have made asses of themselves in the Homestead riot case would fall in line." The picture shows several figures each with a label: Governor Pattison, "delay in calling out militia"; Palmer, "incendiary speech"; Voorhees, "wild talk"; a donkey-headed "agitator"; two more donkey heads and another down a long line labeled "free trade editor" . . . The second picture portrays Public Opinion in feminine personification delivering a mandate to Governor Pattison: "Write that letter!" with an explanatory label: "Letter ordering out the militia in the interest of law and order." Below was the added comment: "And he wrote it."

My third pictorial preachment on Homestead is headed: "Dana Shames the Small Democratic Editors." The cartoon depicts the New York editor in a silk hat pointing an admonitory finger at a group of boys as they stand abashed at the foot of a scarecrow labeled: "Homestead riot scare to frighten voters." Underneath is a long quotation from Dana's paper, the *New York Sun,* which was Democratic but not wedded to the idea of free trade; thus:

"We regret to notice that some (nearly all) of our Democratic contemporaries are treating the Homestead incident in a partisan fashion, for which there is no excuse. They assume that because Mr. Andrew Carnegie and his associates at Homestead have been engaged in an industry protected by the tariff, and because a dispute as to wages has arisen between the employers and employed, protection is responsible for the murders and mischiefs. . . . If strikes were never heard of in unprotected industries; if, in fact, the greatest strikes in the country had not occurred in the unprotected industries, like the steam railroads and the horse railroads; if free trade England were not a country of desperate strikes, and if these facts were not known to everybody with education enough to read large print, these assumptions might be worth contradicting. As the case is, they are so far fetched and wildly absurd that we fear they will bring discord upon the Democrats in the national campaign."

John P. Altgeld, who had been chief justice of the Cook County Superior Court, was running for the governorship on the Democratic ticket. He was anathema to the *Inter-Ocean,* as probably any Democratic candidate for that chair would have been then. I look back over the anti-Altgeld cartoons in my scrapbook now with a deep sense of shame. Two cited here will be sufficient to typify my assaults upon that clean man's character in those far-off days of youth.

One is headed: "Eighty Per Cent Wrong," and underlines quote the *Streator Free Press* as saying: "Judge Altgeld's record on the bench is about the worst in modern history. Ten cases were appealed from Altgeld's court, eight of which were reversed on account of error by the Judge. He couldn't have been wrong oftener if he had tried." In this picture Altgeld is seen leaning on "his barrel" (then the political symbol of wealth) which is labeled "Wrong Argument," and a string is fastened to one of his legs, which is being pulled by Mike McDonald, political boss. Back of Altgeld on a wall are numerous signs: "Says the wrong things at the wrong time . . . The wrong kind of man to nominate for Governor . . . Does wrong by his poor tenants . . . Combs his hair the wrong way . . . Makes his tenants pay in gold coin only, which is wrong . . . Has wrong views on the labor question."

That was how I was making good with the *Inter-Ocean* and the Republican party. It seems unbelievable at this distance that we assailed a candidate because he combed his hair the wrong way, but that is a part of the record of mud-slinging in American politics. And I was a participant on the front page of a leading newspaper.

But for sheer abuse the following is perhaps the prize cartoon:

"Shades of Departed Governors, Has It Come to This?" Shades of Yates (1862) and Edwards (1812), tall men, stand beside the Illinois executive chair, while Altgeld, shown as a diminutive figure, is climbing onto the dais with his hands on the chair-arm. On his back is a keg labeled "$$$ Barrel to Buy Votes," and on the floor are papers with these inscriptions: "Attempted robbery of Chicago . . . Slander of state institutions . . . Alliance with thugs and bum element."

Altgeld had attacked the prison contract labor system, and he had charged Governor Joe Fifer's administration with gross extravagance, alleging, for instance, that there were institutions in Illinois where "it took $600,000 to pay and keep employees to expend $400,000 on the inmates of the institution." In answer the Republican press, with the *Inter-Ocean* among the loudest, denounced Altgeld as a liar without conscience. The editorial writers assailed his charges as "the deliberate and malicious falsehoods of a brazen demagogue," they called him an Anarchist, a gold-bug, a fomenter of "foreign know-nothingism," and asserted that he was "never in the army at all!"

In all this smoky conflict I followed the *Inter-Ocean's* editorials and trusted the editor who had given me my job and H. H. Kohlsaat, the owner. They were mature men and as such I felt ought to know the truth. The *Inter-Ocean* called itself a paper for the home, and it was careful not to print anything except what was "moral." Sometimes, it is true, I detected flaws in the Republican armor; but I consoled myself with the thought that no human institution was perfect. Perhaps politics was just sordid, unpleasant, and a necessary evil; when I got away from the office at night I was glad to forget about the campaign.

Despite all our bitter opposition Cleveland was elected President and Altgeld Governor of Illinois, and afterward the *Inter-Ocean* had the federal and state administrations to attack instead of mere candidates. We got excited once about the hardships of life at West Point, which I deplored in a cartoon called "Straining at a Gnat and Swallowing a Camel." This depicts the Democratic Congress swallowing a camel labeled "Southern harbors appropriations," with an underline: "Not one cent for soap at West Point, but millions for the improvement of Southern harbors."

We found time, too, to hit at the misdeeds of the Democratic municipal administration. In one picture entitled "A Ruler Afraid to Rule," a feminine Chicago points to "Gambling dens running wide open," and Mayor Hopkins replies: "You'll have to speak to the chief of police about that." . . . John Burns, British labor leader, came to the city, and I quoted him in a cartoon as saying "Your streets are vile, horrible!" and city contractors, inspectors, and subcontractors answering: "They suit us, see?"

So ran my first year on the *Inter-Ocean*.

When time had moved along to 1915 the State of Illinois got around to erecting a monument to Altgeld's memory in Chicago. Writing then in the *Metropolitan Magazine,* for which I was covering Washington, I apologized for having ridiculed the courageous little Governor in my adolescence as a cartoonist.

"Almost every act of Altgeld's offended the capitalist powers of the state and nation," I recalled. "He was an idealist, therefore an 'insane statesman.' He believed in the rights of labor, was a friend of common people, and showed his friendship by his deeds. . . .

"I thought he must be a political Beelzebub because respectable, well-dressed people said so. I soon learned, however, that well-dressed, respectable judgement is not reliable; indeed, it is generally wrong."

Chapter 16

I WORK WITH THOMAS NAST

ONE of my chief compensations in working on the *Inter-Ocean* was that I got to know Thomas Nast intimately. Long a friend of Mr. Kohlsaat, the publisher, he had come to Chicago to act as judge in a contest staged by the paper for a drawing which would best symbolize the spirit of that fast-growing city. He had cut loose from *Harper's Weekly* at the end of 1886 because of the limitations which George William Curtis, the editor, put upon his work. After the contest in Chicago, he stayed on to do some special cartoons for a bigger and better *Inter-Ocean* which would soon make other newspaper editors in the Middle West sit up and take notice.

In that autumn of 1892 the *Inter-Ocean* made its big forward step.* It had installed the first color press in the country, and began to print a colored supplement with its Sunday issue. In this Nast and I were presently appearing with full-page pictures, and it was gratifying to see my name featured in advertisements with that of the artist I had admired so much in the dream-days back on the farm.

While color-printing has of course been much improved in forty-seven years, the productions of that first color press, viewed in copies of the supplement which I have preserved, compare favorably with the fast color printing seen in comic supplements and feature sections of newspapers today. Our Sunday circulation was immediately increased by many thousands, and the editors of the other seven-day papers were given something serious to think about.

---

* The *New York World* has often erroneously been given credit for producing the first colored supplement. Walt McDougall, in his autobiography, gave the date of that "first" in the *World* as September, 1893; while a New York City publication, *Highlights of the Nineties*, timed simultaneously with the opening of the 1939 World's Fair, reproduced an Atlantic Garden Saturday Night Scene from the *World* of November 19, 1893, calling it "the first page of color appearing in any American newspaper." But I have pages from the *Chicago Inter-Ocean* colored supplement dated as early as September 18, 1892.

Nast's cartoons in the supplement were usually political. Mine dealt with various topics in addition to politics. One was entitled "Let Uncle Sam Be the Arbitrator," and portrayed our venerable red-white-and-blue relative making Capital and Labor shake hands. Another was called "In Darkest Chicago," showing crime slinking along on badly lighted streets. Occasionally I illustrated feature articles, such as "Highwaymen of the Past."

That then marvelous color press had been acquired at a propitious time, enabling the *Inter-Ocean* to celebrate impressively the dedication exercises at the World's Columbian Exposition, which took place in October. For more than a year an army of workingmen had been speeding the construction of the great edifices, lagoons, waterways, islands, fountains, remodeled landscape, roads, and docks to comprise the dazzling White City which would commemorate the landing of Columbus on American soil.

All Chicago's people seemingly caught the spirit of that daring enterprise, and felt its thrill, as did the multitudes across the hinterland—for it marked the rebirth of a community that needed to cast off a dingy skin. Architects with soaring imagination from various cities, engineers with unfettered vision, sculptors and painters competent to work on a scale of immensity until then unheard of, were given leave to work out their dreams, with ample money and materials, the one handicap being the pressure of a time-schedule.

There was a glow of idealism about the rising of all that wonderland; at least so I, and most people, thought. I did not know that hundreds of workers on the Fair were injured in accidents due to the speed-up, nor that eighteen of them died from those injuries in the first few months. Such unfortunate circumstances were always kept in the background.

It was inspiring to do pictures of those monumental palaces and pavilions as their towers and domes rose against the sky. Drawing now for reproduction in much larger space than ever before, I could see my draftsmanship definitely improving. I found myself taking more pains with this work which would appear in color than with the daily front-page political cartoons—which I had learned to turn out between

PRE-VIEW OF WORLD'S COLUMBIAN EXPOSITION. Members of Congress visit the scene in Chicago as work on the buildings is rushed.

4 and 6 p.m., and which were done conscientiously enough in that limited time, but which had become routine exercises.

Other memorable things were happening that year. John L. Sullivan lost the heavy-weight championship to Jim Corbett in New Orleans. Nancy Hanks did a mile trot in 2:04. Work was begun on the Drainage Canal, to be followed in time by the changing of the current in the Chicago River, so that it would flow away from Lake Michigan instead of into it, and no longer pollute the source of the city's drinking water supply. And prominent Baptists dedicated the first building of the University of Chicago, toward which John D. Rockefeller had given a small fortune.

Meanwhile the fighting in the national political campaign steadily grew hotter. Backing the Republican candidates, President Benjamin Harrison and Whitelaw Reid, the *Inter-Ocean* was straining every sinew to defeat Cleveland and Stevenson. The Populists, too, were putting on a campaign, and were "viewed with alarm" and denounced frequently by the press serving the old parties. There were Prohibition and Social Labor tickets in the field also, but to the press in general they didn't seem worth worrying about.

I did at least one full-page cartoon in the Sunday supplement assailing Cleveland for his free trade doctrines, and in the week-day issues I kept throwing pictorial shafts at all the vulnerable spots in the Democratic party's anatomy. One of the daily lampoons is titled "Election Day." A character identified as Demented Democracy is speaking to another labeled Voter. The former is a frowsy man standing alongside a downcast horse called Wildcat Banks, leading him with a strap bearing the words Free Trade. Mr. Voter is on a sprightly steed named National Banks and Protection, with a paper in his pocket headed Sound Money. Demented Democracy is saying: "Don't you want to change?" and Mr. Voter says: "Not today."

Reading the *Inter-Ocean's* dispatches from the political battle fronts, to the exclusion of opposition newspapers, one would gather that only the Republicans had any real chance of winning. All over the country, it appeared, the voters were lining up in huge numbers for the party of Abraham Lincoln.

But on election night the sad news came that the Democrats had run away with the apple-cart. Cleveland and

Stevenson had won 277 electoral votes, while Harrison and Reid got only 145, and the Populists (first minority party ever to poll any electoral votes, boasted of 22). Six states gave the Populists a majority, and their national total was 1,065,191 votes. The new alarm at this, voiced now by both the Republican and Democratic press, was probably genuine. Headed by James Baird Weaver, who had been the party's Presidential nominee in 1880, when the *Inter-Ocean* had flown its banner, the Populists had waged a determined campaign on a platform demanding government ownership of railroads and telegraph, telephone, and express systems; free coinage of silver at the ratio of sixteen to one; the initiative and referendum; restricted immigration; an eight-hour workday; and election of U. S. Senators by direct vote of the people.

Altgeld and the whole state Democratic ticket also had won, swept into office despite the supposedly strong Republican press. The Governor-elect had gone into half a hundred counties meeting farmers, miners, and small-town people on their own ground, discussing their problems, talking their own language with them, rather than making many public speeches. His editorial foes of course looked askance at all this, harpooning him for his "political handshake" and giving the impression that there was some skullduggery afoot when a gubernatorial candidate came down from the platform and shook a voter's hand when that hand was grimy with coal dust or locomotive oil. This close contact with the plain people by Altgeld was combined with attacks on the trusts, and with exposures of Republican extravagance in state institutions and of the dark abuses under the system which permitted the contracting of convict labor in the prisons.

That defeat at the polls saddened the *Inter-Ocean's* official family on election night and next day, though the gloom quickly wore off. Officially the paper foresaw calamity for the nation under Democratic auspices, but privately the editors didn't seem to mind. And sometimes I was moved to wonder about the consistency of a newspaper's emotions and actions during such a campaign. Was Cleveland actually the national menace that the *Inter-Ocean* called him? I had seen and sketched him when I was on the *Daily News,* and he seemed a decent, level-headed individual. And was Altgeld truly muddle-brained and Mike McDonald's tool? I noted that despite the detailed instructions given by William Penn Nixon for cartoons charging the Democratic ticket leader with manifold villainies, Nixon, after working hours, would readily concede that Altgeld had numerous good points.

I could see that working on a daily newspaper when a campaign was on was a good deal like being a soldier in a war, on one side or the other. One's personal attitudes, if one had any attitudes, were shelved for the time being if they happened to run counter to those of the publication on which one was employed. True, there were men on the *Inter-Ocean,* as there had been on the *Daily News,* who frequently damned the owners for their policies, but kept on working for them just the same and never walked in and expressed their opinions to Melville E. Stone or H. H. Kohlsaat. No more did I. All of us obeyed.

When the smoke from the political artillery had drifted away, I felt it was time for me to do something tangible about getting my Hell book published. It had been completed weeks before, save for a few finishing touches which I attended to over the next week-end. When Eugene Field advised that I do my own narrative for that volume, his opinion of me as a writer was better than mine. He had seen few samples of my word-handling in the infrequent news stories I had written for the *Daily News* city desk when dealing pictorially with some event—hardly enough to judge by. But anyway, I had taken his advice.

Pictures and text totaled only 100 pages, but that seemed enough to do justice to the subject in that day, and Field, Webster, and others were enthusiastic over my manuscript. There were only a handful of book publishers in Chicago, and I got a ready acceptance from the first one to which I went. Francis J. Schulte and Company brought out the first edition in time for the Christmas trade.

Hell Up to Date was the title of that edition, purporting to deal with *The reckless journey of R. Palasco Drant, special correspondent through the infernal regions, as recorded by himself: with illustrations by Art Young.* I dedicated this highly moral work to Clarence Webster "in the hope that it will make him a better man." The frontispiece was a full-page portrait of the author with bandaged head, standing alongside a bust of the first explorer of the flaming empire. Farther on was another portrait labeled "Mr. Dante of Italy," showing him with a generally damaged and discouraged look as if he had just had a run-in with a denful of devils. Of all the pictures in that report of my initial survey of Gehenna, that one of the pride of the Alighieri family gave me the most satisfaction. The cover title was in bold red ink on black.

Issued at $1 and displayed by stores, news-stands, and train butchers, the book's immediate sales appeared brisk, but the cash returns to the author-artist were disappointing. My royalty checks amounted to only about $500, and I had paid for the engravings. Schultes' put out another edition for the Canadian trade, in paper covers, for 50 cents. There also was a *de luxe* edition with the title softened to *Hades Up to Date*.

But if my profits on that venture were small, it did not diminish my interest in the natural history and the social and economic conditions in the woeful region farthest down, and I returned to the subject in after-years.

I sent a copy of my book to A. B. Frost, then living in Convent, New Jersey. I had never met Mr. Frost, but had long followed his work in the delineating of American types, particularly rural, in the magazines. He replied at some length, despite the fact that his eyes were giving him trouble and limiting his correspondence. There was great encouragement for me in these words:

"I think you have a strong and decided talent for caricature, and what is particularly refreshing in these times, your work is your own; and does not remind one instantly of some one else's. I like your feeling for movement and action very much."

Governor Altgeld was ill when inaugurated in January; he managed, however, to go through his speech; then was taken hastily to his new home in Springfield and went to bed, where he stayed for weeks. The strain of travel and battle had told heavily on his slight physique. There were hints in the air that he might not survive, and the newspapers ceased firing at him.

After President Cleveland had been inaugurated we shot an occasional shaft in his direction; but there was less reason now than during the campaign. Almost immediately he withdrew from the Senate the Hawaii annexation treaty which his predecessor had signed after "an uprising by Americans and the better class of natives," and offered to restore the deposed queen, Liliuokalani, on conditions that she rejected. That gave us an excuse for a cartoon headed "Another Version of the Song," with this underline: " 'Two little boys that are blue'—black and blue." This was a take-off on the then popular ballad, "Two Little Girls in Blue." The boys in the picture are named Grover and Walt, the latter being Walter Gresham, Secretary of State. Both are crying, and holding their behinds, as Uncle Sam leaves after whipping them with a bunch of birch rods labeled Public Criticism. Above them is a bust of the Queen marked Lil, with tears flowing from her eyes.

Interest among all the city's newspapers that spring shifted largely to the opening of the World's Fair, scheduled for May 1. We of the *Inter-Ocean* staff were called upon frequently to visit the transformed Jackson Park, where the magic white metropolis was being rushed to completion. New wonders greeted us each time we went. By virtue of a command from the board of aldermen, the Illinois Central railroad, which would carry the bulk of the traffic to the Fair, was elevating its tracks, and thus would increase its speed and eliminate the danger to life and limb at grade crossings. The hotels and restaurants were preparing for the expected influx of people from all over the world, and real estate values were booming.

On Sunday, April 30, Page 1 of our Sunday supplement featured a colored sketch by Nast—showing the world's nations, personified in the figures of John Bull and the other males which we cartoonists used as typical, romping around a May Pole in honor of the lovely feminine figure of Chicago, who bore the magic slogan "I Will" upon her bodice. In Nast's bold style, the picture bore the words: "Opening Day of the World's Fair."

Into the vast Court of Honor poured some 450,000 men, women and children, who presently were milling on rain-wet ground to hear if they could the words of the notables on the platform flanking the east wall of the Administration Building. Here stood President Cleveland, members of the Spanish nobility, Mrs. Potter Palmer, Governor Altgeld, General Nelson A. Miles, Mayor Harrison, and executives of the Fair.

The President whose election the *Inter-Ocean* had so bitterly fought touched an electric key, and all the silent waiting machinery of the Exposition sprang into life—flags were unfurled on all those gleaming palaces, crystal water flowed from every fountain, heroic statues were automatically unveiled, cannon roared from warships out in the lake.

And what astonishing things to tell of to faraway relatives or friends in letters, or for the people in the country towns to read of in their newspapers—633 acres in the Fair grounds, four times the area used by the Paris Exposition, which I had seen in 1889; the Ferris Wheel, 250 feet tall; the Palace of Manufactures, 1,687 feet long by 787 feet wide; the Palace of Fine Arts, crowded with aesthetic treasures; the magnificent searchlight illumination of the Grand Basin; the replicas of Columbus's three caravels; the reproduction of the Convent of La Rabida, where the explorer applied for alms before starting for the Indies; the Venetian gondolas, with singing Italian pole-men, on the canals and lagoons; the Midway Plaisance, with its Street in Cairo and undulant dancing girls; the lovely tall German building; the Japanese and Javanese villages; and many scenes that typified other far-off countries. . . . Opposite the Fair grounds, on the west side of Stony Island avenue, Buffalo Bill's Wild West had set up its weather-beaten tents. There was no room for that show within the Exposition confines. As a supplemental attraction, it prospered.

And what do you think I liked best? The art galleries, of course—the native art of many countries. But for sheer fascination the Javanese village and its theatre of native actors got to me strongest. And next in appeal to me was Robert Burns's home—a replica, I believe, of the simple house in which many of his familiar poems were written or inspired.

Almost every week during the ensuing five months there were pictures of some phase of the Fair to be drawn. Those assignments were pleasant; for me they amounted to a liberal education in the history, productions, possessions, and customs of the world's peoples. It gave me an illuminating insight also into the habits of human beings, when gathered in crowds. Among the masses of visitors there was a certain curious madness which I too have felt when in some intriguing gallery or museum—the tendency to try to see everything there in a single day or hour. Actually it would have required six months of constant attendance to have seen all that was shown at the Exposition of 'Ninety-three. And to me those glorious edifices gave a lift of spirit which I had not felt at the Paris Fair.

Chapter 17

ALTGELD PARDONS THE ANARCHISTS

WILLIAM PENN NIXON was chairman of the Amnesty Association, which for three years had been striving to obtain pardons or commutations of sentences for the three Anarchists in the Joliet penitentiary. It will be remembered that Fielden and Schwab were serving life terms, while Neebe had been sentenced to fifteen years. Union labor was strongly represented in the association's membership of 100,000 in Chicago, but it also embraced numerous prominent business and professional men.

Countless Chicagoans, including individuals in high places, had come to doubt the justice of the verdict which had sent four other defendants to the gallows and led one to suicide. One of various reasons for this doubt was a charge made by former Police Chief Ebersold, in an interview in the *Daily News*, that Captain Michael J. Schaack had manufactured a great deal of the evidence against the Anarchists. That interview was published in 1889, a year after Melville Stone had sold his interest in the paper to Victor Lawson.

"It was my policy," Ebersold said, "to quiet matters down as soon as possible after the 4th of May. The general unsettled state of things was an injury to Chicago. On the other hand, Captain Schaack wanted to keep things stirring. He wanted bombs to be found here, there, all around, everywhere. I thought people would lie down and sleep better if they were not afraid that their homes would be blown to pieces any minute. But this man Schaack, this little boy who must have glory or his heart would be broken, wanted none of that policy. . . . After we got the Anarchist societies broken up, Schaack wanted to send out men to again organize new societies right away. . . . After I heard all that, I began to think there was perhaps not so much to all this Anarchist business as they claimed, and I believe I was right."

And the *Herald* had revealed, in a front-page story which no one took the trouble to deny, that a secret organization of 300 capitalists, formed immediately after the Haymarket tragedy, had for five years contributed from $50,000 to $140,000 annually to the police "to crush anarchy in Chicago." In 1891 this organization ceased these contributions, according to the *Herald,* because it had reason to believe that "anarchy no longer exists." The finance committee which had disbursed the money gave out no more, but issued a report in which it averred that $487,000 had been expended and that "all we had to show for it was the hanging of four men, the horrible self-murder of one, the imprisonment of three others, and the unearthing of an alleged plot against Grinnell (the prosecutor of the Anarchists) and Judge Gary."

An unnamed "attorney of great prominence," who had furnished the *Herald* with the information on which its story was based, declared that a police raid on a meeting of *Arbeiter-Zeitung* stockholders in Grief's Hall "was simply a scheme to show men who had been putting up money to keep down Anarchist movements that the followers of Parsons and Spies were not yet dead."

A strong showing had been made to Governor Fifer that no evidence in the trial had connected Neebe in any way with the Haymarket bomb. But Fifer had refused to act, although it was understood that he leaned toward clemency for Neebe. Pressure of the opposition forces was too heavy.

Altgeld's election gave fresh impetus to the activities of the Amnesty Association. And shortly after the new Governor rose from his sick bed a petition for pardons for all three prisoners, signed by more than 60,000 Illinois citizens, was placed before him. The top signer was Lyman J. Gage, financier, who later served as Secretary of the Treasury under McKinley. Two other leading Chicagoans, who with Gage had been active in circulating that plea, were aged Lyman Trumbull, friend of Lincoln, and E. S. Dreyer, a banker who had been foreman of the grand jury that indicted the Anarchists. Many of Chicago's men of affairs joined in the appeal —financiers, railroad heads, merchants, lawyers, physicians, clergymen. Governor Altgeld said he would weigh the arguments in the petition carefully, and would get the trial record and study it.

While that study was in progress the *Century Magazine* for April came out with a long article by Judge Gary upholding the Haymarket trial verdict and defending his own procedure. Champions of the Anarchists promptly answered Gary, in pamphlets and magazine articles, assailing his method of reasoning and accusing him of bias. Other individuals took up verbal cudgels in the judge's behalf.

There was no police interference when 8,000 persons assembled in Waldheim cemetery on Sunday, June 25, to witness the dedication of a bronze-and-marble monument over the graves of the four hanged men and Lingg. Justice in bronze, with no bandage over her eyes, is seen laying a laurel wreath upon the head of a worker who has gone down fighting for his kind.

Out of a clear sky next day came a bolt which rocked the nation—the announcement that Governor Altgeld had pardoned Fielden, Schwab, and Neebe, and that they would all be out of prison that afternoon. Not only did he exonerate and free those three men, but he issued an accompanying statement 17,000 words long in which he demonstrated clearly that the jury had been packed, and pointed out that the prosecution had never established who threw the bomb, and that there was no evidence that any of the defendants ever had any connection whatever with the person who did throw it, nor that he had acted on any advice given by them. Emphasizing the charges that Judge Gary had been prejudiced against the defense, he said he did not care to discuss that feature of the case "any further, because it is not necessary."

Newspapers all over the country, regardless of political affiliations, denounced Altgeld for this action. Among the most bitter were the *New York World, Times, Evening Post, Herald, Sun,* and *Tribune;* the *Philadelphia Press;* the *Washington Post;* the *Louisville Courier-Journal;* the *St. Louis Globe-Democrat;* and the *Chicago Tribune* and *Inter-Ocean.*

Editorial prose was not sufficient to express the *New York Sun's* emotions. It published an apostrophe "To Anarchy" which ended with this stanza:

O wild Chicago, when the time
   Is ripe for ruin's deeds,
When constitutions, courts, and laws
   Go down midst crashing creeds,
Lift up your weak and guilty hands
   From out the wreck of States,
And as the crumbling towers fall down
   Write ALTGELD on your gates!

All the old derogatory epithets were hurled, and others added. The little man with the close-cropped hair and beard was portrayed as an Anarchist himself, a bomb-thrower, an enemy of society, un-American, a reckless demagogue, a wrecker of democracy. In one town he was hanged in effigy. There was talk of starting a movement for his impeachment. Many of the newspapers took umbrage at Altgeld's implied criticism of Judge Gary. The *Inter-Ocean* was one of these; conceding that the Governor was within his legal rights, it called his arraignment of Gary "outrageous." This was the paper's official attitude; William Penn Nixon, its editor, obviously thought otherwise. Judge Gary and Prosecutor Grinnell declined to comment on the pardons. It was noticeable also that Altgeld made no answers to any of the widespread condemnation of his course. He had said all that he had to say in the pardon message, and he stood his ground.

I was beginning to admire him now, though I was not yet ready to admit that we were all wrong in our crusade against his policies during the campaign. I could see that even with all the new cannonading against him, his silence gave him the advantage. And there were a few voices sounding which called the Governor brave.

Mayor Carter H. Harrison's paper, the *Chicago Times*, held that "Governor Altgeld has done no more than right in giving them freedom for the rest of their days." The *Chicago Globe* was confident that time would prove the "righteousness and justice" of the pardons.

It took years, however, before my mind got straightened out on the question of where justice really lay in the Haymarket case. That mental clearance had to wait until after Altgeld died, as this narrative will show.

Chapter 18

MAYOR HARRISON IS SHOT DOWN

THERE was an uproar that summer over the question of the World's Fair remaining open on Sundays. Church people, reformers, the Fair directors, the courts, and Congress were all involved in this momentous issue. Congress had originally specified that the Fair grounds should be closed on the Sabbath, in authorizing the selling of Columbian souvenir coins to the tune of $2,500,000 to help cover Exposition costs. Facing a heavy deficit, the heads of the Fair figured that a seven-day operating week would be a life-saver. Their lawyers found a technical reason for contending that the Congressional stipulation was not binding. Fearing a deficit, the Fair officials got around that—as business men usually do—and Sunday opening was announced, to the horror of the moralists.

Meanwhile the reformers, not to be outdone, obtained an injunction against Sunday operation of the Fair. It was contested in the district courts and the ban was upheld. A higher court reversed the decision. The Fair was now running seven days a week, attendance increased daily, and the moral issue was lost in the shuffle.

I continued to do large pictures of Exposition scenes for the *Inter-Ocean* supplement—of the Eskimo Village, and of the buildings and people representing various states and countries. Countless unique objects lent themselves to news stories and illustrations—the Liberty Bell, borrowed from Philadelphia, the long-distance telephone to New York, LaFayette's sword, Miles Standish's pipe, John Alden's Bible, the Japanese tea house on Wooded Island, a Bolivian Indian 25 years old and nine feet ten inches tall, and the moving sidewalk, 4,500 feet long.

There were elements of humor also in the scene. Near the Connecticut building wooden nutmegs were sold as souvenirs at five cents each, a little joke harking back to the days of an ingenious swindle in spice selling by Yankee peddlers in that state. But the demand for the wooden souvenirs was greater than the supply, and when these ran out the vendors took to selling *real* nutmegs to the unsuspecting public, representing that they were wooden. This hoax presently being discovered by some one who thoughtfully grated a souvenir to see what kind of wood it was made of, purchasers now began clamoring indignantly for the return of their money on the ground that they had been defrauded.

The incident furnished a nice illustration of real and artificial values. Bona fide nutmegs were then worth perhaps two for a cent at retail; the wood in a synthetic nutmeg was worth much less, but the five-cent value of such a souvenir was built up by the cost of the labor involved in shaping and coloring the facsimile, the chuckle in the thought of how the old-time peddlers put it over on customers that would never see them again, and the novelty of the 1893 buyers having something odd to talk about with their friends.

Downtown, for years before the World's Fair was thought of, there was a popular department store called The Fair. This four-story emporium extended from State Street to Dearborn Street on Adams. As I write, forty-six years later, it has grown to much larger proportions. But in that day, it was something to see for its vast display of goods.

A farmer from Wisconsin, looking up and down State Street, one day in 1893, asked a passerby: "Say, Mister, kin you tell me where's the Fair?" The one spoken to thought he meant the big store, which was near by, and pointed it out to him.

The farmer spent three days looking around this establishment, from kitchen utensils in the basement to furniture on the top floor and back again, several times. Then he returned home. The natives of course asked him how he liked the World's Fair.

"I enjoyed every minute of it," he said.

Pressed for specific information about the Ferris Wheel, the Midway, and the ostrich farm, his mind was blank. Though he had been looking at the wrong Fair, it was good enough for him.

Visitors from the country at that time flocked to the Palmer House to see an exhibition of money which was regarded by many of them as one of the world's wonders. In the barber shop of that hotel the marble floor was imbedded with hundreds of silver dollars. Potter Palmer, the owner, once said that that was the most profitable form of advertising he had ever tried.

On Wabash Avenue, near my first lodging house, "John Brown's fort" was on exhibition. This was the fire-engine house in which Brown and his army of twenty-two men barricaded themselves when they raided the town of Harper's Ferry, Virginia. Many bullet holes were in its walls, made by the state militia in its siege. Some years later Kate Field, the lecturer and journalist of Washington, D. C., raised money to have the "fort" taken back to Harper's Ferry, where it stands on the grounds of Storer College, a school for Negroes.

October 9, anniversary of the great fire in 1871, was set apart as Chicago Day at the Exposition. Seven hundred thousand spectators crowded through the gates, women fainting in the crush, children getting lost or mislaid—by far the greatest turnout the city had ever seen. Mayor Carter H. Harrison and visiting dignitaries spoke, in celebration of the *I Will* spirit with which the community had risen out of its ashes.

For nineteen days the elation of that gathering lingered as the World's Fair moved toward its end. Then it was shattered by a tragedy.

Summoned by a ring of the doorbell in his home, the popular Mayor Harrison was shot down by a disappointed office-seeker named Prendergast, who had a mental twist and thought the mayor had plotted to keep him out of a job. Mr. Harrison died in a few minutes, and the city he loved was plunged into gloom.

Certainly the regret of every Chicago newspaper worker for his death was whole-hearted, and his bitterest enemies in life did not hesitate to laud him now for his good sportsmanship and his invariable on-the-square attitude.

Harrison, like Altgeld, had made it a point to get out among the plain people and learn what they were thinking about, and what they were up against. Repeatedly he had taken the side of the workers when they were being exploited by employers or beaten down by the police. He was a wholesome man of the people in spite of his shortcomings. Among newspapermen, I used to hear them say that before an audience of Bohemian workingmen, he would tell them he had Bohemian blood in his veins; and when talking to Irish, Czechs, Poles, Italians, Russians, Syrians, Greeks, or Jews, he would claim a similar identity with them. This stretch of his imagination appealed to me. At least it was an indication of a lack of racial prejudice, though interpreted by his enemies as demagogy.

Carter Harrison was a man I could not help liking, though he was a Democrat. Earlier I had illustrated the *Evening Mail's* stories of his journey around the world. Those pictures, drawn on chalk plates, were in humorous vein, showing the mayor meeting Queen Victoria and smiling upon her, hobnobbing with Bismarck, giving diplomatic pointers to the Sultan of Turkey, and encountering the inevitable discomfitures of foreign travel in the Eighties.

The *Inter-Ocean* of course kept on criticizing the acts and policies of President Cleveland's administration. But not all my cartoons of Cleveland had to do with politics; some dealt with his passion for fishing and other diversions. And because we were not now trying to defeat him in a contest the criticisms were usually not so harsh as they had been in the campaign. Two years earlier his daughter Ruth had been born, and various photographs of her had been published. I took occasion to put the child in many of my Cleveland cartoons, a touch of sentimental contrast to her bulky father, who wore a size 19 collar. I was told by our Washington correspondent, White Busbey, that Mrs. Cleveland saved all of my pictures in which Ruth appeared.

Hard times followed the closing of the Fair. Real estate values dropped, great numbers of workers were made jobless by the closing of mills and factories, many men begged food on the streets with watchful eyes out for the police, and the newspapers made much of "the tramp problem." They generally regarded all homeless and unemployed men as tramps, assumed that all these wanderers were opposed to work, and pictured "the tramp" as a menace to society. Supposedly he was what he was because he had a shiftless nature.

Kohlsaat sold his control of the *Inter-Ocean* in May, 1894. The identity of the new ownership was vague, but an official announcement said that the policies of the paper would remain unchanged, and that the *Inter-Ocean* would "continue to serve the best interests of Chicago in its onward march." We of the editorial department were assured that our jobs were safe, and things went on as before.

I made it a point to sketch and interview celebrities who came to town, and to find out, for my own information if not that of the paper, what was in their minds. Some day when I got around to it, I figured I would get up a book containing pictures of well-known people I had met.

W. T. Stead had arrived in Chicago in February, intent upon a crusade against drink, gambling, and commercialized prostitution, which he had fought in London. Clarence Webster and I went to see him at his hotel, and he readily remembered the page of pictures of the last night of the Paris Exposition which I had done for his *Pall Mall Budget,* and Webster's writings for the *Budget* and Stead's other publication, the *Pall Mall Gazette.* He was exploring the slums in our city, he told us, and was gathering material for a book on his findings. This man, with his bushy red beard and burning blue eyes, struck me as fearless, and sincere.

He wrote his book with white-hot ardor, and when it was finished he had me draw a cover design for it. The title was *If Christ Came to Chicago,* and it shocked the city, for it contained names of distinguished citizens, some of them pillars of wealthy churches, who owned buildings in the red-light districts and leased them to the madams at high rentals. And he listed also the names of wealthy but respectable tax-dodgers and grafting politicians then known as "boodlers."

Stead had intended to go to other cities in the United States and expose similar conditions, but the outcry against "the mouthings of this alien interloper" was so loud and the power of the gentlemen attacked so far-reaching that he found his way blocked at every turn.

The press threw cold water on his fiery crusade. The publishers and the business interests they served couldn't allow such "bad advertising" for Chicago. Another thing Stead did to arouse antagonism was to declare his belief in the innocence of Samuel Fielden, one of the Haymarket prisoners whom Altgeld had pardoned. Fielden was a countryman of his, having been a Methodist minister in a small English town.

When I drew a picture of this militant journalist, relaxing in his room after a strenuous day in the slums, he wrote beneath my drawing: "These are my legs, but the face is too tranquilly benevolent for W. T. Stead."

CHAPTER 19

I MARRY ELIZABETH NORTH

THERE had long been an unspoken agreement that some day Elizabeth and I would marry. That was the usual understanding in a small town when a young man and a girl had been "going together" for several years. And as Christmas approached in 1894 I was in a romantic mood. Having seen some of my friends evidently happy with their children clustered about them, I had visualized a similar happiness. Yet I hadn't thought much of marriage as an actuality in my life.

But it seemed that this was a good time for Elizabeth and myself to make the venture. I was now nearly twenty-nine years old. I had saved up considerable money, and the future looked bright. For seven years my sweetheart and her sister Kate had been keeping house for their uncle, Len Cheney, in Wauwatosa, a suburb of Milwaukee. Elizabeth and I were home in Monroe for the holidays, and I took occasion to suggest a quiet wedding soon.

The idea was agreeable to her, and we were married in Uncle Len's house on New Year's Day, 1895, by a clergyman friend of Elizabeth's family.

I wonder if any bridegroom ever really feels ecstatic during a wedding ceremony. I didn't. I felt self-conscious, and victimized by formality, and there seemed something fateful, like the clicking of a key in a lock, in the sound of the words: "Do you take this woman to be your lawful wife, for better or for worse, until death do you part?" and in my answer: "I do." But my embarrassment gave way to a feeling of comic sadness that every young man was expected to go through marriage; now it was my turn. We honeymooned in Chicago. Returning, we stayed on at Wauwatosa. The Cheney house was neat and cheerful under the deft hands of Elizabeth and Kate, and their Uncle Len was a genial host.

Uncle Len liked to paint in oil. His canvases he called

"merely impressions"—and Elizabeth, with playful sarcasm, would say quietly to me, *"merely* impressions." He had invested a good deal of money in a silver mine near Cripple Creek, Colorado. He would read the letters from the company aloud to us. All the mine needed now was another shaft or an ore-crusher, and the company president or treasurer invariably closed his communication with "Thanks for the check." Through seven years the girls had become so familiar

ELIZABETH NORTH, who became the author's wife.

with these letters that the phrase, "Thanks for the check", had become a household joke, and Uncle Len himself would laugh with us, although I do not think he ever lost faith in the mine.

I had married without much deliberation as to the next step. We had no definite plans yet for home-making, and decided it would be best for Elizabeth to continue living in Wauwatosa for a while, and I would run up from Chicago for week-ends. This was a pleasant arrangement. Through each week I would look forward eagerly to the moment on

Saturday when I would hasten to the depot to catch the late-afternoon train. We spent some of these week-ends in the parks, and then extended our walks to the surrounding country. Always I carried a sketching pad in a pocket, and made pictures of my wife in many poses, and of any likely subject that we came upon. The next time we visited Monroe, my brother-in-law, Clyde Copeland, said: "This ought to be a good time for us to burn that 'No wedding bells for me' masterpiece of yours." I made a lame joke about it, saying: "I didn't have any wedding bells. We were married in a house, not in a church."

While the glow of our honeymoon was still upon us, I began to note signs of an impending upheaval in both the editorial and business departments of the *Inter-Ocean*. There had been some change in control behind the scenes, rumor saying that Charles Yerkes, the traction magnate, who had been grabbing up street franchises right and left, had bought a majority of the stock. Some time later his control of the paper was public knowledge.

Working schedules were tightened, office rules rigidly enforced, deadlines pushed ahead, and everybody was made uncomfortable. Old editors, writers, and artists were being displaced one after another. Nobody knew where the axe would strike next. Some of the boys found other berths and resigned before they could be pushed out. Each time a man was given the sack he was assured that this was "no reflection upon your ability, but simply the working out of new office policies." Victor Murdock was one of the reporters on the *Inter-Ocean* then. Later he was elected as a Representative in Congress from Kansas, and succeeded his father as editor of the *Wichita Eagle*.

My future being uncertain, I pondered what move to make next. Clarence Webster was planning to go to San Francisco, having been offered a place on one of the leading dailies there by a friend who had risen to the top since his journalistic days in Chicago. And presently I also received an offer—from Lansing Warren, a former member of the *Inter-Ocean* staff, who had become editor of the *Denver Times*, an evening paper owned by David H. Moffatt, the banker. He wrote that the *Times* was willing to take me on as a cartoonist at the same salary I was then getting.

Colorado seemed far away, out in the vast beyond—an unknown quantity to me as a spot in which to live. But here was a job worth considering. So I took the first train for Milwaukee to discuss the situation with Elizabeth. After weighing all the elements involved, we agreed that I'd better go alone to Denver, try it out for a few weeks, and if I liked the work and the location I would send for her.

Denver was then a bustling community of 125,000 population. It still had a certain frontier rawness, though here and there were evidences of up-to-date ambition. The air was not at all like that of Chicago. On a summer day, if you stepped into the shadow of a telegraph pole you felt as if you were freezing; step out into the sun, and you were frying.

My sponsor made me at home in the *Times* office. After he had introduced me to the staff and explained the paper's program and the kind of cartoons it wanted, he took me to lunch at the Brown Palace Hotel, the show-place of the city. Here I spent a leisurely and profitable hour, while my host pointed out local persons of importance and gave me the highlights of Denver history. This hotel and this dining room had had as guests General Grant, the Prince of Wales, Sarah Bernhardt, Edwin Booth, General William T. Sherman, Oscar Wilde, John L. Sullivan, Emma Abbott, and the Duke of Manchester—and of course I was duly impressed.

Warren had stories to tell also of Eugene Field's years as columnist on the *Denver Tribune*—his comment on the Shakespearean efforts of John McCullough: "He played the king as though he feared somebody would play the ace"; his entering a stray mongrel in a dog show and winning a blue ribbon with it; and his Oscar Wilde hoax. Field dressed up a friend in a velvet coat, with lace cuffs and a sunflower in his lapel, and drove him about town in a carriage a couple of hours before the poet was due to arrive. The pseudo-aesthete bowed to onlookers along the way and raised a plumed hat resembling a British admiral's in salute. Wilde was ready to bite nails when he learned of the impersonation, and delivered his scheduled lecture that night with resentment showing through the words.

Coming out of the dining room, Warren said: "See that man leaning over the desk?" A broad-shouldered elderly person with a black slouch hat, drooping moustaches, and an old frock coat, was asking some question, and the clerk's answer was a negative nod. The inquirer turned glumly away.

"That," said Warren, "is ex-Senator Tabor, who used to be the richest man west of the Mississippi. He was cleaned out when the silver market hit the rocks." Walking along the streets Warren pointed out the landmarks which the Senator had built in his heyday—the Tabor Block and the Tabor Grand Opera House, in which he had objected to a drop curtain bearing the likeness of William Shakespeare, demanding to know: "What did he ever do for Denver?" and having his own portrait substituted for that of the Avon bard.

The *Times* had lately been taken over by Moffatt, and though he was reputed to have plenty of money, the paper had the look of being on a precarious footing. It was trying to cut into the field of the *Rocky Mountain News,* a property which was doing well, and which was controlled by Thomas M. Patterson, attorney, politician, and afterward United States Senator. The *News* was a morning sheet, like the *Republican,* which had merged with and absorbed the old *Tribune,* on which Eugene Field had written his lively quips. Our only rival in the afternoon field was the *Post,* which also was struggling along.

Immediately I began drawing a daily cartoon, in three column-width, and the *Times* featured these. Some of them dealt with silver and gold coinage and other aspects of politics, but a good many had to do with purely local events. My scrapbook includes one on a vital business issue, captioned: "Denver Holds the Bag—the Others Bag the Game." This shows a hunter personifying the Colorado metropolis holding a sack labeled High Freight Rates, while other hunters (Kansas City, Chicago, Omaha, Salt Lake City, St. Joseph) are bringing down birds with guns labeled Low Rates. . . . Another is headed: "Still They Come to the Great Convention City," with a pictured procession revealing the Amalgamated Order of Chinese Laundrymen, the United Order of Hot Tamale Peddlers, the National Asociation of Street

Bands, the Mystic Order of Phrenologists, and the National Order of Veteran Sports. I am not sure how much benefit, if any, the Queen City of the Silver State derived from that free advertising, but the idea I was trying to convey was that Denver, being the ideal convention city, welcomed all comers.

The *Times* didn't think much of the government's policy in dealing with the aboriginal Americans. There was some trouble with the red men just then, and I drew a cartoon headed "That Bannock Indian War," with an underline: "We think Poor Lo has the laugh on you, Uncle Sam." Uncle is seen on a still hunt with a gun, while an Indian brave is hiding behind a rock. . . . The opening of the muskmelon season was recognized pictorially under the caption: *Rocky Ford's Great Day,* that town being the center of a vast and fertile farm region where luscious melons were grown.

Once the business manager got an idea from somewhere that some of my pictures might be useful in appeals for circulation. He would write the words to go with the illustrations. As a writer he was a good deal of a loss to the *Times*. Whenever he sat down to struggle with the English language great beads of sweat stood out on his brow. One of our collaborations showed a lot of frogs around a pond croaking the words: "Hard times!" The caption went *Stop Croaking and Read the Times,* and beneath the picture was this poetic atrocity:

> If croaking croakers who sit all day
> And fill the air with their sorrowful lay
> Would only stop croaking for a minute or two,
> How much better 'twould be for me and for you.

I soon learned that they preferred me to fill my cartoon space with glorifications and boostings of Denver—the city a mile above the sea, with 300 cloudless days a year, the greatest health resort in the West, and kindred claims. Colorado's scenic wonders also received their share of attention.

There were other features of Denver life and industry, however, that the *Times* did not touch upon, but which I glimpsed in evening walks with Warren and others after dinner in the Brown Palace, or the Windsor Hotel, where the legendary Horace Tabor had held forth in the days when he threw money away like water. The city was wide open. "The powers-that-be figure it's good business," fellow staff-members explained. "Plenty of chance for the flush boys from out of town to spend their money, or lose it on games of purported chance. It all means that that money comes into Denver, and gets into general circulation. Somebody gets a cut for protection, and everybody is happy."

Down in the night-life section, known as The Lowers, various *salons de joie* were well patronized. Sounds of well-pounded pianos came from all sides. Warren pointed out the favorite establishment of state legislators who didn't want to be lonesome when they visited the capital. In the gambling houses one could find any game that his heart might desire, and there was no limit on the stakes.

In the afternoons after I had finished next day's picture, I would wander about town looking for ideas, dropping in at the hotels to see if any odd characters were around, talking with any local old-timers who happened along, and searching out the city's landmarks.

On Larimer street I came upon an institution full of romantic appeal—Tammen's Free Museum.

All sorts of relics of the Old West were here—mementoes of Indian and cattle wars, of prairie schooner journeys, of bad men and vigilantes, horse thieves and quick-on-the-draw sheriffs, legal hangings and lynchings. Bows and arrows, arrow-heads, stone hatchets, scalps, outlaws' guns, deathbed-confessions, dead bandits' boots. The public was welcomed to come in and see these historic trophies without charge—but every curio in the "museum" was for sale. A thrilling show, all of which looked real to my unsuspecting eye. But I was not moved to buy any of those articles.

"Your instinct was correct," a former Denverite assured me some years later. "If you had bought Jesse James's favorite six-shooter, there would have been another just like it, and with the same label, on display within a month. Tammen had a factory nearby turning out that stuff for the visiting trade."

Fortunately, however, there were some things in Denver to feed the intellect. Occasionally I went to hear a militant independent preacher named Myron Reed, who gave Sunday lectures in a theatre. My recollection is that he had been ousted from a regular pulpit because of sermons assailing the methods by which many rich men had gained their wealth. He drew big audiences, and the faces of his hearers lighted up as he talked. To me, he gave something that one couldn't get in a regular church—for he dealt with the realities of that day instead of the dim happenings of 1,900 years ago.

A tall, lank Scotchman, Reed made a deep impression upon me. His eloquence was simple, but he said things which one remembered on the way home. He raised questions about justice in the world, the rights of the poor, the laws that were made by the strong to keep the masses "quiet and content."

Listening to this clear-speaking man, and thinking about his words afterward as I walked along the streets, I began to wonder about the justice in the attitude of the newspapers generally toward happenings like the march of Coxey's Army, and the American Railroad Union strike, in which Eugene Debs had seen sent to jail. The movement set going by "General" Jacob Coxey had failed, it was true; but had it

THE VANGUARD OF COXEY'S ARMY. Led by Carl Brown on a white horse, it enters Washington.

ever been given a chance to succeed? From the start the press had heaped ridicule upon it; and another countless army—of paid molders of opinion—had seen hilarious comedy in the spectacle of thousands of ragged and hungry men beating their way across the country to demand relief in Washington.*

* By the same token, a multitude of theatre-goers through five years have laughed uproariously at the comedy in *Tobacco Road*, evidently without perceiving the underlying tragedy in the dramatized lives of Jeeter Lester and his impoverished family in the back country of Georgia. Max Eastman explains this phenomenon in his *Enjoyment of Laughter*.

But what was wrong in that attempted protest? I recalled the editorial bleating of outrage when Coxey's followers commandeered freight trains to speed their progress. That was trespass, of course; or confiscation, if you preferred the word; yet what was there so terrible about it? Weren't the editors and captains of industry really incensed because the Coxey migration showed up the vast poverty and degradation in the United States? Wasn't it in the nature of a mortifying "scene"—like that of a neglected wife berating her husband in public? *

I reflected, too, that one Chicago newspaper, the *Times*, had held that the treatment of the Coxeyites by the Washington police was "vicious and brutal" and "a blunder." The *Times* had been owned by the assassinated Mayor Carter H. Harrison and had since been operated by his son Carter Jr. and another son.

That paper, too, had taken the side of the railroad workers in the great Pullman strike when George M. Pullman had answered their demands for a living wage by saying: "There is nothing to arbitrate."

It was in such a mood that I went to hear an address by Keir Hardie at a labor mass-meeting. I had read about him, and he had appealed to my imagination. I knew that this Scotsman had been a coal miner and a union leader, and that he was a member of Parliament, representing a London district.

Early that summer Hardie had stood up in the House of Commons and attacked Chancellor of the Exchequer Sir William Harcourt, Leader of the House, and his fellow-members for refusing to express a vote of sympathy to the bereaved families of more than 250 miners killed in a South

---

* The eminent Mark Sullivan, in *Our Times*, declares that Coxey's Army marched to Washington to "take control of the government in the interest of the people—or what Coxey thought was the people's interest." Mr. Sullivan is one of those casual historians who pick up their "facts" here and there. I doubt if any of Coxey's critics in 1894 ever went so far as to accuse him of any intention to take over the government. The manifest purpose of Coxey and his legions of the dispossessed was to demand that Congress provide aid for unemployed workers and their families. That of course was a startling proposal in those days long before the New Deal. If the federal authorities had had any tangible evidence of subversive plans, the leaders of the march surely would have been prosecuted for treason, instead of being jailed for walking on the Capitol lawn.

Wales colliery explosion. That happened because the grasping mine owners had not provided adequate safety devices.

Harcourt had moved a vote of condolence to the people of France when President Carnot was assassinated the next day, and called upon the House to congratulate Queen Victoria upon the birth of her great-grandson, who in time became King Edward VIII. But the Chancellor ruled out of order a move for an expression of antipathy to the system which made mine disasters inevitable.

In a speech which nearly caused apoplexy to many of his hearers and which brought bitter denunciation to him from the reactionary English press, Keir Hardie stood unwavering and said:

"The life of one Welsh miner is of greater commercial and moral value to the British nation than the whole royal crowd put together. . . . Two hundred and fifty human beings, full of strong life in the morning, reduced to charred and blackened heaps of clay in the evening! . . . Only those who have witnessed such scenes, as I have twice over, can realize what they mean. . . .

"Coal must be got cheap—even if twelve hundred sturdy miners are murdered yearly in the process—twelve hundred hearths made desolate."

He was shaggy looking like a Scotch terrier, his head, chin, and cheeks covered with brownish curled hair—and his strong voice deeply burred. Thirty-seven then, he looked considerably older. One could see at once that beneath this rough exterior was a man of learning. The thing that he brought home most forcibly to me that night was the fact that a strike or a lockout or an industrial disaster was not an isolated event; it was part of a struggle, a war, which had been going on for decades, and knew no national boundaries.

"The employers and their henchmen," he said, "have a trick of appealing to your sense of local patriotism. They blame unrest on 'outside agitators,' and infer that if it were not for these evil interlopers everything would be lovely in your community and that nobody would be complaining. That trick is as shoddy as the other one of setting two groups of people at one another's throats by stirring up their religious differences."

He quoted a line from Robert Browning: "God give us

no more geniuses, but elevate the human race!" I had never read anything by Browning, and this aroused my interest in him. But I could never find such a passage in any of his books.

That gathering was notable also because its chairman was Governor David Hansen Waite of Colorado, who had been elected by the Populists. A calm enough appearing individual, who looked like a fine old farmer, he had been jeer-

Denver Times

KEIR HARDIE, dealing with the class struggle in a Denver speech.

ingly characterized by the press as "Bloody Bridles Waite" for a speech he made at the state silver convention two years before.

India's mints had stopped coining silver, and immediately the Colorado silver producers had shut down their mines. It was then that Waite, addressing that convention, was quoted thus:

"If the money power shall attempt to sustain its usurpation by the 'strong hand' we will meet that issue when it is forced upon us, for it is better infinitely that blood should flow to the horses' bridles rather than that our natural liberties be destroyed. . . .

"If it is true that the United States is unable to carry out its governmental policy without the dictation or consent of foreign powers; if we are a province of European monarchies, then we need another revolution, another appeal to arms."

But he talked sensibly enough at the Hardie meeting, and had none of the look of a fanatic which one might expect from newspaper descriptions of him.

As the weeks went by I kept postponing my decision as to whether Elizabeth ought to come to Colorado. Though it made a good deal of noise, the *Times* did not seem to be making much actual headway, and I felt that my position, like that of the rest of the staff, was not secure.

For recreation I took a week-end trip farther up into the mountains, to Silver Plume, went riding along rugged trails on a burro's back, and did some sketching and water-color painting—as well as a lot of thinking about the future. The novelty of Denver and its holdover atmosphere from frontier days was wearing thin. I missed the crowd-surge of Chicago. Perhaps the time was ripe for me to go to New York as a cartoonist and illustrator instead of as a student. I would weigh that possibility further. About all I had accomplished in Denver was a reputation for boosting a locality.

A newspaper publisher in Pueblo, a hundred miles south of Denver, who had got me to draw a boosting cartoon for his city, annoyed me by failing to pay for it despite repeated duns. The more I dwelt on this publisher's audacity, the angrier I became. Finally I sat down and wrote him a threatening letter, saying that I was about to get out a revised edition of my book *Hell Up to Date,* and that I intended to put in a Department of Dead Beats with him in a front seat fully identified. By return mail I received an answer: "You win. Here's your check."

Chill autumn weather came, and I felt drawn toward home. Denver had a feeling of isolation about it, for I remembered pictures in *Harper's Weekly* of trains snowbound for days in the mountains of the West. I didn't like the thought of being caught and held in Colorado through the winter. And the Denver newspaper field seemed to lack life; the dailies dealt with all sorts of trivialities, reminding one of a small town like Monroe. So I gave two weeks' notice of leaving. Warren was sorry; we had become good friends.

CHAPTER 20

HELPING THE YELLOW PRESS START A WAR

ON my way back to Wisconsin I kept thinking that it would be best for us to live in New York. I must get into a broader field. Elizabeth readily assented when I rejoined her in Wauwatosa, and in a few weeks we were packed up and set forth. Whether I would seek a regular job or free-lance was still an open question, but I was keen for some arrangement whereby I could do steady production.

Constantly in my mind was the realization that it was a mistake for a man like me to be married. I had chosen a lovely, intelligent girl for a mate, and yet I had a feeling that the freedom I had enjoyed when single was no more. I was no longer an individual thinking in terms of one. Every thought, every plan, now had to include another, and later on probably it would have to include three or four. I am sure that Elizabeth tried hard to understand what kind of a man it was to whom she had entrusted her future. Still I felt there was something wrong in the idea of our signing a contract agreeing to love each other forever—when Nature obviously was opposed to such compacts.

Yet Elizabeth was patient. She saw humor and beauty in life, and our journey to the metropolis was an enjoyable one. I found fun and novelty in showing my wife the sights of New York. We lived first on Washington Place, a few doors from Washington Square, where we had a comfortable apartment. As soon as I got down to work here things took on a brighter hue, and I began to feel that maybe married life would turn out all right after all; perhaps it was just a matter of adjusting myself to the changed conditions.

Later we lived in the top studio of the Winfield Scott Moody home on Ninth Street west of Fifth Avenue. Moody was one of the editors of Scribner's, and his wife was a writer for the *Ladies' Home Journal* and other magazines. Afterward, for a time, we had a cheerful hall room in a boarding house on West 16th Street, opposite St. Francis Xavier College.

Here I began to see that Elizabeth could be helpful in suggesting ideas for drawings. Two pictures among others for which she gave me the suggestions come to mind. One, published in *Life,* bore the caption: "Willie Jones—as he seems to his teacher—to the cook—to the cat—to his mother." Another, used in *Judge,* portrays a farmer who looks at his turkeys as they stand sadly awaiting the Thanksgiving Day axe, and beholding the long necks and general

"THE TIE THAT BINDS."
Farmer—"Mother, I hain't got the heart ter do it. It 'd seem too much like killin' one o' the family."
Judge

A COMIC SUGGESTED BY MY WIFE.

resemblance to his own kin, says: "Mother, I haint' got the heart to do it—it's too much like killing one of the family."

At that time I had my first experience with the type of man who might be termed a "city slicker." He was a Wall Street speculator with an office in Exchange Place. My wife met his wife in the boarding house and we all became sociable. Free with cigars and with an air of prosperity, he got into my good graces by praising Elizabeth's character and looks. And one day he mentioned that he might be in a position soon to put me in the way of making considerable money. He was just waiting for an expected turn in the stock market to cash in on it in a large way.

Presently he announced that that turn had come, and if I could put up $300 he would invest it for me so that I would make a fat profit. By adroitly leading Elizabeth on in conversation, his wife had learned that I had some $3,000 in a savings bank, which I had drawn out of a Chicago building and loan association. My sense of caution led me to balk at giving him the sum he asked, but I let him have $200—with which he bought the rising stock, only to have it go down like a punctured balloon next day. I never got any of the money back, and counted the experience as a valuable lesson.

In this boarding house lived Volney Streamer, who worked for Brentano's as an expert in English bibliography. He wore a wig, had been an actor with Booth, and was now dyspeptic and a misanthrope. My brother Will, who had come east a couple of years before and was on the *World* staff, had met Streamer on several occasions, and one evening when we were sitting in the parlor Streamer came in. Will in his cordial manner said: "Good evening, Brother Streamer!" Scowling darkly, Streamer retorted: "I'm brother to nobody!"

I made no move to get a job in New York. Free-lancing appealed to me now much more than tying up to office routine, and in the long run, I thought, I would make more money in the open market.

My drawings in that period of frequent change of residence were done anywhere—in bedroom or living room or wherever I could slant a drawing-board, and usually I had difficulty in finding a good light. It was not long, however, until I bought a simple collapsible drawing table, which I still use. For forty-odd years I have drawn most of my cartoons on this table. Later, in relatively prosperous days, I bought a larger one, of an expensive type used by architects, on which I drew with a feeling of being less restricted in area —and this I also have in my Bethel studio.

When I was a boy I remember writing to Bernard Gillam of *Puck* asking him what kind of a pen and what kind of paper he used in doing his cartoons. He didn't answer. Nor was the question so momentous as I thought. I didn't ask him what kind of a table he used, but details concerning the tools of any profession loom large in significance when you're young—less so as one gets older. My friend T. S. Sullivant of *Life* was one who never got over his keen interest in implements and materials. He would be jubilant for days over the discovery of a certain quality of paper or a new pen which worked just right.

During those first years of married life and trying to succeed I found that I could not make sufficient income to meet our living expense. Gradually my bank account was dwindling, but not through other reckless loans of money for speculation. Some months I would break even—then have a slump. If I received a check for less than I thought I ought to get from *Life*, I would spend hours trying to write a tactful letter to John Ames Mitchell, the editor, explaining that I had expected at least ten dollars more than he had paid me; and invariably he would send me an extra ten. But generally I had no heart for arguing about money and would take what I could get.

Soon I came to know the personnel of the inner sanctums of *Puck, Judge,* and *Life,* and what was quite as important I knew those stationed at the outer gates, so that I wasn't kept waiting when I called to see the editors. Frequently I had dinner with one or more of them—Tom Masson of *Life,* Grant Hamilton and James Melvin Lee of *Judge,* young Joseph Keppler, Arthur Folwell, and Bert Leston Taylor of *Puck.*

The elder Joseph Keppler, whose cartoons in that weekly had been a national institution for so many years, had died in February, 1894, and I had done a memorial cartoon of him then for the *Chicago Inter-Ocean*. Young Joe thoughtfully gave me a fine collection of prints and humorous European magazines which his father had owned. Looking them over is one of my pleasures today.

I still called myself a Republican, and the anti-Democrat atmosphere of the *Inter-Ocean* office still clung to me as the 1896 national campaign got into full swing. McKinley and Hobart were appealing for votes on the promise of "a full dinner pail for every workingman." That struck me as a vulgar issue, and I told Grant Hamilton, who did most of the full dinner-pail cartoons for *Judge,* that a plea to the worker's stomach, as if that was the only thing the laboring man could understand, was insulting.

But I remembered the hard times under Democratic rule, which was being emphasized in Republican campaign literature, and I was pleased with the opportunity to propagandize for the Grand Old Party—I was working for the nation's "best people"—the same party which, led by Herbert Hoover years later, appealed to the workers with the slogan: "A chicken in every pot."

W. J. Bryan had been nominated by both the Democrats and the Populists, who termed themselves the People's Party, and to us Republicans that proved there was something wrong with him. He had won the nomination by a speech in Chicago, which was being repeated by other orators as if it were a trumpet call to save the nation—that speech which had this grandiloquent climax:

"You come to us and tell us that the great cities are in favor of the gold standard: we reply that the great cities rest upon our broad and fertile prairies. Burn down your cities and leave our farms, and your cities will spring up again as if by magic; but destroy our farms and the grass will grow in the streets of every city in the country. . . .

"Having behind us the producing masses of this nation and the world, supported by the commercial interests, the laboring interests, and the toilers everywhere, we will answer their demand for a gold standard by saying to them: You shall not press down upon the brow of labor this crown of thorns, you shall not crucify mankind upon a cross of gold."

"Just a demagogue's play to the farmers and labor, the seductive words of a master-hypnotist," the Republicans said. Bryan as a Democrat was crusading for Free Silver, on a 16-to-1 coinage ratio, and the pro-McKinley press saw a great danger in that. I was never quite clear about the silver-and-gold coinage question, and in fact I would be hazy about it now if some visiting foreigner were to ask me point-blank to explain it. But as the candidate of the Populists the Commoner from Nebraska stood for government ownership of the railroads, the telegraph, and the telephone systems—and that practically meant Socialism, or Anarchism, according to the newspapers and magazines which spoke for the Republican party.

Judge was in the forefront of the attack. Its methods were far from scrupulous, as I view them now, though at the time I was not so critical, the attitude of all those around me being that anything was fair in politics. Typical of *Judge's* onslaughts was a full-page front cover cartoon in colors, drawn by Grant Hamilton, and captioned "The Sacrilegious Candidate." This portrayed Bryan, bare-armed and with torn shirt, standing with booted foot on a Bible, with a cross of gold in his left arm and a crown of thorns in his right hand. Speeches "plagiarized from the Bible" protruded from his pockets. Beneath the picture were the words: "No man who drags into the dust the most sacred symbols of the Christian world is fit to be President of the United States." Nearby a tatterdemalion figure in a French Revolution cap was waving a red flag labeled Anarchy.

But if *Judge's* editors were horrified by the idea of dragging sacred symbols in the dust, its advertising department was not. For in the same year that periodical ran an advertisement reading: "The modern Joan of Arc polishes her boots with Brown's French dressing," with a half-tone cut of Joan, sword in one hand and flag in the other.

As a result of all this valiant effort, our noble candidates won. The villainous Democrats who had been responsible for all the hard times were sent up Salt Creek by vote of the people, and in came a new era of prosperity and full stomachs for the workers—that is, if you read the Republican press.

But my own income was still low, and the economic problem was pressing. Mornings I spent at the drawing table, and in the afternoon I would set out to visit editorial offices or to cultivate contacts through which I could learn the political inclination of editors who were buying pictures. I would study current magazines for their "policy"—for each had some definite slant. Most of this studying was done at the periodical counter in Brentano's basement, where I would browse at length and finally pay out money for a single magazine—as a sop to my conscience for having had such an educational feast.

I had been working at intervals on pictures and text for a book to be called *Authors' Readings*. This was intended to comprise recitations from the work of sixteen well-known writers, with a short biography of each, and sketches showing

FROM AN EARLY ART YOUNG BOOK. Literary notables of the day. The one whose name is not shown is C. B. Lewis, widely known then as "M. Quad."

them in characteristic attitudes, as I had seen them reading their works. Frederick A. Stokes liked the idea, but thought my manuscript contained enough material for two books.

So a single volume of 215 pages was published, dealing with nine individuals—Eugene Field, James Whitcomb Riley, Bill Nye, Hamlin Garland, Ella Wheeler Wilcox, Opie Read, Will Carleton, Mary Hartwell Catherwood, and C. B. Lewis, who wrote under the nom de plume of M. Quad. There was a foreword implying that a second volume would be issued to cover the others, who were named.

Both the publishers and I were expectant of substantial sales. But the returns were small, and so the plan for the second volume went into the discard. It would have celebrated the literary creations of General Lew Wallace, Captain Charles King, Joaquin Miller, Octave Thanet, John Vance Cheney, Lillian Bell, Henry B. Fuller, and Robert Burdette.

I had a notion that the West was breeding writers who in time might stand the test of enduring worth as well as the New England breed. Some of my selections were amateurish —but they were the best I could find at the time.

After the battleship Maine was blown up I made several cartoons for *Leslie's Weekly* in line with its advocacy of war with Spain. For months various New York newspapers had been emphasizing the tragedy of the Spanish domination of Cuba, against which the Cubans had revolted, and calling for intervention. The killing of 257 American seamen in Havana harbor intensified the editorial demands to the point of hysteria. It was instantly assumed by the Hearst papers and others not ordinarily thought of as yellow that Spain's hand was behind that explosion—although the court of inquiry never found any tangible evidence of that, simply reporting that in its opinion the explosion was due to a submarine mine.

But it was easy for me to believe, as everybody around me did, that Spain was guilty. Such an act seemed in line with its treatment of the Cubans, and its surly attitude toward American protests against its policy in the Caribbean area. No one seemed to realize that it might have been perpetrated by some Cuban who wanted the United States to intervene. And on all sides the press and public men were thundering that it was a sacred duty for this nation to chastise Spain and put her in her proper place. The Hearst papers were interspersed with small red-white-and-blue American flags with the words: "Cuba Libre!" and "Remember the Maine!" And boys and men were wearing celluloid buttons on their coat lapels bearing those slogans and another: "Remember the Maine, to hell with Spain!"

Instead of spreading my war cartoons across several issues, as I had anticipated, *Leslie's* combined them into a full page and ran all at once. That was gratifying.

Those drawings illustrated quoted passages from speeches by four United States Senators—Thurston, Proctor, Gallinger, and Mason—all calling for revenge.

In one issue *Leslie's* asked that the public suspend judgement on the guilt in the blowing up of the Maine until the wreck could be raised and the truth about the cause ascertained. But that, I believe, was its only judicial utterance in that period. Week after week it whooped up the war spirit. If there were indeed any voices objecting to our coming to grips with Spain, they were lost in the din.

To me that war, when it presently came, was equally as just as the war waged by the North to free the slaves. Even though I knew that the South had fired the first gun in 1861, I was still confused about that conflict. I was not aware then of the economic causes which lie behind most wars. . . . Spain needed a lesson, I thought, and needed to be soundly whipped.

But when the stories began to come through from Tampa of the "embalmed beef" fed to the American troops, of soldiers dying like flies of fever and dysentery in unsanitary camps, and then of others dying in battle, some of whom had been my friends and acquaintances, doubt entered my mind. Was war, after all, the best way to settle international wrongs? And how far, I asked myself, was a cartoonist or an editorial writer who advocated such a war, responsible for the deaths of those soldiers? It was chiefly members of the working class who were being killed and wounded, and not the sons of the meat packers or of the other wealthy men who were making big profits on sales to the War Department.

Even with those doubts, I was thrilled when the news came of Dewey's victory in Manila Bay. Most of the reports in the press were highly dramatized, and throughout all the news and editorials the note was sounded insistently that this was a righteous war. There were acts of individual daring, like that of Hobson and his men sinking the collier

Merrimac in Santiago harbor to bottle up Cervera's fleet, which made patriotic hearts beat faster—and I was still a super-patriot—my country right or wrong.

Teddy Roosevelt leading the Rough Riders up San Juan Hill was great stuff—reading the papers one got the idea that Teddy was practically the one who won that war.

Occasionally, however, there were notes of discord—for instance, Stephen Crane's dispatch to the *World* which told

THE TERRIBLE TEDDY.

of the Seventy-first New York Volunteers, a militia regiment, lying down to keep out of the way of bullets while other regiments pushed forward to cope with the Spaniards. Mr. Hearst's *Journal* promptly assailed the *World* for this dastardly reflection upon the bravery of local boys, although its indignation was soon deflated when the redoubtable Teddy confirmed Crane's story.

All the heroes came home—except those who had died afield—and New York yelled itself hoarse. I went to hear Roosevelt speak on the night of his return from Cuba, everybody, including myself, shouting: "Hurrah for Teddy!" . . . Lieutenant Hobson was kissed by countless young women; Admiral Dewey moved up Fifth Avenue and through the Victory Arch, acclaimed by the greatest throng the city had ever seen; the Hearst papers collected pennies from school children to buy a house in Washington for Dewey and his bride; and Theodore Roosevelt's political fortunes prospered because of his war reputation.

After T. R. became President the Russian painter Vereshtchagin visited Washington and spent many days at Fort Meyer painting a big canvas showing the charge up San Juan Hill. The belligerent Teddy was revealed in the thick of the fray, on a white horse. This simply proved that the great Russian artist had read the early dispatches about that battle, and not the later corrected accounts, which brought out that there were no horses in the San Juan assault. The painting, with the white horse still in it, is said to have been sold in New York for $10,000 a few years later. . . . In 1917, when he was touring the army camps, T. R. got a laugh in his speeches by saying of the Spanish-American imbroglio that "it wasn't much of a war, but it was the only war we had just then."

We got the Philippines, which seemed the right thing, on the theory that if we didn't step in and protect the helpless Filipinos, no longer under the Spanish yoke, some grasping nation like Japan would go in there and take over the islands and exploit the natives. Thus Uncle Sam was being magnanimous. I didn't know until long after the fact that 600,000 men, women, and children died in Luzon alone as a result of the American-Filipino War which followed the Spanish-American conflict.

To those who may view this statement as incredible, I suggest that they read the evidence on page 121 of *The Conquest of the Philippines by the United States,* by Moorfield Storey and Marcial P. Lichauco (Putnam, 1926). The charge is based on an estimate made by Gen. J. M. Bell, who spoke from first-hand knowledge. That figure represented one sixth of Luzon's native population.

Two sentences from General Bell's comment on his own figures clearly illuminate his attitude toward the situation: "The loss of life by killing alone has been very great, but I think that not one man has been slain except where his death served *the legitimate purpose of war.* It has been thought necessary to adopt *what in other countries would probably be thought harsh measures.*" The italics here are mine.

CHAPTER 21

MATRIMONY HITS A REEF

SOMETHING was wrong with me, I didn't know what. I was listless, found it difficult to concentrate on my work, and lay awake nights. So I went to see a doctor. "Nothing organically wrong," he said. "Just a case of 'nerves.' You've been working too hard. How about a change of scene for a while?"

I knew of one place where I could go for an inexpensive outing. A couple of years earlier Father had bought forty acres of timberland in Southern Alabama, which the Mobile and Ohio Railroad had been selling cheaply. He had spent two winters down there, clearing the land with hired help, and planting almond trees. His plan was to have an almond grove for each of his four children, so that when the trees matured we all would have a profitable inheritance. He stayed in a hotel in Citronelle, the nearest town, during those visits, and Mother was with him through one of the winters. A couple employed by Father did the general work on the farm.

I took a train for Alabama, and in a few days Elizabeth joined me. We occupied a little house just outside Citronelle, which was set amid healthful wooded country. Here one saw incredibly tall and straight Caribbean pines in great profusion. And there was fine sketching material hereabouts, both in the landscape and among the primitive white folks and the happy-go-lucky Negroes (thus I thought of them then, not knowing of the hard lives of which their apparently care-free attitude gave me no hint). We soon got acquainted with the neighborhood pickaninnies. Some were named after perfume brands and others after labels on package groceries. I liked to talk with them, their vocal tones and their dreamy ideas about life delighting me. The name of one little girl, so she insisted, was Pickle Lily.

I sold a few comic pictures at that time to *Judge*, for ten, fifteen, or twenty dollars. My income was nothing to brag about, but rent was low, food cheap, and fuel cost nothing. Pine wood, to be had simply for picking it up, made an excellent cooking fire.

The almond farm was miles back from the railroad, and to get to it one had to travel with a team over miry roads through bad swampy country. Elizabeth and I visited it a few times, and the thought of reaping a comfortable living from nut groves in future years was gratifying—but I was not tempted to do any of the work on the farm, although Father was busy all the time. Clearing that land for nut cultivation was back-breaking toil, and I was satisfied to let the hired help earn their pay.

After several months in Alabama, I felt much refreshed, and we returned to New York. My brother-in-law Clyde Copeland also went to Citronelle for a few weeks, to help along the almond project and for a vacation. But I never visited Alabama again. The almond trees did not thrive, and presumably the soil was not right for them. In time Father gave up the idea, and sold that land.

"Well, it was a change anyhow and a good way to escape Wisconsin winters," he said, the next time I saw him. "But I guess I'd better stick to the store business."

We took a small upstairs apartment in West Ninety-third Street, and I resumed picture production with considerable vim. Frank Nankivell, illustrator, Percival Pollard, then a well-known magazine editor, and Robert H. Davis had the first floor. Hearst was then buying talent away from Pulitzer's *World,* and Bob Davis was one of the young editors and artists from the West who were making the *Evening Journal* look lively. All kinds of sensational features were being tried out.

Davis was running the *Journal's* editorial page for a while and I wrote a few editorials with illustrations for him. I suggested that they be printed in facsimile typewriter style, and he thought this a worth-while innovation. But I couldn't keep it up. When it came to pouring out my thoughts in words on paper I lacked the necessary ability to keep going and sustain my theme. I could spurt now and then, but routine writing has always been too much for me.

I made the acquaintance of other editors whenever I had a tangible excuse, and occasionally opened up a new market. A few years before I had met Arthur Brisbane when he was on the *Sunday World*. In *Puck* and *Life* I had caricatured him as "Whizzbrain." Now he was managing editor of Hearst's *Evening Journal*. One evening after the theatre I ran into him in Allaire's restaurant (Scheffel Hall) on East Seventeenth Street, where the beer was excellent even if the food, being German-cooked, was a bit heavy.

We talked at length. Brisbane had been particularly impressed by pictures of mine which touched upon social problems—tenements, hungry people, child labor, grafting politicians, low wages, and kindred topics. There was one drawing of mine in *Life* that had attracted wide attention, and he made much of that. It was called "The Outcast," and depicted an old man in rags and broken shoes standing in the rain, with these lines by Shakespeare below it:

> *Famine is in thy cheeks,*
> *Need and oppression starveth in thy eyes,*
> *Upon thy back hangs ragged misery,*
> *The world is not thy friend, nor the world's law.*

Shortly after that talk Brisbane suggested that I go to work regularly on the *Journal*. He wanted me to draw cartoons and illustrate editorials. He had shoved aside the long, heavy editorials of the Greeley-Dana and Watterson types and substituted easy-to-read summaries of popular issues. His offer of $100 a week and his outline of the kind of cartoon material he sought appealed to me, and I readily accepted.

Next morning I reported at the *Journal* office at William and Duane Streets, and Brisbane installed me with my drawing outfit in William Randolph Hearst's private sanctum, which was next to his. Hearst was then in California. Brisbane brought in a plentiful supply of brushes, pens, pencils, and drawing ink, and said: "Go to it."

This spacious room was quiet and well appointed, with mahogany furniture of simple design. One slight disturbance lingers in memory. Frederic Remington kept bobbing in day after day, a bit tight and somewhat voluble, asking: "Where is Mr. Hearst?" I gathered that he wanted some money from the absent owner, and when told that he was out of town, would shake his head sadly and say over and over: "Can you beat it?" *

Hearst stayed away a month. When he came back a desk and chair were assigned to me in the art department, in a

ARTISTS AND EDITORS. Top, left to right: Frederic Remington, Arthur Brisbane. Bottom: Thomas Nast, Bob Davis.

room with Frederick Opper and T. S. Sullivant. Here the atmosphere was less conducive to concentration than in the chief's secluded sanctum.

Lunch-time would usually find Brisbane in an "exclusive" restaurant just south of the stone arches of Brooklyn

* Remington died at the age of forty-eight in 1909, soon after he had built a house and studio for himself near Ridgefield, Conn. His need for money in the days when I was with the *Journal* is recalled in contrast by a news report on May 14, 1937, telling of the sale at auction of a Remington painting, "Custer's Last Stand", for $7,700.

Bridge. He favored thick mutton chops, and invariably matched coins with some one seated at a table reserved for newspapermen to see who would pay for the meal.

Around four o'clock he would begin pounding out editorials for next day on his typewriter. He did this with precision, and ordinarily was finished in a couple of hours.

In the art department I enjoyed the frequent badinage—that joshing indulged in by newspaper artists while "the fac-

FREDERICK B. OPPER.

tory" is turning out comics and political cartoons. The characteristic sound of an art department is scratching—the scratch of pens and the scratching out of mistakes in the making of pictures, not unlike the scraping sound in a barber shop when a razor encounters a tough beard. T. S. Sullivant did more scratching on his drawing paper than any other artist I ever knew. We all were amused by it—he was always fretfully scratching out his pen-lines and starting over again. Once Opper turned to me and said: "If Sullivant would scratch his head more and his paper less, he could draw better cartoons."

Things at home had moved along all right for a few weeks after Elizabeth and I had returned from Alabama. But this condition did not last. My interest in the job at the *Journal* office and its future possibilities of greater income did not prevent me from becoming nervous and morose again. I would wake up in the mornings feeling depressed, as a caged bird must feel when it wants to get out and fly and knows it can't. The fact that the bars which formed my cage were invisible made them no less real. I realized that something had happened inside of me when I married that had crippled me—nothing, of course, that one could describe in words.

I had no criticism to make of my wife. There was nothing in her actions to which I could object, and undoubtedly she was playing her part as a wife conscientiously. She had so many good qualities, and I am sure meant well for me all along the line. Her eyes were lovely, she was slim and neat, and walked with feet toeing in just a little. I liked that, as I have always liked any slight deviation from the norm. It doesn't always mean character, but it suggests it. She was fond of good fiction; her favorites included Howells's *Rise of Silas Lapham,* Olive Schreiner's *Story of an African Farm,* George Eliot's novels, and the stories of George Meredith and Thomas Hardy.

Elizabeth, however, had no special interest outside of our home, as I had. She made friends and I accepted them, but she couldn't as easily accept some of mine. We doubtless saw too much of each other; and we lacked the spiritual replenishment that outside and separate friendly contacts would have given us. I was half conscious of this; but somehow I was unable to talk about it with Elizabeth. And I was fearful of those emotional explosions which so often come when the relations of a man and a woman have become strained; it is easier to remain silent.

Searching back in my thoughts through the years of our life together, I would look for some point along the road where I might have taken some different course which would have made for happiness. But I could never find that point short of going back to the days when I was single, the days when I was not in constant fear of being thought selfish for thinking more of my work than of the household routine.

My mind being troubled, my output suffered. And evidently the uncertain quality of my pictures was manifest to Brisbane, for at the end of five or six months he decided that we'd better end our arrangement.

"But I want you to submit cartoons on a free-lance basis," he said. "My door will always be open to you. I think you'll be happier free-lancing than tied down to an office grind. Not everybody is temperamentally fitted for that."

I wouldn't have quit voluntarily just then, for the hundred every week meant that I could take out life insurance and save money. Nevertheless, I felt a great relief when Brisbane dropped me from the staff. It meant that Fate had made a decision for me. I walked to the elevated whistling.

With my working hours no longer tied to an employer's time schedule, I now found it even more difficult than before to work at home. So I invented excuses to be away from our rooms a great deal. I had to see editors, and I had to go to the library to look up things.

Very soon it became clear to both of us that the atmosphere was too tense; we couldn't go on living together in those cramped quarters, though I wasn't sure that we would have been any better off in a ten-room house.

So we separated. Elizabeth packed what belongings she needed, and I carried her luggage to a furnished room which she had taken nearby. There were tears in her eyes when we said goodbye, and I felt a bit tearful myself, but we said little, beyond wishing each other good luck.

My brother Will, who had been watchful of our unhappy state, now asked me to come and live with him in his large one-room studio at 81 Fifth Avenue. He hoped and believed that our trouble would soon be adjusted. I readily accepted his invitation. His quarters were in a fine old mansion with a beautiful massive stairway leading from the entrance hall to the second floor. It was that stairway more than anything else that had made Will want to live there. Boys from the farm, where simplicity is the order, are apt to be taken in by the appearance of splendor. Some rich family had lived in that house in earlier days, but in our time the first and second floors were occupied as a dancing studio by a then celebrated teacher of the terpsichorean art named Koch. What had once been the grand ballroom on the second floor served for his larger classes and for occasional social affairs. Koch had leased the whole house and sublet the third and fourth floors to us tenants.

Our studio had large windows looking out on a little back garden; an ornate marble mantle, a practical fireplace, and a washroom with cold water; and we had the use of a bathroom with hot water. Will had had a cushioned window-seat made for the wide back windows, and for sleeping facilities he had constructed what was probably the largest "cozy corner" in history, built around and over a box-couch wider than a double bed.

The most bizarre India prints to be found in Vantine's were utilized for wall coverings, and for the canopy and side and front drapings, which were supported by antique spears and lances; and wherever possible a Damascus blade, a kriss, a medieval shield, or some other old-world war implement was hung. For fear that there might not be enough cozy atmosphere in these quarters Will had added some Civil War muskets and swords and Cuban machetes. No week went by without his bringing in a porcelain vase or other decoration to clutter up the space. On that massive couch was the most varied and numerous collection of sofa pillows that I ever saw. Several that my brother prized most were covered with fabrics that he had bought from the Waldorf-Astoria when that hotel decided on a new decorative scheme and got rid of its stock on hand.

Other objects in this great room were a tall inlaid mahogany combination bookcase and writing-desk, a golden oak bureau, a green arm-chair, a willow rocker, and a massive carved Flemish oak table and chair set—a typical conglomerate decorative scheme of the period. On the walls among the array of weapons were framed drawings which had illuminated *Sunday World* feature stories that Will had written, and originals done by the artists on the *World* staff; also drawings for the "funnies" of that era, by Dick Outcault, George Luks, Anderson, Bryans (whose silhouette pictures were then popular), Tony Anthony, Gus and Rudy Dirks, Joe Lemon, Walt McDougall; and illustrators such as Will Crawford (he made comics as well, but they always seemed too dignified and artistic to be classed as such), "Hod" Taylor, Al Levering, and others.

Of course a studio furnished so lavishly would be not at all to my taste now, nor to Will's, but I liked it then. The place was a refuge for me, and I could work again.

Will was alert, got around a lot, as a seeing journalist, and frequently brought in new and worth-while people for me to meet. Or we met them in one restaurant or another where artists and writers gathered. At that time Will was on the *Sunday World* staff.

He had come to New York late in 1894, "absolutely unwanted by any publication", as he recalls. After two long weeks of job-hunting he had been taken on as a reporter by the *World* (on the morning daily) at $15 a week. This wage didn't seem much of a compliment to him, for he couldn't forget that he was one of the founders of the *Daily Cardinal* at the University of Wisconsin, and that he had been news editor of the *Madison* (Wis.) *Democrat* and Madison correspondent for the *Chicago Tribune* and a Milwaukee daily. His combined income in Madison had been about $35 a week. But he took that $15 job none the less, thinking of the "prestige" of working on a New York paper.

He stayed a year in that poorly paid berth, then went to the *New York Mercury,* an old-timer that had just been rejuvenated by the injection of $200,000 in new capital; and lingered there until that money had been absorbed and pay-checks were held up, which took only about six months. Returning to the *World,* he was put on the Sunday staff at a time when Hearst had panicked the other papers by buying their editorial talent away from them. The rich man's son from California, who was still regarded by his New York rivals as an interloper, had induced Morrill Goddard, the *World's* Sunday editor, to move over to the *Journal;* Pulitzer had persuaded him to move back; and Hearst had raised his bid still higher, and got Goddard again, all in a single week.

Tom McGill, creator of the comic strip, "The Hall-room Boys", which was credited with big drawing power in the continuing fight for newspaper circulation, also lived at 81 Fifth Avenue when we did. And he lived in a hall-room, too, for that was before the years of big money for the comic strippers.

In the spacious front room on our floor were Gordon Grant, then and ever since a natural composer of pictures and a fine artist withal, and his roommate, Jack Haywood, a successful patent attorney, now dead. Haywood had social connections and he and the well-groomed Grant gave tone to the place. They had a large organ in their studio, which afforded me much pleasure, for I would frequently go in and play on it, thinking of days back on the farm. I've done a lot of restful day-dreaming while playing an organ or toying with the keys of a piano.

Chuck Connors came to our studio several times with Will, though it was hard to get him to leave the Bowery and come to swell Fifth Avenue. It was Will who had discovered this character of the Chinatown district for journalistic purposes, and who had written the Chuck Connors stories in the *Sunday World* that had made the ex-newsboy a notable and led to his national fame. Will used Chuck as the mouthpiece for a wide variety of observations on passing events, and thus Chuck gained as much or more fame than Steve Brodie without going to the trouble of jumping off the Brooklyn Bridge into the East River.

I remember the thrill I felt when I attended the first of a series of Chuck Connors balls in the old Tammany Hall on Fourteenth Street. This was rough and noisy, with beer flowing free, and music that may not have been so good as that in the Waldorf ballroom but was louder. The fun began during the grand march, when Chuck's lady friend, known in Chinatown as "The Rummager", had her train stepped on and torn off. She spent the rest of the evening in a box, where she slept off the effects of too much liquor. On the program I noticed the typical Connors language, which described a waltz as "Grab a rag and twist."

When my old friend the late Walt McDougall wrote his sprightly autobiography, *This is the Life,* he reproduced the names of some of the members of the "Chuck Connors Club", the purported sponsor of one of those balls. Walt had found a program of the event printed in Moss's "History of New York", with George Francis Train billed as financial secretary, and with the club members including: R. F. Outcault, Walt McDougall, Al Smith, Mickey Finn, Charley White,

Steve Brodie, Roland B. Molineaux, Timothy D. Sullivan, Oscar Hammerstein, James J. Corbett, and Bob Fitzsimmons.

"Judge Moss seems to regard the list of members as authentic—and representative", McDougall wrote, "but his judicial acumen should have enabled him to perceive that this was Connors' method of attracting the élite to his low, coarse, and quite disreputable function."

But the formation of that "club" on paper was not the handiwork of Mr. Connors, the "mayor of Chinatown." It was my brother Will who conceived the idea of the Chuck Connors balls and directed the arrangements for them, coaching Chuck in the part he was to play. And Chuck was a responsive pupil. Will suggested the staging of those affairs in Tammany Hall because they made good newspaper copy and added to the gayety of the city.

There was plenty of artistic stimulus at 81 Fifth Avenue and in restaurants, theatres, and bohemian centers which we visited around town. Will frequently had passes for shows, or was assigned to do a feature story about some situation which involved the gathering of a queer assortment of people, and often I went along, watching for both the serious and the humorous angles.

For Brisbane was buying an occasional illustration for an editorial or for an article, while the comic periodicals were taking some of my joke pictures. And in that period, too, I sold some "Snapshots in Hades" drawings to *Life* and began a "Through Hell" series in the *Cosmopolitan*. John Brisben Walker was then publisher of the latter, and at his invitation I journeyed up to Irvington-on-the-Hudson, where he lived. Those Inferno scenes were subsequently incorporated in my second book dealing with the nether regions, which was called *Through Hell with Hiprah Hunt*. This was published by Clinton S. Zimmerman in 1901.

Will went to Chicago in July, 1900, becoming Sunday editor of Hearst's *Evening American* there, taking charge of its editorial page, and also working on the editorial page of the morning *Examiner*, then under the direction of Charles Edward Russell. I remained in the studio alone, and there was a great sense of luxury in basking amid all those bargain treasures and having that spaciousness all to myself, in imitation of one who was wealthy.

I was still a Republican when the 1900 national campaign came along, with McKinley and Roosevelt asking election with the promise of "four years more of the full dinner-pail", duly featured on the front covers of *Judge* and its

Judge, 1900

WHEN 'HIRAM PENNICK' WAS MERELY COMIC. But I also used this character, I recall with shame now, in aiding the widespread campaign of ridicule which killed off the Populist party.

allies. Still a victim of the old illusions. I had not yet learned to think my way to a clear understanding of realities. Now and then some of my bourgeois beliefs had been shaken a bit by some ironic episode in the human struggle, or by some speech like that of Keir Hardie in Denver, but I clung to my inherited beliefs.

That year I served the cause by writing and illustrating a series of articles for *Judge* under the general title of "Campainin for the Millenum", which purported to record the travels and speeches of Hiram Pennick, a Populist of a Don Quixote type, who was shown touring the Mid-West on a decrepit horse. With my pictures were alleged letters in which Mr. Pennick reported his progress in badly spelled words to the editor of *Judge*.

He was for Free Silver and against Imperialism and the Trusts. In one speech he said: "We must bust the chanes that fasens us to the charyot, thats all made out of gold, when one wheel ort to be made out of silver." In another he made this prediction: "When the smoke of battle is cleared away weel see the octipust (the Trusts) thets been chewin at the nashun's vitals ded as a herrin while over the hull scene the flag of Populism is floatin in a breez of victry."

Mr. Pennick was an elderly farmer. I showed him being met by committees of faithful party members, making speeches on street corners and in halls, and enlisting recruits after which the motley procession would move on to the next town. Thus I helped to kill off Populism by poking fun at it.

Other cartoonists and writers used the slapstick on "Sockless Jerry" Simpson, Representative from Kansas, who was reputed to be eccentric in his footwear, and journalistic winds fanned the whiskers of Senator Peffer of Kansas, also a Populist. And again the sandbag and bludgeon were used against Bryan. I had heard him shout: "You must not put the dollar above the man!" and I was beginning to feel that here was something to think about, even though I was helping McKinley and the big-money Republicans.

Chapter 22

I BECOME AWARE OF THE CLASS STRUGGLE

IN December that year my brother returned to New York to be married on New Year's Eve and to have a brief honeymoon. His bride was Adelaide Oehler, whose father had a shoe store at Sixth Avenue and Eighteenth Street. I felt that they were well matched. Anyway Adelaide was good to look at.

Both were evidently happy, and they became anxious about my lone state of existence. Several close friends, too, had been worrying about that. They seemed to think it wasn't right for Elizabeth and myself to remain apart. Indeed I suddenly found myself the center of a private domestic relations conference, in which I was urged to rejoin my wife and "try it again." Adelaide, Will, and Mr. and Mrs. Winfield Scott Moody held that our separation was simply due to some lack of understanding which could be righted if both of us would show a give-and-take spirit.

They all painted a rosy picture of possibilities. At first I was skeptical, but in the face of their well-meaning concern I didn't want to be stubborn. They offered to go and talk with Elizabeth, and endeavor to smooth the way for a reconciliation; afterward I suspected that the Moodys had already talked with her. Anyhow, I agreed; I let myself be optimistic, and I was ready to meet Elizabeth half-way. As a result of all this we were reconciled (sentimentally at least) to the obligations of the marriage certificate. Then we moved into a studio apartment on West Twenty-first Street.

At the time of our reunion we had not discussed nor even admitted the existence of any differences between us. We simply started all over again, with a sincere effort on both sides to avoid serious misunderstandings. Elizabeth was thoughtful of my sensibilities, and I of hers, and I got along well with my work.

When warm weather came we went to Leonia, New Jersey, where we found a vacant barn to live in, within shouting distance of Peter Newell's home. New and dry and clean, this barn made a good dwelling for us. We shared it with Alfred Z. Baker (an artist whom I had known in Paris) and his wife. Baker was then contributing quaint animal drawings, signed B.B., to *Puck*.

Elizabeth and Mrs. Baker occupied themselves by making the barn ready for housekeeping and decorating it with curtains and other feminine essentials. Baker and I had studios in New York and went back and forth daily. In the evenings we would often assemble in Newell's house, talk about our work, grow reminiscent over old days, quote poetry, have some music, and then back to the barn.

Peter Newell was one of my favorite interpreters of the homely characters of American life—Negroes, farmers, and various types of simple folk. He also did many drawings of a curiously imaginative flavor and a quaint humor. His pictures were drawn for the Harper publications. A likeable, religious, homey fellow from Illinois. In some Valhalla get-together of artists, I want to see that tall, lanky man smile at me and say: "Welcome, Art! . . . As we were saying—"

After the summer near Leonia, we moved into an apartment house called the Corona, at Ninety-Ninth Street and Riverside Drive. Here I settled down to work with a fairly free mind. After all, I thought, maybe I'm adjusting myself to married life. But this new equilibrium was upset when Elizabeth announced that she was going to have a child. She had known it for some time, and had been hesitant about telling me.

I tried to seem cheerful—but I wasn't. All the old feeling of being caught in a net came back. Of course I couldn't quarrel with Elizabeth about her condition, nor blame her. Thinking about the whole situation, in the streets or lying awake in the dark at night, I knew that any friend would say that I had gone into marriage with my eyes open; and that it was customary for married people to have children. But I was more and more unhappy (and not proud as any normal man should be), as the date for Elizabeth's confinement approached.

The cry of a new-born child! . . . Yesterday there were

two of us—now there are three. What a thought to have pounding against the walls of my mind! In Riverside Park I pushed a baby carriage—and I really liked the baby, whom we had named North. I like all babies—to look at, but not to push. And yet the experience was a good thing. Every man ought to go through with the duty of pushing a baby carriage for one summer at least. This new son of mine was a good-natured child, who in due time cooed at the passing steamers on the Hudson and was not afraid of dogs. But the sight of the steamers made me moody. They were all going somewhere, up the river to Albany or southward down the coast, and I was chained here to one place. Would I ever get a chance to travel again? To escape from such thoughts I would go back to my drawing board and plunge into the making of pictures.

And now I found a new means of escape—lectures and libraries. Both enabled me to get away for a little while from my discontented thoughts because of loss of freedom through wedlock. Lately I realized anew that my education was inadequate. So many questions came up that I couldn't answer, and I needed to fortify myself with such answers. By listening to the lectures and reading a wide variety of books I nursed the seed which had been planted in my mind by Keir Hardie's speech in Denver, and by Myron Reed's discussions of the human struggle there.

England was fighting the Boers, and my sympathies were with the weaker nation of bearded Dutchmen who were putting up such a courageous fight to preserve their independence.

Speakers for the Social Democratic party provided me with much food for thought. They attacked the whole capitalistic system, showed how its different units combined to exploit the producing masses to the nth degree, and how the press distorted or suppressed news to protect this system, of which it was a part. Being loyal to the press, my first reaction to this denunciation was one of resentment, though I had to concede that some of the charges were true.

I remembered hearing in Chicago, in talks among the reporters, of department store elevator accidents in which people were killed, and not a paper printed a line about it. I recalled instances of news stories which I knew were far from the truth, written to order to carry out a newspaper's policy. How much justification, if any, was there for the *Inter-Ocean's* attacks on Altgeld, in which I had played an active part? Altgeld's administration as Governor had been creditable in many ways, I could see now; he had taken the side of labor, and had achieved numerous reforms.

It must have been about this time that I first heard Eugene Debs speak. He was facing an audience which packed the Academy of Music. On that same stage Henry Ward Beecher had stood and upheld the cause of the Democratic party in a tense campaign. Some one interrupted with a rude question: "How about Cleveland and free love?" This of course referred to the affair of the candidate for the Presidency with Maria Halpin. And Beecher answered: "Let him who is without sin cast the first stone."

I had been greatly interested in seeing Debs, for I had read and been told much about him—of his fearless leadership in the railroad strike of 1894, his term in jail as a consequence, and his fighting spirit. But I was disappointed that night—not by what he said, but by his manner. I thought him too much like a school-boy elocutionist.

In after years, however, I attended several mass-meetings at which Debs was the main speaker, and he who had once been amateurish had become a real tribune of the people and a master of chastisement of the profit pharisees. No question about it—an inspiring man because he was himself inspired. He was emotional, and used the logic of understanding born of long experience with workers. When one heard him voice a natural sympathy for the enslaved, one felt that here was a champion who would go to the stake rather than sacrifice his own beliefs.

Listening to lectures on the class struggle (after I discovered that such a struggle had been going on for ages), I found that I had a great deal in common with the everyday workers. In other years I had felt that as a newspaper artist I was a member of a profession which enjoyed important privileges and in which a man might possibly rise to fame and fortune. But I saw now that everyone who did productive work of any kind was at the mercy of those who employed him. They could make or break him whenever they so willed. . . . I was living in a world morally and spiritually diseased, and I was learning some of the reasons why.

When McKinley was shot down by Leon Czolgosz in September, 1901, and important newspapers suspected an Anarchist conspiracy, I found myself analyzing their assertions. The police rounded up a lot of Anarchists with a great deal of publicity, but found no evidence of such a plot. Meanwhile the *New York World* laid the blame for the assassination directly to William Randolph Hearst because of the editorial attacks in his papers on McKinley. One of those editorials said that "if bad institutions and bad men can be got rid of only by killing, then the killing must be done." *

But I believed then, and time has strengthened my belief, that accusing individuals of being accessories to, or instigators of, murder because they wrote or said something which might have planted homicidal thoughts in a culprit's mind was stretching legality to the last degree of absurdity. And law is absurd enough without dragging in "suspicious" influences. Many a man and woman has been accused of being an accessory before the fact because he or she rented a room to a murderer, or was seen talking with him three weeks before the deed. The logical end of such net-work finesse in getting evidence would be to arrest the slayer's father and mother who brought him into the world and indict them as accomplices.

Joseph Pulitzer was "wild and impetuous" in his youth, and was assailed by newspaper foes as holding "anarchistic beliefs". Nor was he tame in attacking public men. There was not much sweetness and light in his thoughts when he felt it necessary to condemn men in positions of high responsibility. Turn, for instance, to an editorial in the *World* for September 3, 1913. It was about that time that the directors of the New York, New Haven, and Hartford Railroad had been through a Congressional investigation, and President Charles S. Mellen of the New Haven and the Rockefeller-Morgan interests, who controlled the stock, were accused as the arch-criminals who had got away with the loot and had ruined thousands of stockholders. And to make matters worse there was a frightful wreck in New Haven, the White Mountain express ploughing through a Bar Harbor train and killing and injuring many passengers. The *World* editorial said:

* *New York Journal*, April 10, 1901.

"No Rockefeller is ever killed in any of the wrecks of the New Haven Railroad.

"No Morgan is ever killed.

"No director is ever killed.

"None of the bankers who have bled the system white is ever killed. . . .

"This is Wall Street's wreck, and the blood of the victims is on the hands of the highly respectable financiers who for their own profit have converted a great railroad system into a shambles."

But no maimed victim of that wreck who may have read the *World* editorial took a pot shot at any one of the highly respectable men mentioned.

With like indignation Pulitzer lashed out at John D. Rockefeller Jr. after the Ludlow massacre in Colorado, when the miners employed by the Colorado Fuel and Iron Company were on strike. On April 23, 1914, the *World* said:

"Mr. Rockefeller recently testified that he was willing to sink his entire investment in Colorado rather than yield to the demand of his employees that they be permitted to organize.

"He has not sunk and he does not intend to sink his entire investment, but he has debauched an American commonwealth, and the blood of women and children is on the hands of his barbarous agents, private and public."

In quoting these as samples of the inflammatory character of newspapers, I am merely pointing out the guilt of those who perhaps thought themselves innocent—like Pulitzer—but there were many editors who let loose at times with innuendo or sensational anger as they saw fit. No one connected with the big dailies, however, so far as I know, was ever prosecuted as Albert Parsons of the *Alarm* was in the Haymarket case when some violent crime followed an editorial outburst. But the *Alarm* was a small radical weekly, and not a large daily upholding the capitalist system.

Perhaps no editor has been so guilty of stirring up the baser passions of human beings as Hearst. Often in his early years as an editor and publisher, he did some political arousings on the side of the workers. It helped him get circulation. Gradually, however, he evolved a policy which prevailed over all liberal doctrines that he might advocate—devoting his publications to the will of the big moneyed interests to have and to retain everything that they possessed and to insure their hopes of getting more through their "superior intelligence."

But to hold him responsible for the killing of McKinley because of a bitter editorial, a poem, and Frederick Opper's cartoons of "Willie and his Papa" (Willie being the President and Papa being Mark Hanna, both favorites of the big, overfed trusts) was far-fetched.

Altgeld died in Joliet, Illinois, after collapsing at a pro-Boer mass meeting, and 50,000 people moved sadly past his casket in the Chicago public library; many of those thousands had stood for hours in the rain waiting to do him honor. The changed tone of the press toward this man was amazing; newspapers which had been the most inimical to him now lauded his deeds without indicating that they had reversed themselves. Among his former enemies which now spoke well of him were *Harper's Weekly* and the *Nation*. The latter at that time had not yet come into liberal hands. This was in 1902.

There was an Altgeld memorial meeting in Cooper Union, the place being packed to the doors. Many notables, of all shades of political opinion, paid tribute. Emphasizing the Haymarket case as the high light in his career, the speakers lauded the courage of the little man who had dared to antagonize the press and the courts and to do all that lay within his power to correct a terrible wrong.

Many well-meaning persons who had thought the Chicago Anarchists guilty or who, like myself, had wavered in their attitude toward the accused men, now found occasion to read—or re-read—Altgeld's *Reasons for Pardoning Fielden, Neebe, and Schwab*. This message was now available in most big libraries, in pamphlet form. I had read it, in substance at least, at the time of the pardons, but it was overshadowed then by the prejudiced interpretations of hostile newspapers.

Considering it in 1902 in a calm environment, I could see the real values in Altgeld's presentation of the Haymarket affair. He showed, with ample documentation, that the eight defendants were convicted by a packed jury; that they were never proven guilty of the crime charged (conspiracy to commit murder); that no evidence had ever been produced to show who threw the bomb, and that there was no proof that the defendants had had any connection with that crime.

The Governor also pointed out that at the close of the prosecution's evidence, State's Attorney Grinnell admitted to Mayor Harrison that he did not think he had a case against Neebe, but that his associates objected to dismissing him because it might influence the jury in favor of the other defendants; and that all the circumstances indicated that the throwing of the bomb was an act of some unknown person who was taking his revenge against the police for their wanton clubbing and killing of workers.

Altgeld brought out the point that this jury was not chosen in the usual manner, by drawing names out of a box, and thus getting a selection from the general voting public. Instead Judge Gary had appointed a special bailiff to go out and summon any men he liked. And a prominent business man who was summoned attested that this bailiff said to him, in the presence of others: "I am managing this case, and know what I am about. These fellows are going to be hanged as certain as death. I am calling such men as the defendants will have to challenge peremptorily and waste their time and challenges. Then they will have to take such men as the prosecution wants."

The court records, scanned by Altgeld, showed that many of the talesmen said they had been pointed out to the bailiff by their employers, to be called as jurors. Many of them declared they believed the defendants guilty, then each was examined by Judge Gary "in a manner to force him to say that he would try the case fairly". Even a man related to one of the policemen killed by the bomb was passed by the judge as competent. Several of the jurors who were eventually chosen to serve, after the defense had exhausted its challenges, "stated candidly that they were so prejudiced that they could not try the case fairly," Altgeld found, "but each, when examined by the court, was finally induced to say that he believed he could try the case fairly upon the evidence."

Documents cited by Altgeld included the interview with former Police Chief Ebersold published in the *Chicago Daily News* in 1889 which told of Captain Schaack's desire "to keep things stirring", of his wanting "bombs to be found here, there, all around, everywhere."

"It is further shown here," the Governor stated, "that much of the evidence given at the trial was a pure fabrication; that some of the prominent police officials . . . not only terrorized ignorant men by . . . threatening them with torture if they refused to swear to anything desired, but that they offered money and employment to those who would consent to do this."

Reading and weighing all this, and recalling what Altgeld suffered, I felt a deep sense of shame for my part in the newspaper assaults upon him. I took a new view now of his opposition to Cleveland's sending federal troops into Chicago in the 1894 railroad strike, when neither the mayor nor sheriff had asked for soldiers. On the *Inter-Ocean* I had been infected by the widespread indignation against the strikers for "interfering with the United States mails" when they prevented trains from running. That had seemed sacrilege then. But, I asked myself now, was there anything more criminal in stopping the mails than in an employer cutting wages and shutting off the milk supply for a worker's children?

And with this feeling, I poised in my mind some other questions as to the soundness of beliefs I had long held, based upon copy-book maxims drilled into one generation of American children after another: "Merit wins . . . Survival of the fittest . . . You can't change human nature . . . The best people . . . The poor you have with you always . . ." and the whole long line of rubber-stamp moral precepts. What were these but glittering emblems set up by the moneyed class to serve its own purposes? Born bourgeois, my brain had been filled from infancy with the nonsense of super-patriotism, with the lily-white virtues of imperialism added in due time. I had harbored these false values because I didn't know any better. I had been a drifter, innocent and sheep-minded long enough.

I was to get more light on the Haymarket case in later years from Charles Edward Russell, who covered the execution of Parsons and his comrades for the *New York World*, and who subsequently spent several months on an assignment from that paper investigating to see if he could find any tangible evidence of the purported dynamite plots.

"The truth is," Russell wrote in summing up the results of his work, "that Chicago was at no time in more danger of an Anarchist uprising, in more danger of an outbreak by violence, in more danger of destruction by dynamite, than any other American city was then and is now. . . . Slowly the conclusion was forced upon me that the idea of an Anarchist conspiracy was purely a dream."

Altgeld has been widely quoted as saying, when he pardoned the Anarchists, that it would spell his political death. Yet when he died in 1902, the *Inter-Ocean*, which had fought him so ferociously (now no longer under Kohlsaat control), said that "he left the Governor's office the most influential Democrat in the West, and with his bitterest opponents conceding his personal honesty and his political strength." And Kohlsaat, in his memoirs, published in 1921, said that Altgeld was the dominant figure at the 1896 national Democratic convention, and that if he had not been foreign-born and thus ineligible for the Presidency, he would in all probability have been the nominee.

Now that I was awakening to the realities of the economic struggle, I realized that I could no longer conscientiously deal with certain subjects in the way that editors wanted them handled. I had ideas for pictorial attacks on institutions hooked up with the money power, but there was no sale for these. The few papers which dared strike at the system were small, and had no money to pay for my product. And I had to live and support a family.

Where was I headed? I didn't quite know. I had talent, facility, and a desire to produce—but steadily my market was diminishing. I fell back on illustrated jokes, and even here struck a snag. Tramps were no longer so funny to me as they had been. And my attitude toward the farmer had changed—I no longer wanted to depict him as a mere comic character. His life was all too often bound up with tragedy. The Populists had been right in many of the things they had said about the farmer's plight.

To be sure, my farmers of the Hiram Pennick series were not the straw-chewing by-heck type made familiar by the caricaturist Zim, but came from my sketch-books. They were the folks that I was raised among out in the Middle West, but it was ridicule none the less of men who tilled the soil around Monroe, and in other farm sections I had visited. I had had the temerity to have Hiram Pennick date one of his *Campainin for the Millenum* letters from Oneco township in Illinois, where I was born.

The circulation of *Judge* in this Presidential campaign was enormous—it penetrated to all parts of the country. If I should go home again, I reflected, and should meet any of the farmers there, I would have to explain that it was all done in fun; but would any of them believe that? I wrote a letter to a friend in Wisconsin, enclosing a sketch of myself arriving home and being pursued by farmers with pitchforks ready to lunge at me while I tried to explain.

Letters and news clippings sent by my father told of the campaign Robert M. LaFollette was making to be re-elected as Governor of Wisconsin. That gave me an inspiration. I was a bit tired of New York, and needed a change in order to take new reckonings and re-shape the course of my working life.

LaFollette's friend Isaac Stephenson had established the *Milwaukee Free Press* chiefly, if my memory is correct, to back the Governor's political program. I wrote volunteering my services as a cartoonist during the critical weeks of the contest, asking only that my railroad fare both ways be paid. This offer was accepted, and I immediately left New York and got into the fight. After a conference on strategy with the *Free Press* editors, I went on to Monroe to visit with my folks and sent my cartoons by mail.

My appearance had an effect upon the enemy which amused me greatly. The *Milwaukee Sentinel*, principal mouthpiece for the "Stalwart Republicans", a rival faction in LaFollette's own party, published a long editorial about "the desperate situation" of the LaFollette following indicated when the campaign committee "had to hire a high-priced cartoonist to help." But evidently it was his foes that were desperate, judging by the amount of abuse hurled at him, especially by the Stalwart crowd.

To that effort in LaFollette's behalf I gave everything I had. I believed that he represented the honest Americanism which flowed from the pioneers. He was for the farmers, whether Swedes, German, Swiss, Irish, or what; and for the industrial workers, native and foreign-born alike. His record was replete with activity in the interests of both. As District Attorney, as Representative in Congress, and as Governor, he had served intelligently and conscientiously.

Speaking at county fairs, chautauquas, and other gatherings all over the state, he showed up the rottenness in his own party, exposed appalling inequalities in the Wisconsin taxing system, and the vital importance of public supervision of railroad rates. And now he won re-election as he had won all previous contests for public office. All the mud-slinging had failed to stop him.

Chapter 23

ANOTHER CHILD AND NEW WORRIES

MY wife and I both stemmed from healthy stock. And yet I always had foolish misgivings that our children might be born with some kind of a handicap—blindness, or a lesser affliction. Out west they used to tell a lot of stories about Abraham Lincoln, a good many of them raw, of the variety known as "men's stories." Some of them were undoubtedly inventions. But I recall one that to me seemed true to his quaint humor and imagination. When he had a law office in Springfield and his wife was expecting their first baby, Abe went over to his home to be near during the event. On his way back to the office, a friend who had heard the news hailed him and asked for more information, and Abe answered:

"It's a fine boy. . . . I was afraid it might have one of my long legs and one of Mary's short ones. But it's all right."

Another baby was scheduled to arrive late in 1904, and Elizabeth's sister Kate came on from Wisconsin to live with us and help take care of our growing family. We needed more room, and moved into a larger apartment (five rooms instead of four) at 936 West End Avenue, near where Broadway joins that thoroughfare around 107th Street.

Our second son, Donald, was born in December. Again Elizabeth was pleased, saying: "Now North will have a playmate." And Kate was elated. To me this addition to the household spelled another problem, although I was glad to see such a fine body of a boy. This meant being even more obligated to tread a path of duty. Friends congratulated me, and spoke of the "proud father", making jokes more or less humorous, mostly less. Of course I responded with a synthetic smile, and handed out the customary cigars. How many men who have not discovered how to make a continuously good income are really proud fathers? Yet somehow, as the months went on, I managed to pay rent and grocery bills, although more of my drawings had lately been rejected than in the past.

Admittedly Don was a handsome and inspired looking infant. (My portrait of a youngster often reproduced with the caption, "Every child is a genius until forced to surrender to civilization," is Don at the age of three.) But that didn't lessen my gloomy thoughts.

I worked harder than ever now, and increased my efforts to sell pictures. Constantly, too, I was reading history and economics, to improve my understanding of causes behind the human struggle. No longer could any defender of the prevailing system tell me that there were no social classes in this country.

One evening I had been reading in the Cooper Union library. On my way out I passed a large room off the main hallway, from which I heard the voice of some one making a speech. I stopped to listen. Certain sentences in the declamation interested me, and I quietly edged into the room. Here were young men of varied races and many nationalities learning to talk in the English language on the issues of the hour. The instructor would sum up the merits and defects of the speakers as to good English, construction, delivery, and all that makes for effective speaking in public.

I decided then and there to become a member of that free night-class in parliamentary law, oratory, and debate in this institution founded by Peter Cooper. I had read about this great American philanthropist who had "queer" ideas of reforming our national currency and who was one of the first of the Greenbackers. Whether he was right on the money question I do not know. But his idea of free education for all who wanted it seemed sensible to me. And today I would have less excuse for my attacks on the educational system if colleges were free and democratically administered.

For a long time I had felt the need of learning to think and speak on my feet. When I drew a cartoon on some controversial theme, and an editor rejected it and said it was illogical, I was usually unable to argue against the objections. But Cooper Union, I was certain, would show me how to defend my point of view.

JUST ALIKE

Some of the sessions on debate nights brought me great illumination, stirred me deep within, made clear what was valid evidence in support of contentions on one side or the other of a vital question. My early efforts at argument in class were awkward, but I persisted. Soon I realized that an essential thing in debate was preparation. Often the contests on the floor had the aspects of a battle—each contestant determined to win. Many times our instructor had to pound with the gavel and say: "Come now, you are getting angry. Anger will defeat you."

And as I went along with my reading and debating I became increasingly conscious of widespread social injustice. All the veils of illusion were being stripped away from the thing called civilization, and I saw what a shameful tribute man must pay to her whom John Swinton called "the bitch goddess Success." I had no desire just to be a fluent talker like a lawyer, politician, or salesman. I, too, was seeking success, but it would have to be of a kind consistent with my way of thinking.

Throughout this course in debating I would always take the side which seemed to me *right*—if for no other reason than that I couldn't argue convincingly on the other side. I was sure that the Cooper Union training was going to help me at least in ordinary controversies. And I was now coming to the conclusion that I would no longer draw cartoons which illustrated somebody else's will. Henceforth it would be my own way of looking at things—right or wrong, I would figure things out for myself. If success came, well and good; but to win at the price of my freedom of thought—that kind of success was not for me. Though I perceived that much of life was compromise, in dealing with world affairs or with my own, I would have to sink or swim holding on to my own beliefs on questions of vital importance.

More and more was I aware that I was totally unfitted for married life. I could not adjust myself to the routine of domesticity. There was a feeling always that I was shut in— that I didn't belong to myself. I missed my old solitude, the easy-going way of having my meals any time I wanted to, of going to bed at any hour and getting up when I liked—

unless there was special reason to arise early to do some drawing for which an editor was waiting. Day after day this kind of living annoyed me. Why must I stop for lunch at twelve o'clock if I happened to be right in the swing of an absorbing cartoon? To be courteous? Which comes first —I kept asking myself—dutiful domesticity, or draftsmanship and dreams?

In our family relations I seldom protested, for I preferred at all costs to avoid a scene. Outwardly everything was all right. There was something so ridiculous in bickering about the jarring trivialities while living together in a state that had been blessed, certified, stamped and sealed for all time. I could show anger over issues like government and religion, but not at the pin-pricks of everyday life.

Yet these things continually irked me, and left scars, and I was envious of artists who could "let go" when their emotions got pent up, who could raise hell if interrupted at their work by foolish questions or if blamed for something they couldn't help. I even suppressed my whims (harmless enough I am sure), if I thought they would upset the daily round of married life. But if others felt their whims had the right of way I made no objection. It ought to be said here, however, that I was never a victim of nagging. Nevertheless there was deadly discord—and I had not found the key to harmony.

What with this continued repression, the struggle to make both ends meet, and the feeling that the freedom I knew as a young man was dying from neglect, I was on the verge of becoming a hopeless neurotic, and that should be avoided at all costs—for I was the provider for my family. I felt that I was living a grave mistake. But married life seemed all right for some artists—why couldn't I make the necessary adjustment?

Uppermost was the thought that I ought to resign myself to wedlock at all costs. Was it not the natural and accepted relation of man and woman? And above all things I ought to keep the tradition of the Young and North families inviolate, for most of them knew how to marry, stay married, and be contented. Such was the hold of a conventional upbringing—and I fought day and night to keep contrary thoughts out of my mind.

Spring came again, with fine weather, new ideas, new stimulus, and the pressing conclusion that the city environment was all wrong. Cities crushed people's souls. All these monolithic piles of brick and stone, these hard pavements, the nerve-tearing noise, made it a torture chamber—an inferno. Certainly New York streets were no proper place for children. They were entitled to better surroundings in which to grow up. The country might be the solution of my own problem and Elizabeth's. For I was not blind to the fact that she had a problem.

I began day-dreaming about open roads and fields—the soil, rippling streams, and the sunshine as I knew them in boyhood. If only I could go barefoot again, wade in a creek, and feel the cool touch of plowed ground. If only I could let the warm sun soothe the back of my neck while I stood with naked feet on a grassy knoll,—that would be the true polarity of health, sun and soil meeting in my system, and I would be well again mentally as well as physically. And to watch horses, cows, birds, and trees—the thought of it! I had heard of crippled city horses that had pounded their feet on cobblestones for years being restored to usefulness by the cushioned pastures of the country.

Too much city—now for the country! Elizabeth and Kate both hailed the idea enthusiastically, and we began hunting through the advertisements of farms for sale in the Sunday papers, marking the likely ones. Then we took stock of the family finances. Elizabeth had some money available that had been left her by Uncle Len, and I had a few dollars remaining from the proceeds of sales to magazines.

We inspected several of the farms offered, but all had something wrong with them—they were too far from a town, or were on land too rocky, or had no good water supply, and all too often did not bear out the representations of the real estate dealer.

But each time we fared forth hopefully. And one day we went to Connecticut to look at a place south of Bethel, two hours by train from New York. "Maybe this will be the one," said Elizabeth. Mr. Platt, who lived a quarter of a mile from the farm we were going to inspect, and who was acting as agent for the owner, met us at the depot with a team and a two-seated buggy, and drove us out. We turned to the right at Shaker's Corner, and moved on along Chestnut Ridge Road which climbed amid enchanting wooded hills.

The place we went to see comprised four acres of land; a gurgling creek which ran half-hidden through the brush; a two-story frame house badly in need of repair, with a cellar and attic; a good barn, painted red; and an orchard which was worth the price asked, just to look at. The land sloped "every which way", as New Englanders say. The house was on a higher level than the barn, with a plot of fairly even ground between which was suited to gardening. Back of the house was a trail leading upward to a huge gray boulder, not rounded by a million years of glacial rolling, but still with sharp edges and a pointed apex, as if it might have been tossed around no more than a few thousand years. On that summit one could stand in the breeze and survey the surrounding foothills of the Berkshires. There was a sense of isolation here, of protection from the tearing clamor of the outside world. I stood on that high rock a long time that first day, thinking and hoping. . . . It was amazing how much ground-space there could be in four acres. And the area seemed even larger when I set out later to cut the grass and weeds with a scythe.

We called on neighboring farmers to inquire about the history of this little homestead. Old Mr. Hickok, who lived down the road, said: "There hain't no better garden ground and no better well-water in these parts." After climbing to the lookout rock again and feasting our eyes further on the whole prospect, we returned to Bethel, and went to the town clerk's office to look up the deed. That being clear, we paid Mr. Platt a few dollars to bind the bargain and said we'd bring the family up in a week and take possession.

I felt happier that day than I had in ten years. And Elizabeth was gay. It was a real holiday for her, away from the responsibility of caring for the children. She wore an attractive light blue frock and a flower-trimmed hat to match, and seemed no older than when I came back from Colorado.

Packing our belongings was no task this time; it was sport. During the week I visited several editors and boasted about my back-to-the-farm movement. I would be able to do better work in the country air, I was certain. On the strength of my glowing expectations I got orders for enough drawings to cover the expense of moving—so our migration to Connecticut was made auspiciously.

What did me the most good in all this was the hopeful feeling that I could find myself again out where there was an absence of confusion. In the city my real self was being rubbed out by the friction of conflicting thoughts. You don't know who you are unless you stand alone among the hills and trees. Hills and trees don't argue with you; they take you for granted.

We all stayed for a few days in Mr. Platt's house, until our household goods arrived. They came by freight. I was much concerned about the piano and a large Swiss music-box which had been given to me by a Chicago friend—but everything arrived in good order, and soon was moved up to our hill. For another day we were busy placing furniture, tacking down carpets, putting up curtains, and disposing of various little tasks.

Then I took off my shoes and stockings, rolled up my pants, and reveled in the contact with grass and earth. North joined me, while his mother and aunt were in the house putting minor things to rights. Then we climbed to the big rock, and North was excited over being up so high above our house. Between us and the house the apple trees were in blossom, and the air was fragrant. We went down to the creek, which was beyond the barn, and North tried to catch frogs and minnows, which were always too quick for him. The barn was a lure, and we explored that, watching the doves which had cotes inside the south door; they had been thrown in with the farm.

I did no drawing that day, for there were too many odds and ends to be done before we would be settled. But my brain was active with planning. I arranged to have Mr. Hickok bring his horse over and plow up the garden. In the evening I walked in to Bethel and bought seeds. Mr. Hickok would come the following week, we would plant the seeds as soon as the ground was ready, and I figured out from the directions on the seed-envelopes just how many days it would be before we would be eating our own vegetables. But something happened that year so that the garden did not turn out well—too much rain, or maybe it was drouth; I've forgotten which.

As the days wore on I began to feel quite at home in the

new environment. I remembered the cartoons I had promised the editors. I put my drawing table in the northwest room upstairs which looked out on a hill of apple trees. Picture production had begun again, and I could hear North at his play—and later at the supper table his reports of discoveries of insects and such queer things (to a city boy) that he had found down by the creek. He had captured a small turtle and had put several fireflies in a glass jar and was going to investigate the mystery of their light. The quaint, genius-like observations of children as they voice them before they have been told what their elders think they know on any subject makes child-thoughts sound like the highest wisdom—and hence are real poetry.

After Hickok finished the plowing, a barefoot walk in the moist loam became a daily rite with me before breakfast. Then a footbath in the creek. If there is any greater thrill of health than this I have never felt it. And many times I climbed to the gray rock, inhaled deeply, and saw new scenes in the surrounding countryside; in changing lights and atmospheres the beauties of the view were inexhaustible.

When the vegetables began to show themselves, of course the weeds sprang up to beat them. I hoed earnestly then and with more interest than I ever had on my father's farm. But as weeks passed hoeing became a nuisance, and the crusade against weeds was one more lost cause. I busied myself in one way or another around the old house, giving an imitation of a carpenter.

Then I found it convenient to set up a studio in the loft of the barn, where I could work without being disturbed by North's romping. Entrance to that was by ladder, and I installed a trap-door at the top to close myself off. Not much needed to be done to make that loft comfortable for me. It was dry, the roof being sound. And by leaving the wide hay-door open I could have good light by day and a view of the hills to the East that seemed often to change. After I had swept the hay-dust from the floor, Elizabeth contributed some small rugs so that the place wouldn't be too bare.

My books were in the house, filling many shelves, and in the evenings I would be there, in what we then called the sitting room, reading while Kate and Elizabeth were busy with their own devices, perhaps crocheting, playing crokinole, or telling stories to North. We three grown-ups would vie with one another to find amusing anecdotes in the magazines or newspapers that were worth repeating. Sometimes we would pop corn or have a candy-pull, as we used to back in Wisconsin. And the glee of North over these simple treats reminded me of my own childhood.

In the fall I went down to New York to see editors, but stayed only overnight, and was glad to get back to the farm and the clean smell of earth, the early morning chorus of birds, the peaceful quiet of back roads.

We had rural free delivery, with mail in the mornings. But frequently I would walk to the village, a mile away, late in the afternoon, to mail drawings before the postoffice closed. In the village I would talk with old-timers who had long since retired from whatever work they had done, and would ask them questions about local history. Being a good listener, I was willing to let them do most of the talking—and often I would sketch them as they gave me the low-down on village happenings in the past.

The best of their stories had to do with P. T. Barnum. That great showman, three times member of the state legislature, and mayor of Bridgeport, first saw the light of day in Bethel in 1810. The house in which he was born still stands.

When we moved to the Chestnut Ridge place, there stood in the center of the village in a triangular grass plot an ornate bronze fountain which Barnum presented to his home town in 1881. I have read his presentation speech, and seen photographs of the occasion—and for memory reflections, recalling names and incidents of his boyhood, I have never read a similar extemporaneous address to compare with it.

"And now, my friends," he said in closing, "I take great pleasure in presenting this fountain to the town and borough of Bethel, as a small evidence of the love which I bear them and the respect which I feel for my successors, the present and future citizens of my native village."

But there followed a good deal of criticism of the gift. Some said he "gave it to Bethel because Bridgeport didn't want it," and others that "it took too much water to keep it going." Still others who were suspicious that P. T. might

CONNECTICUT CRIME AGAINST ART. Bronze fountain given by P. T. Barnum to Bethel, his home town. Razed by village authorities in 1920 to make room for this atrocious war-statue.

try to humbug them, opined that "like as not it hain't bronze at all."

Unfortunately this heroic figure of a Triton blowing a horn with spouting dolphins around the base—such a fountain as one sees in public parks in Europe, and which Barnum had had cast in Germany—is no more. I think it sad that the village selectmen one day around 1920 had the fountain demolished. They said it was cracking and sold it to a junk dealer. Then what? In its stead they erected one of those libels on American youth, a big bronze male out to kill—typical statue in American towns to commemorate the "war for democracy". If such memorials are intended to stimulate and revere heroism, they are jokes; but worst of all they are insulting to anyone with a sense of the artistic. The Barnum fountain had at least the merit of classic form.

Passing the old cider mill near Shaker's Corner, and proceeding north along Plum Tree Road for a couple of miles, one comes to a lane which leads to Ivy Island, the five-acre tract which Barnum's maternal grandfather, an inveterate joker, deeded to him at his birth. As young Phineas grew into boyhood, the grandfather and other relatives often reminded him that he was "the richest boy in town." Not until he was perhaps eleven did he get to see this fabulously valuable property of his.

Then he persuaded an Irish farmhand, on a Sunday, to take him to Ivy Island. When they arrived at his estate, Phineas burst into tears when he discovered that it was just a piece of worthless swamp-land. He was chased by a black-snake, according to his recital of that disillusionment, was stung by bees, and sank to his waist in mire. . . . But many years later, when Barnum was buying Scudder's Museum in New York—he blandly put up Ivy Island as part of the security—and it was worth just as much then as it had been on the day when he first saw it. Today it is still worthless.

Three miles north of Bethel lies Danbury, the county seat, an old circus town rich in memories. Barnum was a prisoner there for sixty days, in the old jail, still standing. As a young man he was publisher of the *Herald of Freedom* in Bethel, and got into trouble by criticising one Deacon Seeley editorially. Convicted of libel, he was jailed. But he had a good time during his confinement. The sheriff was a friend, and provided his guest with comfortable quarters on the third floor, where the windows afforded pleasing views. P. T. continued to edit the *Herald of Freedom* from his jail quarters, and when he was released a large delegation of citizens waited outside to welcome him. They put him into a carriage, drawn by plumed horses, and with a brass band at its head, a long procession escorted him through the principal streets of Danbury, and then home to Bethel.

As an editor Barnum assailed slavery, and later as a legislator bore down heavily on the New Haven railroad. An ardent temperance lecturer, he fails to mention in his autobiography, *Struggles and Triumphs,* that he had a brother Eben who was the town drunkard and who used to sleep off his jags sometimes on the grass plot where the Barnum freshwater fountain was erected.

When that work first appeared, a book agent invaded Bethel to solicit orders for it. He knocked at a certain door, and when it was opened by an elderly woman he launched into a description of the book's contents, saying that "every American" ought to know the story of P. T. Barnum's life.

"Young man," she said, "I know more about P. T. Barnum than you can ever get into a book. I'm his mother."

I learned during my early residence in these parts that Danbury and Bethel, which in a manner of speaking were for many years "all one place", had a historic background worth knowing about. Much of renown and interest beside the world's most famous showman is associated with these hills.

Over on Redding Ridge, I heard, there was a place where Gen. Israel Putnam camped throughout a winter with his ragged soldiers during the American Revolution. It was only a few miles from my home, and one day I walked over and saw a serried half-mile stretch of camp-fire sites. Here were a lot of the old stones which encircled the fires around which the boys sang and cursed—but knew with some degree of certainty what they were fighting for. That area has been conserved, and is now known as Putnam Park.

Many Tories lived in this part of the state in Revolutionary years. One patriarch informed me that his grandfather told him that *his* father went to a church "right here in Bethel"—one Sunday in those anxious days—and after the sermon the minister said: "Now I'm going to ask all those who are for the cause of the Revolution to go out of the door on the left, and those opposed to go out on the right." The old-timer didn't know what the count revealed. But it was one way of trying to find out who was for a monarchy and who for a radical change in government.

Our nearest neighbor on the road south going toward Redding was Mr. Agnew, a good carpenter, who had built many houses in and around Bethel. He would often stop at our gate on his way to and from the village, and was always ready to do odd jobs of carpentry. Sometimes he would work for hours and laugh it off when I tried to pay him. I don't like to think of it, but those men who enjoyed doing things for others with no thought of pay have mostly passed out of the scene—to make way for the go-getters in all professions.

Mr. Agnew had never been to New York City since he stopped there sometime during his service in the Union Army. One day he made up his mind to go in and visit a relative living in "the Bronix." When I next saw him I asked if he had been to the big city. He had—for just one day. This was his story:

"I went to visit my cousin in the Bronix. After dinner I thought I'd better take a look around the city. First I went to Grant's Tomb, and the folks told me I ought to look at Central Park—so I went there and hung around till three o'clock. Then I decided I'd take the four o'clock train back to Bethel. Shucks! I don't suppose I seen half what there was to see."

In discussing the Civil War with Mr. Agnew, I spoke of John Brown. He laughed—and I suppose that laugh was the same kind that was heard in many places when Old Osawatomie was mentioned back in pre-Rebellion days. Then my neighbor said:

"I seen him up in Torrington, where he was born. He'd been living and fighting out in Kansas, and folks said he came back to Torrington to buy knives and guns."

"What kind of a fellow was he?" I asked.

"Crazy as a bed-bug," said Mr. Agnew.

One evening I was taking a walk on a back road. Apparently no one lived in that part of the countryside. But finally I came to a worn path which led to a weather-beaten shack by the side of a swamp. No sound except at intervals the croak of a frog—and off in a dark grove a screech owl would shiver the doleful air in reply. In this scene of somber desolation, with the twilight almost gone, I saw a man sitting by the shack. I ventured over to him slowly. After the "good evening" salutation I found that he was willing to have a little conversation, in the course of which I learned that he had lived in this same place "nigh onto thirty-one years." I asked him if he had ever been to New York City.

"Once," he said. "There for three days—but the place is too dang lonesome for me."

I made a picture with similar dialogue which was published in *Life*.

Early in this century there was still some real farming in this region like that I had known out West. Not on such a large scale, of course, but small farms on which a hard-working man with a small family could live, provided he kept a cow, horse, chickens, and enough pigs for winter meat. Then it was possible to survive even in stony Connecticut; so if the worst came to the worst I figured I might be able to do the same on my four acres.

But gradually as the years went by the sturdy American yeoman, not only in this state but all over the country, was giving up the idea of making a small farm pay or even assure a subsistence. The reason is well known to those who follow the trend of economic determinism. Some of these small Connecticut agriculturists had begun even around 1906 to see the futility of farming, so they would do their chores early in the morning and late in the evening—devoting the interim hours to work in one of the many hat factories in Danbury and Bethel.

One fine day I was thinking what a great advantage it was to have escaped from scenes of debate, controversy, and taking sides—that the quiet countryside was the right place to be—away from it all—when George Agnew, son of my neighbor, called. George said he had been asked by his fellow-workers in the Short hat factory to see me about an important matter.

Would I serve as an arbitrator in a serious conflict between the owner and the employees?

He said my decision would stand, as both parties concerned had agreed to that. I was an outsider, so to speak, and would be impartial. He showed me several typewritten sheets explaining how much per dozen hats the workers had received under a previous contract, how much the boss would pay if another contract were drawn up—if the workers would agree to this and that and other things—and so on *ad infinitum.*

After casually looking over this array of facts and figures, I said: "I'm willing to act as arbitrator, but frankly I can't be impartial. I'm for labor, first, last, and all the time." But George was keen to have me serve in spite of my bias. So I read the document carefully and rendered my decision, pronouncing the workers' demands reasonable and justified according to contract. The decision was accepted all around and I was pleased to know that an outsider could do a little to help the cause of labor, if only to the extent of a few cents per day.

During the years that I have lived near Bethel there have been repeated strikes and lockouts in the two towns—a few flush months, then gloom for the rest of the year.

But this once strong union sector of labor was demoralized following a strike in 1902, when the D. E. Loewe Company, hat manufacturers in Danbury, sued the members of the local hatters' union *as individuals* for injury to the corporation's trade because of a boycott used to aid the strike. The suit was brought under the Anti-Trust Act. Backed by the National Manufacturers' Association, the Loewe company claimed damages, and was awarded $74,000 by a jury in 1910, the law permitting it to collect as much as three times the amount of the award. Under this judgement the company attached the workers' homes and bank accounts—if they had any to attach.

Many sad stories are told around here of the desperate straits of those workers as a result of this ruthless assault, the obvious purpose of which was to break up labor unions in the United States for all time. Organized capital had decided that it would no longer tolerate organized workers. This was to be one of the final tests of strength.

The judgement was appealed and carried from court to court. In 1915 the United States Supreme Court affirmed the jury's verdict, which entitled the plaintiff to take $222,000 from the defendants—which meant taking everything they had.

But in this long-drawn fight the boycott persisted despite the Supreme Court, and Loewe himself lost his business and died a financial wreck, though he received a pension from the

National Manufacturers' Association up to his death. It had used Loewe for its own purpose, and the courts did their part in upholding the right of capital to use any kind of a club to knock labor helpless.

Chatting with the townsmen of Danbury and Bethel, I would sometimes meet up with one of the older generation who liked to talk about James Montgomery Bailey, "the Danbury News man," who died in 1894. When I was a boy out west "the Danbury News man" was known to everybody —like Josh Billings, George W. Peck, and Bill Nye. It was pleasant to hear those who had lived when he was here in the flesh tell about him.

"You know," said the veteran Ezra Judd, "Monty was in the Civil War. Got his reputation writing letters home to the *Danbury Times*—some comical, some pretty darn sad. When he come back him and Tim Donovan got hold of a little money and bought the *Times*, and a few years later they changed the name to the *Danbury News*, and said they were going to keep politics out of it, and Monty began writing about anything he wanted to. I've been 'round the old Danbury postoffice when they were mailing out the *News;* they used to say thirty thousand copies went out every week —pretty good for a country-town paper."

"What kind of a fellow was Bailey?" I asked him.

"Great big six-footer—good-looking—never wore a neck-tie—they say he had spells of the blues—and would stay home drunk for a week. He liked children, but didn't have none of his own. Every time I saw him he had a big dog, sometimes two or three, with him. Everybody knew he'd help them if they ever got in trouble—didn't care for money. Mr. Young, Monty Bailey was as fine a man as ever drew breath, and you can say that Ezra Judd said so."

In my library I have one of Bailey's books, *Life in Danbury*, and I'm old-fashioned enough to enjoy the homespun humor of his time. Taking that volume from the shelf, I open it casually and see this one among the locals (which is typical of the Bailey manner of saying things):

"A Sharon man stole a peck of dahlia roots under the impression that they were sweet potatoes. He feels the deception keenly."

Mark Twain made his home in Redding during the last six years of his life. This is the next railroad station three miles south of Bethel. Once I talked with him at an Illustrators' Society entertainment in his honor in New York. I was then illustrating epigrams called "Shots at Truth" for *Life,* and I told him he ought to publish the sententious remarks of Puddinghead Wilson and other short passages from his writings. I don't know whether I had anything to do with it, but about a year later I saw a Christmas brochure

MARK TWAIN

of brief quotations from the works of Mark Twain, with emphasis on Puddinghead's philosophy.

There are many stories in circulation about Twain's life in Redding. He was becoming sick and depressed in those years. I asked Albert Bigelow Paine, his biographer, whose home was near the humorist's then, if his heart trouble (angina pectoris) was caused by his incessant smoking. Paine said: "It is not the cause, but it aggravates it."

Two thieves broke into Mark's house late one night

when everything was still, and stole a bag full of precious silverware. They were caught next day, and their trial was subsequently held in the old schoolhouse in Redding which was used for the administration of justice. Louis Ohlweiler, the Bethel barber, went down to attend the proceedings. When he arrived, he told me, Mark was walking slowly back and forth in front of the schoolhouse and smoking a cigar.

During the trial, the judge asked the author of *Huckleberry Finn* the date and approximate hour of the burglary. Mark drawled out an answer—but the judge, after talking with the sheriff, said: "Mr. Clemens, I think you must be mistaken," and named a different date and hour from the official record.

"All right, Judge," Mark replied, "have it your own way. I'm always wrong. That's how I got my reputation."

CHAPTER 24

BUT THE BACK-TO-NATURE EXPERIMENT FAILS

THE experiment of going back to the soil did not work out as I had optimistically planned. As the months went on it became evident that there was an excess of conventional sameness in my life. Each day was too much like being on a treadmill. I had hoped that the new arrangement, in which I had more room to myself with less interruption, and where my wife and her sister saw less of me—would help to break the terrible restraint I felt as a man married. But try as hard as I could, even praying to the God-of-all-wisdom for guidance (a desperate manifestation of my troubled self), I could not justify my nature with marriage. I knew many artists who were married and apparently happy, and I blamed myself for being queer—a non-adjustable, misfit egoist. Evidently I didn't belong among normal people.

Day after day the situation grew worse. I was miserable, couldn't concentrate on my work and was turning out pictures which I knew were far below my standard, and nightly I lay awake for hours.

I realized now that daily contact with plowed ground, the blowing clover, trees and birds, and above all two bright children, couldn't save me. I'd have to tackle the world with a fresh outlook as I did when young—free to be myself, even if wrong. I had no yearning for the gay life, and no woman was waiting for me in the background. I was simply no longer equal to the duties and courtesies of married life. Only through release from its conventional routine and binding exactions could I function as a provider for my family.

It had become impossible to combine domesticity and creative work. I was capable of doing a small drawing now and then with some concentration and good results—but sustained effort was beyond me under the existing circumstances.

For some five years we had gone on with our second effort to live together in harmony. I did my best to have it succeed, and I am sure Elizabeth did. But the result was failure. Now I was through. All I wanted was to be alone to continue my work.

During all the harrowing conflict which went on within me, I felt that neither of us could be definitely blamed for what happened. We were in the grip of forces over which we had no control. Here were two natures, each the product of countless centuries of combining physical and emotional attributes and defects. With some other man Elizabeth might have been supremely happy, and he with her. Or if we had married in youth, when my love was strong and possessive, it might have turned out all right—*if*. That word if. I made a picture which was published in *Life* of that word *if* as a huge rock in the turbulent sea which I titled "The Grave of Our Dreams." Elizabeth seemed to see in clear outline the reality which confronted us, and did not try to fight it. Elizabeth, the sweetheart of my youth, now so far away, is my favorite heroine. What she went through in her years with me is her own untold story.

An artist is one who can put himself in another's place. There is no art without feeling, and the better the artist the more intensely he feels. He is sympathetic and imaginative to a degree that makes him "queer" to the world of "normal" human beings. Seeing others in despair is his own despair.

One thing I had learned through that long drawn out ordeal was this: When a revolution comes, whether in the life of an individual or of a nation, it is seldom justifiable to those who must endure the brunt of abrupt change. Some will say "it could have been avoided"; others that "I don't object to it, but to the way it was done"; still others deplore "the innocent sufferers." Oh yes, many sad things occur as a result of a vital change in private or social living. But often it is pride that is injured most. People who cannot see the true inwardness of our personal problems are apt to think us heartless for conduct that they see only from the outside. It may have required every bit of our moral courage, but for some other act requiring no strain of morals or ethics in the doing, we are thought heroic.

I came back to New York and took a room in an office building rented out for studios on Twenty-fourth Street.

Under the same roof were John Cassell, the cartoonist; Jim Condé, picturesque illustrator of the *Uncle Remus* stories and other animal books; Philip Dillon, writer and dilettante in politics; and Morgan Robertson, then at the height of his production of sea stories.

Jim Condé introduced me to one of the first stool-and-counter lunchrooms in New York, around the corner on Sixth Avenue. "Let's go over to Minx's," he would say, "and sit on a stool like a frog on a lily-pad." His favorite dish was rice pudding because you got so much for your money.

My studio was up five flights. The elevator stopped running at 6. There were bedbugs to fight on summer nights, and life was far from being one long sweet song—but I accepted the hardships willingly as part of the price of my new freedom.

The building in which we lived and worked had poor heating facilities. In winter it was hard to wield a pencil with freezing fingers. Late one cold December night I happened to go to Jim's room. He had retired—in a cast-off barber's chair, one of his studio accessories. Tilted back and fully dressed, with newspapers tucked in around him, he had arranged an electric light bulb so that it touched his chest. In his colorful language, he said:

"By the billy-horned Moses! I had to figure out some way to keep warm on a night like this."

In a short while after my return to the city the doors of opportunity were opening to me again just as in my youth, and I soon began to send money to Elizabeth. That had been my first thought. But I was now developing a hatred for all bourgeois institutions in addition to marriage, and trying hard to live up to my own ideas of right and wrong. Henceforth no one could hire me to draw a cartoon that I did not believe in. This had become an obsession.

Once I sent back to *Life* a check for a hundred dollars, though I needed it badly, because, after drawing a cartoon at John Ames Mitchell's suggestion, I decided that the idea expressed in it was not true. *Life* had been attacking what it called the theatrical trust, contending that this combine was exclusively Jewish and that these Jews were crucifying the art of the drama.

My picture showed a swooning woman, The Drama, nailed to a cross, with various Jewish men typifying the theatre owners looking on with delight. After the picture had been delivered to the office of *Life* by messenger I realized that it was untrue to my convictions. I asked myself: Why did I draw that cartoon? Why hadn't *Life* asked some other cartoonist to do it, who didn't bother his head about the ethics of ideas so long as there was money in them? I felt that

A SUCCESS.

the editor's suggestion had been conceived in a spirit of animus against a race, and that idea I never could believe in.

Anyone who believes something sincerely usually can make me believe it for a little while if he is a good talker, even if his idea is basically wrong, but when I think it over alone I discover that his thoughts were not mine at all. In this instance I knew I had been trapped by my own tendency to oblige. It is this tendency, plus the damnable coercion of economic need, that leads to the deterioration of creative minds.

When I told Mr. Mitchell that I was returning his check

and that I positively did not want *Life* to publish that drawing he was a bit peeved, but said "All right, if that's the way you feel about it." And I said to myself: "That's the end of me as a contributor to *Life*." But I had thought the whole question through and was ready for anything. And I knew this: that I would not sell my talent to be used for anti-Semitic propaganda. Certainly commercialization of the arts was not by any means an exclusively Jewish sin—there were plenty of old-family Americans and members of other races ready to sacrifice anything for profit. Then, too, I wanted to save such a tragic concept as a crucifixion for a cause greater than that of the drama—and I was now convinced that it should be reserved for use in some stark crisis of the under-privileged, in general the poor and despised of earth, who were everywhere being nailed to the cross of profit at the behest of the moneyed interests.

But that incident did not close *Life's* doors to me; on the contrary, as time went on, Mr. Mitchell seemed even more receptive to my work than before. Had it come to an argument, however, I felt now that I could hold my own. Because of the training I was getting in the Cooper Union debating class I was more and more able to justify my point of view.

Despite *Life's* occasional anti-Semitic slant, its editor had reverence for that Jew whose other name is Christianity. In conversation with me Mr. Mitchell once said: "The average business man finds one great fault with Jesus; he thinks it too bad that he wasn't practical."

"That would make a strong cartoon," I answered. "A picture of a group of business men calling Christ to account for being an impractical man."

He told me to go ahead and draw it. I did, and he voiced his approval and sent a prompt check in payment. Yet I could see that his sense of good taste was a little upset by the finished drawing. Week after week I watched the pages of *Life* hoping to see it appear, but it didn't, though later work of mine continued to be used. More than once Mr. Mitchell was apologetic, saying: "We're trying to get up nerve enough around here to publish your Christ picture."

Likely that cartoon is somewhere in the archives of unpublished works of art among the effects of Life Publishing

Company. It was drawn with enthusiasm because of its truth.

From my reading I would cull meaty phrases and maxims, and illustrate them. Batches of these quotations were printed in *Life*, under the general title "Shots at Truth." At

SHOTS AT TRUTH. Under this general title I illustrated a series of epigrams for *Life*, which ran singly. Captions for the above, in obvious order, were: "Fear follows crime and is its punishment" (Voltaire); "It is difficult to rise if your poverty is greater than your talent" (Juvenal); "The great are only great because we carry them on our shoulders; when we throw them off they sprawl upon the ground" (Montandre); "He who abuses others must not be particular about the answers he gets." (Anonymous.)

the same time I was also drawing for *Puck*, principal competitor of *Life*. My friend Bert Leston Taylor, then an editor of *Puck*, didn't think much of these "shots" in the rival weekly. One day Taylor said: "Say, Art, why don't you illustrate *Bartlett's Quotations?*" I told him that a good illustrated Bartlett would not be a bad idea, and for a long time I entertained the thought of doing *The Best of Bartlett*,

Illustrated. Had I been given any encouragement by an editor or publisher, I could have found many epigrams in Bartlett worthy of such handling. Back of this idea of illustrated quotes was the belief that if a title credited to Shakespeare or some other famous man was put under a drawing of mine, it would have more weight than any title I could devise.

In the debating class we dealt often with the doctrine of government operation of utilities. The theme appealed to me, and I joined the Municipal Ownership League and began making speeches for it around New York. This was during a political campaign. Carrying an easel and drawing paper, I would frequently illustrate my speeches with simple diagram cartoons drawn while the audience watched. Cab hire necessitated by the easel cost a good deal, and not until late in the campaign did the arrangements committee ever pay for my cabs. Being an unpaid speaker, I was considerably in the red when the campaign ended.

One of the arguments used by the opponents of municipal ownership was that it would be unjust to take away the franchise held by the utility corporations—that legally or ethically the city could not compel a corporation to forfeit such a franchise no matter how tyrannical that corporation had been.

"People who argue this way," I said in my speeches, "remind me of the small boy who bought a green pepper at a grocery, thinking it a pear. A gentleman meeting the little fellow a few blocks down the street noticed the boy screwing up his face in disgust. The gentleman said: 'What's the matter?' . . . 'Oh,' said the boy, 'I bought this for a pear and I suppose I've got to eat it.' "

Only five years earlier I had been poking fun at Hiram Pennick for his "campainin for the millenum" and "against the octipust" and now I was crusading for one of the chief demands of the Populists. And often my audiences were not much larger than the handful of listeners which I had shown following in Hiram's wake. Changing the world was a slow process; people in mental darkness were slow in seeing the light, as I had been; crusaders for the betterment of human society needed extraordinary patience.

After that local campaign I had a new burst of productive energy, for I must earn additional money and build up a financial reserve to keep my family going. The easiest material for me to sell then was the illustrated joke, which occasionally satirized the passing show, but didn't tread on individual toes as my political cartoons had done.

Thus I produced a series for *Puck* called "Things That Hit Our Funny Bone." A typical specimen of this series shows two pictures—first, Chester Van Daub, artist, painting a

ALL IS VANITY. Wife reading local paper: "Ezra Whitcomb was seen yesterday driving his new rubber-tired carriage." (Note the "Well, I guess" wiggle of that leg.)

canvas in his studio, and second, Mr. Wright Mush, critic and authority on pictures, gushing over the same canvas to some awed museum visitors. Van Daub at work says: "I d' know wha' thish picture means (*slashes on a brush-full of burnt sienna and pink*) but it looks like a Hungarian goulash. T' hell with art anyway!" . . . Mr. Wright Mush says: "Ah, this is Van Daub's 'Moonlight Splendor', a wonderful conception; the meaning of the artist is so clearly and intellectually expressed and shows such a firm grasp of his medium. As I said in my review, such a picture is born only in the brain of one who is intensely devoted to his art."

One of my dialogue pictures in *Puck* reveals people seated at two tables in a cafe. A soulful woman is saying to her escort: "Those men over there are all brilliant writers. Wouldn't it be a treat just to hear their conversation?" . . . And one of the brilliant writers is reminiscing just then: "Gus, do you remember those sausages we had in Berlin? Talk about—but say, they don't know *how* to cook in this country!"

Other illustrated jokes I sold to *Puck* dealt with The Reward of Virtue, showing the lawyer who resolved never to defend a client he believed guilty (and thus remained poor) and the lawyer who didn't (and got rich); Street Signs in Plenty Where Nobody Goes (in the realty developments) and No Signs Where Everybody Goes (in the center of a city); Santa Claus discovering the convenience of using a dumb-waiter instead of a chimney; and automobiles scaring farmers' horses.

I note that once I poked fun at my own back-to-nature ideas, working out in pictures this theme: "Henry Wilbur Puddin reads Dr. Dippy's book, 'Getting Back to the Earth', and tries the bare-foot exercises recommended (doing them at night in the snow). He gets back to earth in three weeks." His tombstone read: "He had a gentle trusting nature."

In the editorial waiting rooms I would meet other cartoonists and illustrators and exchange small talk with them. There was no other regular meeting place to which I had entree. Cartoonists and writers didn't know much about each other's personalities then. There were few social or fraternal organizations in New York which I could have joined that were not too expensive. Thomas Nast once had urged me to come into the Players' Club, but the cost was too much—and the Salmagundi Club likewise was beyond the reach of a struggling free-lance. Bills that I couldn't pay have always been a big part of the hell that has surrounded me in most of my years.

In a later period, when I happened to be making money above expenses, I was almost persuaded by C. D. Gibson and Frank Crowninshield to become a member of the exclusive Coffee House Club. Here I could have chinned with Joseph H. Choate, Chester H. Aldrich, George Arliss, Winthrop Ames, Paul Manship, and others, and no doubt it would have been much to my liking. But I had learned to avoid the club habit, with its monthly dues staring one in the face like a bugaboo in the night.

Some of us got together now and then at dinners—particularly in Chinatown on Saturday evenings. Robert Ryland, Sydney Shaw, Andrew Schwartz, Howard Smith, and other kindred souls would attend—all painters, and some of them *Prix de Rome* winners and others with prize records. At those informal affairs there was sparkling talk and keen repartee. And after the chow mein and trimmings had been disposed of, and many cups of tea had been downed, we would walk home through dim back streets to our uptown studios.

These gatherings grew larger as the years went by—and the last time I took part Mahonri Young and John Held Jr., both from Salt Lake City, and many more of the rising generation of painters and illustrators were there. The group had expanded to fifty or more—too many for real *cameraderie*. With only six or a dozen at a table the talk was intimate, and all of us could be in on it. But when the number of diners multiplied the Chinatown dinners became confusing. Our friendly little exchanges had become institutionalized, and for me the lure was gone. An announcement of one of those later conclaves described it rightly as "a dinner to make believe we are having a better time than we are having."

And I met a few painters in those days whom I had read about in my youth—for instance, Walter Shirlaw (a great artist now neglected)—and was introduced to John LaFarge once when he was out walking with his Japanese servant. I knew the picturesque DeLeftwitch Dodge, who was one of the promising wizards of sensual and fantastic murals even in the days when we were both at Julien's in Paris. The last time I saw him he was teaching at the Art Students' League —and in one of those casual street talks with him it was plain that the tendency of the younger generation to see some merit in the new cult of Picasso and the other modernists aggravated him.

After our breakup, Elizabeth and Kate and the children remained on the farm for about six months. Then they departed for California to make it their home. Both sisters had been left small legacies by their Uncle Len.

We kept up a fairly regular correspondence in which the

progress of the two boys was the principal topic. Several years after going to the west coast, Elizabeth indicated that she would like to sell her share in the Chestnut Ridge place, and I agreed to buy it and pay for it in installments during the following year.

Around 1910 Elizabeth and the youngsters made a visit to Wisconsin, and my father expressed pride in the brightness of the boys and the consideration they showed for their mother.

Chapter 25

ALL TOO SLOWLY I SEE THE LIGHT

FAITHFULLY I continued to attend Cooper Union. Each Saturday night we debated such subjects as the tariff, immigration, woman suffrage, public ownership of utilities, taxation, states' rights, and others of timely interest.

GRADUATION NIGHT AT COOPER UNION, 1906. Class in oratory and debate. I rise to the occasion.

In the spring of 1906 I graduated, on the platform where Lincoln made his historic speech just before he became President. That speech in which he expressed what was then an unpopular view among the best people of the East, that the federal government had the right to exercise control over slavery. "Never let us be slandered from our duty," he said. ". . . Let us have faith that right makes might, and in that faith let us to the end dare to do our duty as we understand it."

And from this same platform more than half a century later, President-elect William Howard Taft had been confronted with a challenging question:

"What would you advise a man to do who is out of a job and whose family is starving because he can't get work?"

There was little comfort for the unemployed in Taft's answer:

"God knows. Such a man has my deepest sympathy. . . ."

On the night of my graduation, there was a debate: *"Resolved, that a tax on income is vital to the welfare of the American people."* I was selected as one of the four debaters from a class of more than 100. I was at my best that evening, and our side, the affirmative, won. The late Judge Morgan J. O'Brien was judge of the contest, and presented the diplomas.

I enjoyed the mind exercise I was getting in those days; there were thrills in it such as I imagine people have when they fly in airplanes. Disappointments too. Sometimes I would read an illuminating book, and having finished it, would lean back in my chair with the satisfied feeling that I knew enough to last me for awhile. Next night, perhaps, I would hear a lecture by some better informed individual than I could ever hope to be, and would realize that I had climbed only the foothills of understanding.

I stocked up with Socialist pamphlets, and read, or tried to read them. Often they were in language too deep for me; in technical terms familiar to European Socialists, but not to unconverted Americans. But it never occurred to me to be against Socialism or any other theory because it originated in Europe. I felt that such an objection was just plain silly; that "alien theory", "imported doctrine", and such phrases of contempt were deliberately coined to discredit a growing cause. If this was good reasoning, I figured, why accept anything that originated outside of our own country? That our prevailing religion came from Asia—and many of our accepted political and best scientific ideas had their origin in

Europe—seemed to me ample justification for free trade in theories.

For several years the scathing articles by Lincoln Steffens under the general title of "The Shame of our Cities" had been appearing in *McClure's Magazine*, and they exposed the bribed and the bribing of municipal government. Seemingly one city was as rotten as another. And Ida Tarbell had written "The History of Standard Oil," and turned the searchlight on the methods by which John D. Rockefeller acquired his fortune.

Thomas W. Lawson, outspoken Boston stockbroker, had held the center of the American stage for more than two years with his "Frenzied Finance" series in *Everybody's Magazine*. With spectacular wrath, he tore the feathers out of the buzzards of Wall Street, showing up their evil practices and raising hell generally among his own tribe. This lone bird sought to reform the predatory birds all around him. *Everybody's* leaped to an average sale of 750,000 copies during that exposé. Lawson's brilliant and bitter articles aroused great public indignation against Wall Street. Then they petered out with the crusader discouraged and financially crushed.

Upton Sinclair had come along, a young man with a mighty determination, and against heavy odds forced the publication of his novel, *The Jungle*, based upon his firsthand observations of the conditions under which meat was packed in the Chicago stockyards and under which the workers there lived. And President Theodore Roosevelt, who had testified that he would as soon have eaten his old hat as the canned meat furnished the American troops by the Chicago packers in 1898, appointed a commission to investigate Sinclair's charges. Ella Reeve Bloor was a member of this body. Brisbane lauded the book in two editorials, saying "The Jungle" had done for modern industrial slavery what "Uncle Tom's Cabin" did for black slavery, and had done it better. And the *New York American* began running the Sinclair novel serially.

Many persons lost their taste for meat for a long time because of the horrors shown in that story. Then the newspapers reported that conditions had been cleaned up in the stockyards by the new inspection service installed by the Department of Agriculture at the urging of Roosevelt's commission, and the public clamor died down. But the publicity given to the investigation had painted a dark picture of the whole meat industry in the minds of millions of Americans.*

Moyer, Haywood, and Pettibone were kidnapped in Denver and taken to Boise, Idaho, for trial on a charge of assassinating former Governor Steunenberg with dynamite. The stories that came through on this in the daily press for months gave the impression that these men and their associates in the Western Federation of Miners were red-handed murderers; it was easy to believe that, if one heard nothing of the other

ELLA REEVE BLOOR

side of the story, clear up to the time of the defendants' acquittal.

But there were protest meetings in behalf of the defense in New York, and I attended one of these, where Eugene V. Debs spoke, and he brought home to us who listened the black story of the frame-up against the accused, which was designed to crush unionism among the metal miners of the West. Debs was dynamic as he denounced the mining magnates whose agents had seized the three union leaders in Colo-

The Jungle had a profound effect upon me when I read it in 1906. Sinclair gives a graphic picture of the tenacious nature of the giant evil he tried to blot out, in *The Brass Check* and *American Outpost*. Recalling in the latter book, in 1932, that he aimed at the public's heart and by accident hit it in the stomach, he says: "I am supposed to have helped clean up the Yards and improve the country's meat supply—though this is mostly delusion. But nobody even pretends to believe that I improved the condition of the stockyards workers. They have no unions to speak of, and their wages are, in relation to the cost of living, every bit as low as they were twenty-eight years ago. Yet I don't want to be pessimistic. . . . Some day we shall . . . see the sprouting of the seed we have been scattering all these weary years."

rado without a warrant, carried them into another state, and held them incommunicado for days while the prosecution was building its case against them. His voice shrilled with contempt as he cited Theodore Roosevelt's characterization of the defendants and their friends as "undesirable citizens."

What a nation for Washington and Lincoln to look upon, if they could have returned for a visit then!

Nineteen Seven brought a panic in Wall Street, and hard times again. Factories were closing, countless thousands of men out of work. That autumn a mass-meeting of unemployed was announced under Socialist auspices to take place

ALEXANDER IRVINE

in Union Square. A permit for this was refused by the police, but the crowd gathered anyhow. Policemen poured into the Square, on horse and on foot, and began clubbing men and women right and left, and riding them down.

In the midst of all this a bomb exploded—almost a re-enactment of the Chicago Haymarket scene—one youth being killed and many persons wounded. The police "identified" the young fellow who was killed as the bomb-thrower. His name was given as Sig Silverstein, and he was described variously as a Socialist, Anarchist, and Nihilist. One of those knocked down by the explosion and then clubbed by a policeman was Alexander Irvine, a young Episcopal clergyman and Socialist, who on Sunday evenings conducted an open forum in the Church of the Ascension on Fifth Avenue, where Dr. Percy Stickney Grant was rector. Irish-born, Irvine

Puck, 1909

A contemporary is publishing a series of pictures entitled "American Mothers." Don't forget this one at the right.

had been raised in poverty. He wrote of his life in a book, "From the Bottom Up."

I went to the forum on the following Sunday, and heard him tell of his experience at the Union Square meeting, after which he explained how the capitalists used the police against the producers of their wealth, how they threw the latter out of jobs without pity. Being an emotional speaker and a Christian minister, Irvine was an arousing voice in the wilderness of New York churches, convincing all his listeners except of course the wealthy members.

On various occasions I attended that forum, where speakers on both sides could be heard, and always came away with a clearer insight into the class struggle. Once a bourgeois-minded gentleman was speaking on the virtue of charity. It was winter-time, and he said he had just seen a beautiful illustration of that virtue on Eleventh Street near Broadway. His heart was thrilled as he watched a long line of hungry men receiving bread free of charge.

"The true Christian spirit," he shouted. "My friends, it was beautiful!"

Whereupon a lean figure, who looked like one of "those incorrigible Socialists", got up and said: "Then the longer the line the more beautiful it is?"

At that time I had not thought of drawing any cartoons for the existing Socialist and kindred publications, nor had anyone asked me to. The current periodicals of that type included *Wilshire's Magazine,* published in New York; the *Appeal to Reason* issuing from Girard, Kansas; the *Chicago Daily Socialist; Mother Earth,* Anarchist organ, the *International Socialist Review,* the *Weekly People,* organ of the Socialist Labor Party, and *Wayland's Monthly,* also published in Girard.

I knew where my sympathies lay; but was not yet ready to speak out, although Darwin Meserole and other friends were saying: "With your equipment as an artist, you ought to be a Socialist." Instead I was holding on to such established publications as were receptive to my work, and endeavoring to put across pointed cartoons which would in some way help the cause of Socialism. For *Life, Puck,* and *Judge* would take pictures aimed at firetrap tenements, John

THE IN AND OUT OF OUR PENAL SYSTEM.
The law against them.
The world against them.

Puck, 1910

D. Rockefeller, child labor, grafting public officials, sweat shops, deified money, exploiters of the poor, and related evils.

Meanwhile Arthur Brisbane occasionally reprinted cartoons of mine from *Life* or *Puck* and made them the basis of editorials, sometimes agreeing with my contention, but quite as often as not pointing out that there was much to be said on the other side, and that Mr. Young, "able and well meaning", had erred in thinking that his cartoon was as true as it appeared to be. Now and then Brisbane voiced beliefs that were part of the Socialist party program, but quieted the fears of those among his readers who might object by saying that "perhaps ten thousand years hence these ideas will be adopted by society."

And as I moved farther into the field of social satire Brisbane called upon me to do special work for the *Journal*, and subsequently for the *Sunday American*, when he began doing editorials for what was then the World Events section. My cartoons for this purpose were drawn for full-width use across the top of the page. In that day practically all American dailies were seven columns wide instead of eight as now.

I was striking at effects rather than at causes, and it was never possible to point to the institution which I was now convinced lay at the bottom of all these dark manifestations. Once in a moment of excess confidence, I labeled a fat silk-hatted figure in a picture with the word *Capitalism*.

"We can't do that," Hearst's principal editor said. "Call him *Greed*. That means the same thing, and it won't get us into trouble."

It was around 1910 that I realized I belonged with the Socialists in their fight to destroy capitalism. I had been a long time arriving at that conclusion. Often I have been asked: "What made you a radical?" It was no thunderbolt revelation that hit me like the one which struck Paul of Tarsus. Many elements went into my decision. For years the truth about the underlying cause of the exploitation and misery of the world's multitudes had been knocking at the door of my consciousness, but not until that year did it begin to sound clearly.

Earlier I had devoted a great deal of enthusiasm in certain periods to profit-sharing and public ownership, but I

CHARLES EDWARD RUSSELL. The Socialist Party used this drawing as a poster when he ran for the New York Governorship in 1910.

saw now that while these were moves in the right direction, the ultimate solution of society's greatest problem was the co-operative commonwealth, with production for use as the first point in the program, so that no human would ever again have to suffer for want of food, clothing, or shelter.

Seeing this, I began to draw cartoons hitting directly at capitalism, placing them where I could, or saving them against a day when a friendly editor might accept them. I watched for chances to hook up current injustices to that underlying cause. Mitchell of *Life* welcomed some of these cartoons, although he held that there was a limit to how many of that type he could intersperse in his pages. But in those days, for a magazine that had not declared war upon the moneyed interests, *Life* did pretty well.

One of my drawings used by Mitchell, which now seems daring for that time, bore the one-word caption, "Capitalism," later reprinted with the title, "The Last Supper." High on a precipice, symbolic of his lofty position in world affairs, sits a grossly fat gentleman at a table, which is littered with the leavings from a rich feast which he has just gorged. As he leans back in his chair to drain a big golden bowl for his final fill, the chair is dangerously close to teetering over the brink.

One day after I had turned definitely leftward, I ran into Eugene Wood on the street. I had not seen him since our Chicago days. He expressed gratification that I had become Socialistic in my thinking and said: "Everybody will see the light some day." It was an exhilarating discovery to find that a farm boy from my mid-west country who could write effectively also had some "queer" notions about political economy. Most of the many writers and artists in New York then never bothered their heads about economics or political trends. I felt that I was not so eccentric after all—if Eugene Wood, whose humorous stories about his Ohio home folks were popular features of *Everybody's Magazine*, could accept the Marxian philosophy.

He was a man of true nobility, self-sacrificing, giving everything he had to the cause. As writer, speaker, and teacher he served valiantly. He wrote Socialist pamphlets, spoke in political campaigns, and for several terms taught English and pronunciation to large classes of foreigners in the Rand

SOME DAY. A prophetic cartoon.

School. Simultaneously with that teaching, he worked on the copy desk of the *Daily Call*. . . . The death of his wife was a heavy blow to him; they had been devoted to each other. After that loss we used to meet occasionally in the Union Square district, where we both lived; and his sadness deepened as the months went by. The one joy left in his life was his daughter Peggy, the actress, in whose talent he took great pride.

Like myself, he was born amid the moral restraints of a small community, and was a bit timid about some of the pictured nudes and articles on sex in the *Masses,* and resigned from the staff when some of the numbers displeased him. His best humorous writings in that magazine were burlesques of the old stories in the Bible.

Balfour Ker is remembered for his powerful social satires, and above all for a certain picture entitled *From the Depths.* It shows the terror of revelers in a palace of pleasure as a fist is thrust up through the floor by one of the toilers below whose labor enables the revelers to exist. This has often been reprinted, and has been the subject of many editorials and sermons, but few people nowadays know where it first appeared. It was one of the illustrations which Ker made for a novel called *The Silent War,* written by John Ames Mitchell and published in 1906. The theme was the class struggle.

I find a letter which Ker sent me from London in December, 1910, which has bearing on that period, and I feel that it is well worth including here.

So you have joined in the good fight (Ker wrote)—I knew you would sooner or later. It takes a long time sometimes to just *see* the proposition right, but once that is done the rest of the way is sure if rough. Well, the long time it takes us to see it shows how much the future of Socialism depends on the mass of the people being educated in the idea. Constant reiteration, from press, pulpit, picture, book, platform, everywhere, in every conceivable way, whether it be labeled Socialism or not. We must din it into the public ear, eye, nose, stomach, and purse. You remember Mirabeau said that there were three essentials in convincing oratory: "The first is repetition; the second repetition; and the third repetition." I guess that's about right—and would apply to Socialist propaganda.

No human being could stand out very long against the arguments for the necessity of the complete socialization of the economic machine. It's our business to keep hammering away. And Gosh! But you have a bully old sledge-hammer in that pen of yours. Your work stands head and shoulders above any other work of its kind in the U.S.A. It ranks with the little fine stuff in cartooning in Germany and France. I've received *Life* regularly since I left the land of the free—and have got a pretty good idea of its relative merits and demerits. It's a damn bright able little sheet, and shows up well even at 3,000 miles distance. And your stuff is about the strongest of it all, much the strongest drawing, and it tickles me that you have "seen de light," Brer Young. . . .

How is that capitalist room-mate of yours? Have you converted him yet? . . . Vlag gives me great accounts of his co-op society. Co-operation is an important factor over here, and I think Pete deserves all sorts of credit if he gets it going in the U.S.A. with a Socialist tag on it too. I was a member until recently of one of the largest co-ops in England, but I found that the thing was not really democratically run, but run by and in the interest of a small clique of officials and share-holders, so I cleared out. It was founded purely as a profit-sharing concern, and called co-operative to draw members. Even under those circumstances they gave far better value for the money than the ordinary business houses.

It's my private opinion that only through labor unions, industrial unionism, and some form, or forms, of co-operation, will the people receive the necessary instruction in the common sense and economy of complete socialization of productive machinery.

You should have heard yours truly haranguing British crowds on the foolishness of 'protection' as a cure for unemployment, and on the danger of trusts, etc.—pretty near got my head punched several times for butting into 'tariff reform' speeches and meetings.

I've met some damn nice fellows here in the movement. They compare well with any bunch of men in any profession or class, these fellows working in the dark corners for the better day. Man for man, they are far better than the average gink or capitalist. And some of them are real heroes—men who could get to almost any position they wanted if they would just drop their propaganda work, men who cannot be bought, scared, bluffed, nor humbugged. Men of very real ability and really splendidly educated, plugging away day and night year in and year out educating, arguing, talking, talking, talking the truth into the almost hopelessly indifferent workers. Surely something must some day come of such effort—let's hope it comes soon.

Do you still attend classes at the Rand School? I haven't had a chance for lectures since I came here. I've put in about three hours a day studying drawing though in different schools, and I'm starting to paint again tomorrow with some fellows, one of whom is a cracking fine painter, an old pupil of Whistler's named Clifford Adams. Hope to learn lots, not that I want ever to paint a la Whistler, but Adams knows Whistler's "science" of painting down to the ground, and has offered to teach me. I'm going to keep on studying this time I'm over here until I'm a thoroughly well equipped craftsman. I'm afraid that means some years yet of hard work, but I'm going to stick it. The worst of the damned business is that I have to keep doing pot-boiling, which lengthens the time necessary more than I can really spare. However, my "comrade", as you called her, is of the right sort and willing to rough it and even starve if necessary, so we live very economically and I do as little illustrating and as much studying as possible, and methinks I've learned a thing or two since getting here.

When I look over the field of modern art I have to blush for the painters, a lot of silly upper-class parasites, and yours truly is going to try to show that a painter can be a Socialist and use his brush like the splendid weapon it is, and as hundreds have used their pens, for freedom and light. Gee whizz! Doesn't that sound big? And it's little me—talking. However, since you are a Socialist, I don't mind "talking big" to you. Socialism makes us think of big things and long to do them whether we can or not.

One evening I went to hear Emma Goldman, out of curiosity. She was an emotional speaker, but not nearly so dangerous looking as she had been pictured by the newspapers. Her talk was a bit bookish, and she looked like a *hausfrau,* and more maternal in appearance and manner than destructive. She carried her audience along with her like a mother hen followed by a brood of chicks. Sometimes, however, she rose to heights of flaming anger as she cited crimes of the police against workers or the use of federal or state troops to break strikes.

Chapter 26

AT LAST I KNOW WHERE I'M GOING

NOW I was past forty years of age and I knew definitely where I was going. I was in such a state as our Christian forebears would have called "righteous indignation." My humorous sense had to keep reminding me to look out for fanaticism. However, I was filled with a deep resentment against the social wrongs that were manifest wherever one turned to look. Henceforth my drawing pen must be devoted—in so far as circumstances would permit—to attacking the System which engendered so much woe.

From Twenty-fourth Street I had moved to 9 East Seventeenth Street, on the edge of Greenwich Village, then the radical center of artistic and economic ferment—in a sense the American *Montmartre*. Here I occupied a large skylight studio with my friend Howard Smith, painter and commercial artist. We had to walk up three flights, but I regarded this as good exercise.

There was a new zest for me in just living. Days of real doing had set in. But I still had my own economic problem, which must be solved anew each week. Whatever recognition my talent had had in the few years since I had swung to an avowed espousal of "the cause", none of the radical publications could see any point (if they ever thought of it) in turning me loose against the System and paying me for it, not even if I were able to bring about the industrial commonwealth singlehanded. What money they had went to business upkeep and to sustain editors and writers expert at spreading out columns of wordage on the difference between the *tweedledee* of their wing of the movement and the *tweedledum* of the other wing. Of course these editorial writers had to know Karl Marx, the materialist conception of history, and how to use invective—with such equipment they would write a thousand words to say what a good cartoon could say at a glance. So I had to keep going financially by continuing to draw for the established periodicals.

When I received a good check for a Socialistic cartoon, such as those which *Life* occasionally used, I was as pleased as the Irishman who wrote to his friend in the old country: "Jim, come on over. I'm tearing down a Protestant church and getting paid for it besides." My main support came from the sale of comics to *Life* and *Judge,* with now and then a

PIET VLAG, founder of *The Masses.*

job of illustrating for *Collier's* or some other successful magazine. Once in a while, too, I would get a check for a cartoon illustrating a labor leaflet which would just about cover my week's laundry bill. Add to these a few pictures for book jackets at intervals, and my days were well occupied.

Late in 1910 Piet Vlag, a young Dutchman whom I had met at the Rand School of Social Science, then at 112 East 19th Street, came to my studio and said he was going to start a magazine. He had a restaurant in the basement of the school building. If you saw Piet once you would never forget him. He had the large nose you see in photographs of Dutchmen along the Zuyder Zee, black penetrating eyes, and an irresistible smile. With contagious ardor he explained the policy of the projected magazine and sketched its format. It would have to do with co-operatives in which Vlag was directly interested, Socialism, art, and literature, among other things. And Piet had a backer for the enterprise—Rufus W. Weeks, vice-president of the New York Life Insurance Company.

"Will you contribute to the magazine?" he asked.

"Of course," I said, "here's one now." And I handed Piet a cartoon lately finished.

Various names for the new periodical were suggested, and the question was discussed at some length before all those concerned agreed upon calling it *The Masses*, a name proposed by Thomas Seltzer, who was chosen as the editor. Mr. Weeks was ready to pay the cost of printing and engraving for "a reasonable length of time." Vlag, always an enthusiast in anything he undertook, figured that in six months the enterprise ought to be solidly on its feet. He plunged into it with admirable industry, spending all his waking hours in visiting writers and artists, pledging them to contribute, and talking about the virtues of the forthcoming magazine to everyone he met.

There was no mention of paying contributors, and certainly none of us expected pay. For *The Masses* promised to be a publication for the release of socially conscious anti-capitalist literary and artistic expressions for which there was hardly any demand by the well printed news-stand variety of magazine. And there were artists and writers who felt the need of such an outlet—pay or no pay.

January, 1911, saw *The Masses* launched. It was designed, the publishers explained, to help improve the conditions of the working people, *"whether they want it or not."* Eugene Wood was listed as president of the publishing company, Hayden Carruth as vice-president, and Andre Tridon as secretary.

That first issue included articles on the co-operative movement by W. J. Ghent and Eugene Wood, one on the cost of living by Gustavus Myers, a cartoon by Cesare, and two cartoons by myself. One of mine dealt with the evolution of the store, forecasting a day when the vulture of capitalism would be kicked off the top of retail business and ownership and operation would be taken over by the people for the common good.

While the quality of the material in the new magazine varied widely, some of the offerings had strength, and I was optimistic. There would be improvement as the months went on. Eugene Debs, always ready to aid any effort to extend the Socialist press, lauded it.

Charles A. Winter made the cover drawing. This remarkable artist has been deplorably overlooked since those days when he had but recently returned from study abroad. His work showed a strong classic influence, and Dante Gabriel Rossetti at his best could not have surpassed the richness of his color. Doubtless those superb pictures, which have had all too little attention, are somewhere piled up for release, some time—after awhile.

Each month Piet Vlag would hurry into my studio and say: "Vell, Art, ve got to have a picture for the *Messes.*" His pronunciation was delightful, and I was sometimes worried lest Eugene Wood would take Piet in hand and smooth out his speech into pure English. If I had nothing suitable lying around I would draw a cartoon touching on some current topic. A theme agreed upon, I often found these pictures much easier to draw than those I was selling to the conventional magazines. If you are getting paid for work most editors, like true business men, make it a rule to find fault. Anyhow they offer no praise, for fear you will think they need you and that your money is earned too easily. With Vlag there was no haggling over the way in which I had interpreted an idea. It was up to me, and I felt that an audience was waiting to see what would be in the next issue. For the first time in my life I could cut loose and express my own unhampered point of view.

Louis Untermeyer was contributing poems which dealt with the realities of the class struggle, but which sounded a note of hope. There were articles showing how the workers were robbed through exploitation by employers as the cost of living went up; others against the Boy Scouts, which were viewed as a potential military organization; and attacks on

JUST PEOPLE.

child labor. A good deal was printed about co-operatives. Portraits of contributors were occasionally used with their articles. Vlag's writings had some punch in them, but were not in any sense distinguished. Rufus Weeks's offerings were inclined to be too leisurely philosophical to be appropriate in a periodical designed to appeal to the working class.

Weeks was a quiet, dignified gentleman, an avowed Socialist with an inquiring mind. Rockwell Kent, who knew him better than I, told me stories about him. Rockwell said that on election days in Tarrytown, where Weeks lived, the family carriage would be driven to the polling place by his Negro coachman, who also was a Socialist. Together Weeks and the coachman would go in and cast their ballots for the straight Socialist ticket. Being a vice-president of a big insurance company, I suspect that Rufus Weeks, to his business associates, was one of those fellows of whom people say: "He means well, but he's kind of impractical and up in the clouds."

For a year and a half the *Masses* appeared regularly, but did not become anywhere near being self-supporting, and Mr. Weeks's enthusiasm waned and finally came to a full stop. Vlag's co-operative stores were suffering from too much individualism, and he had lost his usual buoyancy. But he was busy trying to solve the problem of survival for "the *Messes*", and he went to Chicago to look up a man reputed to have a lot of money and a generous nature. That man had just left for a trip around the world, and Vlag worked out a plan to merge his publication with a Socialist women's magazine then appearing in the midwestern metropolis. Impulsively he promised the parties of the other part to throw all of us contributors into the combination. When he returned to New York with a wide smile of satisfaction over having fixed up everything for the future, he was surprised to learn that we artists and writers who had been giving time and energy to keeping the *Masses* alive did not approve of his plan.

There was no September issue in 1912, and Charles Winter, who had been an active contributor, called a small group together for a crisis meeting in his studio. Those present included Alice Winter, John and Dolly Sloan, Louis Untermeyer, Eugene Wood, Maurice Becker, Glenn Coleman, William Washburn Nutting, H. T. Turner, and myself. We were unanimous in holding that the magazine must go on. Somehow we would find the money to pay the cost, from month to month. But who would be editor? There were no candidates for the job among the conferees.

I nominated Max Eastman, who had lately been ousted from a Columbia professorship for his outspoken opinions on the social conflict in classroom lectures. Max and I had met at a Jack London dinner, and we had discussed the possibility of building up the *Masses* into a magazine which would have the bold tone and high quality of *Simplicissimus, Jugend,* Steinlen's *Gil Blas,* and *Assiette au Beurre,* all of which were inspiring to the world's rising young artists. To show how Max could handle words and ideas, I read to the conference a magazine article he had written, describing with charming humor how he had organized the first Men's League for Woman's Suffrage in New York. All the others acquiesced in the nomination, and we all signed a letter to Max, which said: "You are elected editor of the Masses, no pay."

Max was not keen about taking a no-pay editorship of a literary magazine, for at that stage it was to have a literary front, but he thought he might make the job serve a useful purpose, and presently consented to come in. In private conversations with him we who had assumed control made it clear that of course he could have a salary, even a good one, if we succeeded in developing the magazine into a self-sustaining property. But the main thing was the co-operative principle in editing the contents—art and literature. Though we of the executive board were eager to resume publication, it took time to raise the necessary money and to whip into shape text and pictures for an issue that would measure up to the standard we had visualized. So it was December before the *Masses* blossomed again, now with a colored cover, a new make-up, and a fresh note of hope.

Members of the staff listed were: *Literature:* Max Eastman, Eugene Wood, Hayden Carruth, Inez Haynes Gilmore, Ellis O. Jones, Horatio Winslow, Thomas Seltzer, Mary Heaton Vorse, Joseph O'Brien, Louis Untermeyer, Leroy Scott. *Art:* John Sloan, Art Young, Alice Beach Winter, Alexander Popini, H. T. Turner, Charles A. Winter, Maurice Becker, William Washburn Nutting.

And in announcing the revival of the *Masses*, and its policy, we said:

> We do not enter the field of any Socialist or other magazine now published, or to be published. We shall have no further part in the factional disputes within the Socialist party; we are opposed to the dogmatic spirit which creates and sustains these disputes. Our appeal will be to the masses, both Socialist and non-Socialist, with entertainment, education, and the livelier kinds of propaganda.

In February, 1913, the contents of the magazine included two drawings by Maurice Becker and a "little testimonial from Boston" in the form of a letter from the Library Club House saying: "Stop sending us the *Masses*; we never ordered it and do not want it." And John Reed, new on the scene, had written a further statement of policy in collaboration with Max Eastman, which now appeared:

> This magazine is owned and published co-operatively by its editors. It has no dividends to pay, and nobody is trying to make any money out of it. A revolutionary and not a reform magazine; a magazine with a sense of humor and no respect for the respectable; frank, arrogant, impertinent, searching for the true causes; a magazine directed against rigidity and dogma wherever it is found; printing what is too naked or true for a money-making press; a magazine whose final policy is to do what it pleases and conciliate nobody, not even its readers.

Reed became a contributing editor in March, and other new writers and artists came in with us as time moved along, replacing some who for one reason or another withdrew. These additional members of the literary and art boards included Floyd Dell, Arthur Bullard, Frank Bohn, G. S. Sparks, Cornelia Barns, Stuart Davis, William English Walling, B. Russell Hertz, Robert Carlton Brown, Glenn O. Coleman, K. R. Chamberlain, E. G. Miska, H. J. Glintenkamp, Edmund McKenna, Arturo Giovannitti, George Bellows, Howard Brubaker, Charles W. Wood, John Barber, Boardman Robinson, Robert Minor, and Frank Walts.

Having a free hand on the *Masses* to attack the capitalist system and its beneficiaries loosed energies within me of which I had been unaware. I felt as many a Crusader must have felt long ago as he set forth to rescue the Holy Land from the infidels. For the first time I could draw cartoons striking openly at those who took the best years of the worker and then threw him on the scrap-heap. I didn't have to think about whether a picture of mine might offend an advertiser and thus violate a business-office policy.

And one was not confined to assailing generalities; I could and did cast my pictorial shafts at individuals who symbolized the system—financiers, politicians, editors, and others. It was gratifying to have a responsive audience, and also occasionally to hear yelps of pain from the persons attacked. They would register their indignation in public speeches or in newspaper interviews in which the militant labor press would be condemned as a "menace to decent society."

Reference might be made to many of the pictures which I drew for the *Masses* in the next seven years, but it will suffice to mention here a few that attracted wide attention.

"Speaking of bandits, the American soldiers are on the wrong trail" was the title of one cartoon which plainly implied that Pershing's troops should go to Wall Street instead of spending their time hunting Pancho Villa in Mexico.

Three pictures on one page, *all alike,* bore these labels: "Composite photo of boards of patriot organization boosting preparedness. . . . Composite photo of boards of munition corporations. . . . Composite photo of foreign exploitation corporations."

I depicted a preacher exclaiming to a workingman: "You must be born again!" and the worker, tired of the struggle, replying: "Once is enough, Doc!"

"Turning to Christianity" was the title of a scene based on a newspaper interview in which a missionary declared that "one effect of the war (in 1916) has been to increase the individual Turk's respect for Christianity." My drawing revealed a church with cannon sticking from the steeple, a tractor-mortar on the roof, and a big cannon barrel pointed from out of a window.

Early in the *Masses* venture I contributed a drawing which I knew would not be acceptable to magazines which

October 26, 1912   **THE**   Price 5 Cents

The Coming Nation

A JOURNAL OF THINGS DOING AND TO BE DONE

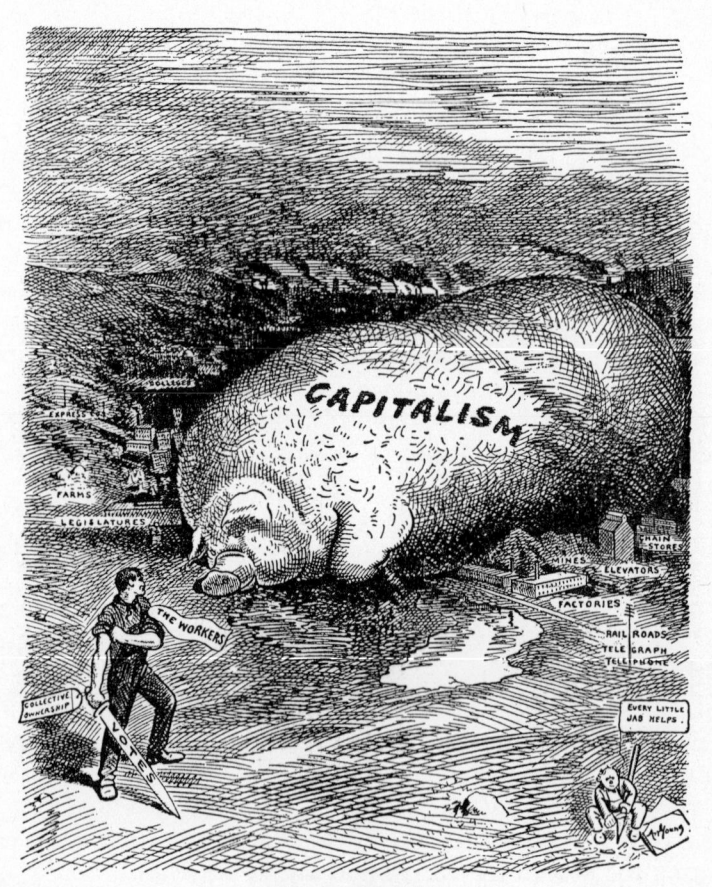

Time to Butcher
For the sake of the beast itself as well as the people

had to uphold the genteel tradition. Some ideas were just bad taste, and none of the old-line editors would think of offending elderly women subscribers. . . . In this production of mine a small boy and his sister are walking along a street in the slums on a star-lit night. Jimmie looks up at the sky and says: "Gee! Annie, look at the stars, thick as bed-bugs!"

But the cartoon which is best known of all the many I made for the *Masses*, and which has been reprinted around the world, portrays a workingman just home from a day's toil. As he slumps in a chair he says:

" 'I gorry, I'm tired!"
And his wife retorts: "There you go! You're tired! Here I be a-standin' over a hot stove all day, an' you workin' in a nice cool sewer."

Editors reprinting that picture and text have persistently altered the opening words to read "By gorry" or "Begorry", evidently assuming that " 'I gorry" was a misprint. But that was the form in which it originally appeared in the *Masses*, and that was the way I had heard that expletive in the brogue of an old Irishman back in Wisconsin.

I found another outlet for creative expression in 1911 and later in the *Coming Nation*, a weekly published by J. A. Wayland and Fred D. Warren in Girard, Kansas. This magazine displayed my cartoons boldly, and now and then I wrote and illustrated an editorial for it.

In its columns, on July 22, 1911, Charles Edward Russell gave me special credit for the corrective effect of a cartoon which I had done some three years before for *Puck*. Writing at length about the episode, Russell said:

"Trinity Church in New York City has now destroyed 156 of the rotten tenements that it owned on January 1, 1908. . . . When the character of the tenements was first disclosed and denounced, the church officers arose in righteous wrath and vehemently denied every charge. . . . Everybody was a liar that said a word against Holy Trinity. . . . The public was assured on all sides that the tenements were among the best in the world and above reproach.

"But almost at once the corporation began quietly to pull down these admired structures. Nothing was ever said in the press about this, but the work was steadily pushed. . . . They . . . will breed tuberculosis and typhoid no more.

"What settled the fate of the Trinity tenement was a cartoon by Art Young. He called it 'Holy Trinity', and it is one of the great cartoons of history. From it there was no

HOLY TRINITY. Charles Edward Russell credited this cartoon of mine with forcing Trinity Church to destroy a vast number of disease-breeding tenements which it owned in 1908.

escape; the wardens might fume and the corporation might dodge and twist; whichever way they turned, there before them rose that tremendous thing, thrusting a finger into their faces: 'Holy Trinity'—Sanctimony praying while in the dreadful tenements below men, women, and little children suffered, and from their sufferings arose the money that made Trinity rich. Terrible picture! And terrible truth! No one that ever looked upon that great cartoon could thereafter get it out of his mind; it had the irresistible and convincing touch of truth and genius, and it did the business."

The cartoon referred to was drawn at a time when Russell was crusading in *Everybody's Magazine* against Trinity's ownership of those disease-laden tenements. He went on to say in the *Coming Nation* that I could feel that thousands of people in New York were better housed and more comfortable because of the power of my pencil. That commendation was the finest reward that had come to me since I had begun to draw.

Chapter 27

IN WASHINGTON FOR THE METROPOLITAN

SOMETHING happened in 1912 which was highly important to me and significant of the spirit of protest that was in the air. I was asked to go to Washington for the *Metropolitan Magazine* and do a monthly review of the political scene in words and pictures. This opened up a broad new field, for the *Metropolitan* had a wide circulation, whereas the *Masses* would have to be content with a rather

Collier's Weekly, 1912

THE LAWRENCE WAY.

exclusive following. The latter had been running a year in revised form, and we knew its limitations for general appeal. Nice people didn't want it around. I had been drawing cartoons (and sometimes writing) for an audience which in the main was already converted, but now I could appeal to those who were "sitting in darkness." It was understood by the *Metropolitan* editors that my pictures would continue in the *Masses* and other magazines.

Up to that time the newspapers and magazines had paid comparatively little attention to the national capital. If Congress had advertised like the theatres, no doubt its personnel and daily procedure would have received ample publicity on the well-known economic principle of reciprocity: "You scratch my back and I'll scratch yours." I knew that the press of England considered Parliament front-page news at all times. I had tried before to interest editors in sending me to Washington to illustrate whatever was informative and picturesque from my point of view, but without success.

The editor-in-chief of the *Metropolitan,* an Englishman, H. J. Whigham, thought as I did—that Congress should be played up as British newspapers featured the doings of their law-makers, and as Toby M.P. (H. W. Lucy) was doing each week in his "Essence of Parliament" in *Punch* with splendid caricatures by Harry Furniss.

When the matter of sending me to the capital came up, there was a debate in the editorial room as to whether my friend Fred C. Kelly, then a Washington correspondent, should not do the writing while I drew the cartoons. Fred told the editors they ought to make me do both. I argued that I would rather draw than write. But they insisted on trying me out in the dual role. I accepted it, and the arrangement continued for more than six years.

What Congress did or didn't do had been of little importance in the daily life of the average American, until just before the war broke out in Europe. As time went on, the newspaper editors observed that there was a growing public interest in this powerful aggregation of law-makers, and that the people were becoming conscious that politics really concerned them, especially when the conscription law was passed and the government reached into the nation's homes for its young men, the citizenry began to ask: "Who's doing all this?"

The editors had come to realize also that an occasional editorial on what Congress was doing was not enough. People wanted to know more about it. Much of the legislation favoring big finance was put over on the American populace while they were unaware of its significance. A long period of public apathy, and concealment of facts or indifference by the press, are largely responsible for the humiliating spectacle of a great

TAFT: "EYES FRONT!" His supporters face temptation on the eve of rival Republican conventions.

nation ruled by the monarchs of money, who have become more of a menace to life, liberty, and the pursuit of happiness than George III and his Tory tyrants were to our forefathers.

Brand Whitlock and I covered three conventions for the *Metropolitan* in 1912—the Republican in Chicago, the Democratic in Baltimore, and the Socialist in Indianapolis. We were given a great deal of space by the editors, and made the most of it.

"And in each convention," Whitlock wrote, "there was a vigorous personality, dynamic and compelling, which embodied the radical principle and troubled the conservative— Haywood at Indianapolis, Roosevelt at Chicago, and Bryan at Baltimore. In each its colossus bestrode the scene, but here the lines of similarity diverge; Haywood forced a compromise and preserved the organization; Roosevelt was defeated and gallantly withdrew to raise his flag elsewhere; Bryan was victorious and for the fourth time in twenty years, wheeled his obstreperous and reluctant party into line."

Battles among the Socialists that year centered around the question of supporting the Industrial Workers of the World in their free speech fight in San Diego and the question of industrial versus craft unionism. And after those issues had been threshed out at length, the report of the committee on labor "confessed the failure of craft unionism but took no decided stand on the subject of industrial unionism, declaring it to be the party's duty to give moral and material support to the labor organizations in their offensive and defensive struggles against capitalist oppression and exploitation."

That committee also stated that the Socialist party had no part in controversies over the question of form of organization, or technical methods of action in the industrial struggle.

Thus the spokesmen for the fighting I.W.W. were able to boast of a victory without dividing the party, and Bill Haywood, in a ringing speech of celebration, said:

"This is the greatest step ever taken by the Socialist party of this country. Now I can go out and talk Socialism from a Socialist party platform to the entire working class, to the eight million women and children who have no votes, . . .

AT THE 1912 SOCIALIST CONVENTION. Brand Whitlock wrote the story, while I did the pictures. Haywood was the dominating figure.

to the blanket stiffs of the West and the timber wolves of the South who are disfranchised by the nature of their jobs."

In the many sketches I made for that article I dealt mainly with personalities, and it was especially gratifying to have a magazine with a huge circulation publish a whole gallery of my portraits of the leading lights in my own party. Some of those I portrayed were: Haywood, "who sees enough with one eye"; Debs, "who hovers over an audience like a big bird"; Dan Hogan, "from Arkansas and proud of it"; Charles W. Ervin, in a characteristic "Well, I'll be d——" attitude; Barney Berlyn of Illinois, veteran Socialist; Victor L. Berger, only Socialist in Congress; Oscar Ameringer, "a man of gestures"; Joshua Wanhope, a big man wearing a cap; Meyer London; and Alexander Irvine.

OSCAR AMERINGER, dean of American labor editors. Publisher of the *American Guardian*, Oklahoma City.

I was in Washington during Woodrow Wilson's first administration and half of his second. Then as now corporation lawyers comprised most of the Senate and House, and they naturally made laws for the benefit of the corporations. I made a cartoon picturing the situation: "Laws for Capitalism go through on wings; laws for Labor go through on crutches."

Until just before the United States got into the war, the policy of the *Metropolitan* was definitely Socialistic, and it was well known that its financial backer was Harry Payne Whitney, a multi-millionaire. Finley Peter Dunne, who was Whitney's close friend, once told me he often twitted "Harry" for backing such a publication. He said he liked to whisper to him through clenched teeth: "Harry, I'm beginning to think you're one of those damned Socialists."

William Mailly was then doing a social comment department in the *Metropolitan*, and Clarence Day Jr. was handling book reviews. Some of the contributors were George Bernard Shaw, John Reed, Morris Hillquit, Ernestine Evans, Algernon Lee, Rudyard Kipling, W. W. Jacobs, Gouverneur Morris, Walter Lippmann, Boardman Robinson, Willy Pogany, Inez Haynes Gilmore, Fannie Hurst, and others.

Usually I did two pages a month on the activities of Congress, for which I got $300 a page. It was of course worth more, for out of that I had to pay my expenses in the Capital, and I still felt it necessary to retain my studio in New York.

On the day I arrived in the city of magnificent distances, the first thing that caught my eye as I stepped out of the Pennsylvania station was the dome of the capitol—the dome which I had drawn so many times in the background of my cartoons but had never before seen. There it was—the same dome which Nast and all cartoonists had used as a symbol of the government of the United States. Throughout most of my years in Washington I lived in hotels around Capitol Park, in the shadow of that dome, though for a few months I roomed a little farther away, north of the Congressional Library, with Isaac McBride, who was then secretary to Senator Harry Lane of Oregon. When I had to go up Pennsylvania Avenue, to the White House or to some government department, I'd roll along in a victoria.

My father used to say that "an artist or a writer has an advantage over a storekeeper because he can carry his capital stock with him." This stock of paper, pencils, ink, and other essentials of my profession, I could carry in a satchel, but I preferred to keep a supply in my hotel or rooming house ready for me on my return from New York, where I was expected to report once, sometimes twice, a month.

It took me a few days to get my bearings when I first landed in the Capital. I knew I did not want the regular run of news that the Washington correspondents were sending out. Usually they just touched the surface of the stories really vital to the welfare of the multitude.

I had entree to the House and Senate press galleries, but the atmosphere was not very cordial. I felt that there was some suspicion that because of my identity with radical publications, I might be a disturbing factor to the morale of the other correspondents, or that I was up to some sinister plot to push over the pillars of the Republic. While some of the newspapermen were friendly, all were aware that I was not a "regular".

I knew, of course, that I could not ignore the conventional subjects of interest—the stars of statesmanship and their ways, and I got the whole Wilson Cabinet except William G. McAdoo, Secretary of the Treasury, to give me sittings of a few minutes each. McAdoo refused, but having seen him on a few occasions, I drew him from memory.

I had a swanky card printed. It was folded—two cards in one. Outside was printed: "The *Metropolitan Magazine* ... Art Young." Turn it over and there was space for writing my request to the Senator or to whom it might concern, and space for his answer.

When I began drawing for the *Masses* it was like the unfolding of wings to soar; but the *Metropolitan* connection gave me an opportunity to circle around and then peer right in at government in the making. Whether it was just a mental heritage, I don't know, but I never could understand the Anarchist philosophy that people could get along without government. I could see no way for them to dispense with recognized laws or rules of some kind. If government was all nonsense, as some of my Anarchist friends believed, now I would try to find out.

A suffragette once asked Bill Haywood, who leaned toward the anarcho-syndicalist faith, if he thought women should have the vote, and Bill said: "Sure, and besides, they can have mine." Such was the indifference to political action held by many who could see no hope in the ballot, nor in the whole set-up of parliaments, but put their full faith in the organization of labor.

During my years in Washington I learned why the capitalists believed in a Congress, a Supreme Court, and in bureaus within bureaus—and I saw their agents swarming at every session lobbying in their interests.

WHEN THE VILLAGE RICH MAN DIES.

It was a privilege to circulate among the "fittest" who had survived in the race for political preferment. Here they were. From President down to doorkeepers, I felt sociable with them, and they didn't seem to object to me. While I found it difficult to select my daily subjects for caricature because there was so much to select from, I soon felt that no one in the wide world ever had such luck. The magazine being a monthly there was no hurry, and I could take ample time to draw for the *Masses* too. Often I would hark back to the cartoons of national politics in *Harper's Weekly* and *Puck* which so absorbed my attention in early youth—and here I was walking through corridors where the glamorous gods of American statesmanship once trod.

I cultivated an old doorman of the Senate, then eighty-seven, who liked to talk about his memories of the long-ago years. He had been employed in the Capitol building since boyhood. I was a good listener, and would ask him: "Did you know Matt Carpenter from Wisconsin? . . . What kind of a fellow was Pig Iron Kelley? . . . Was Roscoe Conkling really so dignified and proud? . . . Was Blaine the great debater they say he was? . . . How about Garfield when he was a Representative—was he really eloquent?"

Almost any question would set him going with delightful reminiscence. Once I said: "Do you remember Senator Sam Houston?" His old tired eyes lighted up. "Sam used to wear a panther-skin vest—quite a man for the ladies." And he would recall that "Daniel Webster couldn't let liquor alone." And that "Stephen A. Douglas was a little feller but a good talker." Over in his room on a side street not far from the Capitol he had many inscribed photographs and other souvenirs of Presidents and Congressmen he had known, dating back to 1850.

I had a sense of well-being then. Nearly every month Whigham or Carl Hovey, the managing editor, would write that my work was "splendid" or "you're doing good stuff." What with my appearance in the *Metropolitan* and in other magazines, surely I was getting on. Occasionally I would find diversion in drawing a few allegorical pictures for other magazines. Late in 1912 Father wrote saying that the minister of the Universalist Church in Monroe had preached a sermon with one of my cartoons as the text. This had appeared in *Collier's*. In the background was a forest of towering, ruler-straight pines, such as I had seen in Alabama. Down in front was one hopelessly deformed tree and a man similarly crippled and leaning on crutches. The caption was "Why?" and the minister had discussed the question: "What is life, and why?" Holding the picture up before his congregation, he said: "Many of you know the artist who drew this cartoon, for his first drawings were made in Monroe."

Life, 1912

SUSAN B. ANTHONY. In 1872 she was fined $100 for voting in Rochester, N. Y. "The spirit of revolt, as shown by this splendid woman," said the caption with my cartoon, "is abroad in the land."

Every week or two I was sending money to Elizabeth in California. In November she wrote from Los Angeles: "The boys are growing fast and doing well in school. Their teacher wants them to belong to a nature club. Donald will be eight the seventh of next month." Then she sent a batch of drawings done by both boys, North having attained the age of ten. Most of them, I thought, were much like the usual child art, but a few were startlingly original. Elizabeth said they were drawn "especially for you", and added that "the boys like their bicycles."

This period of my life on the scene of national politics where I saw so much evidence of lying, demagogy, and downright betrayal of the people, was enough to make me a hopeless cynic; nevertheless, I clung to an inborn faith in democracy. Hundreds of times this faith has been made to look like a stupid error, yet I hang on.

I want the men in a factory to decide who shall be boss. I want the people, by majority vote in periodic elections, to decide issues and choose men and women whom they believe capable of holding administrative positions. When it came to the question of the United States entering the European war, I wanted the people to say whether they wished their government to declare war. When the LaFollette resolution for such a referendum was killed in Congress, I knew it was because Wall Street didn't want to know the will of the people. The people's desire to avoid becoming embroiled in a foreign conflict, as demonstrated in the re-election of Woodrow Wilson in 1916 because he had so far "kept us out of war", might be repeated in another test vote, if the people were given a chance, and of course big business could not afford such a risk.

Democracy is all right if *they* will let it work. By *they* I mean those who don't want it to work. And *they* have many cunning and extra-legal ways of defeating it. Democracy is all right if the issue is fairly clear—but the enemies of democracy are masters of confusion; they stir the water in the spring-fed pool into mud. They take little unimportant truths and blow them up into big important-looking truths. In the chaos of political campaigns you try to find out what you believe, if there is anything to be believed. Nevertheless I continue to hold that even an imperfect democracy is better than other forms of government. Royalty is dying as it deserves, but the first king was called that because he was kind—*king* and *kind* were synonymous in ancient times. Whoever the administrators of the future state, they must be exemplars of kindness—or perhaps my meaning is scientific helpfulness, but helpfulness to the majority who do the world's work; the greatest good to the greatest number.

And that is the dream which must some day come true the world over—a social machinery vastly different from today's so-called democracies, which bring about the greatest good to the few—not to the many. Surely, Washington was teaching me a few things.

I still kept my studio in New York and retained my voting status there. And my work in the national capital did not prevent my running for office in the Empire State in

> 'HE STIRRETH UP THE PEOPLE'
>
> ### JESUS CHRIST
> THE WORKINGMAN OF NAZARETH
> WILL SPEAK
> AT BROTHERHOOD HALL
> — SUBJECT —
> — THE RIGHTS OF LABOR —

The Masses, 1913

"HE STIRRETH UP THE PEOPLE." This portrait of Christ, as I conceived him, also was published with a reward notice describing him as a professional agitator "wanted for sedition."

1913. That fall I was a candidate for the Assembly in the Twenty-seventh District on the Socialist ticket. My running mates were Charles Edward Russell, who sought to be Mayor; S. John Block, who was trying for the Supreme Court; and John Sloan, who was candidate for the Assembly in the Twenty-fifth District.

At the suggestion of the campaign committee, some of my speeches were illustrated with rapid-fire drawings made on big sheets of paper on an easel as I talked. The audiences liked those pictorial attacks on the capitalist system, and demanded numerous encores, but their ballots did not total enough to elect me.

Chapter 28

THE A. P. ROBES ITSELF IN WHITE

WHILE the West Virginia coal strike was at its height in November, 1913, Max Eastman and I were indicted on a charge of criminal libel preferred by the heads of the Associated Press. This was based on a *Masses* editorial written by Max entitled "The Worst Monopoly" and a cartoon of mine called "Poisoned at the Source." On my next trip to New York I appeared in court voluntarily with Max, and Justice Crain of Special Sessions set our bail at $1,000.

Max Eastman's editorial pointed out that the appalling industrial conditions in West Virginia had first become publicly known through a demand by Senator Kern for a Senatorial investigation of stories of atrocities against workers and their families in the coal regions.

For fourteen months, the editorial charged, the A.P. had withheld or distorted news of the West Virginia conflict. Calling the A.P. a Truth Trust, the *Masses* comment went on to say that "so long as the substance of current history continues to be held in cold storage, adulterated, colored with poisonous intentions, and sold to the highest bidder to suit his private purposes, there is small hope that even the free and the intelligent will take the side of justice in the struggle that is before us."

My cartoon which so wrought up the directors of the A.P. shows a man personifying the Associated Press kneeling at the edge of a vast reservoir in which the water is labeled The News. He is pouring into the reservoir the dark contents of bottles of Lies, Suppressed Facts, Prejudice, Slander, and Hatred of Labor Organization. In the background of the picture is a suggestion of cities and towns which depend upon the reservoir for their news supply. The clear water is being discolored by the poisonous dye-stuff from the bottles.

We were not arrested. Efforts toward this end had been

made by the A.P. in August, when one of its counsel appeared in Jefferson Market Court and asked for warrants for the arrest of the *Masses* editors, but the magistrate sitting there overruled the request on the ground of insufficient evidence.

Reporting our arraignment, the *New York Call* said:

"The attitude of the Associated Press on the West Virginia strike was criticized many times in numerous publications, and suppression and coloring of news was generally intimated. These allegations, however, being in some cases in large and powerful publications, backed by big financial interests, were ignored by the association.

"It was not until the occasional, one-sided stories and the long periods of silence from the strike region were the subject of comment in the columns of a Socialist magazine that efforts were made to set the machinery of the law in motion against its publishers." In other words, the great, powerful A.P. picked on a magazine so small that it created wide sentiment in our favor.

At the same time the *Call* did us a signal service by publishing two paragraphs at the end of its front-page story which presumably gave the A.P. bojums pause.

"Socialist and radical magazine men," the *Call* said, "have been working for the past month in several of the cities of the Middle West gathering material in the interests of the *Masses,* and it was stated last night that should the charges of the A.P. really be maintained and the two defendants brought to trial, revelations of such a nature as to make the Associated Press regret that the case ever came to court would be unreservedly made.

"Not only will the charges against the news association under consideration be substantiated, it was asserted, but other facts, now believed to be inside secrets of the Associated Press, will be made public."

Immediately many friends, old and new, rallied to our aid. Various newspaper men who had formerly worked for the Associated Press, and some who were then employed by it, came forward with information and documentary evidence of specific news suppression and distortion by that organization. All this material was turned over to a group of individuals with research experience who checked it minutely before it was handed to our counsel for use as evidence.

Floyd Dell had lately come East from Chicago, where he had been editor of the *Evening Post* literary supplement, and he was promptly picked to be associate editor of the *Masses*, which meant that he would share the work with Max Eastman, who continued as editor. There would be plenty for both of them to do. By this time the magazine's income had reached a point where it was possible to pay each of them twenty-five dollars a week, with something also for a business manager. In January, 1914, we published a long statement about our case, signed by Floyd, in which he explained that after various important publications, including *Collier's* and the *Independent,* had "delicately hinted" that the Associated Press had given the country no fair account of the West Virginia situation, the *Masses* decided to look into it, with the idea that if the stories out of that State were true, they ought to be explicitly told, and not just hinted at.

Now the grand jury brought in a second indictment, this time charging Max and me with criminally libeling Frank B. Noyes, president of the A.P. In February it developed that this was designed as a piece of shrewd strategy. On the 10th our attorney, Gilbert E. Roe, asked Judge Wadhams for an order permitting the defense to take depositions from those in charge of the Associated Press office in Pittsburgh, showing what news was actually sent out on the West Virginia strike. Arthur Train, assistant district attorney in charge of the prosecution, opposed this, and in the course of his argument mentioned that the first indictment, charging libel against the A.P. as an organization, would be dismissed.

But on the 17th Judge Wadhams granted the order for the depositions. Then Train declared that he would oppose such an order in connection with the second indictment, on the ground that the depositions would not be admissible as evidence concerning the alleged libeling of the A.P. president, for the reason that the truth or falsity of Associated Press reports was immaterial to the question of personal damage against Mr. Noyes.

Our friends arranged a mass-meeting in our behalf in Cooper Union on March 5, and 2,500 packed the Great Hall there. Hundreds stood in the aisles, with other hundreds turned away. Inez Milholland presided, and the speakers were Amos Pinchot, who had made a careful study of our case from a lawyer's viewpoint; John Haynes Holmes, then pastor of the Church of the Messiah; Lincoln Steffens, Charlotte Perkins Gilman, William English Walling, Norman Hapgood, and Joseph D. Cannon, organizer for the Western Federation of Miners. Though grateful for the mass demonstration, on that night the two who were accused stayed away from the meeting. We felt that the issue had become too big to make it personal.

"I have had a long acquaintance with the Associated Press," said Pinchot in his speech. "I am perfectly willing to stand behind the charge made by Eastman and Young that it does color and distort the news, that it is not impartial, and that it is a monopolistic corporation, not only in constraint of news but in constraint of truth.

"The Associated Press, through its capitalistic sympathies, is inclined to take the part of capital against labor. It has produced a condition where, during strikes and labor disputes of all kinds, the working people have grown to feel that their case, if given at all to the public, is presented in a grossly distorted form.

"I believe that no one element in American life is so powerfully conducive of bitterness and that feeling of helplessness, which so often results in violence, as the coloring of news during acute conflicts between capital and labor. On the other hand, it gives to men, such as the gunmen recently imported into Calumet by the mine operators, and to the mine operators themselves, a feeling of immunity from public criticism which is inevitably a dangerous element in the case."

Two days later the *Times* commented on the mass-meeting in an editorial more than a column long. Defending the A.P., the *Times* asserted that Mr. Pinchot was careless in his statements, and that it would be impossible for the Associated Press to color and distort the news as we had charged.

"All sorts of newspapers," the *Times* averred, "are served by the Associated Press—Republican, Democratic, Bull Moose, Independent, pro-Bryan, anti-Bryan, some that insist that the corporations are too much abused, and others insisting that they are not abused enough—in short, newspapers *representing every shade of opinion.** Now, if Mr. Noyes

---
* Italics are the author's. An unnamed spokesman for the A. P. had stated in the *New York Evening Post* that "its members, some nine hundred in

should attempt to use his dyestuffs on the news served to all these papers, there would be a deafening uproar and tumult all over the country. The Associated Press would be split into fragments and the views openly expressed of its management would make the cartoon of the *Masses* look like an expression of confidence and esteem."

Amos Pinchot had called for a widespread protest against the use of the federal district attorney's office for the muzzling of those who criticized the Associated Press procedure. "Mr. Pinchot should understand," said the *Times*, "that this is not an Associated Press suit; it is a Government suit, an action brought by the people to punish the lawless."

Meanwhile I traveled back and forth between New York and Washington frequently. One day while I was at work in my hotel room in the capital, there was a knock at the door, and Senator Robert LaFollette Sr. looked in on me. "Hello, Art," he said, "I just want to say that if I can do anything for you in regard to that Associated Press case let me know." I expressed my appreciation of this magnanimous offer, and told him I would keep it in mind if need for his help should arise. LaFollette had long been the subject of vitriolic newspaper attacks because of his stand against the big corporations and the system of which they were a part.

Months passed, and our case did not come to trial. It was apparent from tips we got from friendly sources that the A.P. was in the position of the hunter who had a bear by the tail and didn't know how to let go of it. A year after the accusation the newspapers reported that the indictments had been dismissed, and our bail was returned without explanation by the district attorney's office.

We held a celebration in the *Masses* office, and in high spirits I drew two cartoons for the next issue which conveyed the prevailing sentiments of our editorial and art boards toward our late adversary. In one I depicted the Associated Press as a stout and elegantly dressed woman out for a walk; she was carrying several packages, one being labeled Probity, and a poodle dog called Aristocracy; and out of her armful of impedimenta a legal scroll bearing the words The Masses Case had fallen to the ground. The caption was: "You

---

number, represent every shade of political and economic opinion." This of course was not quite the truth.

Dropped Something, Madam." . . . In the other cartoon, a double-page spread, I pictured the Associated Press as an angel hovering over the news reservoir pouring perfume into it from a pretty bottle labeled Truth.

Since that episode the A.P. and most of the big daily newspapers in this country have been more careful in handling news of strikes and the whole industrial conflict. That of course has been brought about largely by the growing

WHEN I WAS UNDER A CLOUD, as a result of the libel suit brought by the Associated Press.

strength of labor unionism and its better publicity facilities. But I like to think that some of the credit for this improvement is due to the protest which we of the *Masses* made twenty-six years ago.

Some time in 1914 I was proposed for membership in the National Press Club in Washington, only to find that my record was against me, particularly the cartoon attacking the Associated Press, for which I had been indicted. Some of the membership committee (and especially one who had proposed me) dissented vigorously against the attitude of those to whom I was anathema. But it did no good then.

Several years later, however, I was proposed for the club again and was elected as an out-of-town member. By that time I had quit Washington for good, and in a little while I resigned.

Chapter 29

WAR-MAKERS BEAT THEIR DRUMS

SOCIALISM was being frankly advocated by H. J. Whigham in his editorials in the *Metropolitan Magazine* in 1914. He dealt with the European conflict at length in October, asking and answering two questions: "Where is Socialism now? Why did not the Socialists stop the war?" Algernon Lee did social comment in a department headed Tidings of the Times. Two letters from John Reed in Mexico were published, heralding a series of articles on Francisco Villa's war for "land and liberty" for the peons. Lincoln Steffens dealt with the failure of government by "good people."

I had a free hand in portraying the solemn gestures and grotesque antics of Congress each month, often in a double-page spread. Out of the 520 members of both houses, I found that at least 500 were lawyers. Elected by and for the people, the bulk of that august assemblage spent most of its time gumming up legislation instead of working for the benefit of those who elected them. As comedy, if one could overlook the underlying tragedy of the whole scene, Congress was the best show in the country for a cartoonist.

My pictures and text appeared under a different heading each month. Some of the titles were: "Here They Are Again" . . . "Gumshoeing Around Washington" . . . "What's Doing on the Potomac" . . . "Be It Resolved" . . . "Let the Thinking People Rule" . . . "Making History, Such As It Is" . . . "This Tragicomic World" . . . "Can Such Things Be?"

Once I had occasion to remark that "The old judge in the trial scene in a well-known vaudeville act never tried harder to get order in the court by being disorderly himself than does Speaker Champ Clark." . . . Senator Ollie James of Kentucky, who weighed 270 pounds and looked like 400 was always good copy. He never denied any of the many anecdotes about him, most of which concerned his bulk. One told of his dislike for upper berths. Once he drew an upper in starting from Louisville for Washington. A man weighing about 110 had the lower. He looked worried when he saw the mountainous Senator. James grabbed the framework of his bed and shook it violently. "I'm always afraid of these damned upper berths," he said. "The last one I was in fell down with me." The little man was magnanimous. "I'll change with you. I sleep better in an upper."

Mother Jones came to Washington and told a Congressional committee about the terror in the West Virginia coal regions. I pictured her, and wrote that it was not easy to

Mother Jones

portray that "benign and yet so belligerent" face. When she was held captive by the West Virginia authorities she said to them: "You can stand me up against that wall and riddle me with bullets, but you can't make me surrender." Whigham also did an editorial on Mother Jones *versus* Rockefeller.

Jack Reed had written some richly colored articles about Villa's war, portraying him as a man of destiny. After the coal operators' machine guns had rained death upon the miners' tent colony in Ludlow, Colorado, the *Metropolitan* telegraphed Jack to jump to that area. He got there in time to do a trenchant article for the next issue, which said: "There is nothing revolutionary about this strike. The strikers are neither Socialists, Anarchists, nor Syndicalists." The article opened with this excerpt from testimony given before a Congressional investigating commission:

HERRINGTON (attorney for the Colorado Fuel and Iron Company)—"Just what is meant by 'social freedom' I don't know. Do you understand what the witness meant by 'social freedom', Mr. Welborn?"

MR. WELBORN (president of the Colorado Fuel and Iron Company)—"I do not."

Walter Lippmann contributed to the *Metropolitan* an article on President Wilson and Little Business, which I illus-

NOT HARMONIOUS. President Wilson tries to get Secretary of State Bryan in key.

trated. It quoted Wilson's declaration in *The New Freedom*: "I am for big business, and I am against the trust". And Lippmann commented: "He knows that there is a new world demanding new methods, but he dreams of an older world. He is torn between the two." . . . When Lippmann did another article called A Key to the Labor Movement, I furnished a cartoon showing capitalists massed in regiments, with a caption saying: "Employers should organize—sure, that's sound sense—but the workingman should go it alone." Alongside was a companion picture in which a worker stood reading a placard on a factory wall: "TO LABOR, a warning: Be free to work independently—trust the generosity of your employers—Don't submerge your individuality in a union. (Signed) EMPLOYERS' ASSOCIATION."

In one of my articles I reprinted the first two published cartoons of Theodore Roosevelt—one from *Harper's Weekly* by Nast in 1884 and the other from *Puck* in 1886. T. R. was 26 years old and a member of the New York State Legislature in 1884.

"In the 50 years since caricature became a feature of American journalism," I pointed out, "no man has been the subject of so many cartoons as Roosevelt. A cartoon composite of him would include Don Quixote, Tamerlane, Napoleon, Ananias, Cromwell, Wallenstein, Peter the Great, the Wild Horse of Tartary, Dr. Dowie, a prize-fighter, Savonarola, a circus performer, a hyena, a snapping turtle, the Angel of Peace, Ivan the Terrible, Mohammed, and Moses."

Jack Reed and I were assigned by the *Metropolitan* to cover the national political conventions in 1916. And at the same time I was asked by the Newspaper Enterprise Association of Cleveland to draw cartoons at the conventions in collaboration with Charles Edward Russell, who was handling the news end for it. The N.E.A. was then an offshoot of the Scripps-McRae newspapers (now the Scripps-Howard), and through its service my cartoons went in matrix form to several hundred dailies, including the *New York Call, Indianapolis News, New Orleans States, Portland (Ore.) News, Seattle Star, Cleveland Press, Chicago Evening Post, Detroit News, Memphis Press, Oklahoma News, San Diego Sun, Cincinnati Post, Des Moines News.*

In Chicago the work was hard, since there were two conclaves to attend, the Republican in the Coliseum and the Progressive in the Auditorium, several blocks apart. There was always the feeling that while we were at one of these, something highly exciting might happen at the other which we ought not to miss.

Numerous dark horses were in evidence in the G. O. P. ranks throughout that tense week, with the possibility that any one of them might break loose and gallop to victory. So it was real news when Justice Charles E. Hughes of the Supreme Court was nominated on Saturday.

Over at the Bull Moose meeting place I sat just behind William Jennings Bryan and his wife. He was there reporting the affair for a newspaper syndicate. I talked with Bryan during a lull, commending the stand he had taken on the European mess, which had led to his resignation as Secretary of State under Woodrow Wilson. He said: "It's like a terrible fever that will have to run its course."

Newspaper Enterprise Association

WHERE WILL IT STRIKE? Line-up of willing candidates at the 1916 Republican convention at Chicago, where I saw "all the favorite sons, and dark horses, too, waiting to be hit."

I saw the mighty demonstration that had its climax in the nomination of Theodore Roosevelt by the Progressives, followed by the reading of his letter declining to run—unless Hughes proved himself unsound on the issues of Americanism and preparedness and pacifistic, pussy-footed, or pro-German. This was a bitter blow to the Bull Moose legions, since it plainly left them out on a limb. In a long telegram of acceptance that afternoon Justice Hughes expressed his belief in "unflinching maintenance of all the rights of American citizens on land and sea . . . an Americanism that knows no ulterior purpose . . . adequate preparedness . . . the ideals of honorable peace." So T. R. was quickly out of the running.

We went on that night to St. Louis, where the Democrats were assembling. There was no doubt in the air as to where the lightning would strike here; Wilson was a foregone conclusion. But anyhow the delegates went through all the usual motions of a contest. I remember chiefly the eloquent speeches by Senator Ollie James of Kentucky, former Governor Martin Glynn of New York, and William Jennings Bryan. When they referred to the President as "a man of peace" who had "kept us out of war," the spectators in the galleries and many delegates were carried to such emotional heights as to make the scene look like a religious revival.

Cries of "Bryan! Bryan!" from so many parts of the convention hall greeted the appearance of the Commoner in the press gallery at the final session that the chairman suspended the rules to permit him to speak from the platform.

"I have had differences of opinion with President Wilson," he said, "but I join the people in thanking God that we have a President who does not want the nation to fight." Those who had feared he might recall, for purposes of party disruption, their conflict over Wilson's *Lusitania* policy, were now set at ease. Bryan was at this moment the perfect harmonizer, forgetting personal ambition and old quarrels. "As a Democrat," he declared, "I want my party to have the honor of bringing the peace about, and I want the country to give Woodrow Wilson a chance to bring it about."

Peggy and Orrick Johns attended the convention regularly, and Jack and I lunched with them in the Planters' Hotel and spent some pleasant hours in their country home out in the Meramec hills. Orrick harks back to my "declaiming in the manner of a Southern Senator" and remembers how Reed, "a big curly-haired kid wearing dark workman's shirts and the best tweeds, would comment on the wildeyed appearance of the delegates, or tear into the fallacies of the windy monologues."

Often the correspondents for various capitalist papers would tell me of a Congressman or of some one in a federal department who would make good copy for me, but not for them. They had to concern themselves with public men who were strictly "regular," or on occasion those who made news because no one took them seriously.

"Say, Young, you ought to see Lindbergh. There's a man for you," said one of these correspondents. He secretly admired Charles A. Lindbergh Sr., but knew that this Minnesota Representative was frowned upon by his paper because of his political beliefs.

In Washington no observer can escape from the consensus of opinion among the scores of correspondents from all over the country as to what is news of public interest and who should get publicity. Lindbergh, father of a boy then in short pants who in a few years would suddenly become world-famous, was not regular news. Elected on the Farmer-Labor ticket, he was so irregular that he started an investigation of the House of Morgan. Also I had heard casually of a bill he had introduced to provide easy credit for farmers, and of his exposures of the banking system, in speeches and pamphlets that everybody could understand. Being so different, he would naturally be of interest only to a cartoonist and commentator who was himself outside the pale. Such was my reputation for having radical views.

I found Lindbergh in his room in the House Office Building, and told him I'd like to make a sketch of him for the *Metropolitan*. Courteous enough, he seemed neither willing nor unwilling to have me go ahead. He was sitting at his desk, and I said: "Just as you are is all right." A stoical Swede, I thought, as I began drawing from the brow down, as is my usual way. Stoical and a man of home-spun integrity, I felt, as I limned the contour of his strong face and came to the big gnarled hands. I was not long at my work as he sat patiently looking out the window, and occasionally at his desk, where correspondence and memoranda of a Congressman's duties stared him in the face.

My informant was right—"You ought to see Lindbergh." I had seen and sketched Knute Nelson, banker Senator from the same state, a hard-boiled regular, also a Swede. Of him my most distinct memory is that he could make the brass spittoon near his desk on the Senate floor ring with powerful shots of tobacco juice. When the Senate was quiet Knute's echoing sluice was a sure sign that "God's in his heaven, all's right with the world" for the bankers. Lindbergh had vision, while the senior Senator from Minnesota was a prize example of a man without vision.

The younger Lindbergh must have inherited some of his father's imagination—for the son was certain he could do what others thought foolhardy, and did it. Lindbergh senior was farther ahead of time than his boy. But what he ad-

Charles A. Lindbergh

—Art Young

vocated also will be done. The spirit of Lindbergh senior will carry on. He voted against American entrance into the European war, and fought for peace during that conflict. His idea was that human life is at least as sacred as wealth; so he urged the conscription of wealth to pay the money costs of the fighting. He recommended that the government take over the telegraph, telephone, banking, and transportation systems. He hated Wall Street and wrote and published a book, *Why Is Your Country At War?*, which was promptly suppressed and the page plates confiscated by the federal authorities.

So inflamed can a whole nation become through the insidious propaganda of newspapers that on more than one occasion in those days Lindbergh's life was in danger while he was speaking as a candidate for Governor of Minnesota, his last campaign in his home state, where his record for honesty and unswerving principle was known to everybody. "You ought to see Lindbergh," and I saw him—a man who deserves to live endlessly in the history of his country. He was more of a lone eagle than his son. He soared higher and with a nobler purpose, but the bitter unreasoning storm of public opinion was against him.

Wilson's administration was a shining target for the *Metropolitan* throughout the Princeton professor's first term, and the magazine kept on throwing big chunks of criticism at him long after this country was dragged into the war.

"The charge against Mr. Wilson," Whigham wrote in December, 1916, "is that he has poisoned the wells of truth. The one man who ought to be candor incarnate, he has made the written word of the President of the United States a laughing stock of all the world." And a month later, under the heading of Farewell, Old Guard, the editor added: "For four years we have been opposed to the policy of Mr. Wilson and the Democratic party. Long before the war broke out our opposition to Mr. Wilson was based on the fact that his main ideas of government were reactionary rather than progressive."

Theodore Roosevelt, who by this time was being widely advertised as a contributing editor (having resigned as an editor of the *Outlook*), had an article in the same issue entitled "Good Americans Should Support Mr. Hughes."

On the day when Wilson signed the Porto Rico bill I went to the White House, curious to see for once how a President looked when he affixed his name to such a document with three different pens, each of which would be given (like Babe Ruth baseballs) to notables directly concerned with the event. I arrived late, however, because the cab-horse which brought me was tired and the cab needed oiling, and Secretary Tumulty said the ceremony was all over—but that the President was still in the reception room, and said to me, "Go on in," and I did. The President was shaking hands with some of the guests, and when they left him I introduced myself as the Washington correspondent of the *Metropolitan*.

He didn't show any emotion at that, but said, "The *Metropolitan* doesn't like me very much, does it?"

"Well, you may have noticed, Mr. President," I answered, "that I've never drawn any especially harsh cartoons of you, nor written anything libelous about you."

Then I made some conversation about the difficulties of his high office, and told him the Porto Rico bill "ought to improve that situation," and I ended by asking him a question that I heard people ask in Wisconsin in my boyhood: "Do you sleep well?"

He didn't reply to that, but a ghost of a smile crossed his face, and he said: "Good day, Mr. Young." Going out I mentioned to Tumulty that I saw the President and that "everything went all right."

Some three weeks after Wilson began his second term I happened to be in the office of Senator Harry Lane of Oregon one morning. He handed me a newspaper he had been reading, and pointing to a headline which stated that J. Pierpont Morgan was a Washington visitor, he said: "Our government has arrived!"

Official sources had just announced that Morgan had agreed to lend $1,000,000 for the Army, without interest, to permit the continued purchase of supplies for which Congress had refused money. Next day the *Evening Star* stated that "indications grew stronger today that President Wilson will ask Congress next Tuesday to declare that a state of war exists between Germany and the United States."

And a few days later he who had "kept us out of war" went before that body and made a speech about the failure of neutrality. What followed is familiar history—conscription of youth, the beating down of all opposition by a reign of terror, vast profiteering, and a deluge of blood and tears.

I sat in the Senate press gallery when Wilson delivered his so-called peace message to Congress, which in its essence

THE WHITE MAN'S BURDEN.

was a preliminary pronouncement of war. So well groomed that he resembled a fashion-plate, the Chief Executive walked down the aisle with almost everybody cheering as he mounted the dais. Here he shook hands with Vice-President Marshall, adjusted his eye-glasses, looked out over the audience for several seconds, and then began reading the fateful message amid a great silence.

My ears caught scarcely any of his words. I wasn't listening to them; I could read the salient points in the newspapers. But I knew the die had been cast. I was thinking of what inevitably lay ahead, and wondering what my radical friends who had upheld Wilson's course and motives would have to say now. Lincoln Steffens, John Reed, and many others had contended clear up to that point that he would stick to his announced policy and "keep us out of war." But I didn't believe it, and had said so over and over again. I felt he would like to, but I said: *"They* won't let him."

I knew, as everyone handling news did, how the propaganda factories were working ceaselessly to force us into the slaughter. . . . And as I pondered all this, sitting there among the press correspondents, I wasn't looking at Wilson —I was watching the face of Uncle Joe Cannon of Illinois. It was the color of an old plow-share covered with red rust, and he looked at the President as if approving every word he said. Hard-boiled Republican though he was, for once he was in agreement with a Democratic President. And the members of the Supreme Court also were there looking on with satisfied expressions.

Jeannette Rankin had just begun to serve her term as Representative from Montana when the infamous war resolution sponsored by Wilson came crashing into Congress for immediate attention, with the eyes and ears of the world waiting for the verdict. I had been hanging around the Capitol all day on April 5, and had gone home late that night, sick at heart because I was sure the measure was going to pass. About 3 a.m. the vote of the House was taken with 50 members *against* and 373 *for* war.

I heard about the ordeal next day from those who had seen the session through. As the roll was called, and the reading clerk shouted "Rankin of Montana!", there was no response. Then, louder: "RANKIN OF MONTANA!" Visibly overcome and sobbing in despair, she answered: "I want to stand by my country, but I cannot vote for war."

So Jeannette Rankin, in that nest of dominant males, made herself heard. If the manner was essentially feminine, nevertheless it was truly the voice of the maternal instinct which seeks to protect life rather than destroy it.

More disillusionment came to me that spring when the Socialist party's emergency convention in St. Louis split on the question of opposing the war. I had long held the belief that all Socialists would logically oppose a capitalistic and imperialistic war in which the proletarian masses of the countries involved would be the great losers. Ever since the carnage had begun in Europe, the Socialists in this country had been almost unanimously against entering it. I had felt secure in the belief that the party would unflinchingly stand its ground.

But there was bitter controversy on the convention floor when a resolution condemning the entrance of the United States into the European holocaust was offered for passage. After acrimonious debate a majority comprising some three fourths of the delegates adopted such a measure which said:

The only struggle which would justify the workers in taking up arms is the great struggle of the working class of the world to free itself from economic exploitation and political oppression. As against the false doctrine of national patriotism, we uphold the ideal of international working class solidarity. In support of capitalism, we will not willingly give a single life or a single dollar; in support of the struggle of the workers for freedom, we pledge all. . . . We brand the declaration of war by our government as a crime against the people of the United States and against the nations of the world. The Socialist Party emphatically rejects the proposal that in time of war the workers should suspend their struggle for better conditions. On the contrary, the acute situation created by war calls for an even more vigorous prosecution of the class struggle.

Countering this position, a minority resolution upholding the war was insisted upon by the remaining fourth of the delegates, among whom were Charles Edward Russell, John

Spargo, William English Walling, Upton Sinclair, J. G. Phelps Stokes, W. J. Ghent, Charmion London, and George Sterling. The report of these dissenters held that now that this nation was in the war, that war must be "recognized" as a fact; that Socialists should support it and help carry it to a successful conclusion as soon as possible.

Rose Pastor Stokes and her husband, J. G. Phelps Stokes, subsequently resigned from the party to express their opposition to the majority resolution, which in a referendum was adopted by the party membership by a vote of about ten to one. Printed copies of that resolution were confiscated as "treasonable" by Department of Justice agents.

And Clarence Darrow, supposedly a competent thinker, also took a pro-war position. Though I still think that all of that group were wrong, I have never believed that personal antipathy for them, because of their attitude, should have been carried over for a single day beyond the Armistice by any of us who opposed entry of the United States into the war. I have a talent for reserving judgement, sometimes reserving it so long, however, that it becomes a fault.

That session of Congress had opened with an excited determination of many members to reduce the cost of living, which had hit top figures. Many schemes were offered. But only one man in this conclave of statesmen met the issue with a clear, convincing solution. Champ Clark, Representative from Missouri, when asked by a reporter how the people could meet the rising costs of subsistence, said: "Eat mush"—and added that "everyone also ought to keep some hens." So I came out in my *Metropolitan* department for Champ Clark for our next President on a one-plank platform: *Eat mush!*

Later, in a page headed Flopping Around, I had a cartoon of Herbert Hoover tossing out advice so much needed by the millions of families living on $15 a week: "Save the scraps . . . Economy . . . Don't eat unless hungry . . . Don't buy in carload lots."

Memories of industrial turmoil in the Eighties, and the tendency of men to get in out of the storm when the elements battered them too harshly, were recalled by my discovery of an old-timer at a desk in the Department of Labor on which one would always see an orange or an apple mixed up with the documents of business. This was Terence V. Powderly, who in the Eighties was Grand Master Workman (the principal officer) of the Knights of Labor, the first powerful union of workers in the United States. There in Washington, he was assistant to the Commissioner of Immigration. Seldom did his name get into print; he was no longer news for the press which had once regarded him as a force to reckon with in the struggle of labor for a decent livelihood.

Senator Sherman of Illinois was often a good source of copy for me on dull days. He had a large store of anecdotes.

Metropolitan

TERENCE V. POWDERLY. Head of the militant Knights of Labor, he was National Villain No. 1 in the press of the Eighties. When I made this profile in 1918, he was Assistant Immigration Commissioner.

It was easy to get him to slant himself against his desk and start telling stories. One of his tales was about an illiterate man leaning against the frame of a courtroom doorway. Somebody came along and asked him: "What's the judge doing in there?" and the illiterate citizen said: "He's giving his obstructions to the jury."

Roosevelt clamored in the *Metropolitan* for our entrance into the war in an article entitled Now We Must Fight and another called Put the Flag on the Firing Line. After that wish was gratified, T. R. came out in May, 1917, with a treatise on Liberal Russia in which he said: "The great democratic revolution in Russia was successfully carried through just before the United States entered into the war on the side of the Allies. . . . We of the United States most earnestly wish well to Russia. We believe that she has before her a career of really stupendous greatness." And he said also: "We most earnestly hope that the sinister extremists, always associated with any revolution, will not gain control." This was in pre-Kerensky days, and before the Bolsheviki had been heard of in this country.

Whigham continued to criticize the Wilson administration, holding that "our democracy was on trial." "If we want to make the world safe for democracy," he said editorially in July, "there are two things we must surely do. 1. We must so deal with Germany that neither she nor any other great power will ever again think it worth while to start out on a career of world conquest. . . . 2. To make democracy safe we must make democracy self-supporting. Washington at the present moment is rather a deplorable spectacle."

The development of that theme brought numerous protests, and in August Whigham was clearly on the defensive against the pressure of the super-patriots. Under the heading "This Is Our War" he stated the *Metropolitan's* position. Some readers, he explained, had objected to the July editorial as an attack on the national administration. But neither the President nor any of his advisers were sacrosanct, the *Metropolitan's* editor insisted, and it deplored the idea held by well-meaning people that loyalty and patriotism meant standing by the Administration and doing little else. "Whatever the President does toward winning this war in the shortest and most effective way has our enthusiastic support."

Chapter 30

THE CENSORSHIP PICKS ON THE MASSES

ROUGH going had been encountered by the *Masses* in its efforts to remain a medium for free interpretation in a time of hysteria. Because of its pitiless reporting in trying to reveal true causes, its lack of respect for commercialized religion, and its attacks on sex taboos in art and literature, the magazine had earlier been barred from the reading rooms of many libraries, ousted from the subway and elevated news stands in New York, and refused by the large distributing companies of Boston and Philadelphia; and our right to use the mails in Canada had been revoked by the Dominion government.

One poem by Carl Sandburg had caused an issue to be held up in the New York post office for two days, and some subscriptions were stopped on account of it. This was dedicated to Billy Sunday, and the opening lines read:

> You come along . . . tearing your shirt . . . yelling about Jesus.
> I want to know . . . what the hell . . . you know about Jesus.
> Jesus had a way of talking soft and everybody except a few bankers and higher-ups among the con-men of Jerusalem liked to have this Jesus around because he never made any fake passes and everything he said went and he helped the sick and he gave the people hope.

Frequently we reprinted bits from the daily newspapers which needed no satirical comment to give them bite. For example, the mention of a woman who wrote to the *Philadelphia North American* telling how she fed a family of six on $3 a week, and that publication's response: "The *North American* . . . publicly acknowledges its admiration for such a fine manager. A few of this sort in each community in the land would soon put an end to the high cost of living agitation."

For three months after the United States declared war on Germany the *Masses* kept on assailing the jingoists, the profiteers, and the capitalists who caused the beating and deportation of strikers, the Post Office censorship, and other evils which had been loosed in the campaign to silence all critics of the war administration. If anyone questioned the magazine's course, the editors were able to point to a statement by President Wilson for justification. Shortly after the declaration he had said:

> I can imagine no greater dis-service to the country than to establish a system of censorship that would deny to the people of a free republic like our own their undisputable right to criticize their own public officials. While exercising the great powers of the office I hold, I would regret in a crisis like the one which we are now passing to lose the benefits of patriotic and intelligent criticism.

On July 3 the August issue of the *Masses* was delivered to the New York Post Office. Copies of this were immediately sent to Washington "for examination," the editors were informed. Two days later a letter came from Postmaster T. G. Patten of Manhattan, stating that according to advices from the Solicitor of the Post Office Department, that issue was unmailable under the Act of June 15, 1917, which meant the Espionage Act. It was understood that the Solicitor, the Attorney General, and Judge Advocate General Crowder of the U. S. Army had conferred about excluding the magazine from the mails. In a statement in our September number, explaining what happened to the August issue, there was a footnote: "Date of conference unknown; rumor that the Generals, in spite of pressure of war-business, celebrated Independence Day by deciding to suppress the *Masses,* cannot be verified."

Merrill Rogers, our business manager, hastened to Washington and interviewed Solicitor Lamar, who declined to say what provisions of the Espionage Act had been violated by the *Masses* for August, or what parts of the magazine violated that law.

Immediately we retained Gilbert E. Roe as counsel. He had handled our fight against the Associated Press libel suit. On July 12 he filed a motion in the federal court to enjoin the postmaster from excluding the magazine from the mails. All-day argument on this motion was held before Judge Learned Hand on July 21. And now we got a hint of how the Espionage Act would be used as a club against people with anti-war beliefs. Assistant U. S. District Attorney Earl Barnes set forth that the Post Office Department construed that act as giving it power to bar from the mails anything which might interfere with the successful conduct of the war.

Barnes offered as exhibits four cartoons and four pieces of text in the August issue as specific law violations. These cartoons were Boardman Robinson's "Making the World Safe for Democracy," two by H. J. Glintenkamp having to do with Conscription and the Liberty Bell, and one by myself on Congress and Big Business. The objectionable writings were: "A Question," an editorial by Max Eastman; "A Tribute," a poem by Josephine Bell; an editorial, "Friends of American Freedom"; and a paragraph in an article on "Conscientious Objectors."

"But," said Roe, in his argument, "the Espionage Act was designed chiefly to strike at agents of enemy countries, and was never intended to prohibit political criticism or discussion. To permit the Post Office Department to use it as a cover for arbitrary acts of suppression would be to recognize a censorship set up without warrant of law."

Granting a temporary injunction against the postmaster, Judge Hand upheld Roe's contention completely in a memorable decision. That decision, boiled down, emphasized the following points: There was no valid basis for the peculiar construction placed by the postal authorities on the Espionage Act. The *Masses* for August did not violate the specific provisions of the law. Its cartoons and editorials fell "within the scope of that right to criticize, either by temperate reasoning or by immoderate and indecent invective, which is normally the privilege of the individual in countries dependent upon the free expression of opinion as the ultimate source of authority."

Expression of such opinion might militate against the success of the war, Judge Hand pointed out, but Congress had not seen fit to exclude it from the mails, and only Congress had the power to do this. The pictures and text complained of might tend to promote disaffection with the war, but they could not be thought to counsel insubordination in the military or naval forces "without a violation of their meaning quite beyond any tolerance of understanding." The Glintenkamp cartoon on conscription might "breed such animosity toward the Draft as will promote resistance and strengthen the determination of those disposed to be recalcitrant," but it did not tell people that it was their duty nor to their interest to resist the law. The text objected to expressed "high admiration for those who have held and are holding out for their convictions even to the extent of resisting the law." But the expression of such admiration, Judge Hand held, was not a violation of the Espionage Act.

On July 26 a formal order requiring the postmaster to transmit the August *Masses* through the mails was signed by Judge Hand. And on the same day, in Windsor, Vermont, 250 miles away, U. S. Circuit Judge C. M. Hough signed another order staying execution of Judge Hand's injunction and requiring the contending parties to appear before him in Windsor on August 2 to show cause why this stay should not be made permanent pending an appeal which had been taken by Postmaster Patten.

It would be several months before the appeal could be heard. Meanwhile, the *Masses* explained in its September issue, "our attorney will oppose the staying of Judge Hand's order. If he succeeds, you will get your August issue through the mails—unless the Department thinks of some other way to stop it. If our attorney doesn't succeed, we will have to adopt other ways and means. . . . The *Masses* is your property. This is your fight as much as it is ours. We are not going to quit. We do not believe you are, either. We need money to help pay expenses. . . ."

Yes, the fight must go on. Most of us who were co-operatively bringing out the *Masses* were agreed upon that. Some channel of protest must be safeguarded for those who had not been stampeded into dumb obeisance to the world's war-makers. On the back cover of the September issue was a bold pronouncement headed: Challenging the Government, which said:

"Twelve to fifteen hundred radical publications have been declared unmailable. The *Masses* is the only one which has challenged the censorship in the courts and put the Government on the defensive. Each month we have something vitally important to say on the war. We are going to say it and continue to say it. We are going to fight any attempt to prevent us from saying it. The *Masses* has proved in the last few issues that it stands as the foremost critic of militarism."

We had found comfort and confidence in that decision of Judge Hand, even though it had been immediately blocked by another court. Judge Hand's thoughtful and explicit sanction of our course was assurance that there was still some sanity left in the judiciary.

So the September issue of the magazine continued its policy of unremitting protest. A lead article by John Reed headed One Solid Month of Liberty, said that "in America the month just past has been the blackest month for freemen our generation has known." . . . A full-page cartoon of mine entitled Having Their Fling, pictured an editor, capitalist, politician, and clergyman dancing to the music of a devil's orchestra playing instruments shaped like cannon, machine guns, and hand grenades. Placards above the dancers read: "All for Democracy . . . All for Honor . . . All for World Peace . . . All for Jesus." . . . Sweatshop conditions of labor among the women employed in the federal Bureau of Printing and Engraving in Washington were detailed in an editorial.

There was a double-page cartoon spread by Boardman Robinson called Deportations—Take Your Choice, in which he showed the Kaiser and his army driving Belgians away from their homes and a silk-hatted Phelps-Dodge Corporation official and its gunmen herding miners into box-cars in Arizona. . . . Max Eastman had an article assailing the Post Office censorship. . . . Young Lads First was the title of a poem by Willard Wattles, telling of gray-beards who came from councils and set young men's ears aflame with cries of "Honor!" and sent them off to die.

All of these features were of course red rags to the prowar crowd, as were two other cartoons I drew for the same issue. One represented Postmaster General Burleson as a worried knight in armor who had broken his lance in the battle with radical publications. Burleson's tattered banner bore the legend: "Death to all newspapers and magazines that haven't 'the right spirit.' " . . . My other cartoon was a simple portrait of Assistant U. S. District Attorney Barnes, identified as a defender of relics, with a quotation from his argument for exclusion of the *Masses* from the mails: "The Liberty Bell cartoon, sir, to my mind, is objectionable, because it shows that time-honored relic in a state of complete collapse."

It would be hard to find a more illuminating commentary on the American scene in that period than John Reed's article. "With a sort of hideous apathy," he related, "the country has acquiesced in a regime of judicial tyranny, bureaucratic suppression, and industrial barbarism, which followed inevitably the first fine careless rapture of militarism." . . . He declared that Emma Goldman and Alexander Berkman were not convicted of the charges on which they were ostensibly tried; they were convicted by the Assistant District Attorney's constant stress of the term "Anarchist," and by the careful definition of that term, brought out by both judge and prosecutor, as one who wishes wantonly to overthrow society by violence. . . . Reed told of the attack of soldiers and sailors on the Socialist headquarters in Boston; the race riot in East St. Louis, in which more than thirty Negroes, men and women, were massacred by whites; the loading of hundreds of striking copper miners and their attorney, into cattle cars in Bisbee, Arizona, and their being abandoned in the desert, foodless and waterless.

"Out in San Francisco," Reed wrote, "the bomb trials go merrily on. In spite of the exposure of Oxman, the utter contradiction and discrediting of the state's witnesses, Mooney is still going to die. . . . And so the most patent frame-up ever conceived by a Chamber of Commerce to extirpate union labor goes on, and indictments rain upon all who have dared to defend the Mooneys. . . .

"Meanwhile, organized labor lies down and takes it—nay, in San Francisco, connives at it. Gompers is too busy running the war—he has not time for anything except to appoint upon his committees labor's bitterest enemies. I suppose that as soon as Tom Mooney and his wife are executed,

Gompers will invite District Attorney Fickert to serve upon the Committee on Labor.

"The suffrage pickets in front of the White House, set upon by mobs of government clerks, then by the police, arrested time and time again upon no charge, and finally committed to the work-house for sixty days, were, as the world knows, hurriedly pardoned by the President as soon as it was evident how prominent they and their husbands were. But at the same time that he pardoned them for their 'crime,' he intimated that he was too busy over his 'War for Democracy' to give any attention to their petition—which was a petition for the fundamental rights of citizens."

It was inevitable, in the temper of the time, that the *Masses* would be suppressed. In October our second-class mailing privilege was rescinded, and the grand jury indicted Max Eastman, Floyd Dell, Henry J. Glintenkamp, Josephine Bell, Merrill Rogers, business manager, and myself.* We were charged, under the Espionage Act, with "conspiracy to obstruct the recruiting and enlistment service of the United States" by publishing seditious articles, cartoons and poems. If convicted, we faced sentences of imprisonment up to twenty years each and fines up to $10,000 each. And many twenty-year prison terms had already been handed out to dissenters.

Slacker had come into the language as a term of frequent use. Bundles of Hearst newspapers had been burned in Times Square because Hearst was slow in swinging to the Allied cause but in a few weeks he had swung, and American flags were printed all over his daily sheets. So-called pro-Germans were being tarred and feathered by mobs in the West. Frank Little of the I.W.W. executive board had been lynched by business men in Butte, Montana. And new and appalling tales of cruelty to conscientious objectors were coming out of the prisons where they were confined.

The road ahead would be hard. We of the *Masses* staff had no illusions about that.

It was not surprising, in view of the editorial switch of the *Metropolitan* to the side of the war crowd, that my space

* Subsequently John Reed also was indicted.

had in recent months been reduced from two pages to one page, and that now it was cut to two-thirds of a page. I had felt the magazine's policy steadily narrowing, and it had

HAVING THEIR FLING. One of the cartoons for which I was indicted for alleged conspiracy to obstruct recruiting.

become more and more difficult to draw cartoons and express opinions on the situation in the capital that would get by the board of editors. Still I kept on, satirizing the show as vigorously as I dared, under heads such as Following the Leaders and Let the Thinking People Rule.

It was not surprising either when I got a letter from the editors of the *Metropolitan* in the fall of 1917 saying: "You're not catching the spirit of Washington. We wish you would come to New York and talk it over." I went, but I knew what the outcome would be before I entered the office. We didn't go into details in our discussion. Whigham and

Liberator

THE BOSS: "Now, children, all together, three cheers for the Supreme Court!"

This appeared soon after the Keating Child Labor Act of the Wilson administration was declared unconstitutional.

Carl Hovey, the managing editor, both seemed a bit abrupt—and it was all over.

Yet it was a relief to get away from Washington then. For the scene in the capital had become both farcical and sad. Better to be out of it than to remain with my hands tied and brain clamped. The magnificent distances swarmed with business men from near and far patriotically giving their services at "a dollar a year" with a cheerful eye on large orders for their products; Congressmen giving out pompous interviews and making stuffed-shirt speeches; spurred swivel-chair officers suddenly growing omnipotent; members of the Intelligence Service hunting for spies; members of the American Protective League raiding the office files of persons suspected of subversive tendencies, with the aid of building superintendents and janitors by night.

Jeannette Rankin once complained to Secretary of War Newton Baker that she was being followed by a secret service man. "Don't pay any attention to him," said Baker. "Two of them have been following me for three months."

Rents were exorbitant, food prices soared, and every hotel was crowded. One encountered drunken parties in profusion moving about the town by night. When I read new pronouncements by Woodrow Wilson I could hear the voices of all the stay-at-home slogan makers:

"Hundred per cent Americanism."
"Over there—"
"Give till it hurts!"
"Don't be a slacker!"
"Do your bit!"
"Down with the Huns!"
"Kill the Kaiser!"
"Make the world safe—"
"A war to end war!"

Chapter 31

WE GO TO TRIAL IN TENSE DAYS

I FELT, as others among my radical associates did, that the spirit of protest must be kept alive. And with our trial for seditious "conspiracy" approaching, it was essential that we have some dependable medium through which we could present our case to the public.

Accordingly some of us who had been active in promoting the *Masses* decided early in 1918 that we would establish a new magazine of similar format, to be called the *Liberator*. Again Max Eastman was editor, with his sister Crystal as managing editor and Floyd Dell as associate, while the contributing editors were: Cornelia Barns, Howard Brubaker, Hugo Gellert, Arturo Giovannitti, Charles T. Hallinan, Helen Keller, Ellen LaMotte, Robert Minor, John Reed, Boardman Robinson, Louis Untermeyer, Charles W. Wood, and Art Young.

"Never was the moment more auspicious to issue a great magazine of liberty," our leading editorial said in the first issue in March. "With the Russian people in the lead, the world is entering upon the experiment of industrial and real democracy. . . . The possibilities of change in this day are beyond all imagination. We must unite our hands and voices to make the end of this war the beginning of an age of freedom and happiness for mankind undreamed by those whose minds comprehend only political and military events. . . .

"The *Liberator* . . . will advocate the opening of the land to the people, and urge the immediate taking over by the people of railroads, mines, telegraph and telephone systems, and all public utilities. . . .

"The *Liberator* will endorse the war aims outlined by the Russian people and expounded by President Wilson—a peace without forcible annexations, without punitive indemnities, with free development and self-determination for all peoples. Especially it will support the President in his demand for an international union, based upon free seas, free commerce, and general disarmament, as the central principle upon which hang all hopes of permanent peace and friendship among nations."

The Masses

A CASE OF HERESY. Charles M. Schwab, steel magnate, upsets his class by an outspoken speech at an alumni dinner in New York.

That issue included an article by Helen Keller in behalf of the I.W.W.; one by Bob Minor on the peril of Tom Mooney, with a cartoon by Bob showing "the rope still around Mooney's neck"; while Jack Reed dealt with Red

Russia. I contributed two cartoons, one being entitled "A Case of Heresy," in which Charles M. Schwab was being haled into court before old Judge Capitalism for an utterance he made at a banquet:

"Some people call it Socialism. Others call it Bolshevism. It means but one thing, and that is that the man who labors with his hands, yet does not possess property, is the one who is going to dominate the affairs of the world."

Through the following months the *Liberator* contained a good deal about what was happening abroad, and illuminating news material and comment about the class struggle in the United States. Some pieces worth noting here were: an article on an atrocity by a masked mob in Tulsa, Oklahoma, which whipped, tarred and feathered, and deported seventeen men, some of them I.W.W. oil-workers who had been taken from the custody of the city police; a report on the growing propaganda for compulsory military training; and an article by William D. Haywood, general secretary of the I.W.W., telling of the daily life of himself and 105 other class-war prisoners in the foul air of the county jail in Chicago.

Cartoons which I made for the new magazine that year included one in which a capitalist bows his head in prayer, saying: "O Lord, control my appetite if you must, but don't take my pie (private ownership) away!"; another called "Good Night!" in which private ownership of public institutions ("the light that failed") is being buried, amid the weeping of the church, press, colleges, and stage; and a third in which Karl Marx views his triumph in current headlines. Such cartoons I classify now as wishful thinking.

Then I made a portrait of a well-fed, self-satisfied looking man, to illustrate this supposed news dispatch:

"RIDGEVILLE, N. H.—George Turnip, a leading citizen of this town, was given a birthday dinner today in honor of his sixty-third birthday. Mr. Turnip, who is a bachelor, made a strong speech in favor of military training for every male citizen over nineteen and under sixty-three years of age."

Looking over a bound volume of the *Liberator* for 1918, it is easy to discern that the soft pedal was being used, in contrast to the outspokenness of the *Masses*. But the terror against all objectors to the war was in full force, and with our trial coming on, we were not inclined to aggravate the situation further—though we were ready to stand by the written and pictorial expressions which had led to the seven indictments.

On the eve of our trial an editorial in the *Liberator* for May, in discussing it, drew a comparison between our position and that of the *Metropolitan*. While the latter had been aiding the war, it had lately published an article by William Hard declaring that America was not honest in her profession of anti-imperial war-aims, that she was in fact imperialistic. Thereupon some "automaton" in the Post Office Department had issued a mandate to the New York postmaster to exclude Whigham's periodical from the mails. But this action was quickly over-ridden by higher-ups, who explained that it was all a mistake.

Thus, the *Liberator* commented, "the respectable felonies, that enliven the pages of the *Metropolitan*, and the *Kansas City Star*, and *Collier's*, and the newspapers of William R. Hearst, may continue with impunity, as they should of course in a society whose ultimate and really admired ideal *is* respectability."

Our new magazine was being consistently more diplomatic than militant in its utterances, and that issue contained a carefully poised article by Max Eastman headed "Wilson and the World's Future," in which various wrongs in connection with the war were pointed out, in the manifest hope that the man in the White House might deal with them constructively.

"President Wilson conducts his own thinking," this article began, "with a large freedom and interior democracy that is not usual either among professors or politicians. He gives a voice to every new fact and every new suggestion that the current of events and meditation throws out."

Then certain recent actions of the Chief Executive "in the single interest of human freedom" were listed.

"A thing that makes me especially willing to travel [in the same car with him]," Eastman stated, "is that President Wilson has at last turned his attention to those violations of liberty and constitutional right in our domestic affairs which have been making his great words before the world sound so hollow." This referred to an order for a review of courts-martial and sentences dealt out to several hundred conscientious objectors, with a view to remedy by the President "if any be needed."

Moves that Wilson might make to ease the tensity of the whole situation, suggested by the *Liberator's* editor, included recognition of the Republic of Labor Unions in Russia, indorsement of the proposed Inter-Belligerent Conference of Socialist and Labor Delegates, and some public statement to curb "the American Prussians" and to halt the general suppression of publications and the persecution of organizers and agitators with radical opinions.

Patriotic music was being played lustily by an army band in City Hall Park as we of the *Masses* went to trial in the old Post Office building before Judge Augustus Hand in April. Only five defendants were present—Max Eastman, Floyd Dell, Merrill Rogers, Josephine Bell, and myself. John Reed was in Russia, and Henry Glintenkamp's whereabouts were unknown. He had been out of town when the indictment was returned by the grand jury.

Assistant District Attorney Earl Barnes was handling the prosecution, while Morris Hillquit and Dudley Field Malone were our attorneys. Hillquit had been under fire by the super-patriots because he had admittedly written most of the St. Louis anti-war proclamation of the Socialist party; some of the newspapers referred to him as "the unindicted Hillquit." Malone was a liberal who liked to exercise his independent spirit right in the open, but for all that was still regarded as respectable. He was in the case mainly because of the free press issue.

Among the exhibits introduced by the prosecution as evidence against us, these six stood out:

1. Eastman's editorial, "A Question," which praised the moral courage of those who were conscientious objectors to the draft.

2. Letters from conscientious objectors in English prisons, with a foreword by Floyd Dell lauding them.

3. Glintenkamp's cartoon in which Death was measuring a drafted soldier for a coffin, with an excerpt from a news

dispatch stating that a huge number of coffins had been ordered by the War Department.

4. An "article" signed by Reed, which actually was a compilation of quotations from a report by the National Mental Hygiene Committee, which cited the great frequency of mental diseases among soldiers in the prevailing war. This report had been published by the *New York Tribune,* but no editor of that newspaper had been indicted. The only part of

MORRIS HILLQUIT, one of the defense counsel in the *Masses* sedition case.

the "article" which was original with Reed was the headline, "Knit a Strait-Jacket for Your Soldier Boy."

5. Josephine Bell's free-verse poem, "A Tribute," and dedicated to Emma Goldman and Alexander Berkman, who had lately been convicted under the Espionage Act.

6. My anti-war cartoon, "Having Their Fling." This was just one of various pictures of mine cited by the State.

Picking the jury was an arduous task, which often impelled grave doubts of our chances as we contemplated the "peers" who were to decide whether we should spend the next twenty years in or out of prison. Scores of middle class talesmen, many of them elderly and "retired," were examined as to their social views, with practically the same answers from all.

"Are you prejudiced against pacifism and pacifists?" Always the reply would be "Yes."

There was no hope of getting twelve men, or even three, on that jury who were open-minded. The best that our attorneys could get from the talesmen whom we thought looked "human" was an expression of belief that their prejudices "might be overcome by proof and argument." It was chilling to remember that in the Chicago Haymarket case most of the jurors who sent four men to the gallows had voiced the same belief. Hillquit requested Judge Hand to excuse talesmen who had that attitude, but the judge said: "You cannot get a jury anywhere in the United States not prejudiced against pacifism."

My love for music suffered during that trial. While the jury-picking was going on, and through the whole eight days that our fate was in abeyance, the bands in the park below, where Liberty Bonds were being sold, played national airs. To me, who considered myself quite as patriotic in a real sense as those who had to prove it by emotional excess, this music sounded sad, not to say ominous, like the relentless beat of a funeral march.

Once when brass horns blared out "The Star Spangled Banner" right under the court-room windows some one in the room stood up, then others, till everybody present was standing at attention. It was like some solemn religious ceremony with God looking on from behind a cloud. We defendants stood up with the others, knowing that if we didn't we would be mobbed. This patriotic gesture seemed to bewilder Judge Hand. He arose slowly as if saying to himself: "What started all this?" For there was no custom in court-room behavior of standing up for anything or anybody except the judge himself.

We were more fortunate than the Haymarket men, however, in having a conscientious judge on the bench. Judge Hand had not been stampeded by the war mania, and he consistently tried to be fair in his rulings and in his instructions to the jury.

I was amazed anew at the vastness of evil intent which a prosecutor could find in the utterances of defendants representing an unpopular cause. Earl Barnes took great pains to point out to the jury that we were traitors to the principles which guided the Founding Fathers of this nation, that we had entered into a deliberate conspiracy to undermine the pillars of the republic, that we had set out to defeat the purposes of the army and navy which were protecting our country against the mad aims of the Kaiser. He read from the exhibits in awe-inspiring tones, and held up the offending cartoons with a gesture of horror as if he were displaying the pistol with which Booth shot Abraham Lincoln.

Hillquit, in his opening address, contended that "true patriotism, the concern for one's country and its people, is at least as consistent with a desire to protect them from mass slaughter as with honest war enthusiasm," and he concluded:

"These then were our honest views. Were we wrong? Were we right about it? Gentlemen, you are not called upon to pass on this question. History will be our jury. No human being today can assume to render final judgment on the great problems which the world catastrophe has put before us. You are called upon to pass on only one thing: Are these men criminals? Did they conspire to injure their country? Did they conspire with the Imperial German Government in this war?"

At the end of the state's case Hillquit asked the court to quash the indictment against Josephine Bell, arguing that no part of her poem was illegal. Some idea of its character may be gained from this portion:

> Emma Goldman and Alexander Berkman
>   Are in prison tonight
> But they have made themselves elemental forces
> Like the water that climbs down the rocks;
> Like the wind in the leaves;
> Like the gentle night that holds us;
> They are working on our destinies;
> They are forging the loves of the nations.

Judge Hand read the poem thoughtfully, and handing it back to Hillquit said: "Do you call that a poem?" Hillquit answered: "Your Honor, it is so called in the indictment." Whereupon the judge said: "Indictment dismissed."

Each of the remaining four defendants was put on the witness stand. Max Eastman and Floyd Dell discussed at length, in response to our attorney's questions, the fundamental rights of the press and of American citizens as individuals to express themselves freely on issues which concerned their own welfare or that of their countrymen. Merrill Rogers explained the business end of the *Masses,* which largely consisted in finding money each month to meet the deficit.

All three of course denied that there had ever been any conspiracy by those who devised or edited the contents of the magazine, and Eastman and Dell tried to make clear that it had never been possible to get all the "co-operating" editors and contributors together at any one time. (Actually more of us had attended the studio meetings after the indictment than ever before; postcards would arrive from the *Masses* office saying: "Come over to B's studio Thursday night—conspiracy.")

I was called upon to identify my own cartoons and to explain them. In drawing "Having Their Fling," I stated, I tried to show a mad orgy of men representing our country's principal institutions: press, pulpit, politics, and business. I tried to picture them as war-crazy.

"But," said the prosecutor, as if he thought I was holding something back, "when you put that orchestra playing on war-implements in the background of your cartoon and the Devil leading the orchestra, what did you mean by that?"

Nobody but a war-time prosecutor would have asked such a question, but it had to be answered, and I said: "Well, since General Sherman described war as Hell, it seemed to me appropriate that the Devil should lead the band."

Another of my cartoons which had excited the prosecutor's patriotic ire was captioned Iceland Declares War on Africa, and a third depicted Congress as a humble individual asking a war board of financiers: "Where do I come in?" and the board answering: "Run along. We got through with you when you declared war for us."

In cross-examining me, Barnes insisted on knowing what my motives were in drawing these cartoons. "For the public good," I said. On re-direct examination our attorneys sought to bring out just what public good I had intended. I wasn't prepared for that question—my thoughts had not gone that far. There was a long silence, with reporters' pencils poised waiting, and the jurors leaning forward to catch my answer. I felt warm and uncomfortable.

"I intended—why—the good of the public," I stammered.

But evidently that wasn't sufficient. Our attorneys rephrased the question, only to find me still at sea. Then Judge Hand came to my aid. He gave some abstract definitions of public good—which were Greek to me—and asked if I had intended some such public good as he had mentioned.

"That's it exactly," I said, and the matter was dropped. I had reached a stage of weariness with the whole trial where I was in a mood to say, "Go ahead and hang me if you must, but stop pushing."

That weariness culminated one day in my falling asleep in court. Hillquit shook me, with a warning whisper: "Wake up, Art, you'll be arrested for contempt!" Even if that had been my bad luck and twenty years in prison my future, I don't think I could have stayed awake throughout that hot, listless afternoon while trivial technicalities were being messed over. When I was fully awake, I made a sketch of myself as I must have looked during that peaceful nap.

George Creel, director of American publicity forces for the war, was one of several individuals who testified that the accused were of good character. Considering the vilification turned against anyone on trial for anti-war activities, such testimony was thankfully received, especially coming from the chief bugle-blower for war propaganda and the new militarism. Creel had shown some radical tendencies in other years, and had written an article for the *Masses* called "Rockefeller Law," exposing the action of the Rockefeller interests in the Colorado mines.

Various notables attended the trial, sitting inside the rail as guests of our attorneys or because they were known to the court. I remember seeing Dean George W. Kirchwey, Edna St. Vincent Millay, Richard LeGallienne, Amos Pinchot, Edna Kenton, Darwin Meserole, and Savel Zimand. While many in the audience were no doubt strongly against us, I often recognized friends and acquaintances—lawyers, teachers, artists, poets, and Socialists, also I.W.W. members who wisely wore no identifying buttons just then.

Our actions were not those of conspirators, but of "straightforward men," Hillquit and Malone argued. When Max Eastman sent a telegraphic reply to a youngster in New Orleans who was troubled as to what attitude he should take toward the question of fighting in the war, Max wired him what he would do if he were in the inquirer's place; "conspirators were not given to using open language in telegrams," our counsel declared.

"There's Art Young," said Malone in developing his defense. "Everybody likes Art Young. Look at him. There he sits—like a big friendly Newfoundland dog. How could anyone conceive of him playing the role of a conspirator?"

And for the moment I felt sorry for myself—it was a shame, that's what it was, and I hoped that the jury would be duly impressed.

In view of the somber atmosphere of the court when Prosecutor Barnes excoriated us anew in his closing address, we expected a quick verdict and were prepared for an unfavorable one. The best I looked for was several years in prison. Not a pleasant outlook, but I consoled myself with the thought that maybe I would be allowed to draw pictures there. We had told the truth out of turn, and now what? Kate Richards O'Hare had been sentenced to five years for an anti-war speech, and Rose Pastor Stokes had lately been convicted, also for a speech, made in South Dakota, in which she said that "The government cannot serve both the profiteers and the employees of profiteers."

But many hours went by with no verdict, a night, and another day, and still another night. And as the time lengthened we grew more and more hopeful. Somebody was holding out against the war madness. After 48 hours the jurors came in, weary, some of them with bloodshot eyes, and reported that they could not agree.

Ten of the twelve were for conviction; the other two insisted that there was no evidence that we had taken part in any conspiracy. One of the two, H. C. Fredericks, told the others that he would hold out for us "till Hell freezes over." In 1923 I happened to meet Mr. Fredericks, and he told me that, after many years of regular service on juries, he was never again called to serve. Newspaper accounts of our trial related that some of the jurors had complained to federal officials that two "recalcitrant jurors who displayed Socialist and pacifist tendencies" had blocked their efforts to send us to prison. A "federal inquiry" was forecast by the reporters.

While our trial was in progress I had received word from Clarina Michelson, recording secretary of the Socialist party branch in my district, that I had been nominated for the State Senate. To which I had responded, saying: "I am happy to accept, but don't know whether I'll be a resident of New York or Atlanta when election day rolls around."

Thanks to those two jurors who had persisted in doing their own thinking, I was permitted to take part in the campaign that fall as a free man. I made a good many speeches, speaking wherever I was asked to go, but learned afterward that I had never spoken in my own district once. Presumably the arrangements committee didn't think that necessary, and I was told that my comrades in the 13th S.D. gave me "the regular party vote." That, however, was not enough to send me to Albany.

Chapter 32

STIFLING THE VOICES AGAINST WAR

MY world had grown small and shaky. I learned what ostracism means. Men and women whom I had counted as friends found it convenient to pass me on the street without speaking, or were brief and impersonal in their conversation. And often I felt that I was being pointed out as a treasonable being to be shunned as one would the plague. At the Dutch Treat Club, of which I was one of the founders, the atmosphere exuded by some of the members was so cold whenever I hove in sight that I handed in my resignation. Jack Reed also quit; he had been popular and active there, and once he wrote the libretto for a comic opera for one of the club's annual frolics.

Editors of most of the magazines where I had long had entree also shied at my offerings. Sometimes they attempted to explain, but there was no need—it was obvious that they could not afford to continue using the work of one who was being prosecuted by the government on sedition charges. Thus I had difficulty in making a living. But there was one editor who stood by me—Jacob Marinoff, of the *Big Stick,* a Jewish humorous weekly, which also was under surveillance by the federal authorities. Each week he used my drawings, with lettering such as is frequently necessary in a cartoon in Hebrew. I liked this because it gave the pictures a decorative effect that my plain English lettering lacked. And unfailingly each week Marinoff sent me a check, and thus I was able to eat and pay rent.

Early that summer Jack Reed came back from Russia, bursting with elation over the social and economic wonders which were being worked out by the Workers' and Peasants' Government. He brought with him a mass of notes which subsequently grew into his book, *Ten Days That Shook the World.* In the *Liberator* for June he said: "Two months ago, at No. 6 Dvortsovya Ploshod, I saw the new world born." As soon as Jack returned, he notified the District Attorney's office that he would be ready for trial with the other *Masses* defendants whenever called.

Soon after this, he and I went to Chicago to cover the trial of the I.W.W. leaders before Judge Kenesaw Mountain Landis. They, too, stood accused of interfering with enlistment. Bill Haywood and 100 other "Wobblies" * were the defendants—speakers, organizers, editors, corralled by a dragnet covering many states. One of the offenses of this organization, the Industrial Workers of the World, was that it had persisted in striking for decent wages and better working conditions even in war-time—while the American Federation of Labor, headed by Samuel Gompers, had in effect called a truce in its conflicts with employers and had tamely gone with the wind of war propaganda.

Out in the Pacific Northwest the war profiteers had fought fiercely against an I.W.W. strike in the lumber woods for an eight-hour day, shower-baths, and clean bedding instead of unwashed and lousy blankets. The timber-cutters were working eleven or twelve hours a day. Their strike interfered with spruce production. Spruce was needed for aeroplanes, and the West Coast Lumbermen's Association was grieved because the strike cut into profits; spruce was now bringing $90 to $120 a thousand feet in contrast to a price of only $30 a thousand a short time before.

Hot days in this Chicago court; bands below playing national anthems, but nobody rising to their feet here as they had in New York; many of those in attendance with their coats off, and the judge even shedding his necktie. Frank Nebeker, chief prosecutor; he had been counsel for big copper corporations. The defense was being handled by George F. Vanderveer, fearless labor attorney from Seattle; Fred H. Moore of Los Angeles, who had defended Emma Goldman in the free speech fight in San Diego; William F. Cleary, who had been deported into the desert with the striking Bisbee copper miners; Caroline Lowe of Kansas; and Otto Christensen of Chicago.

Jack Reed's description of Judge Landis lingers in memory: "Small on the huge bench sits a wasted man with untidy

---

* The term "Wobbly", said to have been fastened on the I. W. W. members in derision by a Los Angeles editor, had been adopted by them with enthusiasm.

white hair, an emaciated face in which two burning eyes are set like jewels, parchment skin split by a crack for a mouth; the face of Andrew Jackson three years dead. . . . Upon this man has devolved the historic role of trying the Social Revolution. He is doing it like a gentleman. Not that he admits the existence of a Social Revolution. The other day he ruled out of evidence the report of the Committee on Industrial Relations, which the defense was trying to introduce in order to show the background of the I.W.W."

Every one of those defendants could have been a subject for some vivid drama of struggle; they were veterans of industrial battles in half a hundred cities—their names and their testimony evoked pictures of war with exploiting employers in Lawrence, Paterson, Chicago, Spokane, Butte, Seattle, Aberdeen, San Francisco, San Pedro, Everett. From the witness stand one heard echoes of the Ettor-Giovannitti trial in Salem; the lynching of Frank Little in Butte; the Spokane free speech fight; the massacre of I.W.W. members by armed business men and deputy sheriffs on the docks in Everett, Washington; the Mooney-Billings case in San Francisco.

Plenty of publicity—of the wrong kind—was being given to the case by the Chicago newspapers. Whatever the testimony, almost always the inference was that these defendants were guilty of treason. But the reality of the trial was being shown to *New York Call* readers in daily wire dispatches by David Karsner.

Through many days the case against the I.W.W. was built up, mostly with accusations that these men had no respect for property. There was testimony alleging sabotage, copper-nails driven into fruit trees, emery dust thrown into the cogs of machinery, haystacks set on fire—and the prosecution had asked the talesmen at the start: "You believe, do you not, that all children should be taught respect for other people's property?" Various employers testified, and Secret Service men, private detectives, sheriffs and deputies, gunmen, stool-pigeons.

"The wage system," said Mr. Clyne, one of the prosecutors, once, "is established by law, and all opposition to it is opposition to law." And again Nebeker asserted: "A man has no right to revolution under the law." Whereupon Judge

Landis, who occasionally surprised both sides by his bluntness, commented: "Well, that depends on how many men he can get to go in with him—in other words, whether he can put it over."

Jack Reed saw the defendants thus: "Inside the rail of the courtroom, crowded together, many in their shirt-sleeves, some reading papers, one or two stretched out asleep, some sitting, some standing up; the faces of workers and fighters, for the most part, also the faces of orators, of poets, the sensitive and passionate faces of foreigners—but all strong faces, all faces of men inspired somehow; many scarred, few bitter."

Bill Haywood, head of the I.W.W., was on the witness stand four days; and no juror ever dozed in that time; for always the story he told, in answer to questions by Vanderveer, was moving and vital. Through those questions Big Bill, with his large one-eyed head, bulky body, and small hands which seldom gestured, sat there and traced his own life struggle—as a boy in the mines, as an organizer for the Western Federation of Miners in territory where that meant risking death from gun-men's bullets, as a defendant in the famous trial in Boise, when he was one of three accused of conspiracy to kill, and of killing, ex-Governor Steunenberg of Idaho with dynamite; of his helping to organize the Socialist Party, and later the Industrial Workers of the World; and of his part in many of the I.W.W. strikes and free speech conflicts across the land.

John T. Doran, known as "Red" because of his autumnal hued hair, and adorned with a green eye-shade, stood up in court with a chart before him and combined six soap-box speeches into one which lasted five hours. That speech was a liberal education in the details of the class struggle, what the workers were up against, how they were invariably robbed at the point of production. Every juror stayed wide awake during his testimony also. When Red Doran finished, he said: "It is customary with I.W.W. speakers to take up a collection; but under these circumstances, we will dispense with it today."

Ralph Chaplin, bronzed young descendant of New England pioneers of 1638, veteran of the West Virginia coal strike of 1913, when machine-guns mowed down strikers and their families, and editor of the I.W.W. weekly *Solidarity* in Chicago, faced the jury and took full responsibility for an editorial unequivocally opposing the entrance of the United

BILL HAYWOOD.

States into the war. He could have shifted or divided that responsibility, but he chose the harder way.

Among the 101 defendants I was much interested in Meyer Friedkin, a New York boy of wealthy Jewish parents. The color of health was in his cheeks and he had bummed the rails and taken his chances with the migratory workers in many of the hot spots across the country. And there was Herbert Mahler, organizer of the defense committee which had successfully acquitted 74 I.W.W. members of murder charges following the wanton killing of five Wobblies by a business man's mob during a free speech fight in Everett, Washington. No one was tried for those five deaths, but the 74 workers were held for the slaying of two sheriff's deputies. The defense showed conclusively that the deputies were killed by the cross fire of their own crowd.

Stories that were like moving panoramas of the class struggle, each seen from a different angle, were related from the stand by a long line of defendants including Jim Rowan, who had been forced to run the gauntlet of a vigilante line-up and beaten into insensibility near Everett shortly before the massacre there; Vincent St. John, another of the I.W.W. founders, former head of the organization, and once in the thick of the troubles centering about the Western Federation of Miners; Romola Bobba, editor of the I.W.W. Italian paper, *Il Proletario,* who told of conditions among textile workers; Jim Thompson, one of the best of the I.W.W. speakers; Bill Moran, Australian sailor who had recruited new members for the "One Big Union" on all the seas; and J. A. MacDonald, organizer of migratory workers in the harvest fields.

Defense witnesses testified that the I.W.W. had long since withdrawn the pamphlets it once circulated advocating sabotage. It was charged that members had destroyed fruit trees in California, but there was testimony that the organization had widely distributed stickers bearing the words:

"Don't drive copper nails into fruit trees. It harms them."

It was Jim Rowan who was asked a pointed question by Judge Landis. The judge stretched his thin body down from his throne and squinted into Jim's black eyes.

"Mr. Rowan, what is sabotage?"

"Well," said Rowan, "I'd say it's givin' bum work for bum pay."

That jury deliberated only fifty-five minutes, although the evidence against the 101 defendants varied greatly. It found them all guilty, on five counts. But Judge Landis had his own ideas about their relative guilt. He sentenced Haywood, St. John, Chaplin, and some seven others to serve twenty years in Leavenworth; another group got ten years each; a third group drew five years; and a fourth was given terms ranging from one to four years. Landis dealt out these varying sentences on the ground, implied if not specified, that the lesser lights among the defendants had been misled.

One week-end during that trial I went up to Monroe to see my folks. They made me feel at home as always, doing everything possible to insure my comfort. But I noticed that greetings from some of my old acquaintances around town lacked the warmth of the past. They talked with me nervously and seemed to be in a hurry, as if they might be open to criticism if they were seen tarrying with one who had been accused of disloyalty to his country.

My father was perceptibly older than when I had seen him last. And he had changed in other ways. He voiced no specific comment upon my opposition to the United States entering the European war, nor upon my being tried for alleged sedition. But I knew without his mentioning it that he could not comprehend my reasoning. He uttered one sentence which recalled in contrast his liking for independent thinking when I was a boy, and when he would say: "You've got to think things out for yourself."

I had got to talking about some of the atrocities by American super-patriots against unoffending Germans—houses painted yellow, beatings, tarring-and-feathering, and even murder. From my experiences in Washington I cited instances of fake news stories, widely circulated prior to April, 1917, to arouse bitterness against a whole nation and drive this country into the butchery overseas. And I said: "I am proud of the German blood in my mother's veins."

Quietly my father answered: "If I were a young man I'd go to this war."

I said nothing more on that subject, nor did he. I could not debate it with him. Our emotions, I felt sure, were too close to the surface.

His arm lingered about my shoulders as he wished me good luck when I left. He was almost eighty then, still vigorous, and attending to business in the store daily. "But," he said, "one of these days the wheels will stop running."

He died that fall. My mother, then seventy-seven, survived him by four years.

July fourth brought a welcome holiday amid those hot sessions in Judge Landis's courtroom, and Jack Reed and I celebrated by going down to see Eugene Debs in Terre Haute, Indiana. Out on bail on a sedition charge, he was resting at home while awaiting trial. His wife greeted us at the door, and said he was in bed; he had "not been well—not for a whole year." But he immediately got up, and the old fire that I knew came back into the eyes in that worn face as he shook hands with both of us at once.

Jack reported this event in an article for which I made pictures in the *Liberator* of September, 1918. A few excerpts from what Reed wrote are pertinent here.

"The sound of the parade came drifting down. Looking through the darkened windows we watched the people. As they passed the house they motioned or pointed toward it, with expression compounded half of eager malice, and half of a sort of fear. 'That's where Gene Debs lives,' you could see them saying, as one would say, 'The House of the Traitor.'

" 'Come on,' said Gene, suddenly. 'Let's go out and sit on the front porch and give 'em a good show, if they want to see me.'

"So we went out on the porch and took off our coats. And those who passed only looked furtively our way, and whispered, and when they caught Gene's eye, bowed over-cordially. . . .

"Before the war Gene added luster to the name of the town, as well as having an immense personal popularity. In the beginning, practically the whole population, all through that section, was against going to war. . . . But since the war the usual phenomenon has happened in Terre Haute. The whole place has been mobilized physically and spiritually. Except Gene Debs. The simpler people couldn't understand it. The bankers, lawyers, and merchants felt for him a terrible rancour. Even the ministers of the gospel, who had often implored him to address their conventions, now held meetings denouncing 'the enemy in our midst.' "

But Debs was holding solidly to his principles. Jack asked him if he wasn't afraid of lynching. No, that hadn't come into his mind. "I guess I'm psychically protected, anyway," he said. "I know that so long as I keep my eye on them, they won't dare to do anything. As a rule they're cowardly curs anyway."

THE SOWER. Cartoon made for the Socialist Party.

I drew Gene's profile as he sat there in the sun near a porch-box of petunias, and made a sketch of his lean, expressive hands as they punctuated his contempt for the warmakers and his hope for the future: "Socialism's on the way.

They can't stop it, no matter what they do. The more breaks the other side makes, the better for us. . . ."

Debs was tried in Cleveland a few weeks later, with Seymour Stedman of Chicago as his attorney, but he conducted his own defense. He made no attack upon the prosecution's case, so far as the evidence was concerned, but he went ahead to tell the jury about the struggle of men for freedom.

"Chattel slavery has disappeared," he said. "But we are not yet free. We are engaged in another mighty agitation today. It is as wide as the world. It is the rise of the toiling and producing masses, who are gradually becoming conscious of their interest, their powers, as a class, who are organizing industrially and economically, who are slowly but surely developing the economic and political power that is to set them free. They are still in the minority, but they have learned how to wait and to bide their time. It is because I happen to be in this minority that I stand in your presence today, charged with crime."

Not one word of his speech in Canton did he take back or try to soften. Instead he re-asserted the right of any minority, or any individual, to speak out against war or any other act of a nation which that minority or individual believed wrong.

The indictment charged Debs with utterances calculated to incite mutiny in the army, stirring up disloyalty to the government, obstructing the enlistment of soldiers, encouraging resistance to the United States of America, and promoting the cause of the enemy. Then sixty-three years old, Debs was found guilty and sent to Atlanta penitentiary to serve ten years.*

In August I met Jack Reed on the street in New York, and he said: "I've just been up to Croton having a long talk with Max. I'm resigning from the *Liberator*."

He told me why, and in the September issue Jack's letter explaining this action was published. "The reason," he wrote, "is that I cannot in these times bring myself to share editorial responsibility for a magazine which exists upon the sufferance of Mr. Burleson." Then he stated that he didn't want to cease as a contributor, and ended by saying: "And in the happy

* There he contracted the heart illness which shortened his life. President Harding commuted his sentence in 1921, but five years later he died.

day when we can again call a spade a spade without tying bunting on it, you will find me as you have in the past, yours for the profound social change."

Max Eastman's reply also appeared in that issue:

"I haven't a word of protest—only a deep feeling of regret.

"In your absence we all weighed the matter and decided it was our duty to the social revolution to keep this instrument we have created alive toward a time of great usefulness. You will help us with your writing and reporting, and that is all we ask.

"Personally I envy you the power to cast loose when not only a good deal of the dramatic beauty, but also the glamour of abstract moral principle, is gone out of the venture, and it remains for us merely the most effective and therefore the right thing to do."

Recalling these letters, in the *Modern Monthly* for October, 1936, Max makes Reed's attitude clear:

"Jack thought that my editorials, under this policy of getting by with [Postmaster-General] Burleson—I had actually gone to see him in Washington, in company with E. W. Scripps, and deployed my most bourgeois charms against him—were getting a little yellow. (I think so too as I read them now.) But Jack also recognized the value of a 'legal organ,' and testified to it by promising to contribute in the future."

And of course the *Liberator,* as a legal organ, had already shown its value, particularly in enabling us to publish a detailed report of our trial a few months earlier, and showing what the sponsors of a magazine attempting to tell the truth were up against in war-time.

Now we of the *Masses* were ordered to trial again. Reed, who had been in Russia when we others faced the first jury, was eager for whatever might come. All this would help greatly to educate the public, he averred; soon there would be more good people in prison than outside. Glintenkamp had not reappeared, but we heard new and unverifiable rumors of his whereabouts—he was painting in Tahiti; fomenting a revolution in Chile; doing wood-cuts in Cuba; and running a duck farm near Albia, Iowa.

The second trial came in September, with Judge Martin Manton presiding. Again Barnes was prosecutor, but this time we were defended by Seymour Stedman of Chicago, Charles Recht, and Walter Nelles. Before a jury chosen from another large list of middle-class talesmen, the same evidence was set forth, and with much the same kind of argument on both sides.

Prosecutor Barnes, however, added some colorful touches. Citing the name of a lawyer who had been in the army and was killed in battle, he said, pointing reprovingly at each defendant in turn: "He not only died for his country, but he died for Max Eastman, he died for Floyd Dell, he died for John Reed, he died for Merrill Rogers." I was waiting for him to mention me, but he didn't, and I leaned over and asked Reed: "Who was this hero who didn't die for *me?*" Just then a recess was called, and on the way out Reed said: "Cheer up, Art, Jesus died for you."

While Barnes was cross-examining me, he said at one point:

"Now, Mr. Young, you have told us a good deal about your beliefs in revolution and that you believe that the American Revolution was justified, *but, Mr. Young,* do you believe in the theory of the class struggle?"

And I answered something like this:

"If you've got the measles, Mr. Barnes, it doesn't necessarily mean that you believe in them."

Again the jury disagreed, and one juror shed some light on the character of the deliberations when he said to us: "It was a good thing for you boys that you were all American born; otherwise it might have gone pretty hard with you."

Chapter 33

SOME OPTIMISTS LAUNCH ANOTHER MAGAZINE

"NOW is the time for us to start a magazine," said Ellis O. Jones early in 1919. Ellis had been an associate editor of *Life*. The war was over, and the Post Office Department more tolerant. Survivors of the late horror were reaching out to recover their lost sanity, and authors long silent were writing books with the truth in them.

We agreed that people ought to laugh again (or at least try to laugh), and we could help them to find reasons for fresh hope. Other writers and cartoonists liked the idea. One factor which stirred me toward this new move was my feeling of dissatisfaction with the *Liberator*, which was featuring my work but not paying for it.

I had considered it a privilege to draw for the *Liberator*. But a few of us on the staff who had always been ready to contribute for nothing began to feel that it wasn't quite right that engravers, printers, paper dealers, and desk-editors should have their pay or the magazine would not go on, while those who did the creative work had to forego compensation. That was and still is a condition accepted by those who contribute to radical magazines which are not self-sustaining. Yet one's individual economic responsibilities sometimes call for a more fruitful arrangement.

Boardman Robinson and I attended an editorial meeting one evening, the purpose of which was to figure out some way to pay us something for our cartoons. I remember saying at the time that I wanted to know if I was an asset to the *Liberator* or just an ass. I made a plea for at least enough to pay for our drawing paper and ink, as a gesture in the right direction. It was agreed that thereafter more attention would be given to paying a fixed rate to cartoonists—"if possible". Robinson and I left the meeting with those comforting words "if possible" to repeat to ourselves.

I was keen about Ellis Jones's suggestion that a new

magazine be launched. We promptly arranged to hold a conference on the question in Allaire's restaurant. During the war that old-time hang-out of the literati had become sad and pretty much abandoned because it was German, and even after it had been lavishly decorated with American flags, 100 per cent Americans who had once patronized it still stayed away.

It was one of those "be sure to come" conferences, and we gathered at a spacious table where members of the same

CHARLES W. ERVIN, managing editor of the *New York Daily Call.*

group had met often to discuss the tragic aspects of a war which we all felt had been an inexcusable wrong. Those present included Charles W. Ervin, managing editor of the *Call;* Ryan Walker, its prolific cartoonist; Charles W. Wood, then on the *World,* and several others.

We thought it time to satirize the whole capitalistic works. Not with subtle analysis of conditions in essays and the like, but with straightforward exposé in cartoons and comment, and with comedy rampant. Certainly now the people would respond to such truth. But we were conscious of the fact that many radicals and liberals were weary—and worn out with vain hope. After the Versailles treaty many of them had thrown up their hands in despair. Wilson's Fourteen Points, a covenant which promised the beginning of a new and honest deal for the sorrowing world, had been choked to death, to the satisfaction of Big Business. But in spite of this atmosphere of disillusion, we thought the people would see the truth that would eventually make them free.

Was there a chance for a magazine that would try to awaken the Socialist spirit anew, give new hope, and yet keep aloof from the bias of politics? Anyway we would find out. This first meeting was chiefly for the purpose of choosing a name for it. Never mind about the money to keep it going—we would decide on a name, and start from there. The business meetings would come later, and they did, *often*.

I had first met Ellis Jones when we were among the founding fathers of the Dutch Treat Club. For a time, too, he had been on the staff of the *Masses*. He was one of the first to enlist for the voyage on Ford's Peace Ship, and *Life* (which he had helped to edit and contributed to for years) had publicly denounced him for this and proclaimed with pride that he was no longer connected with the magazine.

The conferees discussed the well-known names of existing comic papers—American, English, German, French. Then I said, "Why not call it by some familiar name—some name that we hear every day—?"

Ellis chimed in with: "Like 'Good morning, have you used Pear's Soap?'" which was an advertisment long familiar to the public.

"That's it," I said, "Let's make it *Good Morning*."

There were no dissenters, and I began to sketch out a top for the editorial page (technically known as a mast-head)—with a jovial figure personifying the rising sun as our emblem.

All those present promised to contribute writings or pictures, and we foresaw no difficulty in getting others to help in the same way. We would send out a call for material. That left only the problem of finding money with which to pay overhead. From his experience in publishing, Charlie Ervin figured we would need $10,000 to make a go of the enterprise.

"Certainly there must be money available to finance this kind of a magazine," said one conferee or another. . . . "Satire and ridicule can be more effective weapons than solemn statistics and shrill denunciation. . . . We'll ask the labor unions to take bulk subscriptions. And we'll get unemployed men to sell the magazine on the streets."

Ellis Jones and I came away with the understanding that he and I would canvass certain likely prospects for money, with the other conferees helping "in any way we can." I had high hopes that day, with the keen interest the group had shown at the meeting at Allaire's. At this time I was 53 years old, and a bit battered and sad to look at in my mirror. But I felt that the magazine venture would give me a new hold on life. I needed that as much as the public did—perhaps more.

First I would get in touch with a well-to-do friend who had been enthusiastic over my Washington drawings and articles in the *Metropolitan*. This was Morris Rippenbein, a tobacco manufacturer in Perth Amboy, New Jersey. He had come to this country as a young man from Russia, and as he put it, had "worked like a horse" to get on, and though he had become rich he was unspoiled. Now past middle age, Rip was as radical, using the word in its derivative sense, as any of the flaming youngsters about me, but quiet about it. He had read widely in philosophy, economics, and history; loved pinochle and the theatre; and had a sober sense of the ridiculous.

Long before our planning conference, Rip had hinted to me, one evening when we dined together in the Lafayette, that he might help finance a comic magazine edited by me if I would start one.

So we met again and I put the question up to him. He got out a pencil and paper and began figuring. Yes, he would help, with money and otherwise, but he could not give any great sum of money, he explained; he had to be cautious with his income because he had a large family to support, including aunts, sisters, brothers, nieces, nephews, and cousins here and abroad. He was ready to be one of a group of individuals who would give $75 a month each toward expenses —provided we could raise the essential $10,000 preliminary fund. To have a chance of survival, the project must start with enough cash in hand to carry us safely at least a year without worry.

That was sound sense, of course, and I set out with confidence to round up that money. Systematically I made appointments by telephone and went to see the best of the prospects on the list—and sometimes Rip went with me and explained better than I the importance of the proposed magazine. But the going was tough. If at that time there was any lack of sympathy in my heart for the man who finds it necessary to beg, I've had a full complement of it ever since. No harder work than that.

Some days I would do pretty well, but other days were disheartening. I could always get an entree, but when a tired radical with a comfortable income would say, "Good luck, Art, here's a check for fifty dollars", I would wonder how long it would take the *Good Morning* sun to rise if that was all the encouragement it was going to get. . . . Then I'd have a run of better days. And my spirits would lift again. Eugen Jan Boissevain wrote a check for $1,000 and asked if that was enough; this was compensation for all the weeks of weariness.

Max Eastman, however, was plainly vexed at the prospect of the new publication starting. He felt that our collections were cutting into the *Liberator's* sources of money, for naturally we would appeal to much the same kind of people for support. There was of course no denying that one of the principal duties of the *Liberator's* editor was to raise funds to meet the frequent operating deficit.

After three months I had gathered in about $4,500 in cash. Meanwhile Ellis Jones, who was to be editor of *Good Morning,* was in an office that we had rented in the People's House, mainly occupied by the Rand School, at 7 East 15th Street. He was impatient to go ahead—fund or no fund.

I knew from my investigations that $10,000 was little enough to have in starting a weekly magazine such as we had planned. But Ellis argued that the important thing was to get out the first issue. After that—after people saw that the magazine was a fact and not just a hope—money could be raised more easily. He had been working on the dummy, and was practically ready to go to press, if I would say the word.

Though reluctant, I acquiesced, much to the annoyance

and disappointment of Morris Rippenbein. "Foolish!" he said. . . . "You're right," I answered, "but let 'er go. I'm not a tired radical, but I'm tired of begging for money."

So *Good Morning* arose with this pronouncement on its editorial page: "A weekly burst of humor, satire, and fun—with now and then a fleeting beam of wisdom." The first issue of 10,000 copies was published May 8, 1919, and sold out quickly. It looked like a success. Obviously peeved at the premature start, Rip nevertheless paid in the promised $75 a month, and continued to do so during the three years that the magazine lived. And now that *Good Morning* had peered over the horizon, cheerful letters came in to commend the new day from Hendrik Van Loon, William Marion Reedy, Clarence Day Jr., Stephen Leacock, Horace Traubel, Oscar Ameringer, and numerous others.

After five months, Ellis Jones, who had been writing the editorials and a capital series called "Sinbad and the Old Man of the Sea", which I illustrated, became critical of the business management and resigned. There had been no business management to speak of, but his criticism was well taken. Now it was my responsibility alone. I was editor, publisher, and goat.

We were often hard put to raise money to pay for paper (costly at that time), printing, distribution, and office expense. As I remember, I received $50 a week for about four months, and Ellis Jones received the same during his connection with the magazine. Our stenographer, who was also receptionist, received $25 a week, although later we raised that to $35.

For some time we got along without paying much attention to promotion or the business end of publishing. But there was a tradition in radical circles that a business manager who could get advertising and make a radical magazine a going concern was some kind of a magician, a wand-waver worth more than mere editors. As a consequence, prospective business managers would call on me often, each one assuring me that all that was needed to build *Good Morning's* circulation to *Saturday Evening Post* proportions was his services. Finally I acceded to the idea that a business manager might be useful. But I made it plain that he would have to work more for glory than for money. During its precarious life our magazine had three business managers—the last one, A. H. Howland, generously donating his services most of the time, as I, too, was doing. The receptionist-stenographer was always paid first. Income from news-stand sales and 4,000 subscriptions kept us afloat and in good humor the first year.

But banquets and balls for the purpose of money-raising and a lynx-eyed hunt for an angel willing to take a chance on a promising magazine were vitally necessary—and we staged social functions of picturesque character as often as we thought our public would respond to them.

A GOOD MORNING POSTER, announcing a spring-time dance to aid its treasury.

One of these, a Harvest Festival, is memorable for several reasons, including the funds which it inadvertently failed to produce. This was held in Yorkville Casino on Saturday, November 6, 1920. Dinner and dance, with corn-stalks and pumpkins for decorations. Charles W. Wood was chairman, and a frolicsome note keyed the speeches. Helen Keller spoke, saying:

"I came tonight, knowing there would be no blue devils here. . . . You are all jolly good fellows. You have kept alive, through the bitter winter of the world's discontent, the spirit of spring and youth. Your gayety has blown my own heart into a glow. . . . The world needs more of this dauntless spirit of laughter. . . . While we can meet together and laugh, there is hope for the world. With laughter and hope and the Revolution in our hearts, all the powers of earth shall not prevail against us."

I read my annual report on the status of *Good Morning:*

"Cash on hand, $2.33, also 20 cents worth of slightly damaged postage stamps; assets, about $49. As for liabilities, we are liable to do almost anything. . . . Disbursements have been considerable. Exact figures are hard to get at. Any money that we received was so quickly snatched from us by printers and paper dealers that we couldn't get time to record the transaction. . . .

"One day last week two subscriptions came in the same mail—one from a woman in Iowa, who said she was 'disgusted', and one from a man in Milepost, Missouri, who said he was 'temporarily in an insane asylum,' but that he was 'with us heart and soul.' . . . *Good Morning* was partisan in the late campaign. It opposed Wilson and Bunk and advocated Harding and Hell. Some of our stockholders think we should have stayed out of politics, but our leading contributor, the Poor Fish, said he would resign if we didn't advocate a change. . . ."

Charlie Wood was supposed to have followed my report with an appeal for funds, but everybody was having such a good time that this matter slipped his mind. I didn't notice the omission either.

That night I met a tall young man named John Nicholas Beffel, who had just returned from the Pacific Coast, where he had reported for the *New York Call* and other labor papers the trial of ten I.W.W. members for defending their hall in Centralia, Washington, against an American Legion mob. He had come back lecturing across the country on the class-war in the West.

Tables and chairs were being cleared away for the dance as Beffel told me about talking with Tom Mooney in San Quentin penitentiary and with Carl Haessler, conscientious objector from Wisconsin, in Alcatraz. Then one of *Good Morning's* trusty henchmen hove in sight with a huge colored papier-mache head of the Poor Fish, for which we had paid $30. Instantly Beffel's husky shoulders suggested something, and I, as president of the publishing corporation, elected him to wear that fantastic costume. Helen Keller stood near, and presently her sensitive hands were exploring the contour of the Poor Fish's head, asking whether he was a whale or a shark, and feeding him red apples.

Now the orchestra struck up, and the grand march began, led by the Poor Fish and Polly Markowitz, bobbed Titian-haired youngster, who was then with the Federated Press. I was next in line, with my lovely partner of the evening, Jessica Milne.

By the time we had swung into the dancing, Charlie Wood remembered with chagrin that he had overlooked the main purpose of the affair. In a valiant attempt to save the occasion, he and others who knew what had happened, went among the guests holding out their hats while trying to explain—but too late. The opportune time had passed. Apparently the assembled merry-makers had put all thoughts of money out of their minds. So the harvest that evening was sparse, though as a festival the gathering was one of *Good Morning's* best.

However, other dances and parties for fund-raising kept us from bankruptcy. We had established a cartoon mat service, which was subscribed to by many labor papers throughout the country, but starting as an asset, it turned out to be a liability. Our clients enthusiastically published the material we supplied, but most of them were low on cash, and collections were difficult, often impossible.

Our mainstays among contributing writers were Charles W. Wood and T. Swann Harding, while occasional pieces in prose or verse came from Howard Brubaker, Samuel DeWitt, Clement Wood, Phillips Russell, Mabel Dwight, Miriam Allen DeFord, Art Shields, Samuel Roth, John Nicholas Beffel, and Skepticuss.

Artists who drew for the magazine included Boardman Robinson, Hendrik Van Loon, Robert Minor, Maurice Becker, Reginald Marsh, Cornelia Barns, Peggy Bacon, Clara Tice, Lou Rogers, Will Crawford, Edmund Duffy, William Auerbach Levy, Alice Beach Winter, William Gropper, Adolph Dehn, Frank Hanley, Norman Jacobson, Albert Levering, Frank Walts, John Barber, and F. F. Jerger.

Volunteers were plentiful in emergencies, especially when

we needed to mail out circulars. Martha Foley would often assist in the editing, and once at least she wrote the editorial page. Arthur Cole and Horace Reis, both of whom were then on the *Nation,* would come to the office and help on make-up nights.

Our friends among the writers and artists were glad to contribute; all we had to do was ask them. I knew that none of them expected pay—but once when we chanced to have some extra cash in the bank I sent checks to about 20 contributors as a surprise; doubtless it also was a shock.

SMALL FAVORS THANKFULLY RECEIVED.

I remember letters I received thanking me—and saying they never expected it.

When Woodrow Wilson spoke in Kansas City shortly after his return from Versailles and told the real cause of the war of 1914-18, I made a cartoon about it for *Good Morning,* entitling it "Letting the Cat Out of the Bag." With this we reproduced an all-revealing passage from his speech:

"Is there any man here, or any woman, . . . is there any child here, who does not know that the seed of war in the modern world is industrial and commercial rivalry? The real reason that the war we have just finished took place was that Germany was afraid her commercial rivals were going to get the better of her, and the reason why some nations went into the war was that they thought Germany would get the commercial advantage of them. . . . This war, in its inception, was a commercial and industrial war. It was not a political war."

Max Eastman's annoyance at the launching of *Good Morning* did not cause any break between us, and I continued to contribute to the *Liberator*. Late in August, 1919, Max and I went to Chicago to report for that magazine the emergency convention of the Socialist party, which immediately split off into conventions at which two other radical movements were set going—the Communist party and the Communist Labor party.

Sitting at the press table in Machinists' Hall on South Ashland Avenue on the opening day of the S.P. gathering, we saw a stirring contest for power. Adolph Germer, national secretary, and member of the right wing, was in the chair, and it was evident at the start that he faced an intense fight from the militant left wing. The Socialist party's national executive committee had been expelling branches, locals, and individual members all over the country for conduct which it thought too brash and disgracefully radical.

John Reed was one of the group which was determined to check the conservative trend of the old-line Socialists. It was the idea of Reed, Louis B. Boudin, C. E. Ruthenberg, Alfred Wagenknecht, and other delegates that they could capture the convention and make the party over in the image of revolutionary Marxism as they understood it. It was wild ferment from the beginning.

Just before Max and I arrived, Jack Reed had had a fight with Julius Gerber of the right wing out on the porch of the convention hall. Chuckling as he described it, he told me that it began like a boxing-match and that, after a few bouts, he held Julius off at arm's length clutched by his neck. "It was a great fight. Too bad you missed it," he said. I made a picture of it from Jack's description, published in the *Liberator*.

When it looked as if the militants actually would take control of the convention, the police came and cleared the hall of all persons present except those who were approved by the right wing leaders. One of those ejected was a delegate who had received the largest vote in Kansas. Having been forced to leave, Reed and his allies, in a dramatic walkout, marched to a room on the floor below and opened the first convention of the Communist Labor party. That room not being large enough, they moved over to the I.W.W. hall on Throop street. A third group, made up of members of the Slavic Federations and of Michigan members of the S.P. who had been expelled (all Michigan members had been ousted in a bloc) hastened to Smolny Hall on Blue Island Avenue and there held the convention of the Communist party. (Subsequently, the Communist Labor party faded out and more or less of its substance was absorbed by the Communist party.)

Here Jack Reed was in the most playful and yet the most serious mood in which I had ever seen him. When his group opened their convention they sang the *Internationale* with a gusto which resounded throughout the building and into the street. Both right and left wings claimed credit for victory that day.

I met Victor Berger, who was one of the Old Guard, as we left the scene. "Say, Art," he said, "you tell Jack he better write another book."

"About what?" I asked.

"You tell Jack to write a book about the Three Days That Shook the Left Wing."

Chapter 34

SUCCESSFUL PUBLISHING REQUIRES HARDNESS

AFTER a couple of years there were times when volunteer cooperation reached a low ebb, and I found myself doing most of the cartoons, reading copy, writing editorials, making up the magazine, and falling asleep at my desk when I should have been on the move. Surely *Good Morning* had given me a new interest in life, as I had hoped, but now I knew that the burden of publication routine was becoming too much for me.

Sometimes when my spirits sagged under the strain, I would take long walks through quiet back streets late at night to reflect on the future. At the age of fifty-four the man or woman is lucky who does not have to fight off gloom. When you reach the half-century line you begin to think seriously about how to apportion your time, to get the best out of yourself while the years are slipping away. As a young man you don't care—all the time in the world is ahead.

I would berate myself for not having drawn on the stone to get those variegated values of light and shade which make lithography so fascinating. I wished I had not neglected etching. I was sure I could handle the dry point stylus on the copper plate. And why had I not done, or tried to do, cartoons in oil-paint? Certainly all of the great paintings of the Renaissance were basically cartoons, to propagandize the cause of Christianity. I, too, had a cause—and why not try to put it across in paintings? Several of my fellow artists on the *Masses* had found time to indulge their talent in media which made their work take on the look of permanent value to connoisseurs and critics.

But here I was drawing cartoons on paper with whatever implement was nearest at hand—pen or crayon—when not writing and bothering about a publication with no time to think of anything else. And how much influence did it actually have? Did it any more than touch the edge of its possibilities? Anyway, I knew that starting with only $4,500 instead of waiting until we had raised the whole $10,000—or better still $50,000—was a mistake.

These questions would come into my mind as I sat at my desk laboring over copy. In such an hour of retrospection I was visited by three young men from the Art Students' League. The spokesman, David Morrison, achieved considerable note as a painter a few years later. They came as a

JAMES EADS HOW, millionaire hobo, gave me marshmallows but no money.

committee from the League to ask if I would become an instructor of one of the drawing classes there. When I shook my head they told me of the simple and seemingly easy requirements—just going to the school twice a week and criticizing the work of the students—for which I would be paid something like $60 weekly. But I said no, that I had a magazine to look after which took all my time—and what was more to the point, that I felt I was not equipped temperamentally to be a successful instructor.

On another day when the problem of finances was pressing heavily on our minds, dear old James Eads How, the "millionaire hobo", dropped in. While I was welcoming him, A. H. Howland, the business manager, hastened to remove a pile of newspapers from the extra chair, so that our caller would be comfortable. Then I explained the situation, and tactfully asked How if he could help out with a loan to keep us from bankruptcy. He said something about his funds being "all tied up", but he appeared interested and wrote down the address of an acquaintance who might be able to aid us. As How arose to leave he took from his coat pocket a box of marshmallows and presented it to me. When he was gone and I announced the net result of the conference, "an address and a box of marshmallows", we of the office staff looked at one another silently and solemnly shook our heads—then laughed.

All sorts of queer literary contributions were offered to us by amateur writers, who lived in the city as well as in the sticks—long poems, dissertations on theosophy, cowboy humor by drugstore cowboys, automobile jokes which were familiar horse-and-buggy jokes adapted to the machine age, he-and-she jokes, quips borrowed from vaudeville comedians, bright sayings by children who must have fallen on their heads in infancy, Pat-and-Mike jokes, and jokes about funerals and hangings. Most of the unsolicited manuscripts we received came from persons who obviously were ignorant of the underlying trend of our magazine.

Once an anxious faced middle-aged woman walked in and asked me to read a poem comprising several typed sheets written by her brother. It was filled with saccharine praise for *Good Morning*. When I handed it back, gently breaking the news that we couldn't pay for such contributions, she said: "I'm terribly disappointed! My brother had depended on my selling this to you—*he's got to have his teeth fixed.*"

For some issues of *Good Morning* there was a big demand. Jobless radicals around Union Square, a block away, seized the chance to make some change by selling the magazine on street corners. These young men (and some not so young) were mostly well-read and healthy minded, and were opposed to working like slaves for the capitalist system. I liked them, and knew many of them by name—Dan O'Brien,

Frank Strong Hamilton, Harvey Stork, Curly Daniels, the inimitable Harry Engels, and others.

They swarmed into our fourth floor office around publication days, and I learned things from them. Many of them had traveled widely, as sailors; others had been itinerant workers in the lumber woods, orchards, and grain fields of America, and some had been "over there" in the so-called world war. Certain ones were good soap-boxers, speaking effectively for industrial unionism, Socialism, anarcho-syndicalism, with variations on the pleasures and vicissitudes of the "free life" of the hobo. A few had no regard for business ethics, not even among friends. But all were worth knowing.

FIXING UP THE WORLD WAR SOLDIERS.

Betty Kaye, our secretary and office manager, called my attention to the fact that many bundles of *Good Morning* given out to the street-sellers on consignment were not being paid for. She said I was too easy with them, that the office could not be run successfully without some practical sense, and that I ought to be firm about sales on trust. "All right," I agreed, "we'll be firm." So Betty began to treat the delinquents with peppery resentment. She made it plain that she was going to end this grafting by so-called comrades from Union Square benches.

With such thoughts in her mind and fire in her eyes she looked up from her typewriter one day while I was out, and saw a man enter who was travel-dusty and had the untailored look of a Wobbly. He said he wanted to see me.

"He isn't in," said Betty tartly, "and I don't know when he's coming back. But listen—if you want to peddle *Good Mornings* we're through—do you hear?" "We're through with you bums!"

Soon after I got back to the office there was a phone call from Upton Sinclair saying he was in town, and could we get together for dinner? He had looked in at my office but had "met with a screen of protective coloration." Then I told Betty I wished I had been in when Upton Sinclair called.

"My God!" said Betty, "Was that Upton Sinclair? And I put him out!"

Sometimes the boys would be arrested. One night Harry Engels was trying to sell the magazine to a crowd in Brooklyn. He read excerpts from its pages, held up a double-page cartoon of mine for all to see, and declared that I was "a satirist as great as Voltaire."

A cop interrupted him. "That's enough of that. Come with me!"

Taken to court, the prisoner was dismissed with a reprimand. Next day he sent me a clipping from the *Brooklyn Eagle* citing the offending quotation from his speech, with a note pointing out that those who sold *Good Morning* had to run risks, and that the business office ought to be lenient with them.

Engels had a clever way with audiences, and always put on a good show. From his well dressed appearance, he might have been a rich man's son. He had a friend who owned one of the better makes of automobiles. The two would drive up to a spot where a radical soap-boxer was making a speech to a crowd of workers. Engels would interrupt the other, and would address the audience from a capitalistic point of view.

"Don't we give you parks and free schools and bridges?" he would demand. "Haven't we given you the five-cent fare?"

And when he had got his listeners well steamed up with indignation, he would begin talking about the merits of *Good Morning* as a literary diet for those who were not satisfied with the "gifts" from the capitalists.

In contrast to the rough boys who were continual callers —one day I saw a well-groomed, cultured-looking old gentleman looking over a bound file of *Good Morning* in the reception room and heard Betty call him Mr. Allen. I left my desk when I heard that name, saying to myself: "I'll bet that is James Lane Allen, author of *The Choir Invisible*", and it was! I told him his stories were prose poetry, and we had a mutual admiration chat.

Lincoln Steffens came in soon after his return from the Peace Conference in Versailles, where he had seen President Wilson's fourteen-point plan for healing the wounds of war ridiculed and spat upon by his European rivals in diplomacy, backed by the business interests of their nations.

"You're right, Art," said Steffens, "keep *Good Morning* going. There's nothing to do now but laugh—laugh like Hell!"

Wise sayings of the Poor Fish, a character I originated in the early days of *Good Morning,* attracted wide attention and comment. Carl Van Doren, then literary editor of *Century Magazine,* called it "a classic, a genuine contribution to the scene and civilization." Lincoln Steffens wrote an essay on Poor Fish philosophy, with permission to use it if I wanted to, in a book of pictures and sayings of the Fish—but I never got around to assembling the material for that volume. Many labor periodicals reprinted the likeness of the Poor Fish, in the various poses in which I portrayed him, while emitting his weighty thoughts on current topics. Long after *Good Morning* had ceased to exist, some labor editors continued to use pictures of this character of mine (without credit) but with new sayings which they invented, not always in the naive language of common street talk which I used as the true Fish idiom.

Here are samples of authentic wisdom from the mouth of the Poor Fish, taken from *Good Morning:*

> "Progress is all right, but it ought to stop sometime."
>
> "The Poor Fish says he knows that many of our leading citizens got their wealth dishonestly, but we ought to let bygones be bygones."
>
> "If people would work harder we would not have so much unrest."
>
> "Anybody who is making a good living ought to keep his mouth shut."
>
> "The Poor Fish says that if there are any ex-soldiers

Good Morning

THE POOR FISH. He appeared in many costumes and postures. Specimens of his wisdom are cited in Chapter 34.

mixed up in these bomb outrages they ought to know better."

"If a man has saved up a billion dollars, he is entitled to enjoy it. Instead of trying to take his billion away from him, every man should try to save up a billion of his own."

"Liquor is not injurious if taken in moderation. Unfortunately, the workingman never knows when he has had enough."

"The Poor Fish says agitators just stir up trouble, and what with his two sons crippled in the War for Democracy, and the High Cost of Living, we have enough trouble as it is."

We brought out a God Number of *Good Morning* on July 1, 1920. "Isn't God conscripted to support war?" we asked. "Isn't He exploited at political conventions? Why can't He be put to the good use of the common people?" William Blake, who illustrated his own verse, left to posterity several pictures of God, one of which we reproduced, pointing out that this likeness of divine omnipotence resembled a well-known American, William Cullen Bryant.

"Other Blake designs of the Deity," we recalled, "look more like a composite of an Indiana farmer and Moses. Every artist who has attempted divine interpretation in sculpture or painting insists on a portrait with whiskers. Is that settled? Can't someone think of a new, rejuvenated, up-to-date God? We really believe that God would like to see a new portrait of himself." Our readers were invited to send in such pictures.

"More backbone in the public officials of the Holy Land" was demanded in a contributed editorial represented as having appeared in the *Palestine Times,* conservative organ of the Rome Chamber of Commerce at the time of Christ's crucifixion. Percy Atkinson, then circulation manager of the *Metropolitan,* was the author of this editorial.

"Pontius Pilate cannot be commended too highly," it said, "for having upheld the cause of law and order in the execution of the so-called 'King of the Jews' last Tuesday. All right thinking people will sustain him. Hence, it seems all the more regrettable that he should have shown the least sign of weakness in making his decision. This is bound to react unfavorably upon the rabble who may accept 'I wash my hands of this affair' as an incentive toward further demonstrations. . . .

"We must not forget that there are still apostles and adherents of the new religion at large. Their capacity for harm is by no means at an end. They should be immediately apprehended and summarily dealt with.

"There are rumors that Pilate will be recalled by Rome. In that event we trust that he will be replaced by a strong, decisive, conservative official. At this time we need a business man at the helm, not a weakling or a visionary.

"Another 'sermon on the mount' should be made impossible; further spectacular legerdemain such as the 'miracle' of the loaves and the fishes, upsetting the food market, should meet with stern repression; leniency toward prostitution, another 'go and sin no more' incident, affronting the moral sense of the community, must not be repeated.

"If Pilate cannot deal with these conditions so vitally affecting our business interests and our social and industrial integrity, he should be recalled forthwith."

And in that issue, the Poor Fish said that "God will provide" but "at the same time he feels that the best planks in both political platforms are those which oppose the high cost of living."

One of the most successful issues of *Good Morning*, judged by sales and recorded enthusiasm, was the Harding Inaugural Number on February 15, 1921. For this I made drawings of a grand parade in nine sections stretching across as many pages. I can use space in this book for only two illustrations of this magnificent turnout of notables; description of the others must suffice.

1. First—leading the parade—came the editor, myself, with the business manager of *Good Morning* and the Poor Fish, in an automobile, all ardent supporters of the 'Back to Normalcy' movement.
2. General Pershing proudly perched on a high horse with his chin protruding to denote bravery; President Harding entirely surrounded by the "best minds"—Root, Hughes, Weeks, *et al.*
3. The best people of Marion, Ohio, including Henry Deuteronomy Harding, the banker; Doctor Balaam Harding of Blooming Grove, Cousin Em, Old Josh

THE HARDING INAUGURAL PARADE. *Dramatis personae* are identified in Chapter 34. Top picture is Strip No. 9, and the bottom one is No. 6.

Harding, and others. Also a bandwagon of job-hunters playing, "What a friend we have in Gamaliel."
4. Group of underfed school children doing homage to the Packing Trust (a gigantic garlanded hog). Col. George Harvey and Lillian Russell doing their campaign dance, the Harding Hula-Hula. Representatives of the unemployed strewing roses and chanting the same old hymns of hope.
5. Liberty Bonds getting kicked around and howling, "I want to go back to par." Dollar-a-year patriotic profiteers, including the 57 varieties of trust presidents, with Charlie Schwab sprinkling the street with tears. (Charlie had broken down and sobbed before a committee investigating his profits in the war.) Ku Klux Klan, bodyguard for the profiteers and standard-bearers of race-hatred, reaction, and private vengeance.
6. William Howard Taft, only happy ex-President, dancing the toddle. Old Aunty Blue Law, Herbert Hoover, eating a 41-cent lunch of mush-and-milk to relieve the children of Messarabia. The railroads (a silk-hatted figure in pauper's rags with a plea to "help the poor.") Henry Ford throwing an anti-Semitic fit.
7. Grand Old Mummies of the U.S. Senate taking the air. Touching tableau of American and German capital trying to get together after "the recent misunderstanding." Splendiferous float typifying the progress of religion. (Mammon atop a church equipped with cannon, the devil driving, Jesus and his cross being dragged behind.)
8. Samuel Gompers, accompanied by his valet flying Sam's overalls. And now: Hats off! The Supreme Court (thunder from Sinai), interpreting laws with dignity and respect for the best people. The Tariff Issue coming back to normalcy (a bearded ancient sitting up in his coffin).
9. Dramatic Troupe of Near-Thinkers (they know something is wrong, but are not certain what): Fighting Bob La Follette smiting his breast. Senator Borah, who tries a little to bore from within. The Power of the Press, ably performed by William Randolph Hoist and Arthur Whizzbrain. William Jennings Bryan, playing the heavy in the

new drama, "Resurrection, or Democracy Triumphant". The Fountain of Wrath, Hiram Johnson, rehearsing for his next appearance.
10. The Fag End: a private citizen (Woodrow Wilson) moving his household effects with the help of Barney Baruch, accompanied by secretaries, waste paper, points, presents from King George, and dilapidated principles.

Arthur Brisbane never seemed to mind my cartoons showing him with a bulging forehead and labeled "Whizzbrain". Around that time he published an editorial with a reprint of one of my drawings saying:

"Art Young will die pointing to 'tomorrow' without ever having seen it, just as Marcus Aurelius died, or Karl Marx, or one of the Gracchi, or Madame Roland, just as all the young, ardent souls will die with their longings unsatisfied."

Good Morning had appeared as a weekly up to October, 1919. Then we were compelled to skip some numbers through lack of money, and in January, 1920, we offered 7 per cent preferred stock in our company at $10 a share.* But there was no rush to buy these shares, and in May the magazine became a semi-monthly. We came out regularly for awhile, then had to skip more issues. In August, September, and October, 1921, the magazine appeared only once a month, although the masthead still blandly carried the legend: "published twice a month" and it was our hope to continue as a fortnightly.

But the October number was the last. The burden of raising the necessary money had become too great. There are many pitfalls in magazine publishing. The successful publisher requires a certain hardness, and he needs to surround himself with others possessed of pile-driving energy. The babes who enter the woods of publishing usually are not equipped for big-game hunting and seldom escape the bears.

We made one more effort, however, in the name of the Good Morning Publishing Company. Selecting the best of the cartoons against war that we had used, with articles,

---

* Earlier we had incorporated—hopefully.

A PRIVATE VIEW FOR THE BEST PEOPLE.

Good Morning

poems, gags, and other anti-militarist materials, we put out an issue entitled *The Soldier,* and sub-titled *Good Morning Quarterly.* It included a cartoon of mine showing a disabled veteran watering a small tree that he had planted in a battered shoe filled with dirt—with the caption: "Bonus or no bonus, Private McGinnis is going to have a wooden leg, even if he has to grow one."

Good Morning

Bonus or no bonus, Private McGinnis is going to have a wooden leg, if he has to grow one.

This edition caught the public fancy and was the most popular issue of all. Our Union Square contingent, many of whom had been in the war, pushed that number with the zeal of crusaders, and brought in surprising returns. But we were so far in the red, even after the month's receipts were counted, that I had no heart to go on.

With that longing unsatisfied, I said to myself as I went out for a walk: "Now what, Marcus Aurelius?"

Chapter 35

MY YOUNGER SON PICKS A COLLEGE

JACOB MARINOFF'S purchase of my cartoons for the *Big Stick* continued to be my mainstay. I was still a contributing editor of the *Liberator*, which was then in an old building on East Union Square at the corner of Sixteenth Street. But the *Liberator* had never been able to pay its contributing editors or others whose creations appeared in its pages, and my market was limited.

Though *Life* and *Judge* were friendly, it was seldom that I could produce anything to their liking. Everything was topsy-turvy in magazine land; old editors were frequently being kicked out for new. In the course of three years *Life* had tried out, I think, six editors—and not one of them knew what he wanted. For a time the two Bobs, Sherwood and Benchley, tried to keep that publication, which Mitchell had so long guided, from slipping into "innocuous desuetude," but that's about all they could do—hold it, and issue some brilliant numbers.

But in the spring of 1922 Oswald Garrison Villard opened the pages of the *Nation* to me. It had never featured cartoons before. I was permitted to choose my own themes, with occasional suggestions from Mr. Villard or from Ernest H. Gruening, then managing editor. My first batch of pictures appeared in a full page in the issue of May 3, under the title "Looking On." This same title was used on various pages of mine during the next three years. In addition I was asked now and then to illustrate an article written for the *Nation* by William Hard or others. One portrait sketch I did at this time which I like to contemplate because the subject interested me so much was of Rudolph Schildkraut in "The God of Vengeance."

That connection also gave me opportunity to go to Cleveland with Mr. Villard to cover the 1924 Republican conven-

Looking On *by* Art Young

Shall These Be the Guardians of Our Education?

There are those who say that the Dyer bill to prevent lynching is unconstitutional. Perhaps. We are fast learning what is constitutional and what is not. Child labor appears to be constitutional. If an American speculator gets his toes stepped on in a small Latin-American country, it's constitutional to kill a few thousand natives. But when an American gets killed by a mob of other Americans, maybe that all comes under the head of "life, liberty, and the pursuit of happiness."

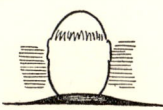

John Wingate Weeks has discovered that Congress has never fallen quite so low as since the nation permitted the incredible folly of direct primaries, popular election of Senators, and similar assaults on the Constitution. In those happy Convention days John was made Senator; later the unthinking rabble refused to return him to the Senate. That proves his case, doesn't it?

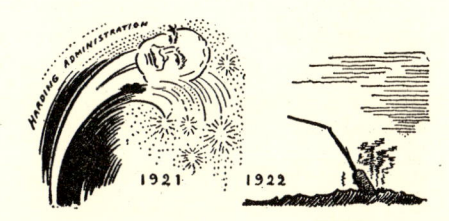

"Up Like a Rocket and Down Like a Stick."

The Juggernaut.

The Nation

LOOKING ON. One of various full pages of pictorial comment on current happenings that I made for the *Nation*.

tion, at which Calvin Coolidge and Charles G. Dawes were chosen as the standard-bearers. For the *Nation* also that year and for *Life* and *Collier's Weekly* I made cartoons calculated to aid LaFollette's candidacy on the Progressive ticket, and some sketches of principals at the Democratic conven-

Convention Notes by Art Young

My impressions of the Democratic convention at Madison Square Garden in 1924.

tion in New York, where John W. Davis and Charles W. Bryan were picked to head the slate.

Brisbane also had continued to give me assignments at intervals. He had me make a six-column review in pictures for the *Evening Journal* headed: "Art Young Sees *Chauve-Souris*—You See It With Him." It was Brisbane's suggestion that I do the theatres three times a week for that paper. I was not sanguine about this, but being fond of the stage, and knowing there was good money in the assignment, was not unwilling to try it for awhile. Meanwhile, however, that wizard of caricature, Ralph Barton, was receptive to the same job, and presently got it. He succeeded Hanz Stengel, who committed suicide—and a few years later Ralph Barton did the same. Ralph was tired of it all.

This boy Barton from Kansas was a better choice for that regular assignment than I would have been, although he held the job only a few months. His work derived, like

The Nation

"Fight LaFollette on every foot of ground in every Northwestern state."—The cry from the Coolidge campaign headquarters.

that of Al Frueh, Covarrubias, and Steinegas, from a school of caricature just begining to be appreciated in America—the arch-exponent of which was Gulbransson of *Simplicissimus* in Germany: the school of abundant emphasis on personal characteristics, done with the greatest possible economy of line and technique. Such caricatures as the subject looks at and says: "O my God! Do I look like that?" Of course people say that about any picture which does not flatter them. But a portrait done by a super-caricaturist is like barbed wit—not many subjects can take it.

In the same month my *Chauve-Souris* review appeared, the *Sunday American* reprinted a four-column cartoon of mine from the *Big Stick* about government ownership in

Russia, to illustrate the first of a series of articles by Frank P. Walsh under the general title: "Russia on the High Road to Prosperity."

Don, my younger son, wrote from Los Angeles in the summer of 1924 saying that he wanted to go to Dartmouth College. Answering, I said: "All right, if that's what you think you need." Yet in a day or two I felt that I had been a little too impulsive in giving that O.K. For I could see that Don's coming East would put a new responsibility on my shoulders. The expense of seeing a boy all the way across the continent, plus tuition and living expenses while being "educated," I knew would be another big financial load for me.

And I had met so many young men, graduates of colleges, who were no better off in the game of getting on than those with a simple public-school training that I was doubtful if the so-called higher education really counted for anything. I had always discounted the value of my own art-school experience. Certainly I had learned much more outside the academies than inside their walls. And what made the modern college seem even less desirable than that of forty years earlier was the pace young men from middle-class homes had to keep up in their association with the sons of the rich.

But I had said yes to Don, and I couldn't reverse myself. I figured it might be well for him to look the situation over for himself. I sent money, and he hastened to New York. We had a good time together for a few days, and then he went to New Hampshire. In Dartmouth he elected to study Spanish, Latin, and Greek, and also took English, history, and botany.

My concern about the pace Don would have to keep up in his new surroundings was borne out by a habit he soon got into, of telegraphing me, usually to this effect: "Please send me one hundred dollars. Urgent." Always urgent.

I had made the mistake of not telling him frankly the state of my finances. Long afterward, when we had achieved a relation in which we could discuss such things, he explained that as he grew up in California he had gained the impression that his father in the East was well-to-do. He had heard legends of large sums paid to artists for pictures, and sup-

Saturday Evening Post
EDITOR OF THE COUNTY GAZETTE
One of a series of Old Home Town types used in the Lorimer weekly.

posed that the rewards to workers in the pictorial field generally were handsome. Thus he had no hesitation in asking for money, by mail or wire, feeling confident that he would get it.

Despite a presumable steady round of social activities, I suppose Don studied as much as a boy could be expected to at Dartmouth, for when I saw him again he told me of his high marks and seemed to have learned a good deal about things he wanted to know. He spent the following summer with me on Chestnut Ridge, and occupied himself steadily with drawings. Not a few of the sketches he made had considerable merit. In the fall he returned to college, but as the weeks went on I saw my bank balance sink lower and lower. For some reason sales of pictures had again fallen off.

So with regret I had to make clear to Don that I was scraping the bottom of my treasury. Naturally disappointed, he accepted the situation none the less cheerfully, and said that he would leave college at the end of October, go down to New York, and look for a job. He managed to keep employed at a fair wage, and after a while began studying in the night classes at the Art Students' League. He pursued sketching industriously and experimented with water colors.

What he really wanted to do was write. Making repeated efforts to put stories on paper, and having trouble with them, he concluded that he had nothing yet worth writing about, and that in order to become a writer of substance he must do some substantial living. So he set out to get experience, and shipped as a seaman on a steamer bound for Buenos Ayres. This doubtless was good for him spiritually, and he seemed to have broadened mentally on his return.

Next he was off to California again, to see his mother, and then got a job with the Associated Press in Los Angeles, tending an automatic teletypewriter, on which news from all the corners of the world clicked out on long rolls of white paper. Don wasn't earning much, but he was paying his own way, and he was proud of that.

North, my other son, showed a definite inclination toward pictorial expression, which I had noticed particularly when both he and Don were active on the Los Angeles High School weekly. Don was editor of that paper for a season and wrote a weekly column, while North did illustrations for it. In short, my progeny seem to have desired the pursuit of the creative arts, though in saying this I cannot lay claim to having had much influence upon their development. Recently North illustrated a book, *Manners for Moderns,* published in Boston.

Shortly after Don had left college things suddenly began to come my way from unexpected sources. To my surprise requests for drawings arrived from respectable magazines which had not looked in my direction before. When I heard from Tom Masson, then associate editor of the *Saturday Evening Post,* that his chief, George Horace Lorimer, wanted me to contribute to that conservative world-popular weekly, I said: "Honest, Tom, you don't mean it!" He assured me that Lorimer *did* want some Art Young cartoons.

I knew, of course, that my kind of propaganda would not appeal to the makers of this magazine with its editorial devotion to Big Business and Big Profits. But I thought of something else which might find favor there. For a long time I had contemplated a series of pictures to be called *Trees at Night.* Often I had made sketches toward this end, after walks under the stars on the roads near my place in Connecticut. The first sheaf of these pictures—eleven of them, as I remember it—were sent for Lorimer's approval, and I got a prompt acceptance. After a few were published, I was asked to draw additional ones. For more than a year the series ran, usually every other week.

My conception of trees showed them as fantastic, grotesque, humanized, or animalized, with trunks, limbs, and foliage tossed in gayety or inert and solemn against the night sky. They were not propaganda as that term is generally understood, but I have heard people who liked them say they read sermons in them all. For this series I received $75 each. I have a large scrap-book filled with complimentary letters, poems, and tree-ideas evoked by these drawings.

One of the best of my tree drawings occupied a double page in *Life.* I have always had a hopeful outlook—even when everything seemed lost. Nevertheless, as an onlooker I had seen so much in human life that revealed the pathos of hope, that I had to put the theme into a picture. Among other tragic hopes I had seen was an old man and his wife

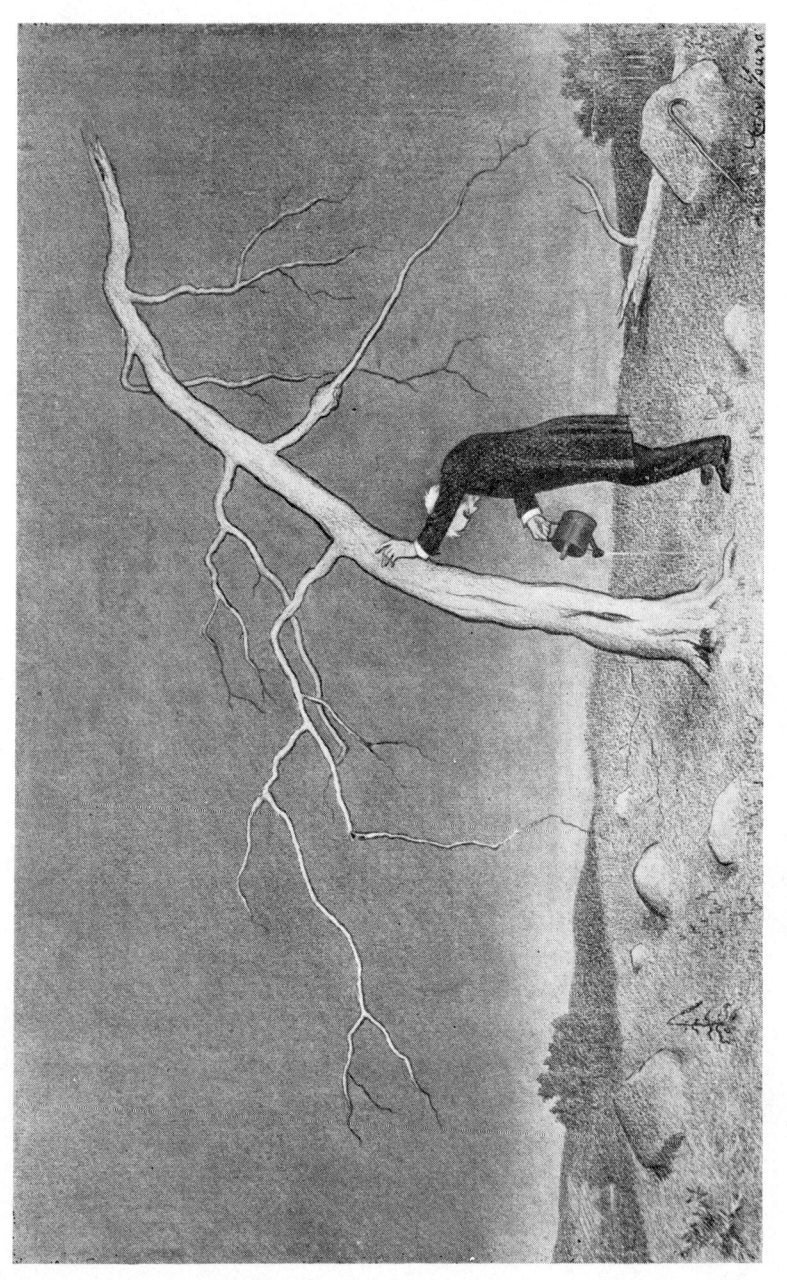

HOPE SPRINGS ETERNAL IN THE HUMAN BREAST

living in poverty, but holding onto stock in one of those kid-'em-along silver mines that they thought might some day bring them joy. In my picture this forlorn old man is out on a bleak hill with his hope symbolized as a dead tree. With a sprinkling pail he waters its roots. The caption, as published in *Life,* was: "Hope springs eternal in the human breast."

Later the *Saturday Evening Post* took another series from me entitled "Types of the Old Home-Town." These pictures I regard as my best contributions to folklore Americana. Here was work which I greatly enjoyed, conjuring up from the days of my youth the characters that I had known back home. And I had traveled enough to realize that they were not just local, but that their prototypes were to be found in hundreds or thousands of towns. The content of the home-town drawings is suggested by some of the captions:

"*Uncle Dave and Aunt Matilda*—Every Saturday they would drive in, hitch the old horse near the court-house, and do their trading: butter and eggs for sugar, salt mackerel, etc. Uncle Dave was a 'Greenbacker'. He said, 'Money is the root of all evil,' but had figured it out that the more there was in circulation the less the evil."

"*Ashley the Lamplighter*—There were eight street lamps in the business section. Our lamplighter's name was Ashley. When he struck his phosphorus the square took on a glow. Not much in kilowatts and such. But—that was thirty years ago."

"*Aunt Nancy Fillebrown*—She went to all the town funerals. No matter what she had said of the deceased in life, she was there when it came to a post-mortem respect. Thus everybody in town was assured of one mourner at least."

"*Pawnee Bill*—Every year the town would be visited by a Pawnee Bill or a Kickapoo Charley, who would sell us Indian medicine made from the roots of wild cabbage and liniment from the bark of the snake-tree. He would cure farmers of their rheumatism right before our eyes. Them were the happy days."

For these types I received $125 a drawing. With this new income and sales to other magazines, I was enabled to make some much needed improvements around my home on Chestnut Ridge. Once more I was tasting the pie of prosperity.

Chapter 36

BATTLES ON THE LIBERATOR BOARD

ACROSS four and a half years the *Liberator*, like the *Masses*, had had a turbulent time of it. It too was a free-lance publication, not affiliated with any political party. Its editors and contributors theoretically formed a united front, and they wrote on many phases of the revolutionary movement, attacking the money-power from various angles. But this united front was a good deal like the "happy family" in P. T. Barnum's museum in New York, which contained a lion, a lamb, a wolf, a boa constrictor, and other oddly assorted creatures.

"And do they always get along peacefully like this?" Barnum was asked by a visiting bishop.

"Oh, yes," said Barnum, "—except that we have to renew the lamb once in a while."

There was frequent conflict among the contributing editors of the *Liberator* over the question of what it should print, as there had been on the *Masses* editorial board. Often these arguments had to do with the relative values of propaganda and "pure art" or "pure literature", but as the echoes of the war receded and the splits in the radical movement grew wider, battles in editorial conferences more often centered upon the matter of tactics to forward the cause of social revolution throughout the world.

Meetings of the Liberator board were irregular and informal. I attended when in town, but tried to keep out of controversies. I was much more interested always in drawing cartoons which would strike at a vulnerable point in the armor of the common enemy than in battling over the fine points of tactics. In my years as a Socialist I had attended meetings and seen members of my party argue hotly among themselves far into the night. I knew tactics were necessary, but I didn't want to be bothered with them so long as I was shooting straight and making a hit now and then.

Often I have been amazed at the tendency of some of the controversialists on the left side of the political fence to detect the darkest motives in utterances and actions of erstwhile friends whose opinions disagreed with theirs. I took but a small part in the internecine cross-fire. I knew my forte was drawing cartoons. Others were better fitted to endure the polemical heat. But I would not be understood as being unaware of the importance of official decisions and correct shaping of social propaganda. I knew that it had to be done with thought and care, but it could become ridiculous and frequently did.

In February, 1919, Eugene Debs was listed as a contributing editor, and K. R. Chamberlain and Minor were missing from the roster. Minor had gone to Russia, and had been writing articles about the situation there, from the viewpoint of an Anarchist. This was the philosophy that interested him most at that time; the doctrine that the individual should be free to live his own life unhampered by governmental restraints imposed against his will.

Robert Minor, son of a judge in San Antonio, Texas, first came into public notice through his strong cartoons in the *St. Louis Post-Dispatch*. These cartoons looked as if they had been done with a blunt marking crayon on any kind of paper that was handy, and were never cluttered with detail —only an eyeful, and just a glance would give you the idea. His work was the forerunner of the crayon cartoons in the daily press of today. In his early thirties he came to New York, to work on the staff of the *Evening World*.

Once I made this comment on him in *Good Morning*:

"When he talks, it is as if he thought a reporter for posterity were listening in, and his words and sentences are formed with precision, and are grammatical enough to suggest that a good college professor was lost to the world when Bob joined the proletarian movement."

Beside Minor, many of the best artists and writers of that period thought of themselves as Anarchists, not as Socialists. They wanted to be at liberty to act as individuals without the restrictions of government, Mrs. Grundy's opinion, or any other frustrating element. John Reed, Lincoln Steffens, and George Bellows also come to my mind as having anarchistic ideas in those days.

But most of the many I knew who respected that philosophy lived to learn that something came before the Anarchist dream. That something was economic freedom, without which one could only give a feeble imitation of calling his soul his own.

I think there is no one on earth who is not in some degree both Anarchist and Socialist. Some there are whose collective sense is confined to their own family. Others go still further and include a community or their country, and still others have regard for the welfare of the whole human race. But within the orbit of every one's social circle is the individual's desire to be a law unto himself.

After Minor returned to New York he was acting editor of the *Liberator* in the spring of 1921, while Max Eastman was in California finishing a book. Max criticised the April issue by telegraph, and Bob wrote a long letter in defense. But to me this was just one more of those hot controversial matters, and as usual I stayed on the side-lines.

As I turn the pages of the *Liberator* for September, 1918, my eye lights on another letter which takes me back to those feverish days.

> Fairmont, W. Va.,
> June 23, 1918.
>
> My Dear Comrades:
> Enclosed find draft for ten dollars paying for the *Liberator*.
> In three weeks we have organized 10,000 Slavs who were in bondage. Put the professional murderers out of business; these Slavs were in bad.
> Tell Art Young I have been raising H---.
>
> Fraternally,
>
> MOTHER JONES

I suspect that the last word in this message was subdued as a concession to the supercritical rules of the Post Office, for

Mother Jones had a delightfully extensive profane vocabulary and did not hesitate to use it in conversation.

In the same issue is the black stamp of censorship, blotting out two items listed among the book advertisements.

Thus magazine editing was a game of quiz—to guess when you were within the law. But no lawyer was smart enough to advise you in advance of publication what you might legally publish.

Whenever Mother Jones came to New York she would let me know. She was moving toward the century mark, but she still had fire in her eye. For hours at a time I would talk with her in her room in the old Union Square Hotel. With a pail of beer on the table, she liked to tell me all about "my boys" (the miners), her experiences in jails, and what happened during strikes.

John Reed and Louise Bryant lived at 1 Patchen place, and I would drop in there of an evening now and then. In memory I can see this dynamic boy, chuckling at some angle of his daily activity and then looking at a pad of paper on his desk as if he ought to be writing instead of chuckling.

One evening Louise told me that she had been talking with one of Jack's Harvard class-mates. And he said to her: "It's really too bad about Jack. He used to write good librettoes for light opera. Now I hear he's writing this humanity stuff."

And this lovely daughter of a Fenian laughed in her contagious way, and we all laughed together.

A few years after Jack's death in Russia, Louise married William Bullitt, long a Washington correspondent, friend of Woodrow Wilson, friend of Jack, and later Ambassador to Russia and then to France. Poor Louise committed slow suicide—went the sad road of narcotic escape. Only a few weeks before she died she sent me a postcard from her Paris studio at 50 Rue Vavin.

"I suppose in the end life gets all of us," she wrote. "It nearly has got me now—getting myself and my friends out of jail—living under curious conditions—but never minding much. . . . Know always I send my love to you across the stars. If you get there before I do—or later—tell Jack Reed I love him."

I had supplied cartoons to the *Liberator* frequently during its existence, and a good deal of my best work, I think, was done in that period. As I open a bound volume, I see one cartoon of mine, entitled *We,* which caused widespread amusement. It depicted two tramps, with feet sticking out of broken shoes, and one saying: "Say, Bill, whadd'ye know about this?—We've got to raise eight billion dollars in the next Liberty Loan!"

The Mollycoddles' Union portrayed a group of workers registering enthusiasm as their employer announced: "Now, boys, you've been very good, and I'm going to give each of you a five-cent stick of candy as a weekly bonus."

That's For Us, Bill showed two disabled veterans looking through a window at a Victory Dinner, $6 a plate, in the Hotel Best People. . . . As the troops came back from France I did a cartoon of an employer telling a one-legged doughboy: "Sorry I can't make a place for you. But you see a soldier gets much of his compensation in glory and in the thought that he has done his duty."

Daughters of the American Revolution Hearing a Revolutionary Speech pictures some of our female patriots registering indignation; "Seditious! . . . I never heard of such a thing! . . . She's terrible! . . . If she doesn't like our government she ought to have the courtesy to keep still about it."

When Woodrow Wilson returned from France, I did a full-page feature on the Washington scene, reporting that about half of the political population in the capital were no longer standing behind the President, "except for the purpose of kicking him." . . . *In Six Months* is a two-sided picture, in which at the left Wilson, holding his sleek silk hat in one hand and his Fourteen Points in the other, stands at the large end of a horn while Fame shines upon him; at the right he is seen with battered topper, crawling out of the small end into the darkness of oblivion.

Early in 1922 Max Eastman felt that he had to get away from it all. He resigned, and Mike Gold came in as the active editor, with William Gropper, another energetic youngster, strengthening the pictorial art in the *Liberator* with lively cartoons. Presently Joseph Freeman, a young writer and "wayward" son of a millionaire real estate operator, joined the editorial staff. Floyd Dell was now spending a good deal of time in Croton, working on a book, but appeared at the office frequently to lend a hand.

Circulation had fallen off, and the going was hard, what with the steadily widening cleavage in the radical movement in the United States. There were vital causes to fight for—Sacco and Vanzetti, Mooney and Billings, the liberation of the remaining anti-war prisoners—but a large percentage of the *Liberator's* audience was displaying great weariness, especially when asked to pay money for subscriptions. It was harder, too, to get people to attend mass-meetings, even when issues of vast import to the downtrodden were to be discussed. Month after month the boys in the editorial office had to go out and find money to cover printing and paper and distribution costs. Often their untiring services were paid for in fragmentary installments—if at all. In the light of my own struggles on *Good Morning,* I could understand their problems.

After a few months Mike Gold reached his physical limit, and departed for California, to rest his torn nerves and write a novel. This left Joe Freeman holding the reins, with Floyd Dell still faithfully co-operating.

In October, 1922, I had a note from Floyd asking me to attend "a very important meeting, at which a decision will be made concerning the future of the *Liberator*—a meeting at which some very good news or very bad news will be announced." This took place in Bill Gropper's studio, three flights up, at 149 West 14th Street. Those present, as I remember it, included Hugo Gellert and Joe Freeman. And here, too, was a genuine soul of a man—Charles E. Ruthenberg, secretary of the Communist party in this country, then known as the Workers' party. He had served a term in an Ohio prison for his anti-war beliefs and had been the Socialist party's candidate for Governor there. Ruthenberg had requested the meeting inasmuch as he was returning to Chicago next day. Invitations had been sent to all those still listed as editors and contributing editors, but only a few responded. Others were out of town, and still others apparently were not interested.

Floyd Dell opened the discussion, explaining that the *Liberator's* financial status was steadily growing worse. The responsibility was too great for those in charge to continue. If we stopped publication it would be a good deal like killing a child. If we changed the magazine into an art and literary journal, catering to those who wanted to escape from thinking, the effect would be decorative but of little purpose.

Ruthenberg indicated that the Communists would like to have the *Liberator,* and Floyd asked us each for our opinions on a proposition to merge whatever was left of the magazine—subscription list, news-stand orders, name, prestige, and good will—with the *Workers' Monthly,* then being published in Chicago. Naturally Ruthenberg was negotiating not only for the *Liberator,* but also for the prestige of its predecessor, the *Masses,* which in memory was bathed in an aura of admiration by its readers as the first magazine of cultural quality in America to espouse the cause of industrial freedom.

"That goes with me," I said in reply to the proposition. But I remember with what indifference I supported the proposal. If a broker for a Wall Street syndicate had been there and had offered a large sum of money for our name, prestige, etcetera, as had been done with other magazines of protest— to make them conservative while outwardly appearing the same—I think I might have approved the sale. With a substantial cash payment, we could have sent Christmas gifts to old contributors to both the *Liberator* and the *Masses* who had never received a cent. I had experienced so much trouble as an editor, publisher, and contributor that on this particular evening I was in one of my what's-the-use? moods.

I knew, too, that the original *Masses,* out of which the *Liberator* had evolved, had receded far enough into history to be thought better than it really was. The *Masses* came along at that well-known "psychological moment," at least for a few thousand people who were tired of the conventional contents of bourgeois publications. By 1922 many of them had forgotten that the time and the innovation had much to do with the loving acclaim as well as the fierce denunciation with which our magazine was received. The devotees of the *Masses* had made it a model, a shining exemplar.

Merging of the two publications was delayed for a time, however, and the *Liberator* continued to be issued in New York, with Minor and Freeman at the editorial helm, and with the board now including several members of the central committee of the Workers' party. But in 1924 the move to Chicago was made, and the *Liberator* name was submerged in that of the *Workers' Monthly*.

Need for a magazine which would be an outlet for news and interpretation of events bearing on the class struggle from the leftward viewpoint, but which would not be the organ of any political party, made itself evident in 1926, and

STEFFENS REPORTS ON HIS VISIT TO RUSSIA.

the *New Masses* was born in May. Sponsored by a broad united front of radical and liberal writers and artists, its initial editors were Egmont Arens, Joseph Freeman, Hugo Gellert, Michael Gold, James Rorty, and John Sloan. In addition to these five, the executive board included Maurice Becker, Helen Black, John Dos Passos, Robert Dunn, William Gropper, Paxton Hibben, Freda Kirchwey, Robert L. Leslie, Louis Lozowick, and Rex Stout.

With the desperate Passaic (N. J.) textile strike, where gas bombs were being used by the employers, as a cause to fight for, the new publication got away to a strong start. It experimented widely with literary and art forms of revolutionary propaganda.

There was a long list of contributing editors, including myself, with both old-timers and youngsters represented. Establishment of the enterprise gave me a sense of fresh hope. The pages of the *New Masses* displayed vitality that was electric in its effect upon me, and undoubtedly upon other creative workers.

Welcoming this magazine and expressing delight that the infant seemed so lusty, William Allen White, editor of the *Emporia Gazette* in Kansas, gave it only six months to live. But it has survived all the fears of friends and hopes of enemies that it might die an early death, and has gone on functioning for the remarkable span of thirteen years.

It, too, has had its internal political upheavals, with a changing editorial board, and repeated financial struggles, yet somehow it has survived all vicissitudes.

I have found satisfaction in numerous pictorial contributions to the *New Masses*—necessarily less often in recent times—and it is good to know that this dependable vehicle of social protest exists.

Chapter 37

AN ART GALLERY AND TWO BOOKS

AS time went on and other markets opened up, I began to plan anew for the building of an art gallery such as I had dreamed of in Paris in 1889, when with the optimism of youth, I foresaw myself as some day having an estate within easy distance of New York, on a broad hill of which I would build a studio and a large picture gallery. In it would be a Louvre Room, a London National Gallery Room, and other rooms for the display of my selected reproductions of the world's great paintings, etchings, drawings, and statuary from the principal museums of the Old World, and of course there would be an American room for my favorite prints of native art, and especially the work of the early cartoonists, including Paul Revere. However crude his cartoons, Revere, besides being the most publicized fast rider in American history, contributed a few notable concepts done on copper plate in behalf of our first revolution. And I would hang on the line Thomas Nast, Joseph Keppler, and Bernard Gillam. There, too, would be my own drawings, not too conspicuous, but in a spot where visitors couldn't miss seeing them.

Basking in the glow of that youthful dream, I had not bothered to figure out the cost in detail. Who does? Whether you are dreamy or practical, building-construction always costs more than you expected. All I knew was this: I had over $6,000 in the bank, the largest sum I had ever accumulated. I was affluent, and friends told me I looked like the typical man of big business whom I liked to ridicule.

Knowing that I was going to spend money on my "estate," acquaintances were free with advice. Not many approved the plan for an art gallery. Some thought I ought to be practical and build a garage; others who enjoyed sports suggested a big swimming pool down by the creek, and a tennis court to displace half of the garden. Still others felt that I ought to build a bungalow or two to rent.

One well-meaning friend said: "Do you know what I'd do if I owned this place? I'd have a chicken farm. There's money in chickens." Another spoke for a goat farm; said there was money in goats.

Then of course there were some with "conservative" proposals. They said: "Now that you are making money, invest it. Put it into *good* stocks or *safe* securities." To me the latter suggestion was the most comical of all—as if you could make a "good" or a "safe" investment.

All of this of course was before the crash of 1929—and it still stands as my opinion of profit-enterprise in general, with more financial crashes yet to come.

I can anticipate criticism of this book on at least one point, by persons who have read thus far—that I am always taking the side of the worker with apparently no understanding of the problem of the employer.

I have already said that an artist is one who can put himself in the place of others. All too often, I think, workers show a talent for seeing the employer's side, which is one cause of their subjugation. They are the apologists for their masters; whatever they, the workers, suffer, they feel is inevitable like bad weather and can't be helped.

On the other hand, the masters apparently do not try to put themselves in the place of their workers—it would not be good business, and they do not intend to be their brother's keeper. That's why it's a class war, whether we like it or not, and whether the contestants realize it or not.

The story goes that Pierpont Morgan the elder was talking with a former employee of his who was relating a tale of hard-luck, his wife and children starving, etcetera. Morgan pressed a button on his desk and said to a flunky: "Put this man out—he's breaking my heart."

I think I have the imagination to understand the problems and obligations of one who employs others to work for him for wages. I had done some employing as an editor and publisher, and had to hire and fire and learn from experience that business responsibility is a headache much of the time— even a small business. Nevertheless, the employed manual worker or artist worker gets the worst of it. He is the underdog. The ditch digger and the concrete layer use their tools to get results and are paid whatever the boss thinks is enough, unless forced by unions to pay more. The draughtsmen use pen or pencil and dig around on drawing paper in another kind of work, for an employer who takes the finished product and pays whatever it pleases him to pay.

Artists and ditch-diggers are alike producers, whatever the tools used—pen, pencil, and brush, or pick and shovel. Those who can handle these tools must work for those whose business it is to make a profit. And there is no legal limit to profit-making. So long as both sides are compelled to struggle for money as their objective, it will be a class war, a war between those who produce and those who prod the producer to work harder and cheaper.

At the age of fifty-seven I had again become an employer —not much of a one, to be sure, but enough to make me understand why the master curses the worker. While my motive was not profit, it was the same in the sense that I had to hire others at a reasonable rate and get a building job done according to agreement.

I knew a versatile New York artist whose rent I had paid twice when he couldn't meet it. He was a sculptor, furniture craftsman, carpenter, painter, writer of poetry, and interior decorator. With a wealth of self-assurance, he prided himself on "making the walls of a room sing" and in doing substantial, artistic construction—"knitting with nails" he called it.

A familiar figure in Greenwich Village, he was striking to look at—with his long black hair, waxed goatee, and moustache—a kind of composite of a mediaeval troubadour and John the Baptist. Friends had said he was not exactly reliable.

One day he came into my New York quarters, and I told him of my plan to build an art gallery and studio on my place in the country. My idea was to have a place for the housing and safe-keeping of my original drawings, as well as the exhibition of them—with a stone vault as a wing of the building, to obviate paying storage as I had done for years. But first, I explained, I was going to put two large statues of toads or devils or something on the massive stone gate-posts out by the road. This was to be the entrance to the proposed gallery, and I must have a grand entrance.

I showed him my small clay model of a toad which I had decided would make the best statues for my purpose, and asked if he could reproduce two of them on a huge scale in concrete or terra cotta. His eyes were wide with enthusiasm as he answered that he had a secret formula for making a kind of cement that sculptors could use like clay—with the advantage that it would withstand the elements for countless years. He had tested it, he said, with a vase of his own making, which had stood a long time outside his studio window without disintegrating. It was a secret process—he repeated—and he was not yet ready to reveal it to the world. But he would not only make the toads for me—he also was keen to help me design, and build, the gallery.

He spent a week of research in the New York public library studying the species and habits of toads the world over—and came back with sketches of a dozen kinds. I told him this was all unnecessary; I knew the common American variety of toad, and my model, though crude, was about what I wanted. He soon agreed and told me he had enjoyed his research studies of toads. His enthusiasm ran up to such a degree that my own began to mount higher for both the statuary and the gallery. His work would be initiated by the setting up of those great squat toads of indestructible clay, or whatever he called it.

It was early spring. We went to Bethel, and immediately he began work on the sculpture. I was not allowed to see him mix his new kind of cement. It must be kept a secret. There was a fortune in it. As soon as he finished the toads, it was understood that he would proceed with the construction of the gallery. I agreed to pay the prevailing carpenter's wage, with room and food free in addition. The building was to be completed by October, and I promised to help if necessary or to hire others if needed on the job.

But the work moved much more slowly than I had expected. It took the painter-sculptor-carpenter a month to model the toads. When they were at last placed on their pedestals on either side of the gate, I sent invitations to neighbors and artist friends in the country surrounding Bethel to come to the unveiling, which I assured them would be "a memorable event in the annals of art."

In the presence of a goodly crowd on a Sunday afternoon, Edna Porter and Theodosia Pearce, both from New York, pulled the covering off the statues. That was the signal for me to march down the path from my house to make my speech. Topped by an old high hat that I wore for fun when such serious functions demanded it, and a Daniel Webster coat that I found in my attic, I thanked everybody for their attendance on this "auspicious occasion." Clive Weed shouted: "Hear! Hear!" The onlookers included Augusta Georgia Cary, her young son Peter, and Dr. A. L. Goldwater.

I then told the audience what I knew about toads, and spoke for ten minutes or so, outlining my plans for the picture gallery toward which this toad entrance led. Some one asked: "Why toads?"

To which I replied: "The humble toad has at last been raised to the dignity it deserves. I plan some day to inset jewels that will shine from the eyes of these toads of mine. Thus I shall pay my respect to Shakespeare, who said: '. . . the toad, though ugly and venomous, wears yet a precious jewel in his head.'"

Three cheers were given for the Orator of the Day—and the event thus passed into history, though unrecorded until now.

Construction of the gallery on the foundation of the barn which had burned down in 1914, while I was in Washington, moved slowly. The old foundation needed rebuilding, for the gallery must rest on a solid wall. I helped trowel the Connecticut field-stones (which in the Mid-West were called *nigger-heads*), and there was satisfaction in observing the massive substance of that wall.

But by the time the foundation was in proper shape more than two months had sped by. The artist-carpenter-mason was often seized by poetic moods in which he was impelled to climb to Lookout Point, the towering rock on the summit of the hill behind my house. I kept saying: "Now remember, it's got to be finished by October," and suggested that we hire local help.

"Oh, no, that's not necessary," he objected. "I can do it alone in time."

Another month passed, however, before this genius got around to the frame-work and the sidewalls on which he was going to show me his way of "knitting with nails." I had to order many truckloads of lumber, sheathing, asbestos shingles, and nails. With their arrival I would look at the bills with alarm. The cost had already run higher than I had figured for the completed job—and his poetry pangs persisted.

"I'm afraid the gallery won't be finished before snow flies."

"Oh, yes, it will," he assured me. "Don't worry."

I paid his daily wage, without thought of his leisure hours on the hill—until he began putting in bills for half hours overtime. Then the employer began to feel injured.

October clicked off all of its thirty-one days, and in the first week of November the four walls were partly in place and the floor was laid in a way—but there was no roof.

One morning on arising I looked out toward "the dream," and saw a blanket of snow over everything in sight. In feathery, drifting white flakes, it was still falling, and most of it seemed to fall into the open top of my studio-gallery.

After I had fortified myself with breakfast I cursed as no employer ever cursed before—using words that sizzled and emitted acrid smoke—and ended my relations with the artist craftsman who could "knit with nails" and "paint walls in a way to make them sing." When I quieted down, I said: "No hard feelings, but I'm through, and so are you."

Early the next spring I employed Mary Ware Dennett's son Devon, an expert carpenter, to carry the work on to completion. Now it moved along efficiently. I noted how well he took hold of the problem, and marveled at the agility and skill of this young man who had a job to do and was determined to do it on schedule time.

For a month his wife was in the Danbury hospital having a baby, yet he managed to see her every day, work on the gallery, and get his own meals. I was in New York much of the time that spring and summer, but late in August I saw the result of Devon's work and was well pleased.

All the gallery needed now was a pair of lamps, one on each side of the main door. These lamps I removed from an ancient victoria that I had bought from a veteran cab-driver in front of the Hotel Brevoort. I have told the story of that purchase in *On My Way*. All that remains of the victoria now, beside the lamps, is an oil painting of it as it stood for many years in venerable dignity amid the high grass under an apple tree. This painting was done by Henry Glintenkamp

my art gallery

when he visited me for a week-end in 1925 to discuss our experiences in the late war and a new way of cooking spaghetti.

However limited the physical dimensions of my so-called gallery, it has been a comfortable place for me to draw more pictures and dream more dreams. As I said in the foreword to *The Best of Art Young:*

"I look around at my own drawings occasionally all alone, and in the quiet communion with my past, feel that I learn something, and that, given another ten or twenty years, I might do better."

Here are drawing tables, large and medium sized; the small collection of reproductions that I bought in Paris in 1889; numerous books on home-made shelves, including a Daumier book presented to me by Erhard Weyhe; works illustrated by Doré and others, including Phil May, to whom I owe much as early guides; a biography of Thomas Nast by Albert Bigelow Paine; a bound volume of the original *Puck* in German; and bound sets of several magazines in which many of my drawings appeared.

On Saturdays and Sundays in summer, my gallery is open to the public. Not on the main highway, it is never crowded. Those who come have heard about the place from others; sometimes they are visitors from far away, who perhaps have driven out from New York or down from Boston, bringing me friendly messages from old-time friends that I may not have seen for years.

If the toads on the gate-posts are not an identification for those who come my way, there is a brass plate on the gallery door that has a history:

One Sunday some eight years ago a man of seventy walked all the way from Ansonia, eighteen miles, to tell me he wanted to make a door-plate for me. He asked that I sketch out an appropriate design so that he, who had worked all his life in an Ansonia brass factory, could fashion a mold from it in brass. I drew a design around my signature, and in a few weeks he came over again and presented me with the finished door-plate, which he had partly hand-engraved. He was familiar with my cartoons in the Socialist and labor papers, and the occasion was one of pride for me. We never know, until some incident like this occurs, who is interested in our work and wants to say so in his own way. That friend's expression of appreciation in metal is one of my valued mementoes.

For more than a year from the time we had begun to build the gallery I had been spending many of my evenings writing down reminiscences and reflections on happenings of the day in a kind of diary. Some time later, at the Hotel Laclede in New York, I showed Mary Heaton Vorse portions of my manuscript, which by that time had run beyond 200 pages of hand-written material. She read a few pages and said: "I'm going to write to Horace Liveright about this."

In a few days a letter came from Liveright asking me to come to see him. And when I was in New York again I went to his office.

"I want to be your publisher," he said. "Mary Vorse tells me you are writing a book. What is it?"

I explained how far I had gone with my reminiscences and reflections. "But," I suggested, "here's a series of pictures

MARY HEATON VORSE

called 'Trees at Night' which have been running in the *Saturday Evening Post,* and I've added a few that appeared in *Collier's* and *Life.* Thirty-five in all. How about publishing these first and giving me a few months more on the writing of the other book?"

Liveright turned the pages of a dummy volume I had made up of the tree drawings. "Good stuff . . . but of course just a picture-book . . . won't sell very well. . . ."

Nevertheless he was ready to take a chance. We discussed terms and in less than a half hour publisher and author had come to an understanding.

For the reminiscences and reflections I had thought of two titles—*All Right So Far* and *On My Way.* After consultation with Tom Smith and Julian Messner, his advisers, Liveright told me they all liked *On My Way* best.

He had enough confidence in *Trees at Night* to issue it at a price of $3, though it contained less than 50 pages. It evoked some gratifying reviews, especially pleasing to me because it meant recognition in a field apart from my politico-economic cartoons. At the risk of violating the canons of modesty, I will cite here some of the published comment on that work.

Saturday Review of Literature: "It is a surprise to find the admirable caricaturist of the old *Masses* in an exercise of pure fancy. His success in the new adventure shows the ready convertibility of great talent. Art Young has let the disorderly arabesque of trees and plants against the nocturnal sky speak to him. They have told him whimsical, grave, at times terrible things. . . . These fantasies are rendered in black wash with a rich and free handling which a Japanese painter would approve. It is a book to put on one's shelves and take to one's heart."

Rockwell Kent, in *Creative Art:* "Art Young's trees, because they represent the playful fancy of a distinguished man, are more convincing with illusion than the graphic imaginings of the whole Rackham school of professional fanciers. A lot of people will like as fairy tales these pictures of Art Young's. We like them because they are drawn with the same very personal power and sensitiveness that has made us like everything he has ever done."

Baltimore Sun: "A fine example, a lyrical cross-section of the work of one of the few real native talents that this country has produced in art."

Edwin Bjorkman, in the *Asheville, (N. C.) Times:* "Art Young stands alone. In the thirty-nine drawings included in *Trees at Night* he has given free rein to his pen and his imagination."

The first edition of *On My Way* was published in October, 1928, with a map showing the main trails of my life-route used as end-papers, and with a drawing of my friend the Brevoort cab-driver conveying me over the Connecticut highways on the title-page. Liveright thought so well of this literary and pictorial enterprise that he printed a

DEFEAT   *Trees at Night*

handsome *de luxe* edition as a private gift book for authors and other friends of the publisher and myself. The regular edition was chosen by the Institute of Graphic Arts as one of the prize illustrated volumes of the year. There was a second printing in February, 1929.

Of course I was pleased by the hand given to my work by the press. Here are selections from some of the many reviews.

Carl Sandburg, in the *Chicago Daily News:* "*On My Way* is the diary of one of the sane and serene souls of the world—sometimes getting het-up and landing a wallop. . . . Art Young is a living definition of democracy, whatever that may be. He is more Jeffersonian than Jefferson, and knows things Karl Marx never had time for. He is onto Omar Khayyam, has Billy Sunday's number, and so lives that each day he is ready for Gabriel's horn. We believe this would be a better country and not so hard to save for those who would like to save it, if *On My Way* could outsell some of the best sellers."

Lewis Gannett, in the *New York Herald-Tribune:* "It has all the sentimental charm of a Currier and Ives print, with the added chuckle and thrust that lie in Art Young's pencil." . . . Heywood Broun, in the *New York Telegram:* "The author has made no attempt to keep his narrative within a rounded whole. No sequence of time is enforced; as the thoughts stray, so does the pen. The effect then, is of some one talking at his ease in front of a log fire." . . . Freda Kirchwey, in the *Nation:* "With cause, Art Young is enormously proud of his talent; yet he is the humblest man that ever became autobiographical."

Shaemas O'Sheel, in the *Saturday Review of Literature:* "He has achieved that most difficult of all things to achieve in letters, utter simplicity—the ability to just tell the thing, not get tangled up in words." . . . Llewellyn Jones, in the *Chicago Evening Post:* "Though the surface of his book is a complex play of ripples in every direction, there is under the rippling cross-currents of the surface, the steady pull of a life that has always kept a consistent direction." . . . Harry Hansen, in the *New York World:* "At my house we are very particular about the books that go on the parlor table. Today I am going to add another book to the pure reading matter under the lamp. It is called *On My Way.*" . . . *Time:* "A merry masterpiece of shirt-sleeve autobiography, sketched by a pen that achieves with words the same quaint economy for which its line is noted."

Right here I think I ought to say that had the press been hostile with reviews such as "poor old Art Young is floundering around where he doesn't belong" or "This picture-maker had better stick to his last"—or had refused to notice me at all, through some "conspiracy of silence"—or had I simply been overlooked in the avalanche of books that pile up on the critics' desks—I was fully prepared. I was ready to take praise, blame, or neglect—for I had become used to all of them. There was, in fact, one review devoid of all enthusiasm; somebody on a newspaper in Louisville, Ky., said (I quote from memory): "*On My Way* is a cartoonist gone garrulous."

As I write the word "neglect" I recall meeting my friend Richard Duffy of the *Literary Digest* in this period. He said: "Why don't you send some of your recently published cartoons to our office? I'm sure the cartoon editor would like to reprint them."

And I answered: "Listen—I've been drawing cartoons for labor papers for many years. If the editors of the *Literary Digest* ever wanted to print any of them, they've had their chance." Then I thought that perhaps the cartoon editor of this magazine, the policy of which was to print both sides of controversies, never saw any of the labor publications. Anyway my parting word to Duffy was: "Tell the *Literary Digest* editors that they have let me alone for 30 years and to continue to let me alone—I'll survive the neglect." This sounds a bit peevish now, but that was the way I felt that day.

When material for the fourteenth edition of the *Encyclopedia Britannica* was being assembled, with various well-known Americans on the editorial board, I was asked to write an article for it on the Theory and Technique of the Cartoon. This appeared in that useful publication when it was published in 1930, and it was accompanied by a full page of my pictures among representative examples of cartooning in this country. Subsequently the same material was used in a large volume entitled *Graphic Arts,* also issued by the Britannica company.

"Materials and methods of reproduction are merely incidental in the world of successful cartooning," I wrote; "the main factors lie in the ability to invent ideas, to compose pictures, and to understand the value of emphasis. Creating ideas can become habitual. As the cartoonist looks about him he sees in the everyday walks of life scenes that he thinks might apply to political situations. These ideas he notes and stores away in his subconscious mind, some day to develop and release as cartoons.

"Like the poet and the dramatist, he gets suggestions from the natural scene, from wide and purposeful reading, or from cartoons that have been produced in another era, endeavoring to improve them. We might say that the cartoonist is like the dramatist and, carrying the simile further, that the surface on which he draws is at once his stage-floor and proscenium arch. Within this area he creates a scene. . . .

"Once the cartoonist has decided on his idea, then comes the composition of the cartoon. Good composing also is something one must feel, as there are no set rules. But just as in literature and all of the arts, to compose well is to feel a balanced harmony or completeness, which means that the cartoonist has relegated to second place the less essential features of the scene and stressed the most important, that he is alive to the value of contrasts and above all knows when it is time to leave off, having said enough."

Chapter 38

I MOVE ALONG A SHADOWY ROAD

POLITICS were seething again in 1928. Another Presidential year, with Herbert Hoover nominated by the Republicans, Alfred E. Smith by the Democrats, Norman Thomas by the Socialists, and William Z. Foster by the Workers' party. That contest was notable for mud-slinging and poisonous whispering. Ordinarily calm Republicans solemnly warned me that if Al Smith should win the Pope of Rome would immediately take over this noble republic. And a middle-aged Scotchwoman whom I met in a friend's home in Brooklyn related in awed tones that she knew "somebody who saw a nun in Staten Island" put a curse on one of Hoover's lieutenants there. The alleged curse involved an elaborate ceremony, with a lot of gestures that savored of black magic. It was evident that the narrator believed this wild gossip.

The opening of this campaign, with all the weird voices sounding, affected me as an alarm bell affects a fire-horse that is tired standing in his stall. I was r'arin' to go. The *New Leader* wanted my cartoons. Edward Levinson was associate editor then, and it was through his friendly co-operation that I did some of my best work. He insisted on large cartoons and printed them large. And as the election drew near my current drawings were reprinted on heavy paper and issued in portfolio form, under the title: *This 1928 Campaign in Cartoons.*

But 1928 was a bad year for the Socialist party, for Thomas got only 267,420 votes, compared with the total of 919,799 that Debs had rolled up in 1920. (There was no regular Socialist Presidential candidate in 1924, LaFollette having received a combination of Progressive, Socialist, and Farmer-Labor votes in various states aggregating 4,822,856.) Foster got 48,770 votes in 1928, and in 1924 his total was

33,361. The whispering campaign had won for Hoover, and the social millennium seemed farther and farther away.

Time marched on, but seemed to take delight in stopping occasionally at my door just long enough to leave something to annoy me. I could expect anything. It would have been no surprise if some morning I had found a lusty, squalling, red-faced infant in a clothes basket on my doorstep.

Still I didn't feel old; just tired, moody, and a bit irascible. Perhaps the great drop in the protest-vote had something to do with my state of mind. It made me realize what a prodigious job of education we radicals still had to do to make the American people see how they were being victimized by the profit system, which the two chief political parties rigidly upheld. The flame of my optimism was burning low.

As always, however, I found a lift for my spirits in work. That, I believe, is generally true with any artist. If he is busy with creative expression, in whatever medium he employs, his mind is at ease.

And in the next few months not a few of my days were brightened by letters, from old friends or new, in response to what they had discovered in the pages of *On My Way*.

When the stock market crash came in October, 1929, and the depression followed, all that downpull had a marked effect upon me. Selling cartoons and actually getting money for them became more and more difficult, and my cash reserve steadily dwindled. Gloom dogged my steps.

It was of course no phenomenon for me to be passing through a financial depression. I had seen many of them, Republican and Democratic depressions, with no essential difference between them. Like the lives of most artists, my life had been one depression after another, with the intervals sometimes only a few months long. A streamline smoothness of financial going for a while—then a big bump.

The panic of 1929 was at first interpreted by many as being merely psychological. It was not really "hard times" that had descended upon us; it was your way of thinking. If you thought that times were hard, why, that's what they were. I was one who had no wealth to lose (in the general crash of accumulated wealth mine made no noise at all) but

I was having no end of trouble in adjusting myself to the havoc wrought by the panic and its effect on my personal affairs.

Before me was the prospect of beginning all over again to peddle my pictures and conserve as best I could my connections with what was left of once prosperous publishing houses on which I had long depended. I had seen so much ruin in the wake of the stock-gambling insanity and the tolerant way in which the people generally took it that I became sick, mentally and physically, as I contemplated what was happening.

Now in my sixties, after all those years of effort, I was poor and ailing, and fearful lest I become dependent on others. I pictured myself as an inmate of the county farm—in the old days we called it "the poor-house," but the name had been changed to make it sound less humiliating. I saw myself with long white whiskers, sitting in a corner chair, with dim-watery eyes, a blueish-pink nose, and with cracker crumbs on my vest—waiting for the end. I could imagine the superintendent saying to visitors:

"There's Art Young over there. They say he used to be quite a noted feller, a c'toonist or something."

And I thought: Well, if that's to be my finish, it's no worse than that of millions of others. But there was small consolation in that.

I was still spending the colder months of each year in New York. Howard Smith and I shared the fourth-floor bathroom at 9 East 17th street with the occupants of another studio on that floor. Early in June, 1930, I was relaxing in warm water in the tub and thinking about going to the country soon, so as to escape from the evidences of the depression in the city. When I got through I found that while I was taking that leisurely bath, a sneak thief had entered our studio and walked off with my best suit of clothes and my pocket-book, which contained $23 in cash and a $100 check. I hastened to have a stop-order put against the check, but no attempt was made to cash it. Also I notified the police. The thief was never caught.

Soon I got away to Connecticut, and my secretary, Jeanne Duval, went along. A cheerful and conscientious youngster, who had studied drawing and painting. She spent that summer on Chestnut Ridge, as she had the previous summer, classifying my drawings, taking care of my correspondence, and keeping the gallery open Saturdays and Sundays for casual visitors. On other days, when not occupied otherwise, she roamed the countryside painting pictures.

Going back to New York in the fall, I heard reports on the general economic situation which caused me to have misgivings about my own future. Cartoons were harder to sell, my market narrower than ever. What pictures I sold brought in little money.

The Socialist party's national office had me do a few more drawings for a new edition of a booklet called the *Socialist Primer*, which I had written and illustrated to aid Scott Nearing's campaign when he was running for Congress in an East Side district. This contained such questions and answers as the following:

"Is this a spider? It is. What is its other name? The Capitalist System. Has he got an ant in his web? He has. What is the ant's other name? Workingman. Does the spider like to have the ants organize? No, he prefers to deal with them 'individually.'

"See the boss and the worker. What are they doing—dividing up? They are. Is it a fair divide? Never mind, the boss decides that.

"Does the man like to jump like a dog for his food, shelter, and clothing? No. But the boss pulling the strings tells him it develops his character.

"See the oil well . . . and the river. . . . Who owns the oil well? A private company of speculators. Who owns the river? The public. Is not oil used by the public just as water is? Of course. Then why doesn't the public own the oil well? That's what Socialists want to know."

Shortly before Thanksgiving Day I got word that my son Don was in jail in Hoboken. I asked my lawyer friend Abe Friedman to see what he could find out about that. He phoned, asking what the charge was, and was told: "Assault and battery—in a street fight."

That puzzled me, for I knew Don was usually able to keep out of trouble. So Abe and I took the ferry over to New Jersey. We found Don in the old city jail in Hoboken—with several other prisoners in the "bull pen." the sight of him as he was led out into an ante-room made me feel ill, for his head was bound with a bloody bandage.

Then we got the story. Don had gone to Hoboken the evening before, to see a friend off who was sailing to Europe on a freighter. While they were walking toward the docks, they were halted by two men who, without identifying themselves, began to ask personal questions which Don answered was "none of your God-damned business." One of the men laid a hand on Don, who replied by soaking the stranger in the jaw. Whereupon the questioners hauled out blackjacks, proceeded to beat up Don and his companion, and when they got through with that, revealed that they were detectives.

Presently Don and his friend were taken before the police magistrate, with Abe Friedman appearing for them. They told their stories, and were released. Thinking of this incident, and what could happen to innocent persons minding their own business on the public streets, I felt weak and nauseated. Don was philosophic enough about it all, charging the incident off to experience, but it took something out of me.

The cold early days of December seemed to chill my bones, and I was low on energy. I would get up after a full night's sleep, quite as tired as when I went to bed. The Seventeenth Street studio no longer spelled comfort. And I was beginning to find that climbing the stairs to the fourth floor wasn't so easy as it had been; indeed, I had never thought of it as a hardship before. Now my heart would have spells of fluttering like a wounded bird.

I could understand artists getting worn out when they had been doing a kind of work under compulsion in which they could take no real interest. But I knew I was not overworked. My kind of labor was fundamentally a conserver of health and youth. Nevertheless something was the matter with me. I was too irritable. Bills for rent, light, telephone, and laundry would make me mad. In the ideal world I visualize, these necessary adjuncts to living would not be such a money-problem as to make them worth worrying about. I remembered the $3,000 that the building of the gallery had cost; I had no regrets about that, but I wished I had that much money again.

Unquestionably I was becoming a case for the wise men of the medical profession. "Maybe I'm one of those terrible neurotics," I thought.

One morning I was crossing Union Square, looking, I have reason to believe now, "like the wrath of God." Half way to Fourth Avenue, I met Eddie Levinson, who appeared alarmed when he saw me, and said I ought to go to a doctor. Immediately I went to see my old friend, Dr. Harry Lorber, who stethoscoped me, and gave me pertinent advice. Then a few days later to Dr. Abraham Stone, who examined me further and then took me over to the Union Health Center. There Dr. George Price and his coterie of doctors led me to a room, where they examined the "artery transit" of my blood stream.

I didn't look at the machine that was registering my trouble, but I saw those doctors watch it as closely as if they were discovering some valuable information that I ought to know. Their eyes registered greater and greater astonishment until the hand of the meter finally stopped. For a normal man of my age the pressure was much too high—I had read that in their faces. I asked: How high?

Dr. Price shook his head, saying: "Over two hundred."

He questioned me about my habits. One thing he told me I'd have to do—"stop walking up those flights of stairs."

"Well," I said, "you advise people to do mountain climbing, don't you?"

"Yes, but not you."

After this, at the suggestion of Samuel DeWitt, I went to see Dr. Solon Bernstein—who fluoroscoped and explored my anatomical jungle. And I had a session with the amiable Dr. A. L. Goldwater, who prescribed for me a strict diet.

I have always had a fondness for doctors, for they are usually fine fellows to talk with, especially out of hours. And I go from one to another without much regard for the ethics of the profession—which, as I understand it, is "one physician at a time—don't mix them."

Eddie Levinson visited me often. He asked me to tell him how I was fixed financially. I handed him my bankbook, which showed a meager balance. Eddie promptly conferred with Adelaide Schulkind, Norman Thomas, and Sam DeWitt. Acting as a voluntary committee, they talked with or wrote to others, and as a result money was raised which assured me of being able to cover my expenses for months to come, and to take ample time in which to get well. I was told that I could loaf as long as I wanted to, without feeling that I had to produce and sell pictures. But loafing was the hardest of all things for me to do.

To eliminate the stair-climbing I moved over to the Earle Hotel, on Waverly Place, recommended as quiet and comfortable by Deborah Camp. A month later Ben Belsky invited me to his apartment on Columbia Heights, in Brooklyn, and I enjoyed some pleasant weeks there.

I looked forward to the warmth of spring. I knew I needed to get away from the city's tumult, and again I longed to have trees and grass around me and to walk barefooted on plowed ground. While I rested in town, Sam DeWitt went up to Bethel and inspected my house on Chestnut Ridge Road, to make certain that it was in proper shape for me as a place of convalescence. He had repairs made, bought some new furniture, and saw to it that the kitchen equipment was complete.

In April I took a train for Connecticut, accompanied by a twenty-year-old nurse who had been engaged in my behalf. It was refreshing to return to the soil, and I felt that here I would surely get well—though my energy was scant, and it was essential that I remain in bed many hours out of each twenty-four.

I got into the sun daily, and that was the best part of the whole scene. Some days I spent a few minutes in the gallery, noted the idle drawing table, and thought wistfully of all the work I had turned out on it, but had no inclination now to touch a pen. Looking at the backs of the books on my library shelves, I saw old favorites that I had long intended to re-read. Yet I opened none of them.

But a bright day came in June when I had considerable more strength than in months, and soon afterward I went down to New York for another examination, which showed some hopeful signs. I was enough better so that it was possible to dispense with the nurse's services.

My chief need at this stage was not a nurse, but a man of all work, especially one who could prepare my meals. Accordingly the committee enlisted an old-time "Soakalist," as he pronounced the word Socialist, a veteran migratory worker named Stahl, who was a familiar figure around the Rand School. He was all right in the culinary line, but he had one idiosyncrasy—he refused to use any of the aluminum pots and pans which hung in my kitchen, holding that such utensils generated poison in food. He insisted on cooking in old tin coffee-cans.

I learned later that Stahl had been a lone beach-comber on the south shore of Long Island for years. He had a collection of reminiscences that were fairly interesting the first time he related them, but he wore his stories thin by repetition, and after two months he had ceased to be either of real help or a novelty to me. So I had to give him notice.

Then the committee sent up a Nicaraguan boy of excellent qualities. He cooked well, introducing appetizing dishes native to his home land. When he could be drawn into talk, he had good stories to tell, and some bitter memories. For he had seen civil war in Nicaragua, and his family were active political insurgents, siding with the cause for which young General Cesar Sandino gave his life. Of those memories, however, he said little, and in the main he was a cheerful person to have around.

Though I was manifestly in better condition physically, and though the group of loyal friends in New York assured me that I needn't worry, that there was no danger of my going hungry, I still had dark hours in which I was fearful of becoming permanently dependent upon others. Days would come when I was weighted down with melancholy that I could not shake off—and nights when I would lie awake thinking of dire things which might happen to me. Often, for no tangible reason, I would feel that I was at the end of my long journey.

Those dark periods were lightened now and then by the visits of friends, some from New York and others who lived elsewhere in Connecticut. They would drop in unannounced, bringing news of the outside world, and we would repair to the gallery and talk over old times, old battles in the class struggle, and changing situations the world over.

On one such day an idea took hold of me which lifted my spirits away up. . . . Before I go to the poorhouse, I told myself, I'll write and illustrate one more book. Though nearly forty years had gone by since the publication of my first volume, *Hell Up to Date,* the curious interest I had had then in the infernal regions once more absorbed my thinking. I had seen so much hell on earth that I was eager now to find out what the ancient theological region was like after the passage of four decades.

Early in September I began to map out the new Hell book. The morning after Labor Day was cold, but I didn't mind that. I took the sun on my bare body for twenty minutes, had breakfast, and got busy on the manuscript. James Rorty happened to come over that afternoon, from his place in Easton, and was a booster for my exploration project. And in a few days Stuart Chase was a visitor, and then Manuel Komroff, each voicing encouragement. . . . So I descended into Hell again, this time finding an entrance in New York City as I had in Chicago in 1892.

During my 1892 exploration of the smoky regions below, I observed that so much mechanization had been effected that in interviewing His Satanic Majesty I asked him if he was not afraid that the capitalists eventually would wrest control from him, and in the interest of progress and profit, force him to abdicate. Satan laughed merrily and asserted that he could handle any emergency.

But he was more confident than clever, for I found in 1931 that he had been compelled to resign his power to the industrialists and bankers. The "malefactors of great wealth" and the "economic royalists" who had gone there since my first visit had arrogated to themselves the right to rule under a constitution written by their lawyers, a Supreme Court of their own selection, and an All-Hell Congress, representing their interests.

Nominally, the new government was a parliamentary monarchy, with Satan at its head. The simple natives still called him king, but to the ruling financiers he was just a rubber stamp. His prerogatives had been restricted to shaking hands, receiving committees, laying corner-stones, and talking over the radio. In fact, the whole domain had become a plutocracy, known today as a state of fascism or military capitalism, with most of the punishments and horrors of such governments which curse the upper world.

Art Young's Inferno

SKETCHING DEVILS.

I had occasion to record in the manuscript of my book, as it grew through the ensuing months, some pathetic reunions and interviews with still sturdy old-timers. Charon, the ancient Greek ferryman of the Styx, had been compelled to retire, being displaced by a young sinner called Charon II, nicknamed "the Snappy," who captained a handsomely equipped passenger boat. Socrates, Plato, and Homer were in a sanitarium for the queer, where I also talked with Thoreau, Walt Whitman, Cellini, Karl Marx, Tom Paine, Louise Michel and many others. None of these sinners was allowed to participate in public affairs. Their segregation was considered a necessary precaution against their upsetting the normal thinking of the Gehenna masses.

Corporations controlling affairs in Hell under the new regime included the Sulphur Toothpaste Company, the Smell Syndicate, United Lava, Vitriol Distilleries, Noise Amplifying Corporation, Cinders Cigarette Company, Pitch Chewing Gum, Allied Alarm Clocks, Juggernaut Trucks, Intestinal Gas Company, Amalgamated Motor Sirens, Pink Bathroom Equipment Company, Allied Poison Gas, and Pitchforks, Inc.

One of the oldest inhabitants complained bitterly to me of the changes in Hell. He was boiled in oil for 3,000 years, but averred that the medieval Hades was preferable to the new one with all its so-called comforts and compensations— modern plumbing, motor cars, movies, jazz, and the radio.

Money, which was unknown there in Dante's time, was now minted, and the problem of the millions of suffering sinners was to get some of it in order to exist. There were a Wall Street, subways, insurance payments on everything, ear-shattering noises, sickening odors, unemployment, profit madness, slums, pay toilets (usually two miles away), rival wars for certain areas of the narrowing open spaces—quite as on the earth's crust.

When the 1932 Presidential campaign got into swing I interrupted my work on the Hell book, and was glad to be in another political contest. The national office of the Socialist party had commissioned me to produce two cartoons each week.

Herbert Hoover was running for re-election against Franklin D. Roosevelt, then Governor of New York, while Norman Thomas was again the Socialist standard-bearer, and William Z. Foster headed the Communist ticket.

One of my cartoons which attracted the most comment in that campaign was entitled "Hoover Mostly Cheek." And another showed the Republican and Democratic parties as sloppy silk-hatted old reprobates lying in a gutter, while a Republican voter was saying to a Democratic voter: "Must we help those two old bums up again?"

This time the spirit of protest was strong again, and Thomas came close to the Debs showing of 1920, tallying

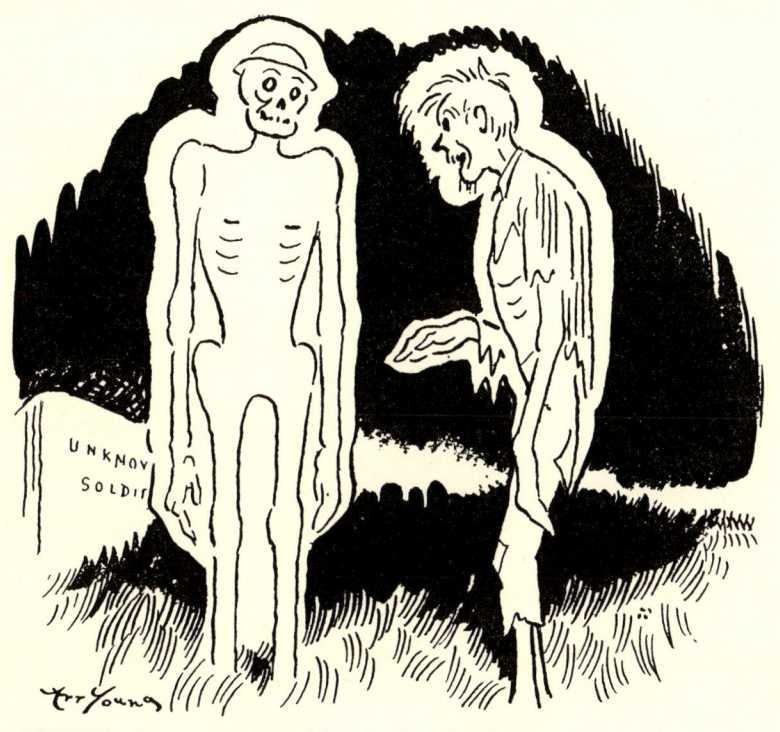

GHOSTS. Cartoon syndicated by the Socialist Party.
"I'm the Unknown Soldier. Who are you?"
"I'm the Forgotten Man. The way I figure it out, they make us famous because we're nobody in particular."

884,781 votes, while Foster got 102,991. Jacob Coxey of the famous march of ragged men was on the national ballot also, under the Farmer-Labor emblem, and was the choice of 7,309 voters.

I went back then to the writing and drawing for the report on my visit to the world farthest down, and early in 1933 it was in final shape. Going to New York, I offered

One bystander to another: "Say, have we got to help those old bums up again?"

Cartoon made for the Socialist Party in the 1932 campaign.

it to four or five publishers, but all turned it down; did not think it would be profitable.

Finally, late in the year, it was brought out by the Delphic Studios. My book was entitled *Art Young's Inferno*. It comprised 176 large pages of text and cartoons; and Jose Clemente Orozco did a brush-drawing caricature head of me for the jacket.

In launching this work, the Delphic Studios staged an exhibition of my drawings which was billed as my "first and last one-man show." Published in a limited subscription edition, the Inferno book received a lot of favorable and gratifying reviews though it never became a best seller.

As the months went on I drew occasional cartoons for the radical and liberal magazines, and some for Vincent Astor's weekly, *Today,* and thus managed to keep afloat. But my income was uncertain, and my spirits were up and down from day to day. As summer waned I realized that I was nearer bankruptcy than ever before, and the specter of the poorhouse rose again before me. I said nothing to any one about this fear. It was never easy to tell people about my troubles—I have always disliked to speak of them, lest I be thought a whiner.

But again at this stage some good friends suspected what was happening to me, asked questions, and thoughtfully came to my rescue. While I was in the depths of gloom a little group in New York City got busy and arranged a testimonial benefit for me. It was staged in the Civic Repertory Theatre on Fourteenth Street on Sunday evening, November 18, 1934. That historic old playhouse was crowded to the doors, and from all accounts it was a memorable occasion. An important factor in drawing that throng was a special Art Young Supplement issued by the *New Leader;* but of greatest value was a quiet but widespread promotion campaign conducted by the testimonial committee under the direction of its treasurer, Adelaide Schulkind, who has endeared herself to thousands in the labor movement as the tireless executive secretary of the League for Mutual Aid.

To show the united-front character of those behind the testimonial, and as an expression of my deep appreciation, I want to set down here the names of all on the sponsoring committee:

Bruce Bliven, Arthur Brisbane, Heywood Broun, Earl Browder, William E. Browder, Saxe Commins, Floyd Dell, Samuel A. DeWitt, Theodore Dreiser, Max Eastman, Morris L. Ernst, Bruno Fischer, Elizabeth Gurley Flynn, Martha Foley, Mary Fox, Al J. Frueh, Lewis S. Gannett, William C. Gassner, Susan Glaspell, Henry Glintenkamp, Michael Gold, William Gropper, Albert H. Gross, Henry Hart, Arthur Garfield Hays, Harry Kelly, Herbert Klein, Manuel Komroff, Walt Kuhn, Margaret Larkin, Dr. Robert L. Leslie, Hiram Motherwell, James Oneal, Frank L. Palmer, Amos Pinchot,

HEYWOOD BROUN

Charles Recht, Elmer Rice, Adelaide Schulkind, Gilbert Seldes, John Sloan, Otto Soglow, Arthur Spingarn, John L. Spivak, Norman Thomas, Carlo Tresca, Hendrik Van Loon, Oswald Garrison Villard, B. Charney Vladeck, Anna Strunsky Walling, Harry Weinberger, Louis Weitzenkorn, Walter White, Alexander Woollcott, Carl Zigrosser.

Unable to be present that evening, I had sent a letter to Heywood Broun, the master of ceremonies, which he read from the stage. In part that letter said:

"Please impress upon the audience, the performers, and the League for Mutual Aid my sincere gratitude for this night of celebration of my 'century of progress.' (Or is it only sixty-eight years? Anyhow, the time doesn't matter.) As a veteran of the radical movement, I'm a little the worse for wear, and am advised to avoid the 'wicked city' and 'undue excitement' for a while longer. So to my regret I cannot be with you to enjoy the comradeship and entertainment.

"But I will try to deserve the festivities in my honor by endeavoring to express myself hereafter with bigger and better bitterness, for it has been truly said by some critics of my work that I am often too gentle with the enemy.

"When one reflects upon the sorrow, misery, and death caused by the profit system, it is doubtful if it deserves any tolerance at all, especially at this stage of its maniacal stupidity. . . .

"And yet, for all that is happening, we have good reason to dance and sing, not only as a brief respite from the punishment of having to live in this inferno, but because the end of Capitalism is near and the principles of Socialism are going to be applied to life and industry.

"I don't know the meaning of 'dialectic materialism,' and many other terms used by the polemical experts, and I try not to get overly excited about them. All I know is the difference between right and wrong. The cause of the workers is right and the rule of Capitalism is wrong, and right will win. . . ."

This testimonial provided a fund which has enabled me to go on for four and a half years without anxiety about income. When the first money from that fund was sent to me, the committee wrote saying: "Be assured that this is given not in any sense as charity, but as a definite tribute to the enduring value of your work."

And my spirit was further warmed by receiving numberless letters of appreciation which had come to the committee with contributions from individuals of all shades of political opinion in the labor and radical movements, from writers, artists, actors, musicians, and men and women in many other walks of life.

Chapter 39

AMONG THE SILK HATS AT BRISBANE'S FUNERAL

MY *Inferno* book had attracted enough attention so that early in 1935 James Henle of the Vanguard Press indicated that he was receptive to the idea of publishing a volume which would contain a representative selection of my pictures, with little text. A contract was signed and the choosing of drawings was begun by an informal committee. A long arduous job, with much re-sifting of material, which took months.

Publication finally came in November, 1936, celebrated by the publishers with a cocktail party in a studio on Fifty-seventh Street. The title of the book was *The Best of Art Young,* and it included an introduction by Heywood Broun, saying:

"Like most efficient radicals, Art Young is utterly conservative in one respect. I refer to his art. The subject might be provocative and wholly distasteful to standpatters, but the line which he drew was tight and stern and as ruggedly individualistic as the mind of Herbert Hoover. . . . Modern art never so much as rumpled his hair. He drew the most shocking and scandalous cartoons, all done in the somewhat nostalgic manner of one who had been frightened by a woodcut in his early life. At a distance an Art Young drawing suggested the illustration for some moral maxim. Closer view revealed the fact that he was saying that every exploiter should fry eternally for his sins."

After that work came out, friends would ask: "Why was such-and-such a picture omitted?" and I could only answer that the selection was based on the best judgement of the committee which made it, and that probably no two persons ever could agree on what was the best of an artist's work during fifty years as a producer.

In 1936 I was asked by a firm of New York art-book publishers to write a biography of Thomas Rowlandson, to be used with reproductions of his pictures as one of a series dealing with significant artists. The series included an estimate of Van Gogh by Walter Pach, and of the elder Pieter Breughel by Aldous Huxley. I assented, signed a contract, and put in many weeks of labor on the job.

That was an unhappy and disillusioning experience. The book came out in March, 1938, copyrighted by an organization I had never heard of and bearing the imprint of a company also unknown to me. I was never paid the agreed-upon advance for this writing, nor did the publishers take me into their confidence in making up the volume. The company with which I had made my original contract had gone into the hands of a creditors' committee, and my efforts to pin responsibility on anybody were futile. The book was wretchedly produced, most of the Rowlandson prints being maltreated and cheapened in the engraving process, in a way to discredit the English caricaturist's masterful designs.

Meanwhile John Beffel came up to Connecticut occasionally, when he could get away from an editorial job in New York, and went ahead with the assembling of notes for this autobiography. I wrote at random on past events; we had agreed that that would be the easiest way. Week by week the manuscript grew. At times I was appalled by the prodigious task ahead—the matter of getting dates correct, for instance. At my age it is easy to be ten years out of the way on some happening when thinking back. And there was the need of recalling names of people important in my life long ago that had faded from my memory.

But there are ways of refreshing one's memory, as I found to my frequent surprise and gratification. Some old letter or newspaper clipping that we came upon in the attic of my house on Chestnut Ridge, or in the studio, would bring a completely forgotten episode back, as clear in detail as a stereopticon picture thrown upon a screen.

Nineteen Thirty-Six also saw me active in the national political campaign. Among other output I did a series of cartoons for the *Socialist Call*, in behalf of the candidacy of Norman Thomas and George Nelson, who headed the party ticket.

In this contest, however, I found that I could not honestly draw cartoons of attack against Franklin D. Roosevelt such as I had made against Al Smith and other past candidates for the Presidency. All I could do was to be mildly critical of an honorable man, one of such integrity and courage as is rarely found in political affairs.

Today I think of Roosevelt's problems as being as vast and formidable as were Lincoln's. I view him as a man holding to his duty as he sees it, while surrounded by national and international chaos, a man who is trying to do his best for his own country and deal as honorably as circumstances will permit in the nation's diplomatic relations with other

Socialist Call

A GREEK FABLE UP TO DATE. Orpheus plays enchanting music, but what can he do to rescue the people? (The New Deal looked a little too optimistic to me.)

countries. And I think of Eleanor Roosevelt as a woman of such human and uncompromising qualities that they make her not just in name but truly the first lady of the land.

One of my cartoons in the 1936 campaign, entitled "Can He Save Them?" portrayed Roosevelt as Orpheus in classic robes playing beautiful music on a lyre in the modern Hell of war, poverty, and kindred evils, charming all who listened, while the long-suffering multitude hopefully expected him to rescue them as the Orpheus of Greek legend had rescued the maiden Eurydice, and all Hell had forgotten its pain.

Yet I would hate to have it said of me that my cartoons never hurt. To live a life as a caricaturist of the kind whose pictures "never hurt" is my idea of futility. It should not be the function of a political caricaturist just to be funny. Sometimes his job calls for downright cruelty, but to produce a cartoon that is nothing but an insulting burlesque of a public man is not my idea of forceful attack. It often happens, however, that a public man serves as a symbol of wrong because of his record, and as such he is properly a subject for lampooning, but to be assailed less as an individual than as a sponsor of the idea for which he stands.

Of course when one feels that everybody, even the most predatory of capitalists, is also a victim of the system of

MY SLOUCH HAT, in distinguished company at Arthur Brisbane's funeral.

which he is a part, one's steel is in danger of not being ground sharply enough for effective warfare. But not to hurt with an idea and his manner of expressing it proves that the cartoonist is nothing but a court jester whom the money monarchs like to have around, and when he dies they will say "he never hurt."

Just now an old clipping from the *Rochester* (N. Y.) *Herald* turned up; under a photograph of myself is mention of the Associated Press libel suit, and the added sentence: "Young is said to be agreeable to know socially, but he puts vitriol into his cartoons."

I was in New York when Arthur Brisbane died on Christmas, 1936, at the age of 72. His funeral rites were held in St. Bartholomew's Church, and I served as an honorary pallbearer. There was a curious feeling for me in being there, suggested in a cartoon I drew later that day, in which my slouch hat appeared alone in a sea of high hats. Those shiny toppers were on the heads of big shots of finance and politics including Governor Lehman. I noted that Mayor LaGuardia and Vincent Astor also were among my fellow pallbearers.

I don't know what was in the minds of the notables around me, but I was feeling sorry not only for the late chief editor of the Hearst papers and his family, but for everybody in the crowded church, the many who had known Brisbane's acts of personal kindness outside of business hours and those who knew that his unusual talent, however corrupted, had often aroused thought for the good and true. I was sorry, too, for everybody who had to die—or live—in this crooked world.

Brisbane's passing gave me much to think about, for we had kept up our contact through the years, ever since those few months when he had me working for him in the *Evening Journal* art department around 1900. I had seen him become more and more cynical and hard, increasingly subservient to the Hearst interests, and a willing defender of and apologist for militarism and the power of money.

The last time I saw him was perhaps in 1935, when I was seldom contributing to periodicals and to all appearances laid on the shelf. Nevertheless I was still drawing and writing, with a view to possible future publication. Always solicitous about my work, Brisbane inquired: "What are you doing now?"

"Oh, trying to express myself," I said.

He gave me one of his characteristic snap-answers: "Nobody's self is worth expressing," and then added a tired afterthought: "But perhaps you're right."

Kenneth Chamberlain, cartoonist for the *Sunday American,* who saw him frequently during his final illness, told me that he was looking over my latest book, while propped up in bed, a few days before his death.

I remembered my first meeting with Brisbane when he was a brilliant young man on the *World,* and Joseph Pulitzer's favorite. He had won his spurs previously under Dana on the *Sun.* I recalled when he went with Hearst and got a bonus for each thousand increase in the *Journal's* circulation, and was soon getting rich. One of his first editorials in that paper created a sensation. Headed "A little truth will do no harm," it had to do with an old woman outcast, whom he described as a victim of our social system.

I remembered his love of pictures—how he could write "all around" a cartoon that ignited his imagination; his capacity for hard work, his gift of imagination, his originality as a commentator on news, his passion for contrasts and striking cartoons, his dislike of ornate diction. But singularly he was attracted by pen-and-ink pictures in which there was an abundance of technique.

He would drop me a line now and then asking me to show him my latest cartoons when he was writing the Sunday spread of sermonized editorials, for he always could write best when he had a picture before him. It was remarkable how he could amplify, quote, and discourse on whatever theme he chose.

He enjoyed looking at the ideas that I carried with me, briefly sketched on a writing pad. Sometimes he would O.K. two or three at a time. He liked my way of putting an idea across the footlights—and often told me so. These cartoons when finished invariably expressed my own thinking, and I was keen to see what he had written about them when they appeared in the *Sunday American*. As a rule he did not violate my meaning, as he might have done in later years when the Hearst policy became brutally Fascist, but held close to what I had sought to say pictorially. In those days I doubt if any other writer could have written under such pressure of time and with such facility and easy-to-read clarity. His secretaries knew that I had the right of way whenever I called to see him; others could wait.

It was Brisbane's idea that modern life was a matter of sheer survival of the fittest, and his conception of the fit were those with brains for business. I had arguments with him about that, my belief being that the acquisitive sense and the ability to succeed as a money-maker frequently made the possessor the most unfit to survive.

Around 4 p.m. in the old days he would start pounding out editorials for the next day on his typewriter. Some time later he increased his high efficiency by installing dictaphones in his office, home, and automobile, even using one when traveling by rail. Once when his car was standing at the curb outside the Hearst building with no one in it, Gene

REMEMBER WHENCE YOU CAME

New York Sunday American

This picture topped a full-page Brisbane editorial admonishing the successful to help weaker persons rise. 1923.

Fowler, then managing editor of the *American* and an incorrigible joker, stepped into it and dictated a half dozen paragraphs for Arthur's daily column, burlesquing the well-known Brisbane style. He dealt with the gorilla's ability to lick Jack Dempsey single-handed, and other favorite themes of Hearst's No. 1 man. Brisbane's temper hit the roof when he read the draft of this stuff typed out by his private secretary.

He was undoubtedly the leading American apostle of

FOR ADOPTION.

speed and success. One day we were talking in his office when he asked suddenly: "How old are you, Young?"

"Fifty-one."

"Just my age," he said, and added: "You'd better hurry."

My friend Walt McDougall, who had done the first daily newspaper cartoons in New York a few years before I did the first in Chicago, found an exit from his chaotic world with the aid of an old long-muzzled horse pistol in 1938. He met his end in the house where he had lived alone on the bank of the Niantic river near Waterford, Connecticut. A diary in his handwriting contained a recent entry telling of "tough times."

Walt had a son and many friends, but somehow had let himself become isolated, and mental depression closed down on him in his old age. I know of people who had been near to him, and who afterward blamed themselves for not keeping a better eye on his welfare. Yet I realize that in recent years, with all the economic stress in the world, many individuals have drifted away from old associates, largely because they have had their own difficult problems to cope with and to take on the troubles of others has become too much for them.

Probably no cartoonist of my acquaintance had more fun than Walt McDougall. Through his long career he was both an industrious worker and a light-hearted playboy, and his autobiography, *This is the Life*, is rich in colorful anecdote.

Chapter 40

OVERFLOW MEETING OF MEMORIES

HAVING written all this, I am conscious of the fact that much has been left out of my story. I skim through folders of letters, newspaper clippings, pages from magazines, handbills announcing mass-meetings called for a long succession of causes, and sheaves of notes on the economic struggle and the passing show—and I am appalled

ROUNDING UP THE UNBRIDLED PAST.

at the realization of how many individuals more or less vital to my life have found no place in this running narrative.

Leaning back in my chair and looking at my living-room wall or off into the green Connecticut hills, I ponder the decades through which I have come, and recall countless incidents which might properly be set down here. If it were possible to take an additional year, all these stray recollections might be assembled in orderly fashion, each in its exact niche. But that essential year is not available.

There is, however, another way out. Hence this chapter, in which many extra memories can be thrown in pell-mell, with no attempt at correct sequence and no bothering to spend more hours checking dates. One's thoughts flow thus, so why not one jumble-chapter in a book of reminiscence?

In putting my autobiography together, I have often stopped short with the self-conscious feeling that some of it perhaps would be regarded by my audience as shameless exhibitionism. Yet I have kept on with the telling anyhow. And I have tried to write honestly, difficult though it be for any man to do that in such a narrative, for he necessarily lacks perspective on himself.

Here, then, are odds and ends dipped from the overflow.

Seeing President Sadi Carnot of France and his wife in the Louvre four years before an assassin stabbed him to death. . . . A night with Jack Reed exploring the Great White Way, which resulted in an illustrated article called "From Omaha to Broadway" for the *Metropolitan Magazine*. . . . Mary Blair and Constant Eakin entertaining people from miles around at an old-fashioned Fourth of July celebration on their broad lawn at Redding Ridge, Conn.; the host in white suit and red sash as master of ceremonies, introducing me in a silk hat as the "renowned Senator." My speech contained all the spread-eagle oratory I used to hear as a boy.

Eugene Field having me write some anecdotes, illustrated with thumb-nail sketches, which he used in his *Chicago Daily News* column. . . . Visiting the famous Hoffman House bar in New York when I first arrived there, to see Bouguereau's painting, "Nymphs and Satyr," which hung beneath a plush canopy. . . . Letter from George Cram Cook asking me to "rearrange your entire plan of life and work" and to play a role in a Greek play put on by the Provincetown Players— "the part of the chief magistrate of Athens summoning the Athenian ladies to desist from their feminist revolt against the war with Sparta." Somehow this seemed to call for too much effort.

Louis Gardy, Sunday editor of the *New York Call,* using a cartoon of mine in a special Child Labor issue in January, 1917—the one in which a devil with a forked tongue touches an infant on the head. "The joke is on you, Baby," said the caption. "They put you here with talent for music, literature, art, and science—yes, and talent for goodness and play. But they make you spend most of your time scheming and fighting for the necessities of life. I don't like to tell you, Baby, but it's a hell of a joke, and it's on you." . . . Ida Rauh sending out a notice in 1913 of a club to be organized, where men and women could eat, drink, and talk—which led to the establishment of Mabel Dodge's salon at 23 Fifth Avenue. . . . Frank Harris holding forth there one evening on personal morals, with especial reference to his own love affairs.

New York Daily Call

THE JOKE IS ON YOU, BABY.

Meeting Jack London at a dinner in New York, when the *Snark* was being made ready in California for his intended round-the-world voyage; his inviting me to "come out and see us off." . . . Sketching O. Henry in Luchow's in New York in 1908, and his depicting me "as an old 'un," as we sat at dinner with my brother Will and Jim Crane. . . . Buying bright colored socks three or four pairs a week till I had an old trunk full of them. . . . Voting for William Randolph Hearst for mayor of New York City on a municipal ownership platform. . . . Attempts of my brother Will, then managing editor of *Hampton's Magazine,* to get me to illustrate stories by Eugene Wood and others (around 1909), and my saying I would not illustrate anything except what I wrote myself—an attitude which I reversed after I joined the *Metropolitan* staff.

O. HENRY

Bob Ingersoll speaking at a rally of the McKinley League in Carnegie Hall in 1896. Big night. Great speech. *New York Sun*, in head-line, says Bob "stripped the tinsel from Bryan."

ROBERT G. INGERSOLL

And as an example of partisan news reporting in that day, its opening paragraph asserts that: "In the sense that the audience was made up of persons too intelligent to be deceived by Mr. Bryan's variety of political twaddle, the meeting was a gathering of the classes." . . . Getting word from a traveling friend that a Texas clergyman was delivering serious lectures on the nether world and using stereopticon slides made from the comic pictures in my first book, *Hell Up to Date*. . . . Gaston Akoun, "concessionaire," writing me in 1907 from Norfolk, Virginia, asking for the privilege of using my Hell drawings enlarged in an amusement enterprise at the Jamestown Exposition to be called *Up and Down*— "not being allowed to call it Hell or any such epithet which might offend the religious element who will attend." . . .

I have always been interested in men and women from other countries, in whatever occupation, that I might learn their attitudes toward fundamental things. . . . About a year before Ramsay MacDonald became Premier of Great Britain, I heard him speak at a banquet in New York and tried to extract from his address some phrase that was definite. But no—if one sounded at all positive, he would, by circumlocution of words, qualify it beautifully in the way of an adept statesman. Put all of his sentences into a sieve, shake them, and they would all go through, leaving no nuggets of convincing quality. That's what happens to one who stays too long in politics; in his youth MacDonald was positive.

Tom Mann, the English labor leader, I saw when he was eighty. He looked more like an ambassador representing an old established government than the leader of a minority group of workers. His speech calling on English soldiers not to shoot their fathers in a bitter strike (which the *Masses* published with a portrait I drew of Mann, and a cartoon of mine to illustrate the context of his earnest appeal) was to my mind one of the most eloquent speeches in history, not excepting those by Marc Antony, Patrick Henry, and Eugene Debs while on trial for obstructing the war. . . . When I talked with George Lansbury at a studio party in his honor in South Washington Square, I felt that he lived up to what I had heard about him; that he was the kind of Christian who would try to persuade Satan himself to mend his ways. Later he wrote asking me to draw cartoons for *Lansbury's Weekly*. Another one of the things I wanted to do, but couldn't get around to doing.

Meeting Finley Peter Dunne on the street in New York after my arrest on anti-war charges in 1917. He was no longer

a dissenter; was writing no Dooley observations now to point out the stupidity being exhibited on many sides by the pro-war crowd, as he had during the Spanish-American imbroglio. He seemed a bit sympathetic toward my point of view, but said: "Art, when the world goes crazy, you have to go crazy too." I said something about trying to stay sane.
. . . A bird flying in through the open door of my gallery in Connecticut, one day when I was sorting pictures there, and then, mistaking the skylight for the real sky and trying

CARLO TRESCA

to fly out again—with such anxious cries, flutterings, and bumpings that I feared it would beat its brains out. But the frightened creature finally found the open door and flew out.
. . . When I was fourteen on the farm, all four walls of my room were papered with cartoons printed in that period, and my drawing table touched my pillow. And so throughout my life. When I get up in the morning, I look first at the drawing on which I worked yesterday.

Stirring speeches by Bill Haywood, Arturo Giovannitti, Elizabeth Gurley Flynn, Eugene Debs, Carlo Tresca, Jim Larkin, Norman Thomas, Mother Jones, Upton Sinclair,

ART YOUNG: HIS LIFE AND TIMES 439

Meyer London, Morris Hillquit, John T. Doran, big Jim Thompson, Ella Reeve Bloor, Herbert Mahler, and others on many platforms, for outstanding causes—the Ettor-

New Masses

Governor Fuller: "Cheer up, Judge, it will soon be over."

Giovannitti-Caruso defense; the I.W.W. war cases; the Mesaba Range case in Minnesota; the great Paterson silk workers' strike; the striking Colorado and West Virginia miners facing machine-gun fire; the Mooney-Billings, Sacco-

Vanzetti, and Terzani defenses; the fight to free the four remaining miners among seven sentenced to life in Harlan County, Kentucky, because strikers defended their lives against an attack by mine guards; the Centralia defense in Washington State; the courageous fighting of Irish and East Indian revolutionists for independence; the Scottsboro and Angelo Herndon defenses; the Imperial Valley strikers; and the share-croppers in the South.

Such speeches added to my education, often moved me to action. Going back to my drawing board, with a vivid conception of some new wrong, I would do a timely cartoon, feeling that it couldn't wait till morning. Thus I made pictures to aid most of those causes, for one publication or another. The list is beyond my power of estimation; there was never time to keep systematic record. Day after day I am reminded of work of mine, dealing with the economic conflict, that I had forgotten for years.

I know that in preceding chapters of this book I have said that "some of my best work was done for" this or that publication. And perhaps I'd better sum up here, and say that that statement applies pretty much to numerous pictorial contributions of mine to *Life, Puck,* the *Masses,* the *Liberator,* the *Metropolitan,* and *Good Morning.*

Calvin Coolidge was the only President I had missed seeing and putting in my sketch-book in many years. Toward him I felt as my Uncle Lem did in 1886 when Grover Cleveland was due to speak in his town: "I wouldn't go 'cross the street to see him." I had seen quite enough of Cal in the news-reels, which had begun to give us Presidents pictorially raw, sliced, boiled, baked, fried on one side or turned over, and served in the juice of publicity. One waxwork figure would have been plenty—so far as I was concerned in the Coolidge kind of fame. . . . I find pages from the *New York Herald Tribune* of May 30, 1926, in which I illustrated an article by Duff Gilfond, "The School for Verdant Congressmen." . . .

Mike Gold phoned me one day in 1926. Would I come over to his place for dinner next evening? Otto Kahn was to be there. The banker wanted to meet a few radical writers and artists. Kahn was well known for his financial help to struggling artists. Mike's apartment was over near Hudson Street—walk up three flights. Informal; about a dozen present. Otto arrived around 9, his chauffeur following and puffing as he made the climb with a satchel filled with bottles of champagne.

I was seated next to the guest of honor, and knowing that his father was a red in Germany in 1848 I asked questions about Kahn senior. Otto seemed to have a great love and respect for his memory.

ALEXANDER WOOLLCOTT

Conversation turned to Italy and Mussolini's rise to power. Something was said about the dictator's financial backing. "You ought to know all about it, Mr. Kahn," Carlo Tresca spoke up. "You lent money to him." Kahn smiled, but made no reply.

The wine had its effect upon all of us, and we unbent a good deal. We had dined well and everything was lovely. After we had left the table Otto began to defend and excuse the capitalist's point of view. He told eloquently of the responsibilities and hardships which a fortune entails upon its owner. Being rich, he explained, meant nothing but trouble and mental suffering. At that I heard Bill Gropper sobbing and saw him wipe his eyes with his handkerchief. The banker took Bill's acting as a good joke, and presently was talking of other things.

Afterward I wished we had asked him if he knew any rich men who had parted with their wealth, to enjoy the serenity of want. But we were drinking his champagne, and while the evening was pleasantly informal, we still followed the rule of etiquette that one must not be too rough with a guest.

Illustrating a book by that brilliant West Coast satirist, Charles Erskine Scott Wood, entitled *Heavenly Discourse*, in 1927. It dealt with conversations by outstanding dignitaries and some interlopers in the celestial regions. For this volume I enjoyed doing some portraits of God, a venerable old gentleman with long white whiskers. I showed him at the wheel of the universe, steering a course through space; in a general's uniform, sounding a call for preparedness; and exhibiting impatience with Aquarius for his unintelligent manner of answering prayers for rain from Denver. . . . Illustrating two trenchant books by Upton Sinclair about education under capitalism in the United States—*The Goose-step* and *The Goslings*. Both of these added materially to my own education concerning the malforming of the thoughts of youth by a system of colleges and schools dominated by the moneyed interests.

Other work I did in various years—cartoons on profit-sharing which I could sell nowhere, and tried to *give* to the Socialist press, in the early years of this century, only to find that Socialist editors weren't interested in profit-sharing. . . . Feature article in the *New York Evening World* in 1907, about my experiences as a juror, when I saw John D. Rockefeller Jr. sitting as a guest alongside the judge, and a stream of misery pouring in from the city prison. . . . Pictures for *Brooklyn Life*, 1906; for *Scribner's*, 1907; for the *Woman's Journal*, official organ of the National American Woman Suffrage Association, 1912; *Intercollegiate Socialist*, 1913; for an article by Walter Prichard Eaton, "A Poor Man's

Bank," in the *American Magazine,* 1914; for the *Sunday World,* 1925; a cartoon for the *Nation* showing a cat labeled Massachusetts Law toying with a mouse, identified as the Sacco-Vanzetti case. . . . Topical drawings for the *Window Ticker,* a periodical leaflet showing "the world in

FOR AN UPTON SINCLAIR BOOK. Illustration used on the cover of *The Goose-Step.*

cartoons" sold to stores for display to passersby, around 1921. . . .

Throughout all the years of the *Masses* and the *Liberator,* when he was a contributor of poems with an elemental sweep, I never happened to meet Carl Sandburg. But I think of him as a voice of the people, and with more reverence for the true Christian spirit and sympathy for the lowly than could be found in an average church full of pious members of the faith. . . . A big day at the *Academie Julien* in Paris, when I won second prize in the weekly competition for painting on a Biblical subject—with a canvas depicting David's victory over Goliath. How proud I was when other students congratulated me on the good qualities in my first real effort to do an oil painting.

Speaking at a dinner to Andre Malraux in New York in March, 1937. First time I ever spoke over the air. I hate to be hurried, and I approached the microphone with the same sense of caution that one feels near a red-hot stove. "I am allotted five minutes. If I speak only four minutes and ten seconds, Mr. Chairman, I hope you will know what to do about it; I don't." And of Malraux I said:

"It is one thing to sit in a quiet room and write or draw pictures of revolt against tyranny, and quite another thing to meet the enemy face to face in armed conflict. Our honored guest not only has studio courage, but he has that noble daring shown by the rank-and-file fighters—those individually unknown heroes in the desperate battle against the insane scourge of Fascism. It is these heroes of the background—the brave men and women of farm and factory, whether on the picket-lines in the United States, or enduring the horrors of Hitler's inferno, or fighting and dying for an ideal on the barricades in Spain—it is all of these that we have in mind when we pay our respects to Malraux. His eyes see what the aroused working people are beginning to see the world over; his will is their will; his heart beats *with* them and *for* them."

If I had no other pleasant memories to recall than those of the beautiful women I have met who were active in progressive or radical affairs, life would still be worth while. I fell in love with Elizabeth Gurley Flynn when as a young girl she aroused uncounted thousands with her clear, ringing voice to the cause of social revolt. When I think of beauty I know that some on my list would not have passed a jury test for what is called feminine beauty today. But as a jury of one I attest that they were beautiful to my eyes, and their loveliness lingers in retrospect.

With no attempt at alphabetical arrangement or making a complete list, I think of Margaret Larkin, Ernestine Evans, Rebecca Drucker, Ruth and Hannah Pickering, Jessica Smith,

Crystal Eastman, Marguerite Tucker, Inez Milholland, Genevieve Taggard, Mary Marcy, Doris Stevens, Louise Bryant, Edna Porter, Leane Zugsmith, Freda Kirchwey, Sara Bard Field, Lydia Gibson, Martha Gruening, Clara Gruening Stillman, Jane Burr, Caroline Lowe, Jessica Milne, Mary Ware Dennett, Harriot Stanton Blatch, Margaret Sanger, Helen Black, Mary Heaton Vorse, Anna Strunsky, Louise Adams Floyd, Helen Keller, Grace Potter, Edna Kenton, Helen Todd, Anne Valentine, Carrie Giovannitti, Rose Hanna, Lucy Branham, and Sophia Wittenberg Mumford.

ELIZABETH GURLEY FLYNN

And these are only a few of the many I have watched as they did their part in the fight to make this a better world to live in—organizing, picketing, speaking to crowds in halls or on street corners, writing, and raising money.

Delving into my note books, I come upon some pages devoted to Edna Porter. She was born in a Socialist environment. Her father and mother were both early members of the party in New Orleans. She went on the stage in her teens in a small part with James O'Neill in *The Count of Monte Cristo*, traveled widely with road companies, and finally toured in *Everywoman*, playing the leading role some 2,000 times. When the Actors' Equity Association was organized, she was in the forefront of its memorable strike.

I knew Edna first at the Rand School when the *Masses* was getting started. And for twenty-eight years I have received at least two postcards from her each month from varying parts of the world. She has a passion for discovering people submerged yet worthy of attention—the lame, halt, and blind. Often she has taken some struggling artist or poet in hand and introduced him to persons in a position to aid and encourage him. One of her services has been typing in Braille magazine articles and even whole books for Helen Keller to read.

It was Edna Porter who, with Dr. A. L. Goldwater and another friend, smuggled a bust of Walt Whitman into the

CLARENCE DARROW

Hall of Fame on May 30, 1919, the day before that poet's birthday. Next morning's papers, especially the *New York Call*, published diverting accounts of the mystery connected with this occurrence. Up to then the author of *Leaves of Grass* had been rigidly barred from that holy section of New York University. By 1932 he had been officially admitted.

I remember when I first met Marguerite Tucker—at a memorial meeting for Jack Reed in Beethoven Hall. She sat near me, and I was struck by the expression on her face as some woman in black on the stage went through the convolutions of a "Dance of Death," which seemed a bit too lugubrious for the occasion. For all our feeling of loss over Jack's end, I felt that he would have preferred less grief and a more cheerful outlook toward the future. Girls went about the hall offering "red roses" for sale, and I heard Marguerite say to one of them: "But these are carnations!" To which the other said: "What's the difference? They're red." Talking with this animate young woman afterward, and thus beginning a lasting friendship, I learned that she was a sister-in-law of Dame Nellie Melba of Australia, and that she had seen copies of the *Masses* on Melba's boudoir sofa in Melbourne.

Florence Kelley's vibrant personality comes back to me clearly. In Washington I often heard stories of the independent ways of her father, "Pig Iron" Kelley of Pennsylvania, who was a member of Congress for thirty years. He got that nickname because of his insistence upon a high tariff on raw iron.

I had a special interest in Florence Kelley because she had been the first chief factory inspector in Illinois, appointed by Governor Altgeld. With admiration I saw her war on child labor, sweatshops, and laws discriminating against women—often in the face of great obstacles, including whispering campaigns of slander set in motion by her enemies. I can see her now on the platform, answering a reactionary opponent who in a debate on a vital piece of legislation, claimed to be "open-minded." She replied that some people were so open-minded that ideas never stayed in their heads.

In all my life from youth to the three-score-and-ten mark I have had mating-intimacy with only eight women. Not a record to boast about when I reflect that one of the American Youngs had eighteen wives—and no doubt other opportunities.

One evening when I talked genealogy with Alexander Young, the New York lawyer, he said that all of us were distantly related to Brigham Young. Perhaps the "distant" relationship accounts for the difference between the American pioneer zeal for breeding and the cautious way of at least one of the modern Youngs. If we could be reasonably sure that our children would not become helpless victims of war or poverty, then abandonment to real love with all its consequences could be as nature willed it. And the arguments for birth-control would lose some of their meaning.

Yet even without these fears, I know that there should be scientific care in propagating children, with a view to

SELF-PORTRAIT OF THOMAS NAST, with note acknowledging a copy of *Authors' Readings*.

quality and not quantity. But my kind of a world would be one in which even the accidents of birth, twins or even quintuplets—legitimate babies or those not quite so legitimate—would be welcomed by their parents. And there would be no reason for dread of their not having decent upbringing or finding places to work according to their individual abilities.

When I sent Thomas Nast a copy of *Authors' Readings* in 1897 he replied with a sketch of himself in an elocutionary posture and this inscription: "Will take the book in but feel out because I am not in it."

Clarence Darrow wrote me in 1928: *"On My Way* is a good book except for one thing—you didn't mention me."

But no one has ever complained about being left out of my *Inferno*.

Of this book I know that friends will say: "But why didn't you mention So-and-so?" No doubt some dear to memory and certain personality notations that might interest the reader have been overlooked and the omissions will come back to plague me in later years. And it may be that some I have included will think there is no honor in once having been associated or on friendly terms with one who has acted with such impropriety against the social code.

Nevertheless, as the curtain goes down on these memoirs I'm thinking of countless friends and acquaintances—most of whom I have sketched and kept in notebooks, and who belong in my life-story. Beside those already mentioned in the foregoing pages and in the revery picture at the end of this volume, others will read between the lines and find themselves.

Epilogue:

WATCHING THE OLD ORDER CRACK

IN my youth I hoped for no higher status in life than to be among those who would follow in the wake of Thomas Nast, Joseph Keppler, and Bernard Gillam, outstanding artists in the field of political caricature. And when in my early twenties I grew familiar with the political and social satires of the graphic artists of England and France across two centuries, these gave even greater stimulus to my ambition. Dreamily I anticipated that my destiny was to succeed as a caricaturist of some influence in public affairs.

Sometimes a prosperous individual will say to me: "Any man can succeed in his ambition if he really wants to. Take you, for instance. Haven't you accomplished what you wanted to do?" And I answer: "Yes—" Then I have a repentant feeling for saying that because "No" would be quite as correct. I tell him that "Yes" is only one small word of a full, honest answer; only a little part of the whole truth.

I point out that I was compelled to waste about half of my life scheming and worrying over the problem of making enough money to keep going, while attempting at the same time to put aside some of it for lean years and old age, like a dog hiding a bone. This exercise of my acquisitive sense, this trying to mix business with creative ability—though it did not strangle my talent—might have done so except for fortuitous circumstances, kind and encouraging parents, limited competition, and an instinct which told me it ought not to be strangled if I could possibly help it. Or perhaps a little bird singing in a tree-top just for joy helped to give me the hint. Finally I achieved a kind of success.

Material considerations thwarted me at every turn. It was my money-earning ability that determined my right to exist, and I got through in a way—but what a way! Having spent so much of my time maneuvering to make enough cash with which to live decently, I count most of that effort a hindrance to my development, both as a man and as an artist. Instinctively most men are proud to be able to provide for themselves and their dependents, and I was no exception to the rule. That duty I accepted willingly. Still it seemed to me unworthy of any one to make that the main reason for living.

It took me a long time to understand why so much that surrounded me was too ugly to tolerate without protest. But eventually I learned the reason. I saw that the conduct of my fellow-men could not be otherwise than disappointing, in fact parisitical and corrupt, and that most of our troubles emanated from a cause which manifestly would grow worse so long as we put up with it.

That cause was Capitalism. Man's natural self-interest, become perverted and ruthless! The motivating principle of business (though not openly confessed), when summed up, meant: "Get yours; never mind the other fellow." I saw, too, that our law-makers and judges of the meaning of the law put property rights first and left human rights to shift for themselves.

Of course clergymen and other paid teachers and moralists admonished us to be upright and unselfish, and for people with good incomes it was easy to condemn those living on the edge of poverty as inferior, impractical, shiftless, and lacking respect for the social code. It was easy to shout *thief* at the other fellow when you had no temptation to steal—I mean steal in a petty way. But stealing in a big way was often accepted as good business judgement.

I found that life was a continual struggle for most of us —and this on a plane not much above that of the struggle of wild animals—and that society dismissed this obvious truth as a negligible factor in determining human conduct as well as our mental and physical well-being. I began to see that this economic battle persisted even in the midst of an exhaustless plenty, and that most humans lived and died trying to succeed in a material sense, in short, to reach the goal of a triumphant animalism.

For that was, and still is, "success." And the more one can acquire of physical comforts and delights the more is this success glorified. I know of course that in these days the measure of a man's real worth is not taken for granted because of the size of the fortune he has piled up. But he is still the envied one—a shining example for having reached "the rugged heights." He is the winner, just as his kind were acclaimed back in the early years of the twentieth century, when individualism was king, and Socialism a mere theory of the crackpots and failures.

I think of myself as a kind of sample of the human race; in some respects a poor sample, and different, if not peculiar. But my problems, I feel, have been in the main much like those of most men and women, at least in this regional habitat of the race, the United States of America.

Every one of us is born with some kind of talent. In early manhood or womanhood each individual begins to see a path, though perhaps dimly, that beckons to him or her. All of us have this leaning toward, or desire for doing ably, a certain kind of work, and only want an opportunity to prove our capacity in that direction. These hunches, these signs of one's natural trend, are usually right, and are not to be thrust aside without regret in later life.

I am antagonistic to the money-making fetish because it sidetracks our natural selves, leaving us no alternative but to accept the situation and take *any* kind of work for a weekly wage. We are expected to "make good," which is another way of saying make money. Therefore we do things for which we have no real understanding and often no liking, without thought as to whether it is best for us, and soon or late find that living has become drab and empty.

The retired millionaire trying to revert to a youthful love for painting or other tendency in the fine arts, is almost as pathetic as the poor man who has worked hard all his life at something in which he has no particular interest and nothing to show for it, in either money or recognition.

We are all caught and hurt by the system, and the more sensitive we are to life's highest values the harder it is to bear the abuse.

I have just looked again at a splash of cartoon-bitterness against the money incentive which I made for an early issue of the *Masses*. It was called "Compulsory Worship." A picture of people in endless droves lashed by the demons of Want and Fear, forcing them to kneel in shameful supplication at the altar of Mammon. It matters not whether you believe in such idolatry—your tormentors compel your prayers. So most of us pray not for riches, but for just enough to assure our living in normal comfort and perhaps a little extra for funeral expenses at the end.

I do not think of myself as having arrived at any degree of achievement commensurate with my potential talent and capacity for work. I am just one among the many who have tried to approximate some measure of integrity in a world that is a sorry bewilderment of wretchedness and affluence.

Through the events of seventy-odd years, as recorded in these pages, one man managed to find his direction. He reached his maturity during the upsurge of individualism, with its so-called "self-made" men (the profit-hounds) and their rise to dominance over government, the press, church, colleges, public business, and most of our country's institutions. Slowly this man grew aware of the wrongs resulting from such sovereignty, and then in his limited way tried to help in the work of bringing about social change.

But he had to learn that many traditional customs and beliefs, however unreasonable and absurd they looked to him, couldn't be changed, and that to compromise with them was no great fault. He saw that there were countless follies and minor wrongs which, while not to be ignored, were not to be taken too seriously.

During the last four decades of his life-journey, as this chronicle has revealed, it became more and more evident that there was one wrong, one thing over all, standing in the way of honest and contented living—the unjust treatment of those who produce the wealth of the world by those who own most of that wealth; and that the continual fight between the moneyed interests and the working people (including artists) was the vital problem of our time. Now, during these recurring and ever-increasing conflicts, is it not obvious that we have to take sides? I think it has come to that, for all of us.

As these final words are written, there is mobilizing and fighting with unspeakable barbarity in many parts of the world—the last drive of investment-finance against further advance of our own Lincolnian ideal: government of, for, and by the people. To describe other outstanding events in recent years of this conflict in our own country would be repetition—the same old fighting, except that the forces of reaction are bolder and more ruthless.

Before finishing, I would like to speak of pleasant and hopeful signs of the times—the splendid work initiated by many federal projects; the awakening to the need of solidarity, especially in the professional fields; the League of American Writers, the United American Artists, the American

Circa 1927

OVER THEY GO. Drawing for an I.W.W. leaflet on labor-saving devices as a cause of unemployment.

Newspaper Guild, and kindred movements. I see much new life and beauty that give reason for rejoicing, but it is obscured from view most of the time by the brutality of other facts—dark realities like the Memorial Day massacre of Chicago steel strikers in 1937, inhuman conditions in the California fruit industry, the fostering of race and religious hatred, suppression of protests and uprisings of farmers in the western states, persecution of southern sharecroppers, the 12,000,000 or more unemployed in this land of opportunity, lockouts, lost strikes, vigilante terrorism;

the countless murders, imprisonments, and suicides caused by the pressure of need for money; and the increase in psychopathic cases growing out of mental anxiety under our crazy economic system.

What can be done about all this? I do not believe that making the world better depends upon each one of us becoming good. That is asking too much in these hostile surroundings. No doubt "inner transformation" is what we need, but outside conditions will not give inner transformation a chance. Yet I *do* believe that man is destined to be released for a more ennobling life, when each one of us can go even farther with our talent or natural ability than we thought possible. First of all, however, our social life must be rightly conditioned before anyone can grow to a decent stature as an honest human being or become a proficient unit in the world's work.

By "rightly conditioned" I mean the common ownership of land and of the means of production and distribution of essential commodities. And this, of course, assumes the elimination of private ownership of our vital industries and the substitution of co-operative business as a public policy, with no concern for profits beyond the self-sustaining limit of each industry and the assured welfare of those who do the work.

This is my own definition of Socialism as I learned to understand it and to believe that to establish it would make the most substantial groundwork for our individual and collective growth. I can see no hope for humanity so long as one's right to live depends upon one's ability to pay the cost of living imposed by those who exploit our daily needs.

I think I know human nature well enough to know that the average individual works better when encouraged and praised, and does his worst when humiliated and looked upon as a slave. Some kind of congenial work is necessary to contentment. From the small boy tinkering with the construction of a toy to the old lady knitting, with no thought in their minds of cash payment—we see the desire of human beings to be doing something with their minds and hands.

If the continual pressure for monetary gain whenever we render any kind of service were removed, I believe people would enjoy working for the common good. This is demonstrated over and over again in time of floods and other disasters when the call to communal welfare is the only incentive.

The horror of unemployment is the final undoing of the worker. When he sees this confronting him he sells himself regardless of the intrinsic worth of his ability. Labor unions and collective bargaining arose to give him some show of power and dignity.

Individual development depends upon mass-solution of the economic problems of everyday living. The inventors, thinkers, and the common man have made this world ripe for healthful leisure, and have created far more than enough goods for all. But through all this progress the business man has assumed the right to the lion's share while those who did the creating and hard work were compelled to fight for whatever they could get—or starve. If money, as it was once meant to be, were a true symbol of individual worth, the problem would be simpler, but no one is so benighted as to believe that in this day it represents true worth any more than it represents mere luck, favoritism, inheritance, or a drunken thirst for money-power.

In the beginning of this narrative I told about one of my first assignments as a pictorial interpreter of events—the trial of the so-called "Anarchists" in Chicago, when the primal reason for hanging four of eight labor leaders was that they had agitated for the eight-hour day and better wages. From then until the present there has been savage and ceaseless warfare. There has been so much purging of labor's ranks by the dictatorship of the privileged interests in an effort to stabilize its power that the record is one long scroll of infamy. But the change is at hand—the old order is cracking. It has been said before that "the cure for democracy is more democracy."

Many individuals shy at the word "revolution" because they regard it as a plea for still more terror—still more blood and tears, as if humanity had not had enough. When I have spoken of revolution in these pages, it was to visualize the cycles merging in the progress of governmental ideas through the centuries.

Having moved from feudalism into concentrated monarchy, then to parliamentary and political democracy, and still further, to include participation of all male and female adults (without property qualifications) in elections, the forces which shape and re-shape society are completing the design in this epoch with industrial democracy. All this evolving did not just happen. It was accelerated by the propagandists, the statesmen, the writers, the artists, and all who believed in the natural trend and inevitable need in each period of changing conditions. It is the opponents of change, those who will not see that conditions demand it, who determine the kind of revolution that is impending—whether it will involve a minimum or a maximum of obstruction and violence.

Trying to turn back the clock of time is the traditional impulse of the Tories. But there is still some hope that they will awaken to the futility of hard negation, and that here in our own country, where progressive ideas have made material headway since 1932 and militant organization of labor has gained more power to hold this progress, we can come out into the light of the new democracy through conscious and planned evolution. This is my hope, not a prediction.

While on trial in war-time I was referred to by my comrades as the only pacifist in the indicted *Masses* group. To be thought such was pleasing to me. Yet I often wondered if I could rightly be classed among the noble men and women of that cause. Sometimes I asked myself: Isn't every moral principle, every good thing in life, in danger of being carried too far? We know it's good to eat, to sleep, to be kind, to be cautious, and to be tolerant. But to overdo any good thing—take tolerance, for example—should there be no limit to that most blessed of virtues?

"Ah!" says the pacifist, "your tolerance can break, of course, but you must not use force." I ponder anew the question: In the long run, is non-resistance the better way to make the world right?

I do not know. This, however, I *do* know—the big war of 1914-1918 was not my war. It was plainly not a war for democracy but for plutocracy; not for peace but for plunder, and to make our country military-minded. It was capitalism's war—not mine.

Times like these test the consistency of a pacifist. One sees the drive to plunge the whole world into carnage. Debate goes on in the press, over the radio, and on the public platform, as to the possibility of the United States becoming involved again in a general war. There are those who contend for an isolation policy, and others who raise the pointed inquiry: Can this country stay above the battle?

As I pen these words, the old feeling stirs me anew, that I would like to see the United States stay out of another international conflict. Yet with all my hoping I know that I am a realist and that new conditions make new truths. To stay at home and be neutral is not so logical nor so possible as it could have been in 1917. If in my time another wide-flung conflict should come, I have no illusions about it. It will again be a war of the investment-capitalists—the aristocracy of wealth in collusion with what is left of that decrepit aristocracy of lineage will be back of the intrigue and diplomacy that decide the fate of the world.

We must be ready to hear of their devotion to political democracy—which they have learned so well how to use for their own ends. And we must be ready to hear of their enmity to the totalitarian state, which is just the kind of state they want, provided it totals in every way to their credit.

This is the truth as I see it. So, if governments haven't learned that peace, not war, is what people desire, my kind of pacifism would succumb to the hope that at last the time had come for a general awakening to the cause of it all, and that the next big war (if there must be a next) would end as the last one came near ending (in Germany, Italy, and other countries) with the rise of workers' republics in many parts of the world.

With more and more governments, however crude and experimental, dedicated to industrial democracy and universal brotherhood, the era of peace and joy in living will come on earth.

Inadequately though it may sum up, if my work can mortise into such a future, whether near or remote, as I believe it will—that thought is consolation and payment. When my time comes I'll lay down my pencil and call it a day.

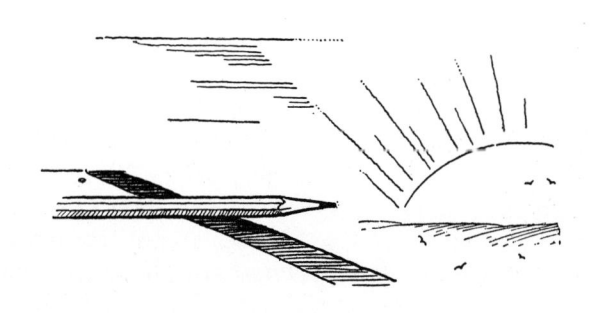

INDEX

A

Abbot, Wyllis S., 139 ff.
Académie, Julian, 4, 8, 9, 135
Academy of Design (Chicago), 62, 73
Ahkoond of Swat, 142-143
Alabama, visit to, 200-201
Altgeld, Gov. John P., 152-153, 154, 159, 160, 161-162, 219, 222; anarchists pardoned by, 166-168
American Field, drawings accepted by, 68
Amnesty Association, 165, 166
"Anarchists," Chicago, trial of, 83 ff., 101-108, 165-168; philosophy of, 387
Arbeiter Zeitung, labor views of, 80
Arkell, W. J., 118
Arnold, Matthew, 109-110
Art gallery, 395 ff.
"Art, song, and music" performance, 139-143
Art Students' League, 120
Art Young's Inferno, 416-418, 419-420, 424
Associated Press, libel suit brought by, 295 ff.
Authors' Readings, 193-195

B

Baker, Alfred Z., 214
Barnard, Frederic, 72, 130, 131
Barnes, Earl, 320, 332, 335, 337
Barns, Cornelia, 328
Barnum, P. T., 123, 233-236
Barrett, Lawrence, 92
Barton, Ralph, 381
Beckwith, Carroll, 4, 120
Bell, Josephine, 320, 324, 332, 335
Bellows, George, 388
Benefit, testimonial, 421-423
Berkmann, Alexander, 323, 333
Bethel, Conn., home at, 229 ff., art gallery at, 395 ff.

Big Stick, 340, 378, 381
Black, William P., 84 ff.
Blaine, James G., 147
Blizzard of '88 sketches, 110
Bloor, Ella Reeve, 256
Boissevain, Eugen Jan, 356
Booth, Charles, editor Monroe *Sentinel*, 31, 114, 136
Booth, Edwin, 92
Bougeaureau, 9, 10
Breughel, Peter, 133
Brisbane, Arthur, 202, 211, 256, 262, 380, 427-431
Browne, Hablot K., 130
Brubaker, Howard, 328
Bryan, William Jennings, 192, 306, 307
Bryant, Louise, 389
Burne-Jones, 127
Burns, John, 153
Burridge, Walter, 72
Business depression (1892), 172-173
Butler, Benjamin F., 102

C

Cabanel, 9
Callot, 133
Campaigns. *See* Political campaigns.
"Campainin for the Millenum," 211-212, 223
Camp meeting, 47-48
Cannon, Joseph D., 298
Caricatures, early, 14, 38-39, 46-47, 52 ff.; new school of, 381
Carnegie, Andrew, 149 ff.
Carnegie Steel Company strike (1892), 150 ff.
Carruth, Hayden, 271
Chalk plates, 69
Chamberlain, K. R., 387
Chatsworth railroad disaster, 98-100
Chauve-Souris review, 380, 381
Chester, England, 127-129
Chicago, life in, 62 ff., 144
Chicago Anarchists. *See* Anarchists
Chicago Daily News, 88 ff., 109-110

461

462 INDEX

Chicago Evening Mail, 69, 83
Chicago Herald, 109
Chicago Inter-Ocean, 109, 123-124, 144 ff., 173, 177
Chicago Mail, 109
Chicago Times, 109
Chicago Tribune, 109-110
Chicago World's Fair, 137, 145, 156-158, 162-164, 169-171
Chinatown dinners, 252
Circus drawings, 46-47
Clan-na-Gael conspirators, trial of, 124
Cleveland, Grover, 92, 148, 149, 153, 158-159, 162, 163, 172
Cockerill, John A., 113
Cody, Colonel (Buffalo Bill), in Paris, 8
Colarossi School, 8
Collier's Weekly, 270, 379
Color printing, introduction of, 155
Coming Nation, cartoons for, 278
Concert episode, 139-143
Condé, Jim, 245
"Conflagration Jones." See Webster.
Congress, United States, cartooning, 282 ff., 302, 315-317
Connors, Chuck, 209
Conventions, party. See Political campaigns
Coolidge, Calvin, 440
Cooper Union, debating class at, 226, 247, 249, 254
Copeland, Clyde, 56-57, 177, 201
Copeland, Mrs. Clyde, 31, 32, 77, 124
Corbett, Jim, 158
Corner, Thomas, 12, 14, 17, 20
Cosmopolitan, drawings sold to, 210
Covarrubias, 381
Cox, Kenyon, 4, 120
Coxey's Army, 182-183
Creel, George, 337
Croker, Richard, 148
Cronin, Dr., murder of, 124
Cruikshank, George, 72, 130, 131, 133
Cruikshank, Isaac, 130
Cuba, war with, 195-199

D

Dana, Charles H., 121
Danbury, Conn., 236 ff.

Darrow, Clarence, 315
Daumier, 10
Davis, Robert H., 201
Day, Clarence, Jr., 288
Debs, Eugene, 216, 257-258, 272, 387
Dell, Floyd, 297, 324, 328, 332, 335, 391
Democracy, faith in, 292-293
Democratic conventions. See Political conventions
Dennis, Charles H., 89
Denver, life in, 178 ff.
Denver Post, 179
Denver Rocky Mountain News, 179
Denver Times, work on the, 177-187
Depew, Chauncey M., 147
Dickens lore, 130 ff.
Doré, Gustav, 10, 52, 120, 127, 133-134, 138
Drainage Canal (Chicago), work on, 158
DuMaurier, 127, 130
Dunne, Finley Peter, 96-98, 287, 437-438
Durer, 133
Dutch Treat Club, 340, 354

E

Eastman, Crystal, 328
Eastman, Max, 275, 295, 320, 322, 324, 328, 331, 332, 335, 356, 362, 388, 390
Ebersold, Police Chief, quoted on Haymarket riot, 165, 220
Economic freedom, 388
Economic struggle, awakening to, 215 ff.
Eden Musee, 119-120
"Edith," 111-112, 114
Education, widening, 215
81 Fifth Avenue, 206-211
Elizabeth, 29, 57, 61, 124, 145, 175-178, 188-190, 200-201, 205-206, 213-214, 225, 229-230, 232, 244, 252-253, 292
Encyclopedia Britannica, article for, 406-407
Engel, George, 86, 103
Entertainment episode, 139-143
Espionage Act, Masses trial under the, 319 ff., 331, 332 ff., 351

INDEX

F

Field, Eugene, 92-95, 113, 146, 160, 178
Fielden, Samuel, 79, 82, 86, 104, 165, 167, 173-74
Fifer, Governor, 166
Fischer, Adolph, 86, 103
Fleury, Tony Robert, 9
Flynn, Elizabeth Gurley, 444
Folwell, Arthur, 191
Foster, William A., 85
Fox, Richard K., 119
Freeman, Joseph, 390, 391
Frick, Henry C., 150
Frost, A. B., 113, 161
Frueh, Al, 381
Furniss, Harry, 283

G

Garden party (Monroe), 31-32
Garfinkle, 125
Gary, Joseph E., 84, 102, 167, 168
Gellert, Hugo, 328, 391
George, Henry, 122
Gerome, 9
Gillam, Bernard, 122, 190, 395
Gillray, 130, 131, 133
Gilman, Charlotte Perkins, 298
Giovannitti, Arturo, 328
Gladstone, William H., 93-94
Glintenkamp, H. J., 320, 324, 332
Gold, Mike, 390, 391
Goldman, Emma, 268, 323, 333
Good Morning, 354 ff., 387
Gould, Jay, 75
Greeley, Horace, Nast cartoons of, 122-123
Gresham, Walter, 162
Grinnell, Julius S., 83, 168, 220
Gropper, William, 390, 391
Gruening, Ernest H., 378
Guerin, Jules, 72
Gulbransson, 381

H

Hallinan, Charles T., 328
Hamilton, Grant, 191
Hand, Judge Augustus, 332 ff.
Hand, Judge Learned, 320, 321
Hapgood, Norman, 298
Harcourt, Sir William, 183-185
Hard, William, 331
Hardie, Keir, 183, 211, 215
Harrison, Benjamin, 146 ff., 158, 159
Harrison, Carter H., 79, 82, 168; murder of, 171
Haymarket riot (Chicago), 82 ff., 101 ff., 125, 165-168, 219-221
Haywood, William D., 257, 284, 289, 330, 341
Hearst, William R., 201, 217, 218-219, 324
Hell Up to Date, 137-139, 143, 160-161
Hill, David B., 148
Hillquit, Morris, 332 ff.
"Hiram Pennick" articles, 211-212, 223
Hogarth, 10, 130, 131
Holmes, John Haynes, 298
Homestead (Pennsylvania) strike, 150 ff.
Hough, C. M., 321
Howitt, 130
Hughes, Charles E., nomination, 306
Huntington, Collis P., 126

I

Illness in Paris, and recovery, 15-26, 136-137
Irvine, Alexander, 258-259
Ismay, Bruce, 126
I. W. W., 330; trials in Chicago, 341 ff.

J

"John Brown's Fort," 171
Jones, Ellis O., 352 ff.
Judge, 61, 189, 192-193, 200, 211, 259, 270

K

Kahn, Otto, 440-441
Keene, 130
Keller, Helen, 328, 329
Kelley, Florence, 447
Kelly, Fred C., 283
Kent, Rockwell, 274
Keppler, Joseph, 122, 191, 395
Ker, Balfour, quoted, 266-268
King, Ben, 125
Knights of Labor, activities of, 75 ff.
Kohlsaat, H. H., 146 ff., 155, 173

L

Labor, early stirrings of, 74 ff.
Labor trial, 83 ff.; 101 ff.
LaFollette, Robert M., 223-224, 299, 379
La grippe, attack of, in Paris, 15-24
LaMotte, Ellen, 328
Lang, Andrew, 93-94
Lawson, Thomas W., 256
Lawson, Victor F., 89, 124, 165
Lee, James Melvin, 194
Leech, John, 72, 130
Leslie's Weekly, cartoons for, 195-196
Libel suits, 295 ff.
Liberator, 328 ff., 378, 386-387, 390-393
Life, 189, 191, 210, 246-247, 259, 264, 270, 379, 384
Liliuokalani, Queen, 162
Lincoln, Robert T., 147
Lincoln-Douglas debates, 33-34
Lindbergh, Charles A., Jr., 309
Lindbergh, Charles A., Sr., 308-310
Lingg, Louis, 86, 104
Lippmann, Walter, 304
London, visit to, 131-135
"Looking On," series, 378
Lorimer, George Horace, 384
Lucy, H. W., 283
Ludlow (Colo.) strike, 303-304

M

McAdoo, William G., 289
McCormick, Cyrus H., 80
MacDonald, Ramsay, 437
McDougall, Walt, 145, 147, 207, 209, 431-432
McGill, Tom, 208
McGlynn, Father Edward, 122
McKinley, William, 146, 147, 191, 211, 217
Mailly, William, 288
Malone, Dudley Field, 332
Malraux, Andre, 444
Mann, Tom, 437
Marinoff, Jacob, 378
Masses. See *The Masses*
Masson, Tom, 191, 384
May Day excitement, 79 ff.
Medill, Joseph, 109, 110
Messonier, 9
Metropolitan Magazine, 154, 282, 287 ff., 302 ff., 315-317, 324-325, 331

Michelson, Clarina, 339
Milholland, Inez, 297
Milwaukee Free Press, cartoons for, 223
Minor, Robert, 328, 329, 387
Moffatt, David H., 177 ff.
Monroe, Wisconsin, 28-58, 70, 77-78, 113, 124, 136-142, 346-347
Morgan, J. Pierpont, 311
"Mother Jones," 303; letter of, quoted, 388-389
Moyer, 257
Municipal Ownership League, 249
Murdock, Victor, 177
Murphy, Charles F., 148

N

Nancy Hanks, 158
Nankivell, Frank, 201
Nast, Thomas, 54, 60, 118, 121, 122, 134, 147, 155, 156, 162, 288, 305, 395
Nation, drawings for, 378
National conventions. See Political campaigns
National Press Club, 300-301
Neebe, Oscar, 86, 104, 165, 166, 167, 220
Nelson, Knute, 308
Newell, Peter, 214
New Masses, 393
Newspaper Enterprise Association, commissioned by, 305
Newspapers, inflammatory character of, 74-81, 83 ff., 89-90, 101 ff., 121, 149 ff., 159, 167 ff., 172, 217, 221, 257
New York, leaving for, 112-114; journey to, 115-117; life in, 117 ff.; return to, 188 ff.
New York Call, quoted, 296
New York Evening Journal, 201-206, 262, 380
New York Graphic, 113
New York Sunday American, 262, 381
New York World, 113, 121
"Nig," 42 ff.
Nimble Nickel, 62 ff.
Nixon, William Penn, 144-145, 160, 165, 168
North, Elizabeth. See Elizabeth
Noyes, Frank B., libel suit brought by, 297 ff.

INDEX

O

Oberlander, 133
Oglesby, Gov. Richard, 102, 104
On My Way, 402-406
Opper, Frederick, 122, 203, 204

P

Pall Mall Budget, 14, 173
Pall Mall Gazette, 173
Palmer House (Chicago), silver-dollar floor, 170-171
Panic of 1929, 409-410
Paris, first visit to, 3-25, 123 ff.; illness in, 15-26
Parsons, Albert, 76, 79, 80, 82 ff., 103, 218, 221
Passaic textile strike, 393-394
Patterson, Robert, 110, 111
Patterson, Thomas M., 179
Peattie, Elia, 98
Peattie, Robert B., 98
Pettibone, 257
"Phiz," 130
Photography, limitations of, 58-60
Piano lessons, 41
Pinchot, Amos, 297 ff.
Pinkerton thugs in steel strike, 150 ff.
Political campaigns: 1892, 146 ff., 158-160, 162; 1896, 191-193; 1900, 211-212; 1912, 284 ff.; 1916, 305 ff.; 1924, 378-379; 1928, 408-409; 1932, 418-419; 1936, 425-426
Pollard, Percival, 201
Poole, William Frederick, 71-72
"Poor Fish" series, 369 ff.
Populist party program, 159
Porter, Edna, 445-446
Propaganda, effects of, recognized, 54-55
Puck, 122, 191, 248, 250, 259
Pulitzer, Joseph, 113, 121, 149, 217-218
Pullman, George M., 183
Push, 143

R

Railroad strike (1894), 221
Rankin, Jeannette, 313-314, 327
Read, Opie, 125
Reed, John, 276, 302, 303, 304, 307, 313, 322, 328, 329, 332, 362, 363, 388, 389; quoted, 323-324, 340 ff.; resigns from *Liberator*, 349-350
Reed, Myron, 181-182, 215
Reed, Thomas B., 147
Reid, Whitelaw, 148, 158, 159
Reilly, Dr. Frank, 93
Remington, Frederic, 202
Republican conventions. *See* Political conventions
Revere, Paul, 395
Rippenbein, Morris, 355, 357
Robinson, Boardman, 320, 322, 328, 352
Rockefeller, John D., Jr., 218
Rockefeller, John D., Sr., 158, 256
Roe, Gilbert E., 320-321
Rogers, Merrill, 319, 324, 332
Rogers, W. A., 121
Roosevelt, Franklin D., 425-426
Roosevelt, President Theodore, 197, 211, 256, 305, 306, 310, 316
Rowlandson, 130, 131, 133
Russell, Charles Edward, 221-222, 278, 305
Russia, Reed quoted on, 340
Ruthenberg, Charles E., 391, 392

S

Sandburg, Carl, 318, 443-444
Saturday Evening Post, cartoons for, 384, 385
Schaack, Captain, 80, 83, 101, 105, 165, 220-221
Schmedtgen, William, 105, 106
Schnaubelt, Rudolph, 83, 125
Schwab, Michael, 79, 86, 104, 165, 167
Scripps-Howard newspapers, 305
Scripps-McRae newspapers, 305
Selanders, J. C., 89
Seltzer, Thomas, 271
Sex, problems in, 36, 50-51, 111-112, 114
"Shots at Truth," 248
Sinclair, Upton, 256
Single Tax movement, 122
"Snapshots in Hades," 210
Snowden, Clinton, 69, 74
Social injustice, awareness to, 222, 227
Socialism, the World War and, 302
Socialist Call, drawings for, 425

INDEX

Socialistic doctrine, growing interest in, 254 ff.
Socialist party, emergency convention, 314-315; 1919 convention, 362-363
Socialist Primer, drawings for, 411
Socialist sympathies, 254 ff.
South Wales colliery explosion, 183-184
Spanish-American war, 195-199
Spies, August, 79, 80-81, 86, 103
Stanton, Theodore, 8
Stead, William T., 14, 173-174
Steffens, Lincoln, 256, 298, 302, 313, 369, 387-388
Steinegas, 381
Stengel, Hans, 381
Stephenson, Isaac, 223
Steunenberg, Governor, assassination of, 257
Stevenson, Adlai E., 148, 150, 159
Stokes, J. G. Phelps, 315
Stokes, Rose Pastor, 315
Stone, Melville E., 86, 88, 104, 106, 124, 165
Sullivan, John L., 158
Sullivant, T. S., 191, 203, 204

T

Tammany Hall, 148, 149
Tarbell, Ida, 256
Taylor, Bert Leston, 191
Tenniel, Sir John, 72
Thackeray, 130
The Best of Art Young, 424
The Masses, 277, 392; beginning and growth of, 271 ff., 282; Max Eastman appointed editor, 275; Eastman editorial in, 295; Floyd Dell with, 297; censorship of, 318 ff.
"Things That Hit Our Funny Bone" series, 250
Through Hell with Hiprah Hunt, 210
"Toby M.P.," 283
Today, drawings for, 421
"Trees at Night" series, 384
Tridon, Andre, 271
Trinity Church (New York) tenements, 278-281
Tucker, Marguerite, 446-447
Twain, Mark, 95, 241-242
"Types of the Old Home-Town" series, 385

U

University of Chicago, 158
Union Square (New York) bomb explosion, 258 ff.
Untermeyer, Louis, 272, 328

V

Vanderbilt, William H., 75
Vanderpoel, John H., 4, 62, 120
Vibert, 10
Villard, Oswald Garrison, 378
Vlag, Piet, 270-272

W

Wabash Railroad, strike on, 75
Waite, Chief Justice, 102
Waite, Gov. David Hansen, 185
Wales, visit to, 129-130
Walling, William English, 298
Wall Street panic (1907), 258
War, *The Masses* policy against, 319 ff.
Warren, Lansing, 177
Washington, life in, 288 ff.
Waterloo, Stanley, 125
Wattles, Willard, 322
Weaver, James Baird, 159
Weber, Grant, 139
Webster, Clarence, 3 ff., 24, 27, 116, 123 ff., 126, 137, 139, 142, 144 ff., 160, 173, 177
Weeks, Rufus W., 271, 274
West Point cartoons, 153
West Virginia coal regions, 303
West Virginia coal strike, 295 ff.
Whigham, H. J., 283, 302, 310, 317
White, Butch, 89, 102, 105
Whitlock, Brand, 284
Whitney, Harry Payne, 287
Whistler, James McNeill, 8
Wilde, Oscar, 7-8, 178
Willard, Frances, 91
Winter, Charles A., 272, 274
Wilson, William L., 148
Wilson, Woodrow, 307, 310 ff., 319
Wood, Charles W., 328
Wood, Eugene, 264-266, 271
Wood, Suzanne Ella, 139
Woodville, R. Caton, 72
Workers' Monthly, 393
World's Columbian Exposition. *See* Chicago World's Fair

INDEX

World's Fair (Chicago). *See* Chicago World's Fair
World War, socialism and the, 302 ff., 310 ff.

Y

Yerkes, Charles, 177
Young, Art, trip to Paris, 3-25, 123 ff.; home life in Monroe, 27 ff.; young manhood, 49 ff.; life in Chicago, 62 ff.; life in New York, 117 ff., 188 ff., 244 ff.; personal attitudes, 159-160, 447-449; life with Elizabeth, 175-177, 205 ff., 213 ff., 225 ff., 243-244; goes to Washington, 282; socialist activities, 222 ff.; later years, 408 ff.
Young, Charles, 37, 42, 45, 61
Young, Daniel, 20 ff., 29, 32-34, 36, 39, 346-347
Young, Mrs. Daniel, 31-32, 33, 35, 347
Young, Don, 225-226, 292, 382-383, 411-412
Young, Elizabeth. *See* Elizabeth
Young, Nettie. *See* Copeland, Mrs. Clyde
Young, North, 214-215, 231-233, 292, 383-384
Young, Will, 45-46, 190, 206 ff., 213

Z

Zeisler, Sigismund, 85
Zim, 122

THIS BOOK IS PRINTED IN
ELEVEN POINT BENEDICTINE
ON LEGAL FINISH PAPER

JACKET DESIGNED
IN COLORS BY
WILLIS BIRCHMAN